DOG OBEDIENCE TRAINING

DOG OBEDIENCE TRAINING

BY **Milo Pearsall**

AND **Charles G. Leedham**

CHARLES SCRIBNER'S SONS • NEW YORK

Grateful acknowlegement is made to the Gaines Dog Research Center to quote briefly from "Touring with Towser" by Harry Miller; to Life to quote briefly from an article by Robert Wallace (February 9, 1953 issue); to The American Kennel Club to quote briefly from "Rules Applying to Registration and Dog Shows," and to reprint "Regulations and Standards for Obedience Trials."

PRINTED IN THE UNITED STATES OF AMERICA
LIBRARY OF CONGRESS CATALOG CARD NUMBER 58-11201

For Margaret and Betty
and aptly enough, two dogs named
Black Charger and Black Douglas
who started it all

INTRODUCTION

Every minute you are with your dog, you are training him. By your every action and attitude, you are teaching him to be affectionate or reserved, courageous or timid, responsive or withdrawn, obedient or disobedient. It is something you cannot escape, even if you should want to, for once a puppy leaves his mother and litter-mates his attitude toward the world will be learned only from you.

If he learns from his first contacts with you, and from all his future contacts, that he is loved and respected, that he has a definite place in the family and that certain things are expected of him, he can be what you have always wanted in a dog, and perhaps even more. It is to this ideal that we have dedicated this book. You cannot spend all your time on obedience training of your dog, but in your training sessions can be established a man-to-dog rapport that is very nearly impossible otherwise. In training, if it is done with kindness and love and respect, your dog will learn to respond to you in a marvelous degree. At the same time, you will learn how to treat him outside of training. He will in addition become obedient, and his obedience to your commands will again color your attitude, making for a relationship that is more than man and pet—it becomes truly man and companion.

What you will not find in this book is a collection of pretty maxims about dog training—neat capsules of methodology which say, in effect, "if you do this, he will do that." What we ask you to do is to think about training, about your dog and his reactions, and then apply the means of approaching each item of training which we have found to be most effective. There is no substitute for thought and understanding in training, any more than there is in any other facet of life. This is what we will ask of you again and again in every section of this book, and this is what we hope you will do.

If there could be any one capsule statement of our ways of training, it would center around the words "praise" and "gentleness". Praise is the keystone, the foundation of training and a good relationship with your dog. He learns through praise, and he forgets the sting of the necessary corrections because you praise him immediately after. Gentleness, too, is an essential. You must, in training, use scientifically applied force at times to demonstrate to your dog what you want done, but the force must be carefully calculated, applied without anger or rancor, and only to the degree necessary. You are working with an animal, the most responsive and intelligent and loyal animal alive, and only through gentle and understanding treatment will you realize his full potentialities.

Do not misunderstand us. This is not a brief for a hesitant and over-protective approach to either your dog or his training. Pampering can have equally as bad results as harshness; too little insistence on the proper performance of any obedience exercise is quite as bad as too much. But there is a middle way—insistence with understanding and knowledge of your dog and how his mind and emotions work. This middle way, the understanding and knowledge that make it up, are what we propound, along with various items of information that we think will be helpful both in and out of training.

The full potentialities of a dog, any dog, are generally nowhere nearly realized by the average person, or the average owner of a dog. A dog is too often thought of as "nice to have around, fun to romp with" and as that only, to be locked in or out as the occasion requires, locked in the cellar when company comes, struggled with and worried about. It is difficult for someone not familiar with obedience to comprehend the ease and pleasure of living with a dog who will respond promptly and willingly to a quiet word, or a click of the tongue, a snap of the fingers, almost to a thought.

Another thing you will not find in this book is magic, or the "easy" way of training. There is no really "easy" way of training, or at least not in the sense of lack of application. To train a dog, you must put forth effort. It is our conviction, however, and it has been borne out through work with hundreds and even thousands of dogs of every variety and temperament, that directing your effort along the lines we suggest will show far more satisfactory results. There are tricks to every trade, and dog training is no exception. Such "tricks" as we explain will sometimes have almost magical results when applied to a dog who has been unable to learn by another method, but there is still no substitute for the thought and understanding behind each such "trick"—these you must have before you can apply them effectively.

There are extremely few exceptions to the statement that every dog can be trained, and certainly no exceptions to the fact that every dog should be trained. Age, after a certain minimum, is no limiter. Whatever type of training you may be interested in, home training, ring training, tricks, tracking—all of these we have treated. All these you can do. It is our hope that now you will do them, for a well trained dog, even at the most basic level, is a joy to own and a pleasure to be with.

ACKNOWLEDGEMENTS

The pictures in this book were taken by Mr. Bill Coursen and Mr. Ken Downs, and much of the chart and diagram material was prepared by Mr. Downs. We are also indebted to the owners and dogs who consented to act as models for these illustrations, and to Mr. Scott Peirsol of the Casa Linda, Daytona Beach for his cooperation.

Also, we are specially grateful to Dr. Dinny Tong, of the Cathedral Dog & Cat Hospital, New York City, for his invaluable assistance in preparing the chapter on Feeding and Health.

CONTENTS

INTRODUCTION   *vii*

   I   *CHOOSING THE PUP* 3

  II   *PRE-TRAINING* 23

 III   *BASIC TRAINING* 60

 IV   *NOVICE* 99

  V   *OPEN* 119

 VI   *UTILITY* 157

 VII   *THE OBEDIENCE RING* 188

VIII   *BRACE AND TEAM* 210

 IX   *TRACKING* 226

  X   *TRAINING PROBLEMS* 262

 XI   *FEEDING AND HEALTH* 294

 XII   *TRAVEL AND MISCELLANEOUS* 319

APPENDIX 349

INDEX 371

DOG OBEDIENCE
TRAINING

CHAPTER 1

CHOOSING THE PUP

To PARAPHRASE the old French recipe: first you get a dog. Then you train him. The kind of dog you get depends on you, of course, and on any number of factors of convenience, temperament (both of owner and dog), what you want a dog for, and conscious or unconscious tendencies toward one breed or another.

If you already have a strong leaning toward one breed, the best we can suggest is that you examine your choice in light of the considerations discussed later. Breed likings can be strong and irrational things, though, not easily subject to examination in the cold light of reason. One owner of a Doberman known to the authors would have none other because of a movie he had once seen in which a lean and beautiful Doberman played a supporting role as the minor villain. The owner of a majestic Great Dane admits his affair with the beast began in a showing of "The Hound of the Baskervilles." This Holmesian epic was equipped with a monstrous Dane leaping over the misty moors in the title role, inexplicably fitted out with a prop set of sabre-tooth fangs.

How many collies found happy homes on the basis of the appeal of Lassie will never be known, but their number is legion, even as the number of German Shepherds inspired by Rin-Tin-Tin and Strongheart. The breed going best-in-show at Madison Square Garden each year inspires its own small flurry of popularity.

There are major cycles of breed popularity for which there is no particularly good explanation. For many years the Cocker Spaniel held undisputed place in American homes as the most numerous pet, then the Beagle, and now the Poodle has taken over as the top dog, according to

American Kennel Club registrations. Within the major cycles there move smaller cycles, many of them regional. On the eastern seaboard not so many years ago the fancy was Scotties, preferably with unpronounceable and obscurantist Gaelic names. More recently the Poodle held sway, and then a rash of Boxers, in turn giving way to Chihuahuas.

Whether you already have a breed in mind, or have just decided that it is time you got a dog, the best possible thing you can do is go to an all-breed show. Once there, you can take a good close look at some of the best specimens of your favorite breed, or simply wander around and window-shop. With an interest in obedience, it is best to pick a show with attached obedience competition where you will have a chance to watch different breeds in action in the ring. Each of the two basic types of show, match and point, has its advantages for the window-shopper. Almost all point shows are benched, which means that when the dogs are not actually in the show ring they are in small stalls arranged by breed groups. Thus the dogs are in one place in some quantity, affording you a better opportunity to look them over. On the other hand, at a match show the atmosphere tends to be more informal. The exhibitors sit, stand or walk around with their dogs on leash when not in the ring, and the opportunities for striking up conversation are greater.

When you have more or less decided on a breed, or on several possibilities, talk to the owners at the benches or at the ringside. Most owners will be glad to tell you anything you want to know about their breed. Remember, though, that when you talk to an owner at a dog show you are talking to an avid partisan of that particular breed. You will learn a great many of the facts of life about dog-owning, and about that breed, but you will also find that his breed is brave, loyal, obedient, resourceful, trustworthy and so on all through the catalog of the major virtues. And you will in all likelihood also find that any other breed is mean, vicious, dull-witted, coarse and tinged with dubious ancestry.

It takes a little skepticism and judiciousness to separate the woof from the warp, but nonetheless you will find out more about dogs and breeds by assiduous conversing and careful looking at a dog show than anywhere else. To find out when and where a dog show will be held near you, look in almost any of the dog magazines, or write to the American Kennel Club (221 4th Ave., New York, N. Y.) for help.

PUREBRED OR MONGREL

Probably the most basic of all considerations is that of whether you want a purebred dog or a mongrel. If the circumstances (of which price is not an inconsiderable one) incline you to a mongrel, all the above advice on dog shows is of course superfluous, as is much of the following material on competition obedience, and on temperament. For when you acquire a mongrel pup, you are taking pot luck of the chanciest sort.

If you get a mongrel pup from a friend, you at least have the advantage of knowing something about its mother, and some clue as to the ultimate size, coat, coloring, intelligence and disposition of the cuddly child you take into your household. But if the pup arrives via pet shop or animal shelter you are deprived of even this. Knowing nothing of the ancestry or age of your acquisition, you may not know until much too late that the lovable bundle of fur has turned into a lumbering giant with hair like a llama. This outcome is unlikely, as constantly mixed breeding tends toward the average, but it emphasizes the uncertainties you acquire with the aptly named "Heinz."

The controversy over the intelligence of purebred vs. mongrel has raged for centuries, but it is neither true that street-roaming mongrels have naturally sharper wits than "pampered" purebreds, nor that constant mixing has somehow scrambled the brains of mongrels. Dog for dog, the mongrel is probably fully as intelligent as the average purebred. The major advantage of the purebred is that the mixed mutt does not offer known instinctual traits. It is these known traits in the purebred that offer such a variety of choice, and such possibilities of temperament-matching to the prospective owner.

Additionally, if you are interested seriously in obedience work, there is the serious handicap that only obviously purebred dogs are allowed to compete in the dog show obedience ring.

PUREBRED DOGS

There are three terms that apply to dogs: purebred, registered and pedigreed (thoroughbred is incorrect when applied to dogs). In general, a dog will be all three, but not necessarily. A purebred is a dog whose ancestry is obviously 100 percent of a single breed; a registered dog is one registered with the AKC as certifiedly purebred, and a pedigreed dog is simply a purebred whose ancestry for several generations is officially attested by a written and signed pedigree.

The American Kennel Club, the ruling authority of purebred dogdom, officially recognizes and accepts for registration 115 breeds. These range from the giant Danes and Irish Wolfhounds to the Chihuahuas and the Mexican Hairless, and encompass anything in size, coat, temperament, intelligence and aptitude that anyone could want.

These are divided into six major groups:

Sporting—dogs used for hunting of game birds.

Hounds—racing dogs and game hunters.

Working—shepherds, guard and rescue dogs.

Terriers—rodent hunters.

Toys—very small pet dogs.

Non-Sporting—catchall group.

In addition, there are twelve breeds officially recognized as purebred by the AKC and accepted in obedience rings, though not for breed judging beyond a "Miscellaneous" class at some shows. It is extremely unlikely that any of these will come under your consideration in the choice of a pup, as the majority are almost totally unknown even to veteran "dog people." The twelve include such exotic breeds as Chinese Crested Dogs, Russian Owtchars, Shi Tzus and Spinoni Italiani.

Any attempt at describing each of the AKC dogs would take a book in itself, and providentially the AKC has done just that. We can recommend highly the AKC's "Complete Dog Book" which has pictures of each breed, a short history of each, and the accepted standard of the breed. This latter can be especially helpful to you when you have gotten down to shopping around within one breed, as the standard sets out in clear terms just what is most desirable in physical conformation and temperament of every breed. If you read it closely and keep the major points in mind while inspecting dogs, you may well avoid serious mistakes in choosing.

SOME BASIC CONSIDERATIONS

Temperament is probably the major factor that will guide you in your choice of a dog. The pup you buy now will be your companion for many years, and it is his disposition and personality that you will be living with rather than his looks. Within the AKC's 115 breeds there is every range of temperament from the lethargic to the hyper-active, from extra friendly to highly reserved, from comic and playful to serious.

It is of course impossible to make any broad generalizations on temperament, particularly as temperament can vary widely within the same breed. Here again the best possible guide is personal observation and whatever advice you can get from friends and people at shows. You should, as much as possible, try to get a fairly close match between your general outlook on life and the known characteristics of a breed. A generally jovial and outgoing owner is not likely to be happy with a moody and reserved dog, and the constant running and whirling of a vivacious terrier could very easily drive a sedentary or nervous master to distraction.

In the young puppy, certain general outlines of character will show. If, for example, you want a very friendly dog, by all means choose from the litter the pup that first runs to you and greets you with glad tail-wagging and licks. If you prefer the reserved type, then choose the one who hangs back and minds his own business despite your opening blandishments. But be careful in this case that his reserved air is not the result of some fundamental defect like illness or deafness, or the result of timidity about the whole world.

There can of course be no guarantee from the actions of the pup as to his final disposition. The basics are there already, but so much depends on his environment while growing up, on your treatment of him, that you can really only establish the basics, and then work from there. Some things should be strictly avoided, such as timidity. A pup who already shows a basic fear of his environment at the age of three or four months will probably never become courageous. But the average happy, active puppy can be molded into whatever you want—and that is what obedience training is for.

If you are firmly set on some particular temperament, the best course for you is to start looking at older puppies, or even at mature dogs. By the time a dog is, say, a year old, his personality will be largely formed, and in buying a dog of this age you can be pretty sure of what you are getting into. But this too has its drawbacks, as will be discussed later.

One friend of the authors' took this "older dog" way in choosing his dog, however, with no ill results visible to date. For reasons best known to himself he wanted a highly aggressive Doberman. Touring the kennels, he looked at pups in the 6-9 months age group, and to each dog he liked the looks of he applied his personal test, which consisted of running suddenly at the dog with a stick as if to hit him. When he found the one pup who nearly tore his chain out of the wall in a snarling return lunge, he had found his dog. It took a good many repeat visits to the kennel, steak in hand, before that pup consented to have anything to do with him, but once a truce was effected they lived happily ever after.

Completely at the other extreme was the young couple who took home a soft and cuddly German Shepherd pup and lavished much affection on him. They were completely inexperienced with dogs, and somehow seem not to have realized that pups do grow up. The inevitable, in their case, happened when one day they found themselves with a year-old, 70-pound reasonable facsimile of a wolf in the household. The day he tried an experimental snarl when they punished him for some misdemeanor, they were frightened silly at the sight of all those big sharp teeth on their erstwhile bundle of joy. The dog, of course, realized very quickly that he had the controlling hand in things, and until the day the couple managed to return him to the kennel (and an unusually accommodating kennel it was) he ruled the household with an iron paw. It happens that in this case one of the authors spent several hours with the dog a few days after his return, and a gentler, friendlier dog could hardly be found. It was simply a case of the owners' having no idea of what they were getting or what they really wanted when they got their pup.

Size is another factor that should figure heavily in your selection. Both for your own comfort and for the happiness of the dog, you should as carefully as possible judge the maximum size of dog you should have. Keeping a large dog in a small city apartment can be literal cruelty. Even in a city house or in a development or suburban area where you may have to keep the dog inside most of the time, too large a dog can be inconvenient. Particularly if he is an active large dog, your nerves might be completely undone, along with your precious bric-a-brac, by ponderous lungings and crashings about. As a fairly good rule, the difficulty of traveling with a dog increases in direct proportion to his size—and the amount of traveling you do is another factor in choosing a size. A Chihuahua can be carried almost anywhere quite conveniently in a small traveling case, but public transportation people tend to get quite stuffy about Great Danes, and a Dane even in your private car takes up enough room for several humans.

If you are undecided whether to get a long-haired or a short-haired dog, your decision can be very quickly made on the basis of the time you are willing and able to put into grooming and picking up shed hairs. The long-haired varieties require constant grooming, plucking, combing, cutting and brushing if their coats are to be kept in even tolerably good condition, and when they shed, the evidence is everywhere in abundance. The short-haired breeds seldom require more than a regular brushing with a good stiff-bristle brush, and when they shed it is considerably less evident and annoying.

MALE OR FEMALE

Almost every dog owner you talk to will give you a different reason for choosing either a male or a female as your dog. In actuality, the difference is small indeed. The male dog of almost any breed tends to be slightly larger, if that is a consideration. In serious obedience work the male has the advantage that he will be eligible for the ring all throughout the year, while the female will be barred when she is in season. On the other hand, the female is less likely to be thrown off in the ring by other dogs' smells, as is the case sometimes with the male. Neither sex is conspicuously the better performer.

Around the house, the female suffers only from the fact that her twice-yearly "season" (10-21 days each time) entails close watching against the possibility of unwanted pups. She may also go into a false pregnancy after a season, and consider herself very delicate and motherly for a few weeks, which can be wearing. And during those seasons you may have the neighborhood males baying about the house until you're ready to call the law. Balancing the scale, the male dog may spend more of his time than you think proper baying about someone else's in-season female, he is far and away more likely to try to pick a fight on the street, and he occasionally will try to drag you off bodily, while walking, on the sweet-scented trail of some female, lo these three days gone.

Another minor consideration, if your dog-walking time is at a premium, is the fact that, once housebroken, the average female will relieve herself as soon as she hits the street, for once and for all, and then will be glad to take as much of a walk as you care to give her. The male is the more ruminative of the two, and if he feels like holding it for a while, no power on earth can persuade him to accommodate your wishes. He will stroll happily around until he has found the half-dozen spots he wants to anoint on that particular day, and time has no meaning for him until he has found them.

ONE DOG OR TWO

Two dogs in one household can be twice as much fun as one, but the problems of keeping more than one dog can increase all out of proportion to the number of dogs, or at least seem to. The major argument advanced in the cause of two dogs is that they will keep each other company, and that playing together they will do less damage to property during the puppy-chewing stage. Both of these claims need close scrutiny, because they are both true and false.

Two dogs may indeed keep each other company, whether the owner is at home or away, but on the other hand they may merely tolerate each other and be just as lonely when the owner is gone as if they were alone. They may, in fact, decide one day that even toleration is too much to ask, have a serious disagreement while you're off shopping, and leave you with one or more badly damaged dogs when you return. Even the most deceptively friendly pair of dogs can have a falling out over a seeming trifle, much like their human owners. But when two healthy dogs decide to disagree, the result is generally more than hurt feelings if there is nobody around to restrain them. It isn't inevitable, but it can and does happen, particularly with two males. A male and a female together offer less chance, and two females together seem fairly safe, but the chance is always there.

The argument that their playing together while you're gone will prevent damage to the furniture is open to serious doubt, indeed. Two rambunctious puppies are just as likely to decide that your possessions make wonderful toys as one. Many a two-dog owner has been greeted at his door by the sight of a room seemingly knee-deep in sofa-cushion stuffing and his beloved pups happily playing tug-of-war with the remains of the covering. Even the perfectly innocent play of two dogs, especially dogs in the medium-to-large sizes, can be nerve-wracking and damaging. One New York City couple with two Doberman pups has trouble because of over-friendliness. The two, a year old at this writing, are happiest when careening around the apartment in seemingly savage mock battles involving much snarling and clashing of fangs. Imagine, if you will, two 70-pound dogs crashing full-tilt through your legs, caroming happily off furniture, clawing into fast turns on your best rug, and all accompanied by blood-curdling sound effects. True, they will outgrow it as sedate maturity comes along, but in the meantime the apartment is about as peaceful as Bunker Hill.

Some of the practical considerations are: (1) two dogs eat twice as much as one; (2) all your inoculations and preventive medicines will cost you twice as much. And as dogs seldom have the consideration to take sick or be injured at the same time, your trips to the vet will double; (3) housebreaking will be more than twice as hard, as the very young puppies will without fail operate on distinctly different schedules, necessitating twice as many rush trips out of the house or to the papers and leaving open the possibility of accident by one while the other is being attended to. Two pups, believe us, are more than twice as hard to keep the requisite sharp eye on than one; and (4) training problems will increase manifold, what with the necessity of training each separately and the almost inevitable difference in learning rate.

Do not, however, take the above as an indictment of the idea of more than one dog. If you're willing to devote the extra time and effort to the cause, you will be amply rewarded, because two dogs can be much more than twice the fun.

AGE OF THE PUP

How old should he be when you get him? Three to four months is the ideal age, for many reasons. By that time, the pup will be well weaned from his mother and fairly well embarked on life. At four months he will be just about ready for housebreaking. The first signs of his personality will have begun to show. Getting a pup younger than three months is a distinctly touchy proposition, especially if you have little or no prior experience with puppies. Before three months, the pup is little more than a mass of instincts, almost totally non-amenable to training or influence, and the number of things that can go wrong physically with a very young puppy are overwhelming.

As the pup gets older than four months, his desirability as a pet acquisition falls rapidly. By five or six months he may have developed strong emotional ties with his kennel-man, difficult to transfer to yourself. The central idea in getting a young puppy rather than an older one or a grown dog is that his first affection, after the instinctual stages, can become firmly fastened on you and you alone, without divided loyalties. Aside from that, the earlier you begin molding the pup's outlook on life to your own, the better your personalities are going to mesh through your life together. A pup older than ten months begins to come into the "grown dog" category in the problems he may present you with. If he has lived in a kennel for ten months he will be completely un-housebroken, and his free and easy ways of taking care of his needs will be much harder to correct than in a four-month-old. Whatever bad habits he may have acquired will have a much greater chance of being well-set, and much harder to erase and replace with good ones. And, again, he may have developed attachments to his surroundings and current owners that will be hard to transfer to yourself and your home.

WHICH DOG FOR OBEDIENCE?

Much has been written, and much more said, about the obedience capacities of the various breeds. If you are interested in serious competition obedience work, you may be looking for the "right" dog, the one who learns and performs best. Every trainer, including the professional, has his own personal choice in dogs for training, and is usually quite vocal about it, but the basic fact is that any breed can be trained in obedience and can achieve the highest degree, the U.D. (Utility Dog).

In 40 AKC obedience trials across the country during one month, the winners of first place in the Utility classes (the most advanced classes) were: Shetland Sheepdog (7), German Shepherd (5), Golden Retriever (4), Standard Poodle (3); Doberman, Boxer, Dalmatian, Pomeranian, Collie, Papillon, Border Collie and Great Dane (2 each); and German Shorthaired Pointer, Miniature Poodle, Weimaraner, Cocker Spaniel, and English Springer Spaniel (1 each.)

Among the winners of other classes in these same 40 shows were: Norwegian Elkhound, Miniature Pinscher, Schipperke, Labrador Retriever, Pembroke Welsh Corgi, Miniature Schnauzer, Welsh Terrier, Samoyed, Chesapeake Bay Retriever, Rough Collie, Pointer, Smooth Fox Terrier, Brittany Spaniel, Irish Setter, Boston Terrier, Dachshund and Wire Fox Terrier.

There could hardly be a greater diversification of breeds than those represented above, with dogs of every size and from each of the six AKC groups, yet each dog outscored all competition in a class open to all breeds.

While any dog can be trained, as shown above, it is true in broad terms that certain breeds are generally somewhat easier to train than others. The most likely candidate for the "easiest to train" accolade is the Working Group. These dogs, the German Shepherds, Dobermans, Boxers, Collies and the like, have a long heritage of working at command, and this aptitude for obedience is an inherited characteristic. Yet the Poodle, member of the catch-all Non-Sporting Group, is generally acknowledged to be the most intelligent of dogs, and the quickest to learn. The Poodle, however, has as a drawback his capricious nature. He may work perfectly one day, and the next day seem never to have heard of obedience.

The size of the dog is something to be considered, from the viewpoint of trainer and handler. Chihuahuas and Danes are as easily trainable as the next dog, but their physiques are something to think about before you start on one. Especially if you are not a particularly large human, you may not feel equal to the pushing and hauling that are in store for you when you tackle the training of a Great Dane, or say a St. Bernard or an

Irish Wolfhound. These dogs are all in the over-100-pound class, and there is no small amount of effort involved in pushing a really recalcitrant giant canine into the sitting position if he happens not to feel like sitting. At the other end of the scale, the really tiny toy breeds require considerable delicacy in handling, because too hasty or forceful a correction could seriously injure a toy.

BUYING THE PUP

By this time you've decided on the kind of pup you want, and the big question faces you: Where do I get it? The answer is, by all means from an established, reputable breeder and/or kennel. There are three good ways to find out about breeders in your area: the AKC, breed clubs, and shows in the area. The AKC maintains a "Breeder Information" service purely as a courtesy service to those interested in buying a dog. They will send you, on request, a list of breeders in your general area handling the breed of your choice (and if it's a numerically unpopular breed, don't be surprised if the nearest breeder is several hundred miles or more distant). Also, the AKC's monthly magazine "Pure Bred Dogs" carries extensive advertising by breeders of almost all breeds. The AKC, however, cannot recommend any one kennel—and their listing carries no guarantee of the quality of the puppies sold. It only means that the kennel or breeder is in good standing with the AKC; that it has not been involved in any deal or transaction that would cause the AKC to withdraw registration or showing privileges from it.

The national breed clubs (see AKC's "Pure Bred Dogs" for a listing of breed clubs) will generally be glad to be of assistance to anyone interested in buying a dog of their breed, and a letter to the secretary will bring you the names of affiliated kennels in your area. At shows, too, you can generally contact breeders, either through just walking around and striking up conversations at the benches, or watching for the kennel signs on the benches.

Pet shops are another matter entirely. While there are many clean, honest and reputable pet shops throughout the country, the ethics and standards of a large percentage are open to serious question. The bouncing, wistful pups in the window have an appeal unequalled in window displays, but they are distinctly not for the buyer seriously interested in a good, life-long pet. While it is undoubtedly true that pet-shop dogs have become excellent, healthy and loyal pets, and that champion show dogs have in rare cases come from such a shop, the odds are distinctly against you. You have no way in the world of knowing the quality of the shop's stock, extremely little chance of finding any former customers to talk to, and a not inconsiderable chance of getting a complete dud. Pet shops are the places where many breeders will get rid of their "culls," poor quality dogs from good litters . . . and you can bet that the cull's parentage is untraceable and he himself unregisterable. This is not, however, meant as a blanket indictment of pet shops. Some are excellent, clean and above-board. Their dogs are healthy and the owners anxious to build and maintain a good reputation. But unless you have some source of excellent advice, don't gamble on the chance of accidentally finding one of the good ones.

Buying a puppy is not very different from buying anything else, except perhaps that a first-time buyer of a dog is generally far more ignorant of the "product" than the buyer of a car or a refrigerator. The major principles to be observed are: find out as much as possible about the breed before beginning to shop; take a good long look around before buying, and don't let yourself be stampeded into buying anything until you're completely satisfied that it's what you want. Always remember that, barring accident, you're going to spend a good many years with your dog, and a dog is not the kind of thing that can be traded in on a new and different model with any great ease.

With your list of breeders in hand, and your desires firmly fixed in mind, you can now start shopping. Be sure to call ahead of your kennel visits, to find out if there is any puppy stock available, and to let the breeder know you're coming. Breeders are not open certain hours daily like a store, and most puppy showing is by appointment. The breeder will be glad to give you as much information as possible over the phone, including directions on how to get there. And when you do get there, remember that the breeder is not a clerk bent only on making a sale; he is an independent businessman who loves dogs, and he is just as eager to make sure his puppies get placed with the right people as you are to get the right pup.

The first step is to look the kennel or breeding quarters over carefully. Satisfy yourself that the "plant" is clean and well cared for. But don't be offended or feel immediately that something is wrong if the breeder asks you not to come right into the kennels proper. He's rightly concerned with the health of his pups, and if you've come straight to him from another kennel on your shopping tour he simply can't take the chance that you might be innocently carrying a vagrant dog-disease germ from the last place. A virulent strain of disease brought in from outside can literally wipe out a kennel—it has happened—and so the breeder is well within his rights in exercising a certain caution. You can tell quickly enough without walking right into the kennels whether everything is clean and in order and if the place "feels" right. If not, make your excuses and walk out quickly.

Up to this point, we'll say, everything has gone well, and the puppies have been brought out for your approval. Right then and there, watch out! The appeal of a clutch of tumbling puppies can be overpowering, and the time to hitch up your sales resistance is right then. Look them over carefully with a skeptical eye and feel perfectly free to ask as many questions as you can think of about their parentage, their health, their prospects and anything else that comes to mind. Talk it over thoroughly with the breeder. He wants to make a sale, true, but he also wants to make sure he has a satisfied customer. A breeder's reputation can be very quickly scuttled by a few vocally unhappy owners of his pups, and this he wants of course to avoid.

Watch the pups carefully. Look for good strong bones. Look for clear eyes and a playful disposition. Watch for a good coat in healthy condition. Snap your fingers behind the pups' backs to check their hearing and alertness. And if you've found one you think is the one for you, don't hesitate to ask the breeder to take his temperature and show you the reading. The temperature of a healthy pup will be up to 102°. Above that watch out, for temperature is the surest known indication of the state of a dog's health.

If you've conscientiously shopped around among the available breeders, and now think you've found THE pup, start all over again. Look very, very closely at this little animal who may share your life for the next 10 years. Watch all his reactions carefully, particularly how he reacts to the people around him. If he recoils from people, he may have been mistreated, or he may be naturally timid. Avoid him like the plague, but don't rule out a dignified pup who is simply reserved about people. You can tell the difference if you've looked at a few litters. Then, start asking questions about his ancestry, if you haven't already satisfied yourself on that score. Most breeders will be eager to show you a pedigree already drawn up for the youngster. Make sure that he is already registered as one of a litter, and that he is fully eligible for registration with the AKC. And be sure to have a clear understanding with the breeder as to who will handle and pay for the official AKC transfer of registration and ownership.

Get all the medical details straight on your pup. Get a written statement from the breeder detailing which preventive shots the pup has had and whether he has been wormed and if so when and how. Get the details of the pup's diet so you can continue to offer him familiar food when he is abruptly thrown into the strange surroundings of your home.

Most important, get him checked by a reliable veterinarian. If at all possible, have the vet come with you to the kennel to give your choice a thorough examination. In some cases, the breeder will allow you to take the pup with you to the vet, but many of them shy away from this practice because they have in effect guaranteed to take the pup back if anything is found wrong with him, and what happens to him between the time you take him and the time he shows up at the vet's is completely out of his control. But if you *do* take him away with you to the vet, and leave a deposit or the full price, have the understanding clearly in writing that the pup is returnable for a full refund if the vet turns thumbs down on him. And whatever you do, take the vet's good advice, even if it means returning the most lovable little bundle of fur you have ever encountered. He won't advise against a dog without good reason, and if you take a sick or weak puppy, you are in for nothing but large doses of trouble. And by all means, if there is any reluctance on the part of *any* seller of a pup to have a medical examination done by a vet *of your choice* before the sale is completed, pick up your hat and politely but firmly do not touch the deal with the traditional pole.

WHAT WILL IT COST

Very generally speaking, a purebred puppy will cost between $50 and $150, with the majority of the prices in the high half of that scale. You will rarely, if ever, find a good pup selling for less than $50, and in some cases the prices are well above $150, depending on the breed, ancestry, and the prospects of the pup. While there is no sure way of telling which pup of a litter is a future show champion, many show apparent good prospects early, and the breeder will set a higher price on these specials, hoping to sell them to someone interested in breed showing and future breeding of their own. If you are looking for a pet and an obedience dog alone, the best thing is to leave these show prospects out of your considerations.

When the question of payment comes up, most breeders will of course prefer cash in hand when they part with the pup, but many will be glad to make arrangements for split payment if you can satisfy them that you are a good credit risk. Dog buying very rarely gets into the true installment range, though. Most breeders simply won't be bothered with small monthly payments and won't want to get into anything beyond a three-payment deal. So if you're not paying cash, plan to pay at least one-third of the pup's price at the time, and the rest in two equal payments, probably at monthly intervals.

Prices vary, of course, within a breed, but you will find that the variation from one breeder to another is relatively slight for an average pup. If you find a pup whose price is unusually low, tread with caution. Dog-buying is one field in which it is never wise for the novice to go bargain-hunting. If the price is exceptionally low, there is a good likelihood that something is wrong somewhere. One extra veterinarian's bill can eat up the difference in price if you get hold of a lemon, or you may well pay many times the difference in price in your disappointment with a poor specimen.

There's very little haggling over price in dog selling. The price is the price, and that's about that. Of course, there are breeders who do haggle, but most of them won't take it very well if you try to knock their price down. Occasionally a breeder will shave his price if he takes a liking to you and if he feels that his pup will find an exceptionally good home with you. Don't count on it, though.

CONDITIONS OF SALE

In most cases, there are no conditions attaching to the sale of a puppy. Once you have paid for him, he is yours to have and to hold et cetera. The breeder may ask you if you intend to show the dog in breed, and it is to him a highly pertinent point. A breeder's reputation rests solely on the quality of his dogs, and the major way that quality is proven is through breed ring awards and championships. Therefore, if he has what he thinks of as a particularly good litter, or pup, he will want it to be shown in order to add to the glory of his line. The breeder may, in fact, refuse to sell a pup unless he has some sort of guarantee that you will show, or that you will allow him to show it. Our advice is that you stay clear of this sort of arrangement, especially the latter sort. A "guarantee" of this sort can involve you in having your dog away from you several times during the year if the breeder takes him for conditioning prior to a show, or takes him on one of the "circuits" of the dog show world. Steer clear of any showing guarantee if you just want a pet and obedience dog.

It is a good idea, too, to avoid any entangling alliances in regard to the future breeding of your pup. The breeder may ask you to allow future use of a male at stud if he turns out well, or ask you to guarantee future mating of a female, or an option on future pups or litters. These stipulations are scarce, but they do occur—good breeders devote a great deal of study to genetics and blood lines and matched breedings to improve the breed, and they like to keep things as much under control as possible. In all likelihood you, as a pet buyer, will never run into any of these things, but if you do, think over the consequences before you agree.

REGISTRATION AND PEDIGREES

As explained earlier, registration simply means that a dog is registered with the AKC. This in turn means that he is certified as a purebred member of one of the AKC's 115 breeds, usually attested to by the fact that his parents were registered, and so on. When a litter is born, the breeder will register the litter as a whole. He may already have an individual registration certificate on each, which he will give to you at the time of sale.

In this case, you have only to fill out the information on the reverse side on change of ownership and send it to the AKC, which will then send you registration papers naming you as owner.

You may have to send in an individual registration application (available from the AKC) on the pup. If you do so yourself, be sure the application has the breeder's signature *and* the signature of the owner of the sire.

Whatever the case, be prepared to wait patiently for your certificate, as the AKC registers thousands of dogs monthly, and the formalities may take as much as two months. And be sure to have an understanding with the breeder as to who will pay for the registration and/or change of ownership, as the AKC makes a nominal charge for this. For your own peace of mind, it might be wise to get the signed application and send it in yourself, for then you know it has been done, although with any reputable breeder there is no question of its being taken care of once the breeder says it will be done.

When your certificate arrives from the AKC it will have on it the name of the dog, the names of his sire and dam, his registered number, the name of the breeder, and your name and address as owner. The registered number is especially vital, as it is by this number that he is kept track of in AKC files for the rest of his life. The code letter preceding it denotes group (W for Working, H for Hound, etc.) and the figures currently run to six digits. If you ever have cause to look into your acquisition's ancestry, you will find that originally the AKC simply gave a number, such as 345,678—but when they got to 999,999 they decided things would get unwieldly in the seven-digit range and began to issue numbers with the prefix "A." Those ran along for a while and then someone saw the handwriting on the wall as registrations poured in, and the present group prefix system was adopted.

The pedigree of your dog is simply a listing of his ancestors for as many generations back as you are interested in. Many breeders will supply you with a pedigree already drawn up (usually three or four generations) at the time of sale, as they are intensely proud of the breeding of their pups. These will usually be on a nicely designed pedigree blank supplied by one of the dog-food companies, and will be signed by the breeder as being true to the best of his knowledge. If you want to go further and have a signed and sealed affirmation of ancestry, the AKC will look up and make out an official pedigree for you if you supply them with name and number, and their pedigree fee ($3 for three generations, $6 for four).

A pedigree is a nice thing to have around the house, and a moderate sprinkling of Champions and/or UD's in your pup's family tree can be a matter of considerable pride to you.

NAMING THE PUP

In 98% of the cases, your pup will come to you already tagged with a long and impressive multiple name, usually including the kennel name of the breeder. Once that name is established with the AKC, it is your dog's name forever and thereafter, as the AKC (for quite good reasons, incidentally) refuses to alter the registered name of a dog. The tendency in the official name of a dog is to the multi-syllabic, to identify him among the hundreds and thousands of other dogs of the breed. Names also run to strong similarity in each breed, being generally of a ponderous or massive nature for the giants, Germanic and fierce-sounding for many of the working breeds, sometimes cute and precious for the toys, and along nationality lines: French for Poodles, Gaelic for Scotties, Chinese for Pekingese and so forth. So, depending on your breed, you may find yourself owning something grand like "Destructor the Invincible von Hohenzollern-Hapsburg" or something so coy and ludicrous you want to hide when you hear it applied to your very own. But there it is—you're stuck with it.

But there is hope in the dog's "call" name, which is what you choose to call him under non-official conditions. If you should happen to acquire Destructor the Invincible there is nothing in the world to keep you from calling him plain Gus if it strikes your fancy, or even Stupid. Frequently, the dog's call name is part of his official name. For example, friend Destructor could be called "Des" or "Vince" as a shortening of part of his name. But it's up to you.

A word of caution, though—try to make his name a little distinctive; away from the Spot, Rover, Queenie line. Also, if possible, make it of one syllable (for ease in calling) and preferably something with a plosive at the front end (p, b, d, or similar consonants). Makes for a stronger sounding word when you want his attention, which will be often enough. Particularly if you are interested in serious obedience competition, make it short and snappy, individual (it could easily confuse him to hear his name called from an adjoining ring while he's in the process of performing in his own ring), and try to avoid having it sound too much like any of the standard obedience commands, for much the same reason. If you want to call your dog "Heel," "Peel," or "Deal," fine and dandy, but he can end up a mighty mixed-up dog if he's trying to do good work in a ring while his name, or something very similar, keeps ringing out from the area next door.

In any case, it's your dog now, and call him what you will—he won't mind much what it is, as long as you call him.

CHAPTER II

PRE-TRAINING

The moment you bring the young puppy home, training begins. As an adult dog, he will represent the total of his experiences with you. What you permit him to do, what you forbid him, what you encourage him in, and what you persuade him to do by active training—these are going to pattern the behavior of the mature dog.

More important than any of these, though, is *how* you permit, forbid, encourage and persuade him. How you treat him will depend entirely on your attitude towards him and on your conceptions of what a dog is and how it works. The dog's mind does work in certain ways, and it does not work in others. If these ways are clearly understood, three-quarters of the problems of civilizing and training will be solved from the outset.

A dog can and does do certain things. He learns certain patterns of behavior, and he learns to avoid other patterns. He learns to respond to words of command, positive and negative. He learns to love and hate. He can learn to do an astonishing variety of things that can easily lead to the conclusion that he has thought the situation through, but it just isn't so.

He cannot follow any extended line of reasoning, equate cause and effect over any period of time, reach rational conclusions about series of events, or do most of the many mental acrobatics some people hold the dog capable of.

No matter about the wonder dog you heard of from Aunt Matilda, who buys the groceries, prices the chops and translates from the Hebrew. Old Shep may be the nearest thing to a human being in the block, but it isn't because he ponders the state of the world, rather that he has a certain combination of instincts, training and an expressive face.

23

(Along these lines there is the experience of one of the authors with a "talking dog" in England. She was a German Shepherd, billed as "Rita the Talking Alsatian," and her specialty was mathematics. She would bark out the answer to the most abstruse problem you could think of as long as it was a whole number, and preferably a low one. There is no sillier feeling in the world than that of facing a dog and saying to her, "Rita, what is the square root of 81" and expecting to get an answer, but she was put to the test and came through admirably. Although she *could* count up to ten, as demonstrated by her barking the right number of times for a number of fingers held up, she couldn't answer any problem her handler didn't himself know the answer to, which pretty well gives the game away after a while. Rita had simply been trained with almost unbelievable patience to respond to minute signals and cues—you could do it with your own pup if you wanted to devote your life to it. We don't recommend it, though. It might be a bit uncomfortable explaining to your friends why the dog handles the family accounts.)

Whatever "thinking" as such can be taken to mean, the dog does not think constructively about training. However intelligent he is, however delicately he may react to your feelings, whatever instincts guide him, you will be avoiding a great deal of trouble in training if you hold fast to the fact that the dog is an animal—a creature of limited intelligence, however lovable, motivated by desire for pleasant sensations and avoidance of unpleasantness. What you want him to do you must demonstrate to him, again and again, without expecting any sort of thoughtful cooperation. He will cooperate to the extent that performance of what you want is made pleasurable to him, and non-performance is made uncomfortable. He has not, and never will have, a conscience. He has no concept of right or wrong, should or shouldn't. He may look guilty at times, but he doesn't feel that way—all that "hangdog" expression on his face means is that he has detected a threatening attitude in you and he's worried about that, not about whatever it was he did or didn't do.

There are many things you should not do when handling and training a dog, and these, along with what you should do, will be taken up with each particular point in training. There is however, one overriding principle to follow in all your contacts with your dog, and that is the basic one of love and confidence. Your dog must never get the feeling that you have withdrawn your love and affection from him. It is something that he will never understand, and will in fact never connect with either performance or non-performance. Insofar as you can manage it, he must never associate unpleasantness with you—and that is easier than it sounds. When it is necessary to correct him, the correction is made to be associated in his mind with his misdeed of whatever nature, and he will accept it as such. It's easy to see that no good will come of giving him the idea that *you* will correct him for misbehavior, for if he should manage to get that idea firmly in his head he'd run wild as soon as you were out of sight.

The object of your training your dog is to make him an acceptable companion and to equip him to live in your civilized world without giving offense, and in the later stages of training, to make him even better to live with and, in fact, actually useful. As to whether training makes a happier dog we have serious doubts. We have never been able to discern any significant difference in inner happiness between a well-trained dog and a messy lout—the difference lies in the reactions of society to him. The ill-trained or untrained dog tends to get booted about and generally disapproved of when he comes into contact with society, while the trained dog gets a pat and a biscuit. And there you have it; the dog is going to be trained for your benefit primarily, and only secondarily for his. You want him around because he's your dog, and it's a lot pleasanter to have him around if he has manners.

When you bring the puppy home, you are faced with a number of simultaneous problems. He has to learn to love you, which isn't too difficult if you're even barely civil to him (and believe us, he doesn't care a hoot about you for a while; he *learns* to). He has to be taught to control himself in the basic sanitary considerations, and he has to learn respect for such things as your possessions and your household routine.

First of all, the pup must have some place in the house that is exclusively his own. In the first days, this is not necessarily the one that will always be his, as the problem of housebreaking will dictate his preliminary quarters. In whichever room you're going to assign as the housebreaking room, make him a comfortable bed out of something old and discarded of yours—a pair of pants, an old dress, a tattered blanket or whatever. Old clothing will serve the dual purpose of giving him something soft to lie on, and of having your smell predominant in his sleeping quarters. You can, whatever his size, make him a low box of sorts, but make it something he can get into and out of himself. Otherwise he will be forced to soil his own sleeping quarters when you're not around to lift him out—and even the youngest pup hates that sort of thing.

Resolve yourself to practice considerable restraint for the first few days and weeks. Let his housebreaking room be his home and *keep him there.* However much it may delight you to see the cuddly little devil shambling about your living room, weakly nosing and investigating things, you will have lost considerable ground even before you start when he relieves himself on the Persian carpet. He's going to have a long life to wander about the house, and he'll be just as cute when he makes those first investigations after he's housebroken.

As soon as you get him in the house, take him to his bed and plop him there. He'll probably be all tired out and ready for a good sleep, as the trip from the kennel will have been a pretty wearing thing for him. If he goes right to sleep, all well and good. If he wants to roam around right away, let him, but only in the housebreaking area. And as soon as he steps foot outside of his bed, housebreaking begins.

HOUSEBREAKING

What you are faced with is a young animal who is only just beginning to have control over the sphincter muscles that control his functions. This control is still weak, and has been building up largely due to the fact of his unwillingness to soil his own quarters. Your job now is to concentrate his attention on further control, and to extend the unwillingness to soil his sleeping area to an unwillingness to make a mess anywhere in the house.

This assumes a pup in the 3-4 months age group. Anything much younger than that will simply not have enough muscular control to do what you want him to. If, for some reason, you have gotten a younger pup (and we advise strongly against it, for this and other reasons) about the only thing you can do is wait for the right age to come along. Almost any attempt to house-train a pup before he is physically ready for it will only confuse and bewilder him, and will set back all your training efforts a long way.

The most practical method of housebreaking, all things considered, involves preliminary paper-breaking for the puppy. He first learns that newspapers spread on the floor are the place to go, and then his attentions are progressively directed to the outside as the preferred place. Pure housebreaking from the beginning is very difficult, particularly for city dwellers who may live on the 17th floor of a large apartment house. The young pup will find it necessary to relieve himself a great many times per day, and if you have very far to go before you hit the street you will become exhausted, discouraged, probably wet, and won't accomplish much.

Despite all the popular lore, housebreaking is neither a hard nor extensive job. Ten days to two weeks will see the worst of it out of the way. True, at the end of that time the pup won't be completely cured, but the bulk of the work will have been done. Keep in mind only that the job requires as constant vigilance as does caring for a new-born child. But if you do it right there's a great feeling of accomplishment, and it's done for his lifetime.

The housebreaking regime we recommend, while not hard, is one which requires constant attention. We realize full well that household chores, child-tending, and other considerations may make it impossible to give undivided attention, even for a week or so, to keeping a beady eye constantly on the pup. What we have laid out is the "ideal" way to go about it—if the pressure of other affairs keeps you from living up to the letter of what follows, it isn't as serious as all that. Follow the instructions as best you can without shattering your domestic life, and omissions and mistakes of a minor sort will, at worst, only prolong the housebreaking period. One caution however—never under any circumstances violate the basic rule of keeping the pup in his housebreaking area until housebreaking is done. This requires no extra effort, and is really the key to the whole thing.

The whole procedure can be helped along from the beginning if you exercise control over the intake as well as the outgo. The young puppy will be fed at fairly regular intervals as a matter of course (see chapter on feeding and health for more on this). He should also be watered only at specific times. Give him his water bowl about an hour after he has finished eating and let him drink as much as he wants then, rather than leaving water always available. About half an hour after the watering, either start watching him carefully or take him out—just about then the hydrostatic pressures in his bladder and bowels add up to "time to go."

It isn't practical to watch the pup *all* the time, and he will have to go at other times, aside from just after eating and drinking. Hence the papers. They are provided only secondarily for sanitation and ease of cleaning—primarily they serve as a focus for the pup's attention. Through them he first learns there is a place to go, and places not to go.

The ideal housebreaking room is the kitchen, combining as it does a linoleum floor (or at least one without a rug), and in many cases a back door leading outside. Even in an apartment, the kitchen is the usual place, simply because of the floor. Whatever you choose as his room and the housebreaking room, put down several layers of newspaper, being sure that you cover the floor space completely. Then, with papers on floor and pup on papers, wait for him to use the facilities. When he relieves himself, praise him, and pick up the sheets he used right away. Sterilize and deodorize the section of floor underneath with a good strong soap or disinfectant so that the smell doesn't draw him back to the same spot.

With one small area of papers used, discarded and cleaned after, the hope is that next time he'll use another papered area. He may, and if he does, repeat the process of praise and cleaning. If he doesn't, and you're lucky enough to catch him at it, try to distract his attention with a firm "No!" and carry him to a papered area to finish. If you weren't watching, take him gently over to the spot, push his nose at it, tell him "No, bad dog" and then take him outside immediately. This will begin to give him a connection between the outside and relieving himself, but don't expect him to light up at the idea right away. If possible, take him to a spot which other dogs use. The smells there, combined with encouragement and "good boy" from you, may even induce him to contribute his own small puddle. Let him know effusively that he's done a wonderful thing by using that spot.

The business of pushing his nose at whatever he did needs a bit of clearing up at this point. The operative word here is "at"—very definitely not "into". The idea is not to shame or humiliate him by pushing his nose into his urine or feces, a fairly disgusting idea, but to let him get some idea of what is going on. If his nose is pushed close enough for him to get a good whiff at the time you're saying firmly, "No, bad dog!" he has a chance to make the connection. Otherwise, unless he's caught in the act, a correction will only confuse him.

Overall, with the papers, what is hoped for is a steady progression toward the door. If you have a back door leading outside from the kitchen, aim him there. If an apartment, aim him at the kitchen door which will eventually lead him outside, even if only past a hallway, 27 floors in an elevator, another hallway and a disapproving doorman. Here again the papers serve as a focus and a guide—through them you can lead him to the door. If you should have the rare good fortune of your pup using first the papers in the far corner and progressing steadily, one sheet at a time, to the door, luck is with you indeed. Otherwise, if he uses the one nearest the door first, replace that sheet with one from one of the corners, symbolically declaring the bare corner out of bounds. Work away from everywhere else toward the door, shifting papers when necessary, until the last set of papers is right by the door.

He is going to make the mistake of not using the papers a good many times. Each time, scoop him up if you catch him and put him on the papers to finish, and praise him. If too late, take him outside to his spot after your correction.

If you are so situated that the kitchen door leads outside, a good trick after the last paper by the door has been used is to put a sheet half under the door to lure him further. When that is used, place one with about a quarter protruding into the room. Keep at it until he goes to that sheet—correcting him all the while for the inevitable mistakes. You will probably find that he will next go directly to the door, looking for the paper after the last quarter sheet has disappeared, and your battle is won. Keep an especially close watch for his searching after the paper is gone, and take him out immediately.

In an apartment, simply watch closely after the last paper is up. When he begins to look around for it, take him out to his spot and wait, no matter how long it takes, for him to relieve himself.

During the paper period, you will be able to see very easily whether or not he has made the connection. To the beginning owner and trainer, there are few sights as glorious as the first time he deliberately uses a paper rather than the floor—he'll probably show his pride of accomplishment in every line of his body. Watch his reactions to the whole process, and adjust the speed of taking up the papers to how well he seems to be getting the idea.

The night is another problem again. You can't keep an eye on him then, and so he *must* be restricted to his housebreaking quarters. If he's been taken out after his last meal and watering, the pressures on him won't be too great, but he still may have to go during the night. If he has used the papers during the night, praise him. If he has used the floor, take him to the spot, chide him, and take him outside quickly. He'll get the night-time idea soon enough.

When the day arrives in which he has kept his room completely clean he is almost ready to be introduced to the rest of the house. Let one more errorless day go by, just to be sure it wasn't chance, and that evening or the next day give him his freedom of the house. Let him sniff around and explore as much as he wants. Keep a close watch still as prevention of a mistake is a hundred times more important and effective than correction after the fact. Keep to his outing schedule after eating and drinking, and be careful not to play too roughly or scare him, as too rough handling or a fright may cause him to lose control involuntarily and wet the floor.

The final, unwatched introduction to the remainder of the house should wait until he has gone several days with no mistakes under your supervision. This applies to night-time also—he should be kept in his housebreaking room for the night until the three or four mishapless days have passed, to prevent accidents. Then, when his day of complete freedom has arrived, issue him his passport to the house. Have faith in him—if you've done everything patiently and well up to now, you may never have another moment of trouble with him.

If something has gone wrong, and it can happen, there is only one thing to do, and that is to start all over again. Allow him one mistake in the house as benefit of the doubt. After the second mistake, take him right back to the housebreaking room covered with papers and treat him as though it were his first day in the house. Don't swear at him—it's not his fault. He may not have quite enough sphincter control just yet, or you may have pushed things a little too fast for him. For whatever reason, the lesson hasn't been firmly enough imprinted in his mind, and the solution is a complete refresher course. Go through the whole thing again, but don't be vindictive. Make the corrections and give the praise just as before. It's rough luck, but sometimes it does happen, and you've just got to sweat it out. When he's through with the second time around he'll be the best-behaved dog in the block and he'll go through the tortures of the damned rather than relieve himself in the house.

HOUSEBREAKING THE OLDER DOG

If you have acquired a dog of over six months from a kennel or breeder, the problems will be much the same as with the 3-months-old puppy. They will be slightly easier because, being older, he will be able to exercise firmer control over himself if he wants to. And they will be harder because of the unrestricted ways he's been used to in a kennel run.

Papers are of little use with such a dog. He is old enough so that he has the necessary concentration for simple corrections. Confine him in the kitchen, or wherever you have that is easily cleaned, and set up a steady vigil. If you can catch him in time, do as with the pup and rush him outdoors. If you don't catch it give him the puppy correction and again outdoors. Here too, proceed with caution when you give him the run of the house, and if necessary start all over again with a second course if he makes a second mistake after his liberation.

With the older dog, suppositories are a help in teaching the fact that bowels are moved only outside. Giving a dog suppositories strikes many people as a highly unpleasant way to go about things, and if you really object on esthetic grounds you can housebreak without them. It's just easier that way. If you do decide to use them, get the help of your veterinarian in the method of administration and in choosing the kind to use. And of course use only a gentle suppository, and with moderation.

About half an hour to an hour after the older dog has eaten, apply the suppository. Take him out immediately thereafter and lead him to wherever you want him to learn to go. Repeat as necessary and your training problems are highly simplified.

STREET AND YARD BEHAVIOR

When, in housebreaking, you take him "outside" it may be your yard, or it may be the city or village street. In any of these cases there should be certain definite spots for him to go. If it's your yard, city or country, you'll want to designate some special corner for his defecation. Whenever you take him out, always take him to that spot and keep him there until he has gone. It requires occasional policing up with a shovel and old papers, but it's preferable to having him litter the yard at random.

In the city or town you'll be faced with the sidewalk-curb situation. In many municipalities, it is flatly against the law for you to let your dog soil the sidewalk. In any case, it is an offense against common decency. When you take him out, take him directly to the street just over the curb and make it understood that that is the place. If on your walks you find him squatting on the sidewalk, pull him firmly but gently over to the street and keep him there. He'll learn quickly enough that the sidewalk is forbidden.

The urination problem is something else again. Females squat and they can be taught only to squat in the gutter. Males, though, eventually learn to lift their legs against some convenient vertical object. It's pretty useless to try to teach them to do this in the street proper, as there's nothing much there to lift against except a neighbor's car. And that is something of an offense in itself as the acid in a dog's urine will corrode chrome or paint quicker than almost anything else. Therefore, it is fairly accepted practice to allow him to lift his leg on fireplugs, trees and telephone posts pretty much anywhere along the sidewalk. There is probably a law against this, too, in some places, but it isn't likely to be enforced if you are only a little judicious about spots. Don't, for example, allow him to use someone's doorway. Or young trees, if possible. Keep him away from people's precious front-lawn shrubs as much as possible, too. Aside from that, you and he will have little or no trouble with leg-lifting.

INSIDE THE HOUSE

It is of such great importance that any spots inside the house be thoroughly cleaned, deodorized and disinfected that we will emphasize it again. The smell of urine, which is so helpful in the gutter, draws the dog to that same spot again and positively encourages him to use it. The male is especially drawn this way to "cover" any such place. If, in later days, when he has learned to lift his leg, he tries an experimental squirt at furniture, attack that spot with fury and clean it to a fare-thee-well. Apply your correction first, of course. There are commercial preparations on the market to remove the stain and odor of urine, and they are mostly effective. But there is no substitute for a thorough scrubbing with soap and water, and disinfecting—a strong disinfectant odor will act very effectively in covering up any residual urine odor.

HANDLING AND PLAYING

During those first weeks, most of which he will spend in the house-breaking room, the puppy is something more than just a housebreaking problem. Like all children he will spend a good deal of his spare time sleeping and quite a lot of it in eating. When he's awake, though, and feeling playful he can still be a lot of fun to have around, restricted though he is.

One of the first things he must learn is the comfort of your touch. When you first bring him home, he has been used only to the feel of his mother, and of the other puppies in the litter, and it may take a while for him to get the idea that being fondled and handled by you is something highly pleasant. To get him into it, try to get down to his level aside from the disciplinary moments involved in housebreaking. Try to be, in your moments of play together, another puppy. He'll be taken in even though you are rather large and odd-smelling for a pup. You can play with him just about as roughly as he feels like, but remember that when it comes to a delicate pup, you literally don't know your own strength. Let him set the pace, and don't force him to play if he seems drowsy or disinterested. Rule: let him come to you.

Don't taunt him by slapping at him, however gently, or grabbing at him. Shove him around all he wants, and tumble him gently, but never, never tease him. Growling isn't a bit cute in the puppy: it encourages nastiness and aggression. Differentiate, though, between playful grumbling and growling, and true aggressive growling. There is a difference and a marked one. If, while you're playing, he seems to be getting serious tell him "No!" and put him back in his sleeping box. He may come right back out, and growl again in a moment. Put him right back in. This is not a punishment, but a correction to let him know gently but firmly that this sort of thing doesn't go.

He likes little better at this stage than chewing on things. When you play with him, he'll dig at your hands and fingers with his needle-sharp baby teeth. There's no need to reprimand him if the chewing is moderately gentle—it is after all just his method of playing with you as another pup. Young pups chew at each other all the time and are none the worse for it. Your pup's mouth and teeth are one of the focal points of his body; having no hands to grab and hold things with, his mouth assumes the functions. It is as senseless to reprimand him for grabbing that way as it would be to punish a human child for grabbing with his hands.

Teeth may hurt, though. So if he begins to lacerate your hands take him back to his bed. As he grows older, he may continue to want to grab your hands, and if he does you can teach him to moderate his grip when you tell him "Easy." This is done by prying his mouth open gently when the bite becomes too hard, repeating at the same time the command "Easy." Choose any command you want to, but "Easy" is a good one that won't conflict with any of the standard obedience commands he'll learn later. After this has happened a few times he'll learn that "Easy" means to let up, not necessarily to stop biting entirely. He will come, in fact, to be able to give all the appearance of chewing his way through your arm in three easy bites while not even denting your skin.

Your pup will never have any real intention to hurt you, but if you have mauled him too roughly in play he may instinctively snap a good one at you. It is his nature to protect himself first of all, at least before he has learned to love you as his master. And snap he will if he feels he's getting the short end of things. But blameless though he may be in this, it is one time where he will have to take the blame for your carelessness. Admonish him with a severe "No!" and take him at once to his bed. And then resolve yourself never to let it happen again.

TOYS

Because of his great and enduring interest in chewing on things it's a good idea to let him have one or two toys that he can keep in his play area. Give him a ball of hard natural rubber, or a strip of hard leather. Wooden toys, soft rubber toys, or anything else that may be torn up too easily are on the strictly forbidden list for a young puppy. Anything that comes loose in his mouth will be swallowed, and a piece of soft rubber can end up blocking his small intestine, which can either make a very sick pup out of him or kill him. The danger of wooden toys is obvious, what with the possibility of splinters cutting his mouth or lodging in his throat or stomach.

Anything you get him from a pet shop or pet department in the way of a toy must be thoroughly examined both before and after giving to him. Before buying it, give it a thorough test with a fingernail. If you can pry up a bit of it that way, don't consider it. And after you've given him something, watch carefully for a few minutes to see what he does with it. If he is able to chew small pieces off, take it away from him and throw it far away. He won't be happy about it, but you can divert his attention to something else and soon he'll have forgotten all about it.

His chewing also serves the purpose of helping along his teething. An excellent toy to give him with this in mind is one of the specially treated natural bones that can be found almost anywhere there is a pet department. It is a section of bone that has been chemically hardened to the point where he can little more than scratch it after hours of arduous chewing. You can let him have one of these in complete confidence, as it's impossible for him to hurt himself by chewing on it. And don't worry if his chewing on it, or on anything else at this stage, seems highly violent and likely to knock out his teeth. That's what's supposed to happen. He'll lose two sets of baby teeth before he acquires the adult set, and the idea of chewing on something hard is to loosen up the old to make way for the new.

Natural bones are of course excellent if judiciously chosen. Any of the beef long bones or knuckle bones, raw, will provide the pup with hours and days of chewing pleasure. Even cooked, if the bone is solid, let him have it. Be careful, though, of the smaller animal bones, and even the soft and/or splintery kind from beef. Rib bones, for example, are bad.

The bones of any of the fowl, or of fish, are about the worst thing you could give a pup.

As a good general rule, don't give him anything as a plaything that is an old version of something new that is forbidden to him. Old shoes or gloves may seem the ideal cast-off for him but you are only casting temptation before him. He has no way of distinguishing between the old and the new. One day it will be the old shoe, and the next you will lose your expensive brogans. And you can't reprimand without confusing him utterly and undermining his faith in you. A shoe is a shoe is a shoe as far as he's concerned.

The exception, however, is an old sock. Tie a simple knot in the middle of it and let him have it. Tempt him with an unknotted sock and reprimand him if he tries to take it. He will very quickly learn that the knot means okay to chew and he won't bother your other socks.

You can also give him a clean old rag to chew on and to tug around. It won't hurt him. With this, and with your finger, and with anything else that's long enough for both of you to get hold of, he'll love to play tug of war. About this you will hear some contrasting opinions. You may hear that you should never play tug with the pup because a) you're likely to deform his teeth and jaw, b) he'll learn the power of his jaws, and c) he'll learn to defy you.

If you observe common sense in playing nothing will come amiss. First, there's precious little chance that he's not going to learn the power of those jaws of his at one time or another. There's no use trying to keep it from him. And in pulling, if you exercise a bit of moderation, you don't stand any chance of deforming his jaws. Hold on only hard enough to be considered a stationary object and you'll do no more harm than if the rag were stuck on something. Pull gently in the opposite direction and he'll enjoy himself hugely. Do not, though, jerk suddenly to try to get it away from him. That's what can do the harm. A sudden, hard jerk can give his head quite a snap, and it will shake him up a bit.

TEACHING "GIVE"

A valid point in objection to tug of war is that it might teach him to defy you. But this, like some other dog-lore, is a maxim designed to keep dog owners from having to think; a little thought and training shows the way out. That way out is to force him to release his grip on the cloth or whatever when you tell him "Out" or "Give." Besides quelling any defiance at this point, the "give" lesson lays the groundwork for future obedience work. To teach this, simply insist firmly and gently that whatever he is holding onto at the moment be released at command. When you're tugging together, say "Give" and then pry his jaws apart with your fingers. This is done by taking hold of his muzzle from beneath and pressing with the thumb and fingers about halfway back along the jaw, forcing the lips against the teeth.

You'll find, if you want to experiment, that it's very nearly impossible to pull his jaws apart by brute force, big as you are and little as he is at the time. What you're doing is pitting yourself against one of the strongest muscles in the world, the masseter, which supplies the immense power of jaws both canine and human. But by squeezing the skin of the mouth against the juncture of his upper and lower teeth, you are applying pressure that he will want to relieve rather than fight. He'll quickly enough open his jaws to save himself discomfort. Try it on yourself a couple of times to get the idea—put the thumb on one cheek and your forefinger on the other and then squeeze hard together. Painful, isn't it? And see how much it relieves the feeling when you open your teeth.

When he has opened his jaws and perforce released whatever he was holding, take the object and praise him highly for what he has just done. Do this occasionally during the tug of war, and also when he's playing with other things like his rubber toy or bone. No matter how much he seems to be enjoying it, tell him "Give," and apply the persuasion unless he releases it at once. A few times of this and he'll let go quickly at the word, and the defiance problem is no problem at all. Don't bedevil him with it, though. Give him the command and the persuasion a few times a day until he has learned it thoroughly, and then infrequently thereafter unless it is used for some practical purpose. Don't jerk or try to jerk anything from his mouth when you say "Give." Nothing will inspire him to hold on harder than a jerk in the opposite direction. Don't be inconsistent about making him release things once the command is given. A command must *always* be obeyed, from the very first time it is being taught. If you are playing and tell him to give, and then go on tugging happily, or josh with him about it, he is rapidly going to get the idea that commands are actionable only every so often, or perhaps only when you say so a second time with your voice raised. Not good.

PICKING UP THE PUP

In housebreaking, in playing, for weighing, and all round, you'll be picking him off the floor a good many times during his youth and infancy. You can, with astonishing ease, undo him by picking him up the wrong way. Be as careful with him as you would with a human baby—although for once the baby analogy is a bad one. The puppy should neither be picked up by the chest and shoulders nor should he be cuddled or carried on his back. Grabbing him, from front or back, by the shoulders and/or front legs can pull that region seriously out of whack. We won't go into the anatomical considerations—but it is a very bad way to go about lifting him. Nor do we recommend the "natural mother" method of grabbing him by the scruff of the neck, logical though that may seem. By the time you get him he'll be past the neck-scruff stage and such treatment will hurt him.

The right and easy way to do it is to put one hand or forearm under his rump, folding the hind legs forward, and the other hand under his chest and shoulders. Keep the hand as far forward on his chest as you can, either from front or back, and his weight will be distributed so that he's safe and sound. Aside from the possibility of physical damage, the "shoulders only" method of lifting will scare him. Animals hate to dangle in space, no matter how firmly they are held by the front. And the same applies to holding him, once lifted, on his back. It's an unnatural position for a dog, and he will panic and try to get himself twisted around. Put yourself in his place and picture yourself being hoisted by your legs and then dangled upside down by a giant.

TEACHING HIS NAME

By constant repetition, the pup will learn that his name means him. When you're playing with him, repeat it to him in a coaxing and friendly tone. Later, you'll be using it with each command you give him. At the beginning, though, be sure that when he hears his name it is always associated with pleasantness. In correcting him for housebreaking or other mistakes, don't use the name at all. Just "No!" Do use his name when you feed him to reinforce the association with something good.

FURNITURE

Some dog owners believe that a dog is a dog, and that his place is on the floor exclusively. Some feel that he is a member of the family; that he should be allowed up on chairs or sofas if he feels like it. And there are attitudes in between that may dictate permission for him to get up on one "favorite chair." Generally the split is between country and city, with country dogs being relegated to the floor and city dogs having the run of the place. You can do it either way, as long as you decide in the beginning and stick to your policy.

If he is going to be strictly a floor dog, then he must *never* be allowed up on any piece of furniture, right from the start. This means that even when he is first allowed out of his housebreaking room you can't pick him up and hold him on your lap on the couch. Being up on the couch with you or solo holds little distinction for him and it will only confuse him later if you deny him the privilege. When he's little, he won't be able to negotiate the height, so there's no problem with him climbing up. As he grows and investigates new horizons he'll try to climb up just to see what's there. Push him off gently and tell him "no" a few times and he'll get the idea. Later, he may perversely decide that the soft couch or chair represents heaven on earth to him and occupy it while you're out of the house. You can't correct him directly, as you'll never catch him up there despite evidences that he was. (There's a wholly apocryphal but still delightful story about a dog whose owners had this problem. They could never catch him up on his favorite chair because he'd hear them coming up the walk and jump off. But they would feel his warmth still in the cushion and chastize him every time. They thought they had him cured until one day, peeking in through the front window on returning, they saw him standing in front of the chair blowing on the cushion.)

The easiest solution is a few light mousetraps covered with a sheet of newspaper, set near the back of the cushions when you go out. Very light ones, though—just enough to give a sudden snap that'll surprise him when he jumps up and convince him that the arm of the law is long indeed. A light trap under newspaper can't hurt him and it'll solve the problem.

If you decide that he's going to be a full member of the household with all privileges the problems are only those of dirt and reactions. If he comes bounding in from a muddy or snowy outside and leaps directly on to your best petit-point upholstery you may wish you could trade him in for a parakeet. It isn't necessary, as he should be trained to wait at the door for a quick cleaning with an old rag after a particularly messy run. By the time he's old enough to bound onto chairs easily he will be old enough to have learned the "Sit" and "Stay" and there the problem endeth.

As far as reactions go, this is really something between you and your friends. Somewhat fastidious friends who come to visit may find dogs on furniture disagreeable, particularly if the dog has to be shooed off the chair they're about to sit in. Again, a later bit of training is the solution to this—in which he is relegated to his quarters while those particular guests are there. If he's a chair-sitter in your house, he may try to be one when he goes visiting with you. And although your friends may be glad to see him, and dog-lovers withal, they may be of the dog-on-the-floor variety. So set up a rigid rule for him—okay at home, forbidden elsewhere. Don't make exceptions with the occasional friend who doesn't mind him up on his furniture. Keep the rule hard and fast and he won't be likely to be confused.

CODDLING

Far before written history began, man and dog came together on the basis of mutual assistance. The dog helped track down game and defend the cave or hut against marauders both animal and human. The man provided shelter and a supply of food. And out of that relationship grew affection and companionship. Withal, the dog has never given up his right to be an individual, standing on his own feet beside his owner and master.

In our opinion, one of the worst things that can happen in dog-rearing is to take away this individuality—to coddle all the "dog" out of a defenseless pup. One of the most painful sights going is that of the dog who doesn't know he *is* a dog—who's been pampered and petted and cooed over until he's good for nothing in the world but more pampering and petting and cooing. True, the working function of the dog has declined sharply and the companionship side of the things is in the ascendant, but there is no reason why the dog cannot be a respected individual within the household.

When as a puppy he has problems, give him a chance to work things out for himself. If he gets tangled up in something, let him try to get himself out unless you see he's about to panic or simply can't manage at all. Let him work out the problems of stairs by himself. If he gets hurt give him sympathy and fix it up, then leave him alone. And above all, don't be afraid of discipline. Good discipline for the pup means a far happier life for both of you, and it doesn't mean continual beatings and/or scoldings. We've seen the people who "just couldn't bear to hit the little dear." Without fail, the "little dear" has been a spoiled monster unfit for human society. We've also seen, at the other end, the poor pounded pooches who crawl warily through life from one restriction to the next, never getting a chance to enjoy life. The middle course between the two extremes is an easy one to find, with a little thought.

The middle course is an essential one for obedience. It is flatly impossible to teach the pampered pup anything without a long period of readjustment for both pup and owner. While we recommend obedience training as the solution for behavior problems, it is a far easier thing for everyone concerned if the behavior problems are never allowed to arise in the first place. In the next chapter we will spend some time discussing corrections for various situations, all of which comes under the heading of discipline. The most severe correction requires a healthy clip under the muzzle for the dog. You probably will have to hit your dog at one time or another—but one or two firm cracks, scientifically and fairly administered at the proper times, can prevent you from ever having to hit him again, and you can save yourself irritation, frustration and endless disappointment in your dog. Throughout this book we will take up one or another aspect of discipline and permissiveness, at the appropriate places,

—and you'll find, as you train your own dog, that he can be allowed an astonishing amount of freedom and status without getting in the way if he is raised in the middle course.

LEAVING THE PUP ALONE

When the pup has come to have the run of the house by himself, he may get lonely when you go out. In his housebreaking room he's never sure whether he's alone in the house or not, and less likely to make lonesome noises. But when he can look everywhere and not find you, he may take to letting all and sundry know that he doesn't like being left alone. It can be a fearsome irritation to the neighbors, but even uncorrected it will wear off in time. To correct it you have to catch him in the act. Leave him one day with all appropriate motions, and leave the door unlocked and even unlatched. Then lurk about in the hall or around the corner of the house and at the first howl or whine charge back in with a firm "No!" and go right back out. That should shake him up pretty badly. It gives him the idea that maybe you're hanging around after all and he'd better keep quiet if he doesn't want his head taken off. After the first correction, hang about a bit more to see if all is quiet. If he tries it again, repeat the correction. But be careful to do a neat job of lurking—he has fearfully acute ears and you might not be fooling him at all if he never seems to howl when you're just outside the door.

Chewing on forbidden items and forgetting his housebreaking while you're away are more serious. For some reason, dogs seem to do both of these very shortly after the owner leaves—perhaps out of pique, we don't know—and this gives you the opportunity to use the same sort of correction as with loneliness noises. It may take a little more waiting, say ten or fifteen minutes, but you're very likely to catch him in the act when you come in unexpectedly.

One word of caution, though—unless you catch him absolutely red-handed, don't do anything about it right away. Whatever he's been up to he'll greet you joyously when you come in. Greet him at least cordially on your part for a moment or two, and then affect to discover what he's done. Take him to it, make sure he knows what the situation is, and give him a very stern "No, bad dog!" If it's a housebreaking misdemeanor, and it happens more than once, you may have to give him the refresher course. If the problem is chewing, try to make a correction with the item chewed on. Give him a whack with it under the jaw—just hard enough so he knows he's been hit and not patted—as long as it isn't hard enough really to hurt him. Be sure to praise him afterward to let him know there're no hard feelings. That may be a bit hard to do if it was your best pillow or pair of shoes, but remember that he has to associate the correction with the wrong and not with ill-temper on your part. The last thing you want to do is teach him to expect unpleasantness from you, except where unavoidable. This is why you must never immediately reprimand him when you come into the house—after a few times he'll get the idea that your coming back means unpleasantness and he'll run for cover instead of greeting you happily.

Illicit chewing while you're there is very easily solved with a light leather muzzle. When you see him happily chewing away on something forbidden, put the muzzle on him immediately after giving him a "No!" Be perfectly kind and cordial all the while, but keep the muzzle on for half an hour, then take it off and praise him. Don't give him the impression that the muzzle is a correction, as you may have need of it later under other circumstances. He'll never like it, but let him get only the impression that chewing on certain things means the minor inconvenience of the muzzle automatically, and he'll learn fast. Don't leave the muzzle on him when you're away, though. He could catch one of the straps on something and either strangle himself or be nearly insane with fright by the time you return. That goes for tying up, too—never leave him tied when you leave.

One thing you should prevent specifically, before it can happen, is chewing on lampcords or other electrical wires. Inquisitive young puppies are quite likely to chew on anything so conveniently sized and available as a wire. They may get away with it, but a vigorous chew can short-circuit the wire through the pup's mouth, which will at best give him a bad burn. Coat all the wires in your house with musterole, citronella or any of the commercial "keeps dogs away" items. A light wipe with any of these will make the wire unpleasant to the taste—just be sure that what you use is simply unpleasant, not poisonous.

JUMPING UP

Big dog or little, jumping up on people should be discouraged firmly from the beginning. It may seem cute at first, but the big dog in later life can knock people down with a firm planting of the front paws, and even the littlest can leave muddy footprints and rip expensive hose. The habit is easily broken by giving him a good thump in the chest with your knee just as he comes up. Don't even correct him verbally. Catch him in the chest with your knee just hard enough to throw him off balance and over, and then sympathize with him over the accident. Keep doing that and he'll be puzzled by the inexplicable thing that happens to him every time he tries it, but he'll chalk it up as one of the many mysteries of life and seek other outlets for his affection. And with no hard feelings between you. The little dogs require the same treatment, but with the ankle or foot—just a shove, not a kick. Make it seem as casual and accidental as possible. And whatever you do, don't step on his toes to try to cure him. This is sheer senseless cruelty when it can be done without hurting him at all.

PROTECTION AND RESTRAINT

As the pup grows older and learns that you are his property, he will begin to feel protective both about you and about your house. Or *his* house as he sees it. He may begin to develop a strong dislike for the idea of anyone else coming in. This should be controlled and directed from the beginning.

To do this, he must learn to go to his quarters when told to. Decide on what you want to use as a command for this. "Place" and "Bed" are possibilities, but you can use any word you feel like. Whatever it is, get in some practice with it as soon as he has the freedom of the house. Tell him "Place" and take him to his bed. Once there, praise him and pet him to let him know all is well. He may want to pop right out again and come into the living room, but don't let him. At every attempt to get out, put him back in firmly but gently, giving him the command each time you make the correction. For the first several times, you will have to stand right by and see to it that he stays put, and then gradually you can go farther and farther from his bed without his breaking from position. Be very patient about this, as it is fundamentally against his nature to be restrained without any physical barriers. Keep up constant kind corrections until he will stay there, however restlessly. Never allow him out until you have given him the release word.

The release word can be "Okay"—and we recommend it as a good one. But you can say anything you like to him to let him know it's okay to come out. But not until you say so can he move.

Continue the "Place" training until he will go of his own accord on command. And again, be patient. By this time he loves and adores you and hates to leave you. The leaving is something he doesn't want to do at all, so you must be firm about it all, and willing to give the lesson over and again. Remember why it is that he is at first unwilling to go, and you'll be less likely to lose your temper and rant at him.

When he has learned "Place" you can use it for the doorbell and visitors. When the doorbell rings, send him to his bed. This will prevent over-friendly rushes at people he likes, and growls and aggression towards those he doesn't like or distrusts. It won't interfere at all with his protective instincts, because once he has learned the "Place" lesson thoroughly you can go on to allowing a certain discretion—in which he is allowed to stand by, or sit by, when the bell rings, and watch what's going on.

Now you can begin to make a differentiation between friends and strangers and delivery boys at the door. When friends come in, release him from his place and introduce them. Literally that. Let him come out and show him your friendliness and acceptance of your visitors. Go so far as to formally introduce them. Even though the words mean nothing to him, your tone and manner as you do so will convey everything to him. And you can convey the right tone best if you are actually introducing your friends to him. If for some reason he takes a dislike to a visitor, never allow him to show any aggression. At the slightest sign of a growl send him immediately to his bed and keep him there for a while. Then let him out to try again. If he still shows active dislike for your guest, send him to Coventry permanently. He'll learn soon enough that your friends are not to be menaced.

Don't introduce him to delivery boys and salesmen. If someone comes into your house strictly on business, make the pup keep his distance. When a delivery boy comes, send the pup to his place and keep him there. Later, he can learn to stand by the door and keep an eye on things. But for the moment let him learn his distinctions by being kept at a distance. If, from his bed, he makes threatening noises at service people, well and good. Neither encourage nor discourage his attitude, but simply make sure that he stays where he is.

All this is extremely valuable groundwork in obedience and in protection of you and your property. As far as the protection goes, remember that his being kept at first in his bed won't affect it. You don't want a dog that snaps at anyone, no matter how sinister. The factor of protection in a dog is his presence, the amount of noise he will make if anything goes wrong, and the uncertainty in the mind of anyone with evil intentions that he won't really have a hand taken off. And as far as your friends and guests go, there can never be any excuse for the slightest show of hostility towards them, unless of course they have actually mistreated him. If a visitor in your house decides to brain you with a chair, or lifts a trinket or two in a kleptomaniac mood, don't expect your dog to make up for your mistakes in judgment. Keep him in his place, make him be friendly, or at least not actively unfriendly, towards your friends, and let him keep his distance from others.

NOISES, THUNDER AND BELLS

The young pup, like the young child, has an instinctive dislike of sudden noises. Curing him of fear reactions can be done by exposing him to noises under circumstances ordinarily pleasant to him. For example, you can make a racket with pots and pans when it's feeding time and he's busy gobbling, starting easy and working up until he will eat happily through a full cantata for dishpan, fortissimo. Get him to understand that there's no harm in loud noises and he'll come to take them like a veteran.

Thunder and telephone and doorbell trouble almost always can be traced to the owner of the dog. If you leap into the air and crawl under the bed when it thunders, don't be surprised if the pup starts doing the same. He thinks it's the right thing to do, and he will quickly sense and absorb the fear you have. If you're really terrified of thunder, keep his welfare in mind and sit with gritted teeth through the worst, patting and reassuring him the while. It might even cure you.

Dogs get panic reactions to the doorbell and phone in the same way. Eventually he begins to associate the doorbell with company and may get excited at the prospect, but that is another matter. If his owner is galvanized into action by a bell, he'll learn the same patterns by association. Next time the bell rings, see if it's you who's teaching him to jump and run in circles.

THE COLLAR AND LEASH

Within a few days after the pup has arrived at your house he will be ready to be introduced, gradually, to the collar and leash. His first collar can be a cheap affair, because he'll outgrow it before long. Get him one of leather, the width adjusted to his size. If he's short-haired, get him a flat collar wide enough so that it can't possibly cut into his neck. If he's long-haired, get one of the round leather variety. The reason for this is that though the flat is the better collar, a wide-enough flat collar will press down and mat the hair of a long-haired dog, tangling it considerably and making life uncomfortable for him. And make it a perfectly plain collar, with only a strong buckle and a solid, one-piece ring for attaching a leash. If you must have studs or other ornaments, by all means have them, but they will only make the collar heavier and more of a burden to your pup. Ornaments on the collar may make you feel good, but they won't impress him or his friends a bit.

Before you put the collar on him for the first time, play with it around him for a while. Drag it over him a few times and treat it as a plaything. If he wants to chew and tug on it a bit, let him. Convince him that it's an entirely harmless object. Then, one of the times you're passing it over and around his neck, buckle it on loosely. Practice the buckling a few times beforehand so you don't make a butter-fingered mess of the process and panic him. If you do it right it'll be on and fastened before he realizes what's happening to him, and the victory is won. He may object, and object strenuously to having it around his neck, but pet him and reassure him, and let it stay. He'll find it doesn't hurt him, and get used to it before long. The first time on, buckle it loosely. When he's a bit more accustomed to it, you can adjust it to just the right fastening —tight enough so he can't slip it off, but loose enough so you can put your fingers between it and his neck without squeezing overmuch.

It'll take him a day or two before he's thoroughly resigned to the fact that the collar is there to stay. Then you can begin to introduce him to the idea of the leash. Here is where the greatest caution, patience and tact are required, for it is not at all uncommon for serious troubles to arise with the first leashing if you don't do it right. A sudden snapping on of a leash and the consequent restraint can give your dog fits and generally send him into a three-layered panic that he won't recover from for some time to come.

The thing has got to be done gently. When he has accepted the idea of the collar, play around him with the leash a bit, then snap it on. Don't hold onto the leash at all—let him drag it around with him and get accustomed to the idea of having it on. Leave it on him for a few minutes, then take it off for a while, then put it on again. All this stage can be accomplished in a day. Even the most timid pup will soon get over any fright if the leash is not used to restrain him right away. If, in moving about, it catches on things, release it for him, and let him drag it about some more. But don't use it to restrain or hold him. You'll see quickly enough when he has become accustomed to the idea. Let him get firmly used to the idea that it will not hurt him, then take the first steps in using the leash as a restraint.

Try holding onto the other end of the leash now. Go about it gradually and gently, and at first do nothing more than hold onto it. When he pulls away, as he will, go along with him wherever he goes. Make as much of a game of it as you can. Then when he is used to the fact that it pulls on him slightly, exert a little gentle pull on your part. Gradually increase your pressure until you are standing or sitting in one spot and he is restricted to a circle with the radius of the leash. Again, he won't like it much, but reassure him when he reaches the end of his tether. The final step is to exert a positive pressure so that he is forced to leave wherever he is and come along where you want to go. Go easy and gradually, and give in to him every now and then if he seems really unhappy, but finally insist that when you pull it means get moving. Don't jerk or yank—just bring up the pressure until he has to move. With little or medium sized dogs it won't be much of a test of strength, and even with the large variety you should be able to pull it off.

Get in a good bit of practice with the leash before you use it the first time on the street. That way you'll both be more confident about things, and you'll avoid public shrieking on his part and tooth-gnashing on yours. You'd be surprised how many nice old ladies can spring out of the ground waving umbrellas and police threats if your in-training pup so much as whimpers on the street. Get the difficult parts over in private as much as possible. And the more you practice with the leash at home, the better off you personally will be. If this is a first dog, the experience of being on one end of the leash will be just as strange to you as it is to him being on the other end. If you're unsure of yourself and your handling of the leash (and it is a minor art) all your unsteadiness will transmit itself right down that six-foot length to the pup and make *him* unsure of things. You've got to be the fount of wisdom and steadiness in his world, so live up to it.

THE TRAINING COLLAR

The training collar, a device consisting of a length of light chain (usually chrome-plated) connecting two rings, can be introduced any time after the pup has become used to his leather collar. Some dogs never have a leather collar to start with and are introduced directly to the training collar, which brings up practically no problem. If the training collar is his first one, put it on just as you would the leather, slipping it over his head with a deft movement at the same time you would have buckled the other.

When you get a training collar for him, be sure that it is of exactly the right length and width. The length is easily determined—measure the distance around his head from his throat to the highest point (the smallest circle that will just slip over his head) and add an inch. And keep a check on this as he grows so you can replace it with a larger model when necessary. The width must be adjusted to the size of the dog. Make it as light as possible but not so light that it will cut into him when you have to apply pressure with it. Be sure also to get a chain in which all the links are rounded—not "jewel-cut" or ground flat along one or two sides. The grinding of the jewel-cut chains makes sharp edges that will catch and pull his hair.

There's a very definite right way to put the training collar on, and it should always be put on this way. To do this, hold the collar with one ring between the thumb and forefinger of each hand. Lift your left hand until it is directly above the right at the full length of the chain. Then let the chain slip down through the right-hand ring until both rings meet. With the right hand take hold of the half of the chain nearest the left-hand ring, releasing the right-hand ring, and separate your hands. The ring which was in your right hand should now slide freely along the chain between your hands, and the collar is ready to slip on the dog as he faces you.

This may seem to be a great deal of trouble over nothing, but it has a point. With the collar on this way, you will have greater control over the dog walking at your left, which is where he should be when walking or in training. When you pull, via the leash, on the correctly placed chain, the body of the chain slips through the inactive loop and pulls itself up tight immediately. With the chain on wrong, a pull simply exerts a pressure on the other side of the dog's neck without tightening. And tightening, plus a quick release, is the whole point of the training collar.

A simple way of checking whether you have it on correctly is to see whether the chain comes *over* his neck and through the inactive ring, rather than under and through. Another check is to pull the collar tight, then let the free end drop at the dog's right. If the collar is on right the whole thing will loosen. Otherwise the loose end will flop over and hang from the inactive loop.

Get him used to wearing the training collar early, as it will be a great help in teaching him to walk correctly with you on the street. And a final point about training collars—*never* put on or attempt to use any variety of "spike" or "pinch" collar with your dog. They are only for extremely unmanageable dogs; if now or at any time later in training you honestly come to believe that your dog is unmanageable without a special collar, you have no business trying to work with him yourself. Turn the problem over to a professional trainer, who is the *only* person qualified to use a spike or pinch collar. In all probability he will not have to use such a thing, but leave it to him. Never, and we cannot emphasize this too strongly, *never* try to use a spike or pinch collar on your dog.

COLLAR OR HARNESS?

Although many people with small breeds of dogs feel that the proper thing for walking is a harness affair, we definitely recommend against it for any breed. With one of the larger breeds you'd be letting yourself in for a lot of trouble with a halter, for a full grown dog of the larger sizes may be literally stronger than you when it comes to pulling. If he knows that a sudden pull means a contest of strength he may hesitate little on

THE RIGHT WAY TO PUT ON THE TRAINING COLLAR. THE CHAIN COMES OVER THE HEAD AND THROUGH THE "DEAD" RING.

seeing a particularly appetizing cat or place to smell down the street. If, however, it means near strangulation to pull against you he'll think about it for a while.

Even with the tiny breeds, including the toys, a light chain collar is far preferable to a harness. Constant pulling against the harness, by however light a dog, can be irritating. It can also pull his shoulders out of shape if he does it enough. The chain, on the other hand, can only make him momentarily uncomfortable.

THE PROPER LEASH

The best possible leash to get is one of flat leather or webbing, preferably half an inch wide or even more. You may have to shop around to get it, for pet stores and departments go in heavily for fancy and useless little plastic leashes, thin leather ones, and, unfortunately, chains. Avoid all these even if the shop owner recommends them with passion. Any very thin leash of whatever material will cut into your hands if you have to use any force on it (and you will) and a chain is suicidal. It will cut rashers off if you're not very careful. Make sure it is of good leather or solid webbing, with a loop, big enough to get your hand through, firmly stitched at the other end from the snap.

The snap itself is of great importance, too. There are two good kinds —one with a sliding rod at the side of the snap held firmly in place by a spring, and one which has two curved metal hooks which slide alongside each other to make a secure catch for the ring of the collar. Avoid completely the fancy snaps you will see on some leashes, especially the kind that comes apart at the tip of the snap and is held together by a spring. That one will come apart one day on a hard jerk and you might lose a dog.

Six feet is exactly the right length for the leash, regardless of the size of you or the dog. In fact, some municipalities that require leashing at all times in public specify that the leash shall be no longer than six feet. Don't waste money on anything longer at present with the idea of giving him a little more freedom—you and he will get all tangled up in it. The longer canvas leashes you may see in pet stores are for tracking, where considerable length is required.

CATS AND OTHER DOGS

There is no natural antipathy between dogs and cats. Dogs are set on cats in the street by witless clods who seem to think it's funny, and the dog's natural prey instinct makes him chase anything that runs. If there's a cat already resident in your house when you bring the puppy home, they'll learn to accept each other, and even like each other, if they're left to themselves. Make the introductions slow and easy, and keep an eye on things. Don't force either of them on the other and all will go well. If as the pup grows older he develops a desire to chase the cat around, put a stop to it, no matter how friendly all seems. In the heat of the chase they might accidentally hurt each other, and things would get serious. After a few trial chases are discouraged the growing pup will get the idea, and the dog and cat will live happily ever after.

On the street, teach him simply to ignore cats. When you approach one while walking, keep the pup in close or tell him to heel (to be learned later) and make him mind his own business. Give him a sharp "No!" and yank him back to your side if he lunges. He'll always keep an eye on cats you pass, but he won't bother them if he is discouraged uniformly from the beginning.

Other dogs on the street constitute more of a problem, because both parties will want to investigate each other. Up until he's at least six months old, strictly discourage any close contact with other dogs in the street. Nobody knows what curious germs a stranger might be carrying, no matter how clean he looks, and a good mutual sniffing is the surest way known to man or dog for transmitting those germs. When he's old enough to meet his fellows, allow the contact cautiously at first. If you let them get together, be cautious about pulling them away from each other, as there is a very strict protocol about dog meetings that you shouldn't violate. Their first stiff-legged contact is a wary one usually, and each is looking sharply to see if the other will flinch. If neither does, and they are of the same political persuasion, they will draw apart in a very dignified manner. But if you suddenly yank one off, the other will take that as abject withdrawal and will want to tear yours apart.

If your pup is aggressive by nature, keep a firm hand on him in dog meetings. A growl or a snap should be discouraged sharply by a strong "No!" and a yank back into position at your side. Remember, though, that aggressive behavior on his part toward another dog is very likely to be one of his ways of protecting you—strange dogs are to him much more dangerous to the realm than most strange humans.

If on the other hand he's excessively timid about meeting his peers there's very little you can do about it. Pushing him at another dog will terrify him and may warp his relations with other dogs for life. Let him be and wait hopefully for signs of courage, or at least manliness. As in all meetings with dogs and dogs and/or cats and/or people, don't ever force the issue.

As far as having other dogs in your house, or taking your pup to another house with a dog, simply exercise caution. Don't visit either way until he's past the six months stage and full to the ears with the proper inoculations. When you go to another house, expect the resident dog to be wary and protective. Let things take a natural course. Follow the same procedure with visiting dogs in your home. It does happen at times that two dogs will take a violent dislike to each other, for no reason apparent to the friendly humans involved. If so, just shrug your shoulders and make the best of it. If they really don't like each other they shouldn't be brought together. They'll probably never hold hands, even after years of forced proximity.

CARS AND TRAFFIC

In the city, where he will always be on leash outside the house, the problem of chasing cars and bicycles is solved simply by a yank back on the leash and a stern command to stop it. Actually, city dogs on leash hardly ever seem to develop this taste in recreation. Country and town dogs, though, quite often have to be broken of the habit. Here, the best correction is prevention. As soon as the pup shows any tendency to chase moving vehicles, set up a situation where correction can be automatic and convincing.

Tie onto his collar a very light chain or rope and fasten a stick about three-quarters of the way between his neck and the ground. Fasten the stick in the middle so it will swing, and then arrange for a car to be driven by, and for someone to ride a bicycle along the road. You can sit by and not say a word, for the stick will do the correcting for you.

When he starts to run, the stick will crack painfully against his front legs and soon drive out any interest he may have had. Repeat this a few times, and then try him without the stick. He should be cured, but if not, put it back on. Repeat until he is through.

Also in the country, you may have the opposite problem—that he hasn't the brains to get out of the way of a moving car. Here again, the situation itself is the only cure. Get an accomplice to drive a car slowly along the road or a driveway and maneuver the pup into the way. If he still sits or stands there as the front bumper approaches, have the driver hoot the horn in the pup's ear. That'll move him off in a hurry unless he's stone deaf.

Traffic in the city may be a problem to the dog who's always on leash outside. He never has a chance to learn the traffic facts of life. You can teach him respect for cars by the method described above, and teach him respect for the street by never allowing him to run out into it, except for his brief excursions to relieve himself. When you're on your walks together, make it a firm practice to stop at the curb before crossing. Make him sit if you want, but at least make him wait at the curb for a word from you before going into the street. Make it consistent— never let him bound ahead of you at the end of the leash, for as he grows older he'll get faster and stronger, and one day might leap out into traffic.

RIDING IN CARS

When you brought your pup home from the kennels the first day you may have had your first experience with the carsick dog. Some dogs take to cars naturally and never have a sick moment. Others are nauseated by the motion of the car and other factors and get sick at the thought of going for a ride. The central problem is one of confidence— he has to be made to feel sure of the situation, and of his surroundings. Consider it from his point of view. Suddenly he is thrust into a strange-smelling monster of steel and padding, closed in a small place which immediately starts moving and bumping about, assaulted in the nose by gasoline smells, in the ears by motor and horn noises, and in the eyes by the frightening sight of the world swaying and rushing by him. Small wonder some dogs get upset.

You can start things out right by not feeding him for an hour or so before taking him for a ride. That takes some of the physical load off his system. And then carry things out gently and in a manner calculated to instill confidence in him. If you're driving alone, by all means let him snuggle up to you on the front seat, pet him and talk to him. Let him sit with you in the car for a few minutes before you start up, until he has gotten used to it. Then start off slowly, reassuring him all the while. Drive only around the block the first time, so you can get him out before he has a chance to get sick. Then increase the length of the rides until he becomes a veteran.

During the introductory rides, keep as close an eye on him as you can and still drive. If he shows any of the preparatory signs of throwing up (usually a sort of slight hiccuping) stop as quickly as you can and get him out. But if he beats you to it, let him go until he is empty. Then go on for a bit and see if he becomes resigned to it. Whatever you do, when he is sick, don't chastise him in the slightest. He simply can't help it, and any attempt at correction or any disapproval will only confuse and bewilder him, and may make him sicker yet. If he throws up on your lap, just sigh and clean it off as best you can. Better, though, to make the precaution of spreading an old blanket or an expendable sheet over the front seat and your lap beforehand.

Once he's gotten over car-sickness, or if he started out cured, you can direct your attention to persuading him to ride where you want him. Your early attentions and permission in letting him ride beside you on the seat won't substantially affect the job of persuading him to take his proper position. Wherever you want him, put him there and make him stay. If he moves, correct him with a firm "No!" and put him back.

Later, as he makes the car his own, you'll run into the problem of windows if he's middle-sized or larger. Most dogs who get to like riding in cars love to stick their heads out of the window like a railroad engineer. You may think this is quite all right, and if so, let him crane for all he's worth. But keep in mind the possibilities that, a) he may get something large and gritty in his eye that way and do it permanent damage, and b) if he learns that poking his head out is okay, he may carry his pro-

tection of the car a bit beyond the bounds of propriety. For some reason, dogs defend cars even more fiercely than they do houses, so think
of the fact that he might just reach out and snap a sirloin off an innocent
passerby who happened to brush against the car while you're parking.
It's better to let him know that the windows are strict boundaries.

For car riding, it is essential to make one very strict rule and never to
let him deviate from it. That is that he cannot leave the car until you
give him permission. When you drive up to home and stop, he'll dance
around in his anxiety to get out and into the house, no matter how much
he enjoyed the ride. Make him sit and stay until you give him the "Okay."
It can save his life, and it can save you the nasty spill you might take
if a large or medium-sized dog came charging out between your legs as
you were trying to disentangle yourself from the car.

TABLE MANNERS AND FOOD REFUSAL

Although feeding and its related problems will be taken up in a separate chapter, table manners and food refusal properly belong under
pre-training. Table manners are simple. They involve his staying away
from the table when you're eating. You can, of course, allow him around
and throw him tidbits from your plate if you want to, but quite a few
people feel strongly about dogs at table, and you may have them over for
dinner some night.

After he's been given the freedom of the house he'll come up to the
table at lunch or dinner and fix you with an appealing, mournful look as
though never a morsel of food had passed his lips these three days
gone. You know it isn't true, and he knows it isn't true, but there's
no harm in trying. Send him to his bed for the remainder of the meal,
and then release him. If he persists from meal to meal, keep sending him
away and making him stay. After a while he'll catch on. He'll just lie
around the house and ignore you completely, and you can eat in peace.

Food refusal is a little more complicated. It's something all dogs
should learn, for their own good and for yours. There are, sad to say,
people in the world who hate dogs enough to poison them just on principle, and many a fine dog and long-time companion has been lost that
way. If your dog trustingly takes food from anyone who comes along, he

stands a fair chance of getting at least a stomach upset, even if he never runs into a poisoner. Doting strangers will try to feed your dog an unholy variety of stomach-turning items, and he'll probably happily gobble any and all such.

For your own well-being food refusal is a good idea. Too many homes have been burgled by someone with the foresight to bring along a handful of hamburger to pacify the household dog. To prevent this, lay the groundwork by never allowing anyone outside your own household to feed him anything. Never, that is, unless you specifically tell him that it's all right. Don't tempt him for a month or so, just to let the idea get firmly established that food flows only from you and yours. Then, if you want, get a friend to offer him some tidbit that he likes specially well. As soon as the friend offers it, tell the pup "No!" quite firmly. By this time he'll know full well what "no" means, which is why it's best to wait until you have some measure of control over him. Repeat this treatment until he will refuse the morsel offered without your having to tell him "No." Then, when he is steady, tell him "Okay" and let him take it. Alternate permission and refusal until he will refuse the food without fail, and take it willingly when you permit it. The reason for this two-way training is that some day you may have to leave him with friends or at a kennel and you don't want him to starve to death just because he has faithfully learned never to take food from anyone but you. Don't allow him to show any aggression toward the offerer, and don't worry yet about his refusing things when you're not around. Just get the basic idea across.

A thief or poisoner can also throw his offering onto the ground, and a dog should learn that he is to eat nothing unless it is in his feeding bowl or he gets it from you or with your permission. It'll also save him from getting sick from tainted food left lying around. For the moment, though, don't take any positive action in this line. Lay the groundwork by never letting him pick up anything from the floor or street to eat. If he approaches something on the ground, sheer him off with a "No!," and if he's grabbed it already, put the "Give" training to use and take it from him.

SOME GENERAL CONSIDERATIONS

There are, as you have seen, a great many things the young puppy has to learn in his first weeks and months in your home. All of them he will learn if you learn to be a good teacher and practice patience and kindness in your teaching. Space out the lessons and don't bedevil him with over-training. Take it slow and easy in all things, for up to now he's having a time on his own sorting out the world around him. On your side you have the fact that he will become quickly attached to you. He will learn to want to please you, not from any innate joy that pleasing you gives him, but from the fact that pleasing you brings him fondling and praise, while displeasing you brings corrections and confinement. There is no natural perverseness in him, no matter how much it may seem so at times. When he sets his will against yours, it is not just for the setting, but rather that his way is dictated by instincts and his otherwise natural way of life. When he opposes you it's for a reason, and try always to look for that reason and take it into account in training.

If you've gotten him safely and well through pre-training, he will be at the barely civilized level, fit to live with but just only so. Basic training as taken up in the next chapter will teach him the elements of behavior above and beyond controlling his natural impulses, and will fit him to be a true companion and member of your household.

CHAPTER III

BASIC TRAINING

A<small>LTHOUGH</small> this chapter is titled "Basic Training" and the next "Novice," both together comprise the work necessary to pass the Novice class work in AKC obedience trials. At the same time, the training taken up in both chapters is what we consider as basic grounding for the well behaved dog above and beyond the elementary manners acquired in pre-training.

We recommend strongly that you train, in following the two chapters, exactly as though you were preparing for the ring, even if at present you haven't the slightest intention of ever going into competition obedience at a dog show. All the exercises included in AKC Novice work are based in practicality (Heel on Leash, Heel off Leash, Recall, Stand for Examination, Long Sit and Down) as we will point out as each exercise is gone over. One of the reasons for our recommendation is that you may easily acquire an interest in ring work as you progress in training. It has happened to thousands of dog owners, and it is many times harder to re-train a haphazardly trained dog to perform all the exercises correctly than it is to begin right. Obedience training to show standards takes very little extra effort and is rewarding in itself.

BEGINNING BASIC TRAINING

The pup should be at least six months old before you begin serious work on obedience training. As with most age specifications, this one is subject to variation depending on the dog. It may be that you have a canine genius in your household, ready for work at the age of four months. Dogs have been started in training earlier, and in fact we know of at least one who qualified for the basic AKC obedience degree, the C.D., at the age of six months. This is the exception—and in this case the trainer was a man of considerable experience in the field who had the ability to recognize extra talent in the very young puppy, and to adapt standard training procedures to his precocious charge. If this is your first dog (since childhood) and your first attempt at training we recommend that you hold off until at least six months. We've seen too many dogs who've had their puppyhood shattered by too-early attempts at the imposition of the concentration and discipline necessary, and who, though trained after a fashion, never worked happily or well.

Most training classes stay several months above the line by refusing to accept dogs until they are eight months old. Professional trainers who take dogs to train for others prefer that they be *two years* old before they begin. At two years, the nominal maturity age for a dog, he will be adult enough really to give his attention to the task in hand and there will be little problem with frolicsomeness and a wandering mind. The various institutes which train dogs as guides for the blind set two years as their minimum age limit. So take counsel from those whose lives are devoted to dog training and wait awhile before beginning on your pup.

Ease of training isn't the only factor in waiting. The puppy is after all a puppy, young and playful, full of the joy of life, sniffing and sprawling and tail-wagging. As a member of your family he deserves to be allowed to enjoy his puppyhood even as a child enjoys his all-too-brief childhood before being intensively prepared to face the world on his own. Training, properly done, can be fun and basically enjoyable for both you and the pup. Still, it involves disciplines and restraints, concentration and corrections, learning and unlearning. Enough that in his first month or so he has had to learn to control his natural functions, to respect visitors, not to chew on your possessions, to release his treasured playthings on command. Let him enjoy the fruits of his elementary civilization for a while before going on to more serious endeavors.

At the other end of the scale, you can totally disregard the hackneyed business about an old dog and new tricks. We have seen dogs entered in training up to the age of 11 years and qualifying for degrees at 12 and 13. The fact that the older dog will be a bit more set in his ways is counteracted by his increased ability to concentrate. If he's been yours all that time your relationship will have become so firmly established that your position as giver of commands will be unquestioned. Unless, of course, he's been badly spoiled and/or unmanageable all his life. But with the average older dog, training is definitely indicated.

DISCIPLINE AND CORRECTIONS

Training requires discipline. Discipline in the case of the dog means attention to the matter in hand and ultimate performance of the required exercises. Discipline also means, equally as importantly, discipline, concentration and self control in yourself. Before the dog can learn what you want to teach him, you must understand thoroughly what it is he is to learn, how he is to learn it and how he feels about it. You must resolve never to lose your temper, never to display anger to the dog, never to correct him for your own mistakes (except in the rare instances we will mention), and *always* to remember that you're working with a dog. That last may seem obvious, but it isn't. People who are having their first contact with training often tend to lose sight of what they are working with. They impute curious and overly human motives to the dog—vindictiveness, obtuseness, spitefulness and other unpleasantly human characteristics. If this major mistake is assiduously avoided, the training processes can be genuinely enjoyable and effective.

As a first rule of obedience training, keep always in mind that the dog is never punished. He is corrected. When possible (and this is nearly always) he is corrected immediately the commission, or omission occurs. He does not, and never will, understand punishment. While you can say to a child, "You did thus-and-so yesterday and I'm going to spank you for it," you can't do it to a dog, for remembrance of isolated mishaps past is beyond his capacity. The dog lives in the moment, with no real understanding of the concept of the past or the future. He will anticipate and expect things that are going to happen soon, but tomorrow, or even later today, is an alien concept to him. And yesterday, or even earlier today, means little more to him except as habit patterns have been laid down, and people or commands or things from the past come to his attention and excite conditioned responses.

We don't mean to say that the dog doesn't remember, for he most surely does. He remembers you, and your friends, and his toys, and the things you have taught him, and your house, and his favorite run in the woods. And while we won't get into the argument over whether he consciously thinks about things when they are out of sight, we will say that one-time occurrences mean less than nothing to him once they are over. Even the veriest novice would reject the idea of punishing a dog for not having sat yesterday. But as the gap between not sitting and punishing grow smaller, the tendency arises to feel that punishment is justified, that "he knows why he's getting it." It simply isn't so—the separation in time of a minute, or even ten seconds, is enough for all connection to be lost in the dog's mind.

Of corrections there are two types: demonstrative and restrictive. We will speak throughout this book simply of "correction" and in each case the type will be apparent, but for the moment let's examine these two distinct types.

The demonstrative correction is one which shows the dog, by physical guidance with leash or hand, what is expected of him. When he is learning, say, to heel—the snap on the lead pulling him back to the proper position by your left side is demonstrative. It is in effect a compulsion, in that you compel him, however gently, to do as you want him to. It can be applied in many degrees of force, and can, when training has progressed, even be a purely vocal correction to call his attention to what he is supposed to do. In pre-training, you will already have applied a good many demonstrative corrections, beginning with the first time you rushed him to the papers or outside.

In the restrictive correction, you prevent him from doing something undesirable. In many cases the line between the two is hazy, as in the example just given of heeling. When you snap the lead to force him back, are you demonstrating where he should walk, or are you preventing him from walking elsewhere? It's a philosophical point in such a case, depending on how you look at it. Generally, the strong restrictive correction will be given literally to correct his behavior. If, for example, he becomes rebellious during training, the strong correction is called for. This may mean firm handling with the leash, or it may mean striking the dog. And this latter requires a discussion of its own.

Striking the dog is something to be done only *in extremis*. When he is struck, he should be hit only in one place, under the chin, and with only one thing, the fingers of your open right hand. He should be struck *only* for positive misbehavior uncontrollable in any other way, and never, repeat *never*, for failing to do something.

There are many good reasons for the place to strike him when necessary. A blow anywhere on the body, or on the side or top of the head can injure him internally. A blow under the chin, applied with the proper force, can only snap his teeth together and shake him up a bit. The chances of catching his tongue between his teeth are slight indeed, as he's a good deal faster on his reflexes than you are. Of course, the force has to be calculated with considerable nicety, all of which leads back to the vital issue of never losing your temper while training. A full roundhouse swing, even under the muzzle, could rattle his brains pretty badly. With a toy breed, even a six-inch swing might, at full steam, nearly snap his head off.

This consideration is behind the "fingers only" restriction. With your open fingers you have considerably less chance of miscalculating your own strength, plus the fact that the open-finger blow is the maximum ever required, regardless of the size of the dog. Try it under the edge of the table and you'll see that you can deliver a pretty nasty crack with your fingers, without even moving your wrist. If and when the time comes, use your good judgment about the force of the blow. Of the hundreds of people who have been taught this correction, there has never been a case where a dog has been injured by it.

Hitting him with the hand, incidentally, won't make him "hand shy," not if you do it right. When you give him this sort of correction he is always on lead and unable to duck. So you connect. One of the things that makes a dog hand shy is being swung at. If the dog can get away, or if you rush at him swinging and hollering, he's going to get distinctly unhappy associations with that good right hand of yours. The cardinal rule in all this is a simple one: don't miss. If he isn't in a position where missing is nigh onto impossible, don't swing.

The other thing that will cause him to distrust you and your intentions with that right hook is the lack of immediate praise after you've corrected him. But more on that in a moment. First we want to lay down a rigid rule—never hit the dog with *anything* but your hand. No leashes, no sticks, no switches, no buggy whips, nothing. The folded newspaper, by the way, is a bit of interesting mythology designed to keep you from having to think through the business of corrections. True, the resounding whack of a paper may scare the wits out of him, and unless you larrup him with the Sunday Times, sports section and all, you don't stand much chance of hurting him seriously. But if you follow this method you are letting yourself in for a) being unable to correct him until you have found and rolled up a newspaper; b) teaching him to be scared of sudden loud noises; and c) instilling a fundamental dislike for newspapers which could seriously affect his literacy.

PRAISE AND PLAY

Praise is the motive power in the training of your dog. In training, it is to be applied in liberal doses, at any and all opportunities. It is administered when the dog does something right, and paradoxical though it may seem, when he does something wrong. Don't fall into the "easy" solution of giving him tidbits as rewards for the performance of exercises. It'll work, the food, but eventually it'll have to stop and then you've got a problem. You'll either have to face him down when you start withholding the goodies, and endure his thoughts of you as a pretty cheap character, or you'll have to substitute effusive praise for the food. In which case you'll be right back with us and praise. It's strictly against AKC rules to give an obedience dog any offering of food in the ring, but praise between exercises is unlimited. If your dog is used to bribery, he may decide in the middle of the ring, no food, no work, and go on strike. For which we wouldn't blame him a bit if he'd been trained to expect worldly goods for his efforts.

Praise when he does right needs little explanation. When he is first learning, give him praise when he has done something, even if you have had to guide, shove and haul him into it every step of the way. All the work in the beginning stages may have been yours, but praise him as though he'd done something colossal. When he gets a glimmering of what you want and tries it experimentally, praise him to the skies. And even after he is a veteran, having performed the same exercise a thousand times perfectly, praise him every time as though it were the first.

Praise him with your voice, telling him "Good Boy!" and "Good Dog!" and even "Well Done!" or whatever. This is one case where there is no reason to stick to a single word or phrase—the tone of your voice will tell him all he wants to know. The words are for you because it's easier for you to sound praiseful while saying "good boy" than while pronouncing "the rains in Spain." You could do it with practice, but why bother? And praise him with your hands. Particularly with your left, of which more later. Pat him, stroke him, fondle him, scratch him. But let him have your touch as a reward and assurance that all is well.

Praise when he has done something wrong may be a bit harder for the neophyte to understand, but it is perhaps even more essential than praise for good work. It assumes a good constructive correction first to straighten out whatever he has or hasn't done. Then praise to take his mind off the fact that it was you who did the correcting. As we have said before and will say again—the correction must always in the dog's mind be a natural outgrowth of the wrong, or of the failure to perform whatever is wanted. If you correct him, then come in immediately with praise; it lets him know that you are still on his side, still love him, and that all is well in the world. Correction, done fairly and firmly, will earn you his undying respect, if followed by praise and unaccompanied by any display of displeasure or withdrawal of affection, however momentary. Take this as another firm and basic rule of training—always praise after a correction.

Play is important in training, too. While the training period itself must be kept businesslike, a period of carefree play and romping should always follow, as something of a reward. As soon as the training period is over, let yourself go and romp with him. While he'll probably never think of it as an actual reward for having been cooperative, the play will establish completely friendly relations between you. No one but an old hand at this sort of thing can maintain a completely icy calm during training, and things may get a bit strained around the edges before the period is over. If so, the play puts things back on the right footing—he'll forget about the corrections in his joy at wrestling or running with you, but the lessons will still be there.

HEEL AND SIT

The goal in the heel and sit, which are taught simultaneously, is to train the dog to walk at your left side, neither lagging nor forging ahead. When you halt, he is to sit quietly by your side and wait for further developments. The practical advantages of this training are evident—walking along city streets is paramount among them.

In preparation for heeling you will have been out on the street with him a good many times. Through hours of having his freedom restricted by it, the leash will have become a nuisance, but a tolerable one, something to shrug and live with. This is of course a general rule, to which there are exceptions. If your particular pup is still at odds with the leash, hold off until truce is declared. There are as many types of dog, and reactions to the leash, as there are dogs in total. Through leash-walking you should by now have a fairly good idea of how he will react to his first lessons in heeling—whether he will take it well, or actively fight it, or get hysterical, or curl up and die at the thought. Keep these first reactions in mind, as the course of heeling training will be largely dictated by them.

Choose as a training area someplace where there is enough room to walk a bit in any direction, and where there will be no interruptions. A field, if you can get to one conveniently; your yard, a quiet sidewalk, or even your living room as a last resort. Put on the training collar correctly, snap on the lead, and take the lead in your left hand. Grasp it as near to the dog as you can without forcing yourself to bend over or strain sideways.

Maneuver yourself around so that he is more or less at your left side (don't haul on him), then do three things simultaneously. Call his name and give the command, "Mike, Heel!," step forward with your *left* foot, and give a gentle snap on the lead. That may be enough to get him moving. If he comes along more or less peaceably, keep going, snapping the lead gently to urge him into the proper position with his shoulder just even with your left side. With each snap repeat the command "Mike, Heel!" exactly at the time you snap. Don't make it a sequence of command and then correction. Make it absolutely simultaneous. Then, immediately after each correction, praise him with a warm "good boy."

He can deviate from position forward, to the side, or to the back.

Forward or to the side mean at least that he is moving in the same general direction you are, and require only continued corrections to get him back into position, accompanied by command and followed by praise. Adjust the force of your lead snap so that it jolts him just a little—enough to call his attention to the fact that he's in the wrong place and give him a nudge back where he belongs. Don't haul him. Make every correction a quick snap and an immediate release of pressure. The over-riding idea is to make it uncomfortable for him to be elsewhere than at your side. When he's not there, snapping and associated discomfort continue; as soon as he's in position the discomfort ceases. The lead is *not* used to haul him anywhere, but as a method of control and administering corrections.

A slightly more serious problem arises when he doesn't move at all, or tries to charge in the other direction once you've started off. Again, snap the lead but don't haul. Continue snapping and moving away from him, snapping just hard enough to jolt him and lift him off his rear a little. If you increase the force of the snap gradually, he'll soon get tired of all the nonsense and decide it doesn't make much sense to sit or stand there and have his head jarred continually. With each snap use his name and the command to heel, and continue to praise him even if he's sitting there glaring at you between snaps. As you go along, you can increase the firmness of your verbal command until it is strong and demanding. But don't raise your voice, don't grit at him, and don't get exasperated. It may take him a few minutes, but he'll get there soon enough.

When he's gotten up to your side and you are striding along together in an orderly fashion, praise the pull-back especially warmly. If he's big enough to reach without bending double, pat him with your left hand, holding the lead in the right to keep up the corrections. Otherwise make your voice give all the praise. While he's in position, let the lead hang slightly loose and give him continuous praise for being where he is. Don't hold him firmly in position with the lead, but always keep a short enough hold for an immediate correction.

PROBLEM DOGS

A real problem is the pup or dog who resents the idea of training to the point where he will take active steps to put a stop to it. The dog inherits from his wild ancestors the instinct to try to become leader of the pack, and he may choose this time to have a showdown with you. No matter how good your relations have been up to this time, it can happen. Usually it won't, but if it does, the time has come to establish for once and for all who is going to be boss in your particular pack consisting of you and him.

First, though, go back to the beginnings and try to regain his confidence in you. Loosen the lead and spend a few days just walking around together companionably, giving him very mild snaps as you turn to go in another direction. Coax him along with his name and anything else that comes to mind. If you can avoid the showdown, all well and good. If he's really set in his mind about being the pack leader it'll come up again, but you do have a good chance of eliminating any contest if you spend a few days in patching things up.

Run with him a little, and when he gets going, use the lead to bring him up sharply. As soon as he's been jolted to a stop, go to him and praise him and apologize for your clumsiness. Tell him what a terrible thing it was that you accidentally held onto the lead too tight. He'll forgive you, not knowing that it's going to keep on happening. Apologize profusely after every time it happens. He'll begin to think you're a pretty clumsy lout, but he'll watch out for the jerks on the collar and he won't get mad at you.

This may cure him. If not, showdown time has come. When you start back into serious heel work, keep a very close eye on him, watching for the first sign of a curled lip or snarl. Work with a very short lead so that your hand is near his collar and ready to hold tight if need be. When the snarl comes, grab his collar with your left hand at the back of his neck, lift him just enough so that his front feet are off the ground, and connect under his chin with a good crack with the right fingers. Just having his feet off the ground will take some of the fight out of him. Immediately, then, loosen the collar and praise him. Keep hold of the collar with your left hand and keep your right hand ready to go again in case it's needed, but praise him effusively with words. Watch him closely. If the resistance seems to be gone, straighten up and start off with a snap and "Mike, Heel!" and go right into heeling. It may take several fairly stiff corrections to straighten him out, but its infallible. If you're firm and quick you stand little chance of being so much as nipped. And praise here after the correction is of extreme importance—to take his mind off the fact that he's been hit, and to let him know that you love him still and all that, but that you're having none of the snarling business.

The two vital things to remember are: do not display any temper or fear, and especially do not use this correction when he is just being stubborn. Only apply it when he makes it perfectly clear that he intends to lacerate you a little if you insist on trying to train him. Then make it good.

Possibly the worst of problem dogs is the hysteric. When the lead is put on for training he may sit, lie down, roll over, or even stand on his hind feet and try to climb up the lead with his front feet. What he is afraid of is the lead and the increasing restriction that is being placed on him through it. The cure is a simple repeat of the original introduction to the lead as he runs free around the yard or house. He'll trip on it and stumble, and tangle and disentangle himself; but let him work out his own problem of getting more used to it. When you put the lead on, attach it to the inactive ring of the collar, the one that will not make the chain pull up tight when he steps on the lead and yanks himself. By leaving him alone with the lead, you allow him to regain his own confidence in the state of the world without having at the same time to worry about you and commands and what to do next.

Gradually, then, take him out for walks, using more and more restriction as you go, adjusting the progress to his own progress in confidence and lack of resentment and hysteria. Don't force him at all—keep things at the pace he sets, and a week or two should see the problem over. Gentle corrections and especially fulsome praise are indicated for this type of dog once you are back in the training schedule.

MORE HEELING

Up to now about all you will have been able to do is give your dog the idea that he is to stick close to your left side while you're walking along. The next thing is to teach him to stick with you when you turn either left or right, or around, and to adjust his pace if you slow down or start trotting or running.

When you begin making turns with him, do the left turns first. This way you are guiding him around the turn with your body. Do the turns gradually at first, forcing him around with nudges from your left leg, and keeping him close in with the lead. After a few left turns have been accomplished, turn to the right, again making more of a small quarter-circle than a sharp turn. In turning right you will have to rely entirely on the lead to keep him with you. Snap him along gently to keep him in place. Praise him and coax him along with you on the turns, remembering to praise after every snap of the lead, and to give the heel command with every correction.

The about turn is simply an extension of the right turn. While walking along, turn around and go in the opposite direction, turning always to your right. Don't spin in position and do a military about face, but turn in a very small circle, giving the dog a chance to be with you. Again, snap him around gently with the lead, coaxing and praising. With all your snaps of the lead, give him the "Mike, Heel!" as you snap.

When you make any turn, remember to take the preparatory short step just before you go into it. Slow slightly to give the dog a small warning that you are going to do something. Otherwise it is extremely difficult for him to stay smartly with you. Try it yourself just to get his viewpoint. Have a friend walk along, taking unwarned sudden turns, and you try to keep with him without bumping or lagging on the turns. Then have him give a slight warning of all turns by slowing a bit. This way you will see the problems your dog faces and will be better able to teach and handle him.

Throughout all your heeling and turns, walk always at an even pace—just fast enough so that he can step along smartly. Don't adapt your pace to his once you've gotten into it. Use the lead to make him keep up with you, or down with you, at the pace you've chosen.

When he has mastered the turns, a matter of several days of training, you can begin the slow and fast. While walking with him at heel in a straight line, slow down gradually until you are moving quite slowly. Keep him with you, using commands and the lead. Then gradually increase your pace until you are again walking normally.

To teach him the "fast," reverse the procedure. From a normal walk slowly increase your pace until you are trotting along at a fairly good clip, again using snaps on the lead and the "heel" command to keep him right at your side. Don't break into a full run, because at this point the temptation will be almost irresistable for him to break into a real lurching gallop. Even with a mild trot you will encounter the problem of his trying to romp with you once you begin going fast. As soon as he breaks his pace, slow down, giving him a strong correction with the lead. Then start up again, increasing your pace more gradually this time. Keep a close lead and keep him well under control as you speed up. You'll have to break him of romping while you're increasing your speed, as it's quite difficult to keep a good snapping lead control and puff out firm commands and praise once you've gotten up to a respectable pace.

Although you may seldom want to run with him at heel, especially off lead, there may come times when you do want to. Teaching him to stay at heel can prevent some pretty nasty work trying to slow down a really charging dog who's gotten worked up to a full run. In the show ring you'll be required only to work up to quite a mild trot, really not much more than a jog—but you must be able to demonstrate that he'll stay at your side whatever your pace.

When going into or coming out of either the slow or the fast, "float" into or out of them. Don't suddenly start running, or creeping along, and don't return to normal pace with a jerk. With his shoulder directly by your left leg he has to have some small warning of your intentions to change pace. If you don't help him out, he'll develop the habit of lagging or forging ahead.

THE SIT AT HEEL

Teaching the dog to sit requires a little more work than heeling. You have to learn to use both hands in smooth coordination and to bring him to the point where he will sit automatically when you come to a halt.

Don't bring in the sit too early. Let him get well accustomed to the fact of walking at heel before you begin on it. Then, once you have started, make it a firm rule that when you come to a stop while heeling, he sits.

Walking in a straight line with the dog at heel, slow to a halt, taking several steps to do it. As you're taking those steps, prepare yourself for the lesson by moving your right hand over to the left which holds the lead, and taking hold. Don't do the move suddenly, as you may startle him and take his mind off his work. Then, just as you stop moving, place your left hand flat on his shoulders and move it rapidly but smoothly down his back until it is directly over the end of his rib cage. Command him, "Mike, Sit!" and at the same time pull *straight up* on the lead with your right hand and press down firmly with your left. Release the pressure of both hands immediately and reassure him with hands and voice. But keep a close watch and keep your hands close to position. If he tries to get up or shies from position, pull the lead up again and push down on his rear gently but firmly and repeat the commands. Follow this command immediately with "Stay!" If he tries again, correct him into position and again, "Sit, stay." Keep him there for a few moments, then start up forward again, always taking the first step with the left foot, telling him to heel and snapping the lead if necessary.

Do not, at this point, attempt to teach him to sit under any other circumstances than in stopping at heel. Getting him to sit while in front of you or at a distance will follow later in a natural sequence of training. Concentrate on the sit now as part of heeling and get it down firmly before progressing to anything else.

The simple "sit" method applies to any breed and size. With large or medium dogs there should be no trouble in applying the simultaneous moves of the hands. With the very small breeds you will have to bend over considerably to get the left hand move done, but do just that—bend over. Don't, with any size, squat or kneel down to teach the sit. Stay on your feet so that he doesn't get the idea that you have to be down with him to get him to sit.

The pull directly upward is important. It serves to stop his forward motion, keeps his head up when sitting, and gives a pressure in the general direction of what you want him to do. Be especially careful not to pull the lead across your body with the right hand, as this will pull his head in that direction and encourage crooked sits. If you are working with a very large breed, say a Scottish Deerhound, you can pull the lead slightly *back* as you pull up to aid you in exerting the proper pressures. Or if the dog really needs a push, still hold onto the leash but move your right hand around to give him a rearward push on the chest as you exert downward pressure on the rear with the left hand.

The position of the left hand is important, too. If you push on him too far forward, in the middle of his back, he will brace his hind legs and resist the whole idea. If you push too far back on his rear it will make him tend to hunch his rear forward when sitting. Keep the hand, after sliding it down from his shoulders, directly over the rear of his rib cage. The purpose of the slide from the shoulders is to reassure him by not bringing a sudden and unexpected pressure to bear on his posterior.

As in all training, adjust your pressure carefully to the dog, using only enough to force the action you want and to demonstrate to him what it is you're looking for. Use as much force as necessary with the big ones

VERY LITTLE FORCE WILL BE NECESSARY WITH THE LEFT HAND IN TEACHING THE "SIT." USE ONLY ENOUGH TO GUIDE HIS REAR DOWN.

and go carefully with the toys and miniatures. They have delicate leg bones and rough handling can either scare them to death or actually injure them.

When you have him firmly at the sit, don't start up immediately into the heel again. Let him sit there for a few moments. It is far easier to teach a dog the wrong thing than the right, and if you start up again right away he'll get the idea that what he's supposed to do on a halt is to bump his rear on the ground and then pick it up right away and start off. By making him wait patiently you're also teaching him to work at command rather than by a learned routine. As he's sitting there, reassure him continually with praise and a repeated "Stay!." The constant repetition of "stay" will keep his mind on his business and lay the groundwork for more intensive "stay" work in future training.

Once he seems to have learned that he is supposed to sit when you stop walking, stop using the left hand. When you halt, give a snap upwards with the lead, commanding "Sit." The free left hand can now be employed to advantage in making him sit straight. Walking along with you at heel, his hindquarters will be in line with his head and the direction of travel, and it is just as easy for him to sit perfectly straight as it is for him to swing his rear around in any direction. From the first time, at the beginning adjusting the direction of your downward pressure with the left hand, and later using it purely as a lateral corrective measure, insist that the sit be straight. Try not, though, to shove his rear around once it has hit the ground. Keep a close eye on proceedings as you are about to halt, and use the hand to guide his posterior as it moves to the ground.

When he will sit with only the lead correction, use it gradually less and less but still retaining the verbal command. Work with him several days, always commanding "Sit" when you halt, before you try to leave commands and corrections out altogether. Then, one day, come to a halt while heeling and see what happens. Ninety-nine chances out of a hundred he will surprise the life out of you by coming smartly to a sit and looking extremely proud of himself. Praise and praise him again, and after a few moments start up the heeling again. If he doesn't immediately sit, use the leash to snap him into position without a command, continue this for a while, and later try him solo again. It won't take long.

Put him through complete routines now. Forward, left turn, right turn, fast, normal, about turn, slow, halt, forward, halt, right turn, halt, and so on. Mix it up thoroughly so that he doesn't get to expect any definite pattern of events, but will follow your lead wherever you go. And always, when you start up again from a halt and sit, use the "Mike, Heel!" command, and always start on your left foot.

TURNS AND FIGURE-EIGHT

By now your dog should be fairly proficient at heeling and halting, and you can begin to sharpen things up. Start going into your turns more sharply while still giving him all the help you can. On the left turns, swing on your left foot so that your right leg comes around in front of his face to let him know what is up. Try giving him a light snap backwards on the leash just as you are about to turn left, to hold him back slightly and draw his attention. On right turns, turn on your right foot and swing the left leg around to guide him. Snap lightly a bit forward and to the right as you are about to go into the turn. Work on these until you can turn sharply to the left or right with him staying perfectly at your side.

The next step is circling completely to prepare him for the figure-eight. As you are walking along, start out by making a very wide full circle to your left, coaxing and correcting him along as you go. Then make a full wide circle to your right. Work with him on these circles, making them increasingly smaller in radius as you go along and he gets the idea. On the right turns, work until you can turn almost in place and have him swing around you at heel. On the left, continue decreasing the radius until he himself is almost swinging around in place as you circle around him back to the original line of travel. Don't let him crowd you or swing wide.

Mix the circles up, going from a full left directly into a full right, and then again into the left, making the circles ever smaller. Then you can progress to the formal figure-eight. For this, place two chairs, or any other similar objects, about eight feet apart on the ground or floor and proceed to walk a figure eight around them with him at heel. When you've both mastered this, go on to doing the same exercise around two members of your family, or friends, standing in place of the chairs. Keep the dog firmly at heel with his mind on his business. If he tries to sniff either chairs or people, snap his head up into place. If he shies away on an inside turn, make the turn wider and then slowly decrease it with constant reassurance until he thinks only of being where he's supposed to be and pays no attention to the objects you're going around. But give him plenty of leeway on the inside turns so that he doesn't have to brush against anything.

With the figure-eight (which is, among other things, preparation for walking along crowded streets and all the consequent turning around people) the training in the heel proper, on leash, is completed. You should be able to walk anywhere with the dog without having to think about his being there, or about his entangling people or signposts with the lead. Such problems as do arise will come up in the first heeling and sitting, and the later practice in turns and circles will simply be a matter of continued application by both of you.

HEELING IN GENERAL

While training, and heeling, wear whatever you will for the training periods. A swirling skirt flapping right beside his head may put him off a bit and make him heel a little wide, but if that's what you're going to wear while walking with him, let him get used to it. Small use it would be always to wear slacks while in training, and then expect him miraculously to get used to the idea of a skirt.

All the work is done on lead. Don't give in to the temptation to take him off lead "just once" to see how he will do, no matter how well he seems to have it down. It will give him the opportunity to make a mistake at precisely the wrong time in the schedule, and will set you back considerably. For every exercise in this chapter, and until you have progressed to the Novice work in Chapter IV, *keep him on lead at all times!*

Make your training periods fairly short—about fifteen minutes at a time. Get in two of these periods a day and he will have just about as much learning as he can absorb without getting thoroughly bored with the whole thing. Give him plenty of praise during the training, and play with him afterwards. Keep it fun for both of you and progress will be faster and better. Try not to train always in the same place—or he'll come to expect that he has only to work when you take him there.

If you always step out with the left foot first when you want him to come along at heel, he will learn to take this as a sort of signal. Later, in the "stay" work, you will step out with your right foot when he is to remain, and it helps him keep things separate.

Mix up the work as much as possible. Keep him from thinking that any one move comes naturally after another, except the sit when you halt.

Work as a team. True, you're training *him* to heel with you, but at the same time you're learning how to walk with him and handle him so it's as easy for him as possible. Don't adjust to his walking pace, but keep in mind that it's the two of you working together, not him working for you.

Use verbal commands at all times during the training. Eventually you will need only to say "Mike, Heel" when you start up from a halt. But work very gradually toward that state. Give your commands clearly and firmly, without shouting. Use corrections only when necessary, and then apply them firmly and properly.

The verbal command you use, the "Mike, Heel!" is a two-part command, and should be used as such. Calling his name is to draw his attention and prepare him to do something. After that follows the command for one action or another, in this case heeling. Later in training he will become accustomed to the situation and to listening for commands, but in these beginning stages, make just a slight hesitation between his name and the command, to give him time to alert himself for what's coming.

THE STAND

This exercise is a particularly important one, and it is important that it be taken up at this point in training, before the down and the stays. Therefore, let's take a moment to see just why it is so practical.

One of the objections that people preparing dogs for the breed ring have against obedience is that it trains the dog to sit promptly when the handler comes to a halt. This could be damaging to the dog's chances of winning in a breed ring, where he is expected to keep up and alert at all times. If the stand is taught now, after the basic work of heeling and sitting, the dog learns firmly that stopping doesn't always mean sitting—

it means it only when there is no contrary command to stand in place. The ability and training to hold a standing pose can in fact be very positively valuable to breed exhibitors, teaching the dog, as it does, to stand quietly before and during an examination by a judge.

Although we have no direct knowledge of the training of Rancho Dobe's Storm, the Doberman who won best-in-show at Madison Square Garden two years running, it could well be that he had some intensive "stand" training. Here is how Life Magazine described his first Garden win:

"During the final judging Storm stood motionless for 13 full minutes while Sims (the judge) looked over an English setter, a Welsh terrier, a wire-haired dachshund, a standard poodle and a Brussels griffon. As Storm held his pose—few human beings, let alone dogs, can stand still for 13 minutes—the eyes of one onlooker after another swung to him and remained fixed, until at last 12,000 people were staring breathlessly at him. Finally Sims approached him, and at that instant Storm turned his head, peered puckishly up at the judge, then resumed his pose. The crowd gave one prolonged roar, and kept on roaring until Sims signaled that Storm had won the show."

We don't intend in any way to detract from Storm's natural beauty as a Doberman (and he is a magnificent dog)—but we quote this as an indication of how a solid pose can tip the scales toward your dog in a close contest in the breed ring.

Another common objection of breed exhibitors to obedience training is that it kills a dog's alertness, his sharpness, the elan which sets a top dog apart from others. This point bears discussion, for it has in the past unfortunately been valid. Earlier methods of training involving punishment, striking the dog, scaring him by throwing chains and other objects at him —all these made for a dog who did indeed, though trained, lose some of his natural spirit. Even today a trainer who loses his temper in training or is over-harsh or proceeds illogically in training will have at the end a dog who, if not actually cowering, has lost his alertness and responsiveness.

We guarantee, however, that a dog trained by the methods we outline, and with the attitudes we urge, will not show these results. So long as the dog is treated with respect and kindness and is allowed to retain his natural dignity and self-respect in training, he will lose none of his show-ring sparkle. He may even gain some. It is simply unfortunate that earlier means of training gave the results they did, and that the prejudice against such training and its results still remains among breed exhibitors.

The stand also has two very practical out-of-ring applications. If, in heeling in muddy weather, you want to stop but don't want your dog to sit in the mess, you tell him to stand as you come to a halt, and he stays on his feet and clean. And for grooming it is invaluable. With the large dog on the floor, or the small one on a table, his training to hold a standing pose for minutes will greatly facilitate the necessary brushing and combing.

The stand is taught from heel. With a medium sized or large dog, as you are walking along, suddenly take a long step out in front of him, holding the lead in the left hand, and turn to face him with your right hand thrust in front of his face, palm open in the universal gesture for stop. At the same time give him the command "Stand!" and then "Stay!" If he tries to keep on going, push your right hand at him again and repeat the commands. If he tries to sit, you will have to resort to the small-dog correction.

For small dogs, as you are walking, suddenly step to your right out of the line of travel and turn to face the dog. With your right hand snap back lightly on the lead to stop his progress and use your left hand to block the forward motion of his right hindleg as you command "Stand!" Don't grab the leg—just use the hand, fingers stiff, to block it. Whatever his size, he will be very unlikely to try to sit, because of the unusualness of the situation. Instead of stopping in place you have moved out of position, and with hand either in front of his face or against his leg, you indicate something entirely different to him.

Once he has been stopped at a stand, keep repeating to him the commands "Stand, Stay" to reassure him and steady him. Move back to your position at his side slowly, repeating commands and praise. Then move off in your original line, commanding him to heel. Take three or four steps and stop, telling him to sit. Start up at heel again, and repeat the stand routine, praising and reassuring.

The stand-stay is taught as soon as he will stand motionless at your side. As it is the first time he is expected to stay in one place or position without having you right by him, use great patience in persuading him to hold his pose. One time when you have stopped and he is standing, use the right hand as an additional stay signal again, in front of his muzzle, and move slowly around his head, holding the lead in your left hand so that it passes over his head. It is especially important that during this first move you keep repeating "stand, stay" along with praise. Keep moving all the way around him counter-clockwise until you are back at heel position.

Despite his steadiness at your side, he may show a desire to move during the circling. After having drummed into his head that he is always to stay at your side, you now want him to stand still while you move. He may try to follow you around at heel as though you were doing a tight circle to the left. At his first move, retrace your steps completely, coming back around his head. If he is badly out of position, heel forward together

IN TEACHING THE STAND, USE LEFT HAND AS SHOWN—NOT HOLDING THE LEG, OR SUPPORTING THE BODY, BUT "BLOCKING" THE LEG.

a few steps, stand him and begin again. If he moves this time, give him a strong "No!" and a snap on the lead back to position. Continue this until you are able to walk all the way around him back to heel position without any major move on his part. A minor move, as in shifting a foot, requires only that you reach down and pick up the foot, moving it back to its place, and insisting that it stay there. The goal is for him to stand rock-still while you circle him, although if he follows your moves with his head there is no cause for correction.

As you come around his back on the circle, he may try to sit in place. If so, retrace your steps to heel position. Then, make a loop out of the end of the lead and pass it under his stomach, being careful with males not to get it under the genitals. Hold onto this loop with your left hand, and onto the lead near his neck with your right, and try the circle again. Keep his rear up with the loop as you go around, correcting him and praising him if he tries to drop it. Do this a few times and then try it without the loop.

When you can circle him and he is steady, try moving, right foot first, out to the front of him. When he is in position, back away from him slowly, repeating the "stand, stay" commands and using your open right hand as a stay signal until you are at the end of the lead. If he tries to move to you, check him immediately with your hand and the lead. Get to the end of the lead by slow stages—first just a foot or two in front of him, then three or four feet, and finally the full length. Modify that "full length" in this stay, and in all the others to come, to this extent—let the lead hang from his collar until it touches the ground and move as far away as you can with the lead still touching the ground at one point. This keeps the lead from exerting any pressure on him other than the weight of a very short section, and keeps you from making any inadvertent tugs that would confuse him when he's trying to keep still.

Don't keep him standing there without you for more than 15 seconds or so. Make it only long enough for him to get the idea. Then when you return, circle around to heel position, passing him on your left and holding the lead in the left hand so that it passes over his head. When back at heel, wait a moment, then take three or four steps forward, with command to heel, and come to a halt, whereupon he should sit.

If you've been following all the steps patiently, insuring that he is perfectly steady at each stage before going on to the next, the stays with you at the side and behind him can be accomplished in the same lesson with the "stay in front".

When he is steady with you in front, move gradually off to the right to the end of the lead, with lead still touching the ground, using the same corrections for moves on his part, again repeating "Stand, Stay" constantly to reassure him. Then from heel position move directly back of him to the lead's length. This will be a little harder, as it is hard for him to keep track of where you are, and he will crane around to watch you. Don't try to correct the head-turning, but concentrate on complete steadiness in the rest of his body. Again keep up the talk to him, to let him know you're still there, and to keep his mind on the business at hand. From the side and the back, don't go around him to heel, but return directly to position. And when you return to position, don't step off immediately in the heel. Wait five seconds or so before you move, rather than let him get the idea that he should start up as soon as you're back at heel.

In all the stand-stays, mix up the work with all the other exercises he has learned up to this point. Do one stand-stay, then heel him around a bit, interposing some stops and sits. Then stand him again, then more heeling. Don't get his mind completely on the stay to the detriment of his other training.

THE SIT AND STAY

The sit and stay is merely a repeat of the methods you have used to keep him in one position while standing. Follow the same procedures— first steadying him while you walk around him, then to the front and then to the side and back. You will probably not encounter any problem of moving, as by this time the concept of the "stay" will be firmly fixed in his mind. He will be sure that you are coming back to him when you step out for wherever you're going, and will sit patiently until you've come around, or from in back. Again, if any problems are encountered in the first circling, *come back around* to make the correction, rather than completing your circle. Again, let the leash touch the ground when you're standing away from him.

In the sit-stay, as in the stand-stay before and the down-stay to follow, there is a very standardized "stay" signal which is universally used. As you give the stay command, the open hand, either one, is chopped sharply toward the dog's muzzle, stopping an inch or so in front. The motion is toward the muzzle from in front, and need be only very short. In first training, the right hand is easier to use, for you can bring it around your body in quite an impressive sweep, then stopping just short. Time your stay command so that it rings out just as your hand stops. Later in training you can use either hand, in quite an informal gesture of palm-before-nose to indicate stay to him, but for the present make the gesture quite large and definite.

THE DOWN AND STAY

It is on the down, which should be the simplest of exercises, that some people have had the worst problem in all training. Some trainers advocate pushing the dog down forcibly. Some do it with the leash, either pulling him from below or using the foot to force the leash and dog downwards. If you have a dog with hysteric tendencies, or one who has fought the leash and training before, any force at this point is guaranteed to send him straight into a six-ply panic. If you try to force him down, either by pushing with your hand or pulling with the lead, he has something to fight, and fight he will. He'll brace his front legs to a fare-thee-well and you're in for a struggle that you'll have to win, and it'll make you mad, and him mad, and the training program will be up the spout.

The way we teach the down without force and without resentment on his part has been used on literally hundreds of dogs, with never a serious problem. It shows him what you want him to do, and it reassures him while you're doing it.

With the dog sitting at heel, tell him to stay, and kneel beside him. Reach over his back with your left hand and take one leg in each hand, thumbs down, and holding on at just below the dog's elbow. Then, lift his front legs slightly off the ground and push them somewhat out in front of him. Hold him there a second to reassure him. Simultaneously, give him the command "Down!" and lower his front to the ground. At the same time, with your left elbow (or forearm or even wrist with the smaller dogs), tip his hindquarters off balance toward you so that he comes down with his haunches sideways under him rather than straight and braced to rise. There is nothing for him to fight, as the hind legs are slewed sideways under him, nipping in the bud any tendency to try to rise to the sit or stick his rear up in the air. And the front, with the legs in the air and out front of him, simply lowers to the ground. All the while you are as close to him as you can get, with your arm around him, praising and reassuring him that all is well.

Once he is down, stay there with him and move your left hand slowly from his leg up to his shoulders, leaving it there with slight pressure, repeating "Down, Stay" and "Good boy." Keep a slight pressure on his hindquarters with your elbow (or forearm or whatever) until he shows no sign of trying to scramble his rear feet back under him. Then slowly move the elbow away and maintain only the pressure with the hand.

When he seems steady in the down, slowly get up yourself from your crouch, keeping the light pressure on with your left hand. Here is where the break is likely to occur—seeing you get up he will try himself. If slightly increased pressure with the left hand on his shoulder doesn't keep him in place, combined with a firm, "No, down, stay," don't fight it. Let him get up and then repeat the entire process. This time make your move to a standing position more slowly and be extra sure that he is steady before moving. Lighten the left hand pressure until the hand is no more than resting on the shoulder, and then take it off entirely.

On the original down, you may run into the problem of the dog trying to walk backwards on his hind legs once you have got the front legs up in the air. You can curb this very easily by putting your left leg and foot or knee squarely behind him as you kneel to take hold of him at the sit. He may back a bit, but he will run into your leg and have no place to go. Once he's stopped, proceed with the down as if nothing had happened.

Throughout the exercise keep a good hold on the lead, close to the neck with your right hand, even as you pick up his right leg. If he shows any tendency to fight the action, you have a good short grip on him and can get in an immediate, firm correction. In this case, fighting you can only mean curling the lip or snarling. Once again, the occasional dog may have let things go this far on suffrance and decide that now is the time

THE FIRST STEP—TAKE
HOLD OF BOTH LEGS
JUST BELOW THE
"ELBOW."

LIFT BOTH LEGS
OUT IN FRONT.

EASE THE DOG TO
THE GROUND.

STRAIGHTEN UP
SLOWLY, STEADYING THE
DOG WITH YOUR
LEFT HAND.

THE LEFT KNEE BEHIND THE DOG PREVENTS HIM FROM BACKING WHILE YOU "LIFT" HIM DOWN.

for a mastery dispute. No method of downing in the world can make him change his mind if he is so decided. If he does, follow the firm correction procedures outlined above under heeling, and proceed with the lesson when the issue is decided.

When you are able to stand erect while he is at the down, you can teach him the release, which is the "sit." Let him stay down for a few moments, increasing the time as you go along, and then tell him to sit. Give him a firm snap upwards with the lead to get him to a sitting position, and if he tries to stand, push his rear down with the left hand in the approved manner. Continue with the down until he will go down on command without any lifting or other touching on your part. Remember to praise him at every point, and to keep praising him as he improves and begins to go down without help.

The down-stay will be even simpler, as he has had previous work with the other two stay positions. Repeat again the circle, the move to the front, and the moves to the side and back. Go slowly until he is steady, repeating the commands and praise until you can leave him in any direction for about 15 seconds without saying anything beyond the original "Stay!" when you step away.

The "down-stay" signal for a small dog—when working from the front, stay close at first to reassure him.

Once again, mix up the down and the down-stay with all else he has learned up to this point. Heel him, fast and slow and with turns, give him a down-stay, more heeling, a sit-stay, more heeling, another down-stay, and so forth. Again you will be teaching him to work strictly at command with no anticipation of a particular order of things. And in between the lessons in the new exercise he will be sharpening up his work in all the others.

When he is quite steady at the down-stay, increase his steadiness by stepping over him as he is at the stay. Give him the stay command, then take a high side-step to your left, over his back, and stand at his left. As you raise your foot and go over, keep reassuring him that all is well by repeating "Stay" and "Good boy." Move only very slowly at first, for a sudden move of a foot over his back will make him break. Then as you are standing at his left, take a side step in the same manner to your right and back to your original position. Be careful that you do not touch him with your feet as you go over, and do not jerk on the lead. This maneuver will teach him confidence in you, and will make him less likely to break because of distractions.

RECALL

The recall, or "come," is done at first from the heel, as are all other exercises in this chapter. While walking along with the dog at heel, suddenly back up three or four steps, calling to come, "Mike, Come!" and snapping back on the lead to get him to come around. He should swing around in surprise at this new development and come straight at you. When he is directly in front of you, facing you squarely, quickly command him to "Sit!" You may have to reinforce the "sit" with a sharp upward snap on the lead, but don't reach over and use your hand to whack his rump down. Let the lead do the work here. He already knows what the sit is all about, and the lead will be enough to get him used to the idea in the new situation.

If the turning causes him to slew his rear out of line, then you'll have to run backward a few more steps until he straightens himself out. Don't use your hand to straighten him out except as a last resort, and never use your feet. If you push him around with your foot to make him sit squarely in front of you, he'll get wary of feet, and what we want is for him to come in as straight and close as possible with complete confidence. Keep the lead shortened as he comes in so that you can get in a good correction on the sit, or if he tries to move on past you on either side. A move to either side calls for a sharp snap with the lead to bring him up short and get him sat. Don't try to haul him back to directly in front of you if he is way off course. Get him sitting, and keep a tighter control the next time.

When he has sat approximately in place in front of you, praise him verbally and tell him to stay. Wait a moment or two, and then walk around him to heel position, reinforcing the previous sit-stay training with continued "Stay, Stay" as you go around. Once he has come into the sit, the walking around is a simple repetition of what he has learned on the

AS YOU STEP BACK, WHILE HEELING, THE DOG COMES AROUND TO WALK IN AND SIT IN FRONT OF YOU IN FIRST RECALL.

sit-stay. There should be no problems at all at this point. If there are, return to the sit-stay corrections.

Don't attempt to get him to come in on the recall in any other way at this time. Your control over him won't be good enough yet to accomplish it without a lot of unnecessary tugging and hauling, all of which will put a strain on relations. And again, mix up the work.

Above all, when he does come at your command—never, *never* call him to you to punish or reprimand him. *Always* go to him to make a correction. This is a major reason that some dogs never come to their owners happily—they have been called and punished. Just imagine how often you would respond happily at the call of a friend if every time, or often, you got hit when you went. The dog feels the same way. *Always* make it a pleasure for him to come to you.

GO TO HEEL

At this point, toward the end of basic training, you can take up the "go to heel," or as we will refer to it, the "heel" as opposed to "heeling." In this, the dog learns to move from his position directly in front of you to a position at your left side—ready to walk at heel or to be left in a stay. He will also learn, almost by himself once he has mastered the basic idea, to move to heel from any position near you.

Having learned heeling, the idea has been dinned into him that the command, "Mike, Heel" means that he is to keep at your left side. It requires little further work to make him understand that when he is at rest away from your side he is to get there quickly at the command. There are, for show and for practical purposes, two ways he can get from in front of you to heel position—either by moving to your right and around to heel, or by moving to your left and swinging himself around into position. Which you use is entirely a matter of personal choice. Our own preference is split—we recommend the "left" heel for small dogs, and the "around" heel for the larger breeds. This is based on the fact that it is easier for a large dog to come around and walk directly into position, while a small one can switch his rear around into place quite handily. One other consideration, this a purely practical one, is that if you have your dog on leash, and an armful of packages, he will wrap the leash around you doing an "around" heel. This is a minor factor, even as are the "ease of movement" ones previously mentioned, and so the choice is simply whichever you happen to like. Neither is easier to teach.

First, the "around" heel. With the dog facing you in front, take hold of the leash quite close to the collar, and give him the command, "Mike, Heel." As you do this, take a short step backward with your right foot and pull him along to your right side. As he gets to your rear, move your foot back into position, reach around behind with your left hand for the lead, and guide him around into heel position at your left side. As he gets there, give him the "Sit" command, and praise him generously. The backward step as you're giving him the first pull is for two reasons—the motion of your foot helps him get the idea of going in

RIGHT FOOT IS BACK TO GUIDE DOG, LEASH URGES HIM AROUND TO HEEL POSITION IN "AROUND" HEEL.

that direction, and it gets your weight farther back so that you can snap him more effectively. You can drop the foot movement as soon as he gets the idea.

As he is coming around, guided by the leash, give him encouragement and repeated commands, and praise him. There is little likelihood that you will have trouble getting him to move. But if he for some reason just digs in and sits there, resisting the whole idea, start him off with a good sharp snap on the lead to get him on his feet. Don't try dragging him around all the way on his rear, as this can develop into a struggle. Snap him onto his feet, then keep him going with further snaps. From the very beginning, insist that he sit straight at your side when he gets there. Use your left hand (switch the lead to your right as he comes around) to nudge his rear in the right direction as he's lowering it for the sit. Don't wait until it's down and then try to move it. Correct the sit as he goes down.

When he is doing everything satisfactorily under lead urging, drop the "Sit" command as he gets into position. With your left hand on his rear and your right on the leash, make him sit, just as you did the sit in heeling, without a command. Then continue your work until he will perform the heel with nothing but the original "Mike, Heel" command.

To repeat the exercise, from the very beginning mix up the way you get him in front of you after each "heel." One time, when he has come to heel, tell him to stay and step around in front of him, then repeat the heel. Next time, walk forward with him at heel and do a recall from heel to get him into position. You are, at the same time, reinforcing his training on both the recall and the stay.

If he is slow in coming around, get him around faster by stronger snaps with the leash, and later by any urging that increases his speed. Slap your left leg with your hand, use his name and praise as he comes around. Soon he will practically leap around to get to heel.

The "left" heel is taught in much the same way. Here, as you give the command, "Mike, Heel," take a step backward with your left leg and pull (or snap) him towards your left and back. Get him back until his rear is just past the original position of your left leg, then guide him around in a half circle to his left and into position as you move your leg back into place. Your leg here is even more of a guide to him than in the "around" heel. If you happen to have a very large dog, you may have some difficulty following to the letter the instruction to pull him back to your left until his rear is even with you, but moderate the procedure to fit the situation.

As he gets into position, give him the "Sit" command just as in the "around," and drop the command when ready. Urge him to move faster by verbal persuasion and snaps on the lead, and correct his sit as he goes down.

WITH THE LEFT FOOT BACK, THE DOG IS GUIDED AROUND FROM "SIT IN FRONT" TO HEEL POSITION IN THE "LEFT" HEEL.

Whichever way you have him heel, be careful that he works only on your command once he has learned what to do. Quite often a dog will quickly catch on to the fact that from a sitting position in front of you, you are going to want him to go to heel soon, and will anticipate your command. Insist that he stay seated in front of you until you give him the command, and snap him back sharply with the leash if he tries to move. To keep his mind on his work, once he has learned the heel, mix it up by not having him heel, occasionally. When he is sitting in front, you go around him to heel once in a while. Then get him in front again, and do a heel. Also, vary the time you have him sit in front of you before you give him the "Heel" command. Wait as much as a minute, no matter how uneasy and anxious he gets. And whatever you do, don't try to fool yourself and him by slipping in a quick "Mikeheel" if he starts to come around before your command.

You will also encounter the problem of the "crooked sit" in front of you when he has learned the heel. Knowing that he will probably have to go to the right, if he goes that way to heel, he will come to a sit in front of you facing toward your right rather than sitting squarely in front. As we suggest in the later Novice chapter for off-lead work, this can be cured by taking a backward step and commanding him again to come when you see his rear going down crooked. Keep taking backward steps and re-commanding "Mike, Come" and guiding him with the lead, until he sits squarely in front of you.

When you have taught him the heel, by either method, add the variation of coming to heel from in back of you. Leave him at the sit-stay and walk straight forward until you come to the end of the leash. Then, commanding him to heel, snap him forward into position with the leash. Later in training, you can if you wish have him move to heel from any position close to you. This can be valuable training for corrections if he later loses his accuracy in sitting. But do not have him do this from any distance, now or later, or he may be confused in the straight recall, and never be exactly sure, even with distinct commands, whether he is supposed to run in and sit directly in front of you, or run from a distance directly to heel. You could, with patience, teach him to distinguish, but there is no practical value in it.

GENERAL BASIC TRAINING

As you begin basic training with him following this chapter, be sure to teach each exercise exactly in the order laid out here. We have given them to you in that order for very good reasons—primary among which is that he learns something in each that he can apply to the next lesson. He learns the sit at heel before he needs to use it as a release from the down; he learns the sit-stay and walkaround before it comes up in the recall, and so on. Keep to the order.

During and between the exercises you and he have learned, there are some general considerations to be kept in mind. An important one concerns the words of command you use and how you use them. The simple and directly descriptive words used in this chapter and the ones to follow are the words in general use—heel, sit, stand, down, stay, come. Surprising though it may seem, those six words are all he has had to learn in all this basic work. They are good commands, none of which can be confused with the other by the dog. You can go to a hundred obedience shows without hearing any deviation from them, but if you want to be individualistic about it there's nothing to stop you. Tell him "Sassafras" instead of "Sit" if you feel like it, or anything else that comes to mind. But once you've started out, stick to the word.

And when you've established the command words, don't embellish them howsoever. In his early training, it's going to be hard enough for him to connect your mouth sounds to actions without you garbling up the words with a lot of associated verbiage. If you have a problem on the sit, for example, don't chatter at him, "Hey, you, siddown, blast it, sit, sir!" It means nothing to him. Or if you insist on being conversational during training, at least have the decency to supply him with a handy reference dictionary so he can translate all that into "sit."

The words you use in praise can be many and varied, of course. There it's the tone that counts for the most part, although he'll probably learn the meaning of "good boy" and a few other associated words. Thinking or not, dogs are intelligent creatures, and he already may know more words than you suspect, just from sitting around the house with his big ears open.

The extent to which a dog *can* learn his required words is sometimes astonishing. Not long ago, one of the authors traveled to Staten Island to look at a year-old Doberman he was considering buying. The dog was shown off, and demonstrated that he had had a thorough course in obedience. Later, while coffee was on and general conversation ensued, the dog wandered around sniffing at things. At one point, the lady of the house said to her husband, "Put the cake down on the table there," and midway in the sentence there was resounding crash as King went to the floor. Out of that sentence, uttered in a perfectly normal tone of voice, he had picked out the word "down" and responded like a shot.

When you're giving your commands, sing them out loud and clear. Don't mumble. And don't shout. As far as the use of his name with commands goes, there's a good simple rule to follow: when you want him to move somehow, use his name in conjunction *always*. When you want him not to move, don't use his name. His name calls his attention sharply and prepares him to do something.

Praise can be given both by hand and verbally. Generally, when he's at your side you can reach down and give him a few good thumps on the left side while you're going along. Otherwise, use your voice as warmly and sincerely as you can. With the hands, use only the left hand for praise as far as possible, keeping the right for signals and correction. It'll help him keep straight later on as you get into the use of hand signals.

The leash is the wonder-weapon of training—without it you would stand slight chance of training anything. But keep in mind that it is a training tool and not a magic device. Just because he has it on he won't obey. You've got to use it, and correctly.

Keep your training periods short. About fifteen minutes twice a day is right. Don't keep at it until he is bored with things. And don't bother him throughout the day with a snippet of work here and there. In a later chapter we'll issue a warning about badgering him around the house with commands to no good purpose, but for the present he's off leash in the house, and you shouldn't say so much as "boo" to him unless he's on lead at this point. Not letting him make a mistake is just as vital a part of training as is showing him the right thing to do. Wait for the practical applications until considerable control off leash is effected.

CHAPTER IV

NOVICE

WHEN YOU BEGIN to work with the dog off lead, in this chapter, you will experience for the first time true control of the dog. Above and beyond the specific arts of heeling and sitting and staying, and all the others the dog will learn in later training, you are working now for control. This is the ultimate goal—to reach the point where your dog will unhesitatingly obey your commands under any circumstances and at whatever distance.

All obedience work is aimed at control, and some of the later exercises we will cover in advanced work are taken up as much for the development of it as for any practical application. Control, too, is the reason behind our continued stressing of precision in all your work. The idea is that your dog must do *exactly* what you tell him to, and not just a near approximation. The situation is quite similar to that of training troops. The constant drilling, with manual of arms and marching in columns and right face and about face, are for the purposes of an army directed primarily at establishing control of the men and instilling instant, unhesitating obedience to the commands that make an army work. Drilling is an exercise in conditioning the mind to work in a certain way—obedience exercises for the dog are much the same sort of conditioning. And where army drilling work is useful in moving bodies of men in an orderly fashion, so the basic dog obedience exercises have their own extremely practical applications.

As one cannot reasonably expect a dog to comprehend, "When I say this, you do thus," desired actions and responses to commands must be drilled in until they become almost reflexes. The dog at first learns his lessons by the application of a primary stimulus, forcing him to sit, for

99

example, and at the same time a secondary stimulus, the command, is given to him. Soon, the secondary means exactly the same to him as the primary did. The best known example of this primary-secondary transfer is the famous experiment of Pavlov on the salivation of dogs. The Pavlov experiment, briefly, involved giving food to dogs in his laboratory, and at the same time ringing a bell. He continued this, day after day, until the ringing of the bell was firmly associated in the dogs' minds with food. Then he rang the bell without offering food. The dogs immediately began to water at the mouth, proving Pavlov's thesis that even unconscious bodily reactions can be "trained" to react to a secondary stimulus. In this case the food was the primary, the ringing of the bell the secondary. It isn't recorded just how disappointed Pavlov's dogs were when the food didn't show up when the bell rang, but probably even in old age they watered at the mouth when a fire-engine went by.

The process of training a dog is a repetition of much the same pattern of primary-secondary substitution. You have been doing it in basic training. The primary stimulus in teaching the "sit" is the combined pressures of one hand on the rear and the other on the leash. Soon the secondary "Sit" becomes in his mind associated with the action. Finally, the secondary stimulus alone will produce the desired action. We want to emphasize this because a full understanding can eliminate one of the major possible difficulties in training—that of a wrong attitude toward your dog. Let us suppose that on one of his experimental runs, one of Pavlov's dogs had failed to salivate at the bell. Pavlov would have looked more than somewhat silly, and would have accomplished nothing, if he had sworn at the dog, "Double-blast you, why didn't you salivate?" You will accomplish just about as much if you blame your in-training dog for not responding properly to your commands. And you will confuse and frighten him to boot. What you must do, when your "experiment" doesn't produce the desired results is to examine your procedure and find where the fault lies in you and your methods—not in the dog.

As you get further along in training you will have to use the primary stimuli less and less as your dog gets into the habit of making the necessary associations. There are, of course, slow dogs who take as much time to learn an advanced exercise as to learn the basic "sit," but in most cases you will find that something really advanced, like directed jumping—

which you probably can't imagine your dog ever learning, will come to him in the regular course of things if the proper obedience foundation has been laid.

Through all of the basic training of you and your dog, you have been establishing the transfer to the secondary stimulus (the command) with leash in hand, ever ready to reapply the primary stimuli when needed. Now, in Novice work, you will be working without the leash, and you must be sure before you start that the lessons of basic training are so firmly in your dog's mind that a command is all that is needed for good performance.

Here, attitude is doubly important. Once off lead, the dog is under no control but that of your voice and command. If he is ready, you must have faith in him, and show him your faith. You must be ready to think like him, to examine the mistakes he makes in the light of what you know about the way his mind works. You must be generous with praise for a job well done, and you must know positively what went wrong before you apply a correction. As the exercises grow more complex, with several different required actions blending into one performance, you must be very careful not to correct at the wrong time for a part of the performance ill-performed, lest he get the feeling that he is being corrected for another part that he did right. Remember that by now a "No!" is to him a strong correction, and be careful how you use it. Be ready to forgive mistakes repeatedly, even as you correct them. And practice patience, patience, patience.

PREPARATION FOR OFF-LEAD

The first step is perfection in the dog's work on lead. He must be able to go through all the exercises, heeling, the down, stand and sit with stays, the recall from heeling, and the heel—without your making any lead corrections. To test this, go through the work with the lead on the dog, but out of your hands. Loop the lead through your belt, or stuff it in a pocket, or hang the free end over your shoulder—always allowing enough slack for the dog to make the turns. Start out at heel and go through all his heeling work. Give him all the praise and encouragement and extra commands necessary as you walk along. Slap your left leg to encourage him to keep in place, but keep your hands completely off the leash.

If the heeling goes well, try the stand, sit and down with stays, leaving the lead again attached to his collar but lying on the ground. Go through the complete routines in all three positions, to the front, the back and the sides.

If he has worked well in everything, with no need for corrections other than verbal, you are ready to take the leash off for advanced novice work, most of which is simply an extension of basic training. However—be very sure of yourself and the dog before you try it. Going off lead too soon has been the source of endless frustration for countless dog owners and train-ers—the temptation is strong to get away from the lead too soon, and then the mistakes begin to pile up. The dog wanders off course, he gets cor-rected both improperly and unjustifiedly, he becomes confused and resentful, the owner loses his temper, and sweetness and light go out of the window with the training program.

Be sure you can go through the *entire routine* without using the lead for *any* corrections—if not, keep the lead on for another week and then try again. During the repeat week, concentrate on the mistakes your dog made that kept you both from going off-lead. If all goes well, take off the leash and go right through all the exercises again. You'll probably be stunned by the fact that he does do it—everything right down the line. Keep the leash in your hand, just to let him know it is there if needed, and for your own peace of mind. In all likelihood you won't have to use it. In fact, many city dogs do their heeling better off lead than on, sur-prising though that may seem. To them, being put on lead has come to mean freedom through being taken to the street on lead. Sometimes it pops up right away, and sometimes the dog doesn't make the distinction until later in training. If you're interested only in obedience around the home, it won't bother you at all.

If minor problems develop in the first heeling off lead, put him back on for a few minutes and apply strong corrections where the faults have shown up. Then try again without the lead. One short application may solve the problem. If it doesn't, repeat the "week on" treatment. It takes patience and determination not to try to muddle through somehow once you've gotten the lead off, but the week or two invested in sureness will pay off many times over in lack of troubles later. Unfortunately, there's just no other way out of it. If you try dragging your dog around by the collar or the scruff of the neck, or have to resort to slapping his rear down on the heeling sits, or anything else, you're beginning a losing battle with trivia. Get it right, on lead.

HEELING OFF LEAD

Once he has heeled successfully off lead there is little more to do but practice with him. Mix up your work together as much as possible, fast and slow, left and right turns, circles to the right and left, about turns. Try stopping from a fast and from a slow. Do your figure eights around trees, people, rocks and holes in the ground, around two cars parked in a lot. Get him used to heeling steadily under all circumstances. Don't be afraid to go back on lead momentarily to solve a specific problem. If, for example, he is nervous about cars, or ecstatic about them, put him back on lead while doing your figure eights around cars. When he is steady, take it off again.

Use verbal commands and encouragement as much as you need to, pat your leg to urge him into place, and be generous with your praise. As you're doing corners and circles, keep telling him to heel if he has any hesitation. As you go along, you'll be able to cut down the repeated commands gradually until you need to say "Heel!" only when you start up. Remember in your heeling, too, always to start off on the left foot. It's a big help to the dog, and if you are consistent about starting with the left, and leaving him on the right, he'll be surer of what to do, and you'll incidentally be laying the groundwork for later work with signals.

THE STAYS OFF LEAD

From the stay on lead to off lead is a simple step—you have only to go further away from your dog, which you are now able to do as you no longer need hold onto the leash. As with all training, work up to it gradually. Leave the leash hooked onto his collar a few times. Beginning with the sit, work your way slowly from the leash's length in front of him.

Take it by easy stages and you'll be surprised to find that within one training session you will be able to stand 30 feet or more away from him without a break. Work up to the same distance away to the sides and to the back, and then progress to the down and the stand. As you go farther away in each position, keep repeating "Stay" and "Good Boy" to reassure him until he seems steady, then drop all but the original "Stay!" command as you leave.

Problems here can only be solved by going back to the beginning and working on lead until steadiness is acquired. Among the problems you may encounter is the dog who tries to come to you as you are walking away, or who waits a few moments and then begins a creep towards you. Go back to the beginning, on leash, stepping only out to the end of the leash. Then, with the leash still on, start upping your distance more gradually this time, coming back sooner from the more distant positions and repeating a firm "Stay!" to keep him where he is. In the sit or down, don't expect him at this point to stay for more than five minutes. Hold your requirements for the stand-stay to about two minutes, as standing motionless is very tiring for the dog—he will slowly learn to be able to hold the pose longer, but don't put too much of a strain on him too soon.

Another problem is the dog who tries to change his position when you have left him—sitting from the down or stand, lying down from the sit or stand. Work this one out exactly the same way as with the dog who tries to come to you.

THE PLAYFUL DOG

When the dog is off-lead at some distance from you, he may leave his position and run around playfully. Usually it is because he is still very much a puppy at heart even at this stage; or it may be that, at whatever age, he finds himself for the first time completely unrestrained and it seems like a long-awaited chance for a good run. This is one of the reasons you must be especially sure that all his preliminary training has sunk well in before you attempt to work off lead. But it happens even in the best of families, and you may have to face the problem. The first precaution, of course, is to do your beginning off-lead work in a place where a serious runaway can't get hurt. A fenced-in yard or section of a park is best, or a field in the country is good. True, it is difficult for the city-dweller to find such places for training, but for the safety of the dog never try your first off-lead work in some place, such as a parking lot, where an unthinking run could take the unsophisticated dog onto a street where serious injury might result.

Wherever you are training, the cardinal and vital first rule of coping with the playful runaway is: *don't chase him!* To run after him is the worst possible mistake you can make, for no matter how much you may shout orders or entreaties at him, he will take your running to him as a gilt-edged invitation to run further and make a great game of tag of it. If you are in an area where he can't come to any harm by running about, stay where you are and try to get him either to come back to you or stop where he is and wait for you to approach cautiously. Using his name with praise and entreaties may get him to come, albeit erratically, to you —provided you stay where you are. Crouch down as if you were ready to play, and he is more likely to come running in. Try also giving him a command to "sit" or "down" just to see if it works. It just might, because by the time the situation occurs his responses to those commands should be almost automatic.

If he does sit or go down at a distance, walk, do not run, to him. Keep his attention by repeating "Stay" and "Good boy" to him as you approach, and don't make any sudden moves with the lead you want so desperately to get snapped onto his collar. He can make a very successful break for it when you have your hands almost on him, so keep it casual until you actually have the leash snapped on. However you get together again, don't under any circumstances attempt to punish or correct him for having run away. He won't connect it with the running away at all; but rather with having returned to you or having obeyed your command to sit and stay. Let this happen once or twice and you'll have a serious problem on your hands, for he won't listen to a thing you say, but will start running hell-for-leather once he gets a good start off lead.

Even if the circumstances are such that he is heading for danger in his run or is making for the tall timber, again don't chase after him. Try to get his attention by shouts and whistles, and then run away from him. Paradoxical though it may seem, that is the best way to get him back. Back-pedal in the opposite direction from the way he is going. If he's running away in play, he'll turn and chase you instead of you chasing him. When he gets close, though, don't make any sudden grabs as he'll only sheer off and keep going. He may keep going anyway, and if he does, just reverse and keep running away from him until he either gets tired of it all and comes to you peacefully or plops down. If possible, with his attention on you, run behind some trees or a building—it'll shake him up a bit that *you* are trying to get away from *him* and he'll come belting over to look for you. And again, once he has come to you, praise him and let him know all is well once you get him on lead. Don't sulk or yank him about to get even for the near heart-failure he gave you, or the next time he won't come back so quickly. Let him know by your attitude that he did a wonderful thing in getting back to you.

Go back again and start the stays on lead, and this time when you would have left him off-lead completely, tie to his collar a long length of light clothesline. String it out along the ground before you tie it on, and then when you leave him at a stay, don't keep the line in your hands but walk along it, keeping one foot on the line at all times. If he stays, all well and good. If not, you've got a foot on the line and can bring him up short if he makes another dash for it. Even if he's big enough to yank you off your feet if he goes suddenly, you'll find that a running dog trailing 30 feet of line is a good deal easier to get hold of than one without. Leave a little slack at his end of the line, so that if he decides to get playful you can let him take a bound or two before he is brought up short. Just as you see the line about to jerk him, give him a strong "No!" Try to time it so the "no" reaches him just as the line pulls him off his feet. It'll get across to him that you are in control no matter how far away he happens to be, and as he saw you leave empty-handed he'll wonder how it all happened.

STAND FOR EXAMINATION

In competition obedience, the idea behind this exercise is that the dog must, on your command, stand still and allow himself to be touched and examined by the judge without showing shyness, fear, resentment or hostility. It has practical applications in breed showing, and for the owner not interested in any sort of AKC work. If your dog is thoroughly trained to allow himself to be handled and looked over by strangers when you tell him to stand and stay, you are a long way towards having solved any problems of over-aggressiveness or shyness in the dog. And this training will not lessen any dog's effectiveness as a watch dog. In fact, the dog who will not allow examination when commanded is such a liability that he should never be considered as a pet or watchdog by anyone but a recluse or hermit with gold under the floorboards. Such a dog, if his reactions are aggressive, is an extreme danger to your friends and neighbors, and a danger to you through the lawsuits that will result if anyone is bitten or seriously frightened. Ritualistic and formal though the obedience-ring specifications for the "stand for examination" may seem to you, we urge strongly that you train your dog up to these specifications in any case.

Proceed with the stand-stay training exactly as you have with the sit-stay and the down-stay until he is steady at the stand while you remain 30 feet or more away for a minute. Then, return to the on-lead status for the examination part. Leave him and step to the front, to the end of the lead. Then go up to him, repeating "Stay" to keep his mind on what he's supposed to be doing. Hold out your right hand for him to sniff, then touch him lightly on the head, on the shoulders and on the hind-quarters. Back off then and return to your position about six feet in front. Stand there a few seconds and return around him to heel position. If there are any problems, start over the stand-stay and work him up to the point of examination more slowly. Minor problems, such as moving a leg or sidling out of position you can correct during the "examination," repeating "Stay" and insisting that he remain immobile.

If he is steady during your cursory examination, proceed gradually to examine him more thoroughly, spreading his lips to look at his teeth, running your hand down his foreleg, running your hand along his back, and giving the hindquarters a gentle bounce or two to test the steadiness of his stand, repeating "Stay!" to him if he wants to move. Keep it up until you can give him a thorough going over without his moving—and each time, be sure to return to your position in front, wait, and then go around to the heel. Release him from the stand each time by the heel-and-sit method. Or, alternatively, you can now introduce the sit directly from the stand. But as you introduce this, be very careful that he doesn't get to anticipate your command and begin to sit as soon as you come around to heel. Make him work at command only, and don't slip in a quick "Sit!" if you see him start to go down. You're not fooling him a bit.

When you are able to give him the complete examination, call in the help of a member of the family, or of a friend who knows the dog well. Leave the dog at the stand-stay and walk to the end of the lead just as before, and ask your "judge" to examine the dog. Be sure that he or she knows full well how to go about it, especially the first move of allowing the dog to take a brief sniff of the right hand before any touching is done. A dog generally figures that anyone who comes up to him with a hand extended, *palm downward,* to allow him a smell doesn't mean any harm. It's an important point.

As the "judge" makes the first light examination of the dog, keep a specially close watch for any moves, repeating "Stay" and "Good boy" to reassure him that all is well and that what you want him to do is stay. The examiner should approach from the right as you have been doing (your right, the dog's left) and when he has finished the examination,

A PRACTICE EXAMINATION, "JUDGE" APPROACHES AT DOG'S LEFT, GOES OVER HIM GENTLY. NOTE LOOSE LEAD.

step back without going around the dog. Keep this up until your dog will submit to a thorough examination. You can then vary the procedure with the "judge" approaching from any side (but not from the back), and circling around the dog in his examination.

When that stage is past, somehow secure the services of a complete stranger (to the dog) to do the examining. Repeat exactly as before, working up from a very light few touches on the dog's head and back, to a thorough going over. For the first approaches of the stranger, stand close in front of the dog with the leash held close, and watch for any signs of fear, resentment, or aggression. Cure these by constant corrections with the lead, and reassurances. In the case of any really shy dog, be very generous with praise and reassurance, and make sure that the examiner approaches slowly and gives the dog plenty of time to take the preliminary sniff, and that no sudden moves are made. Next, if possible, get another stranger to come up and give a thorough examination without any preparation. And somewhere along the line, be sure to have both a woman and a man do the examining. Some dogs, for reasons of their own, will submit to a man examining them, but will shy at a woman, or vice-versa. Try it also with children. The idea is to get him to stand for an examination by anyone, when you tell him to.

With both friends and strangers examining the dog, finish the exercise after every examination by returning to the heel position. At this point, don't attempt to go off-lead or stand far away from the dog during the examination.

RECALL

One of the most useful, if not the most basic, things the dog has to know is coming quickly when called. Despite its importance, we have put the teaching of the complete off-lead recall this far back in the training schedule because of the several other things that have had to be learned before a successful recall can be taught. We don't mean, of course, that you shouldn't have your dog come to you, or call him, before you reach this point. It would be impossible to keep a dog around the house this long unless he responded to your summons in some measure. But the formal, obligatory recall should wait until now. Foremost among the things he must learn is control—and specifically the dog must first have learned thoroughly to stay when told, and to execute a preliminary sort of recall from heeling. The recall from heeling as an introductory step is an especially important one, as it eliminates the necessity of having to jerk the dog up from a sitting position to get him into motion. While heeling he is already in motion and has only to learn that "Come!" means to move directly to you and sit in front. Now he can learn that the familiar command means to get up from wherever he is and start moving.

First, work with him until he can do the recall from heeling well off lead. Then, when he is ready, put him in a sitting position, on lead, and tell him to stay. Walk out in front of him to the lead's length and, facing him, command, "Mike, Come!" Give a gentle snap on the lead to help him understand what you mean, and guide him in until he sits in front of you. Be very patient with this first lesson, as he has learned that when you say "Stay" it means to stay there until you come back, so he may be confused at first. As you urge him in to you, keep repeating the "Come" with his name, encouraging him with "Good boy" and praise to suit. When he will do this on lead but without corrections, take him off-lead and repeat until he will come the six feet to you in good order.

To work out the confusion in his mind over staying and coming, alternate recalls and full stays until you are sure he is working entirely on command. If he tries to get up and follow you as you leave him for a recall, go back on lead for a few repeats of simple stays until he is steady and then begin the recall work over again. When you have moved out to the front, don't ever call him immediately. Wait a few seconds, then more, until you stand for a minute or two before calling him in. If as you're waiting he gets up and starts to come to you, give him a sharp correction and a "No, Stay!," then go back to heel after a few moments. Don't ever call him to you after he has made a false start. If he gets up and runs away, use the methods outlined earlier to get him back under control.

Each time he comes in to you, finish the exercise by commanding him to heel, and then praise him. Don't give him any physical praise as he sits in front of you—it is too much of a temptation to him to jump around and play. A quiet "Good boy" is not out of order at this point, but generally save the praise, once he has the exercise fairly well in hand, for when he has gone to heel.

When he will do the six-foot off-lead recall well, you can advance to distance work. Get a 30-foot length of light clothesline with a snap on the end, and put it on his training collar. Again, leave him at the sit-stay and walk away to the front. Go about ten feet this time, leaving the line loose but ready for a correction, and call him to you. If he hesitates, give him a snap with the line, and use it to guide him in straight. Be watchful that he doesn't try to short-circuit the whole thing by coming in and going directly to heel. He's intelligent, and it seems logical enough to him to try to go directly to heel without all the bother of stopping in front to stare at you. So watch for it—it happens with almost every dog sometime in the course of training, and requires only insistence on your part that he sit in front. Check him sharply with the line if he tries it, and make him sit properly.

The major problem you may run into here is that of the dragging recall. The dog gets up, yes, and comes to you, but with no will at all, drooping along as if the temperature were 107° in the shade. Almost without exception this results from faulty training—you have punished the dog when he came to you, or committed some other cardinal sin of training that makes him reluctant to come when you call. The one-two solution for this is to examine your training history to find out just what it is that makes him reluctant, and then cure the habit by making him come in faster. Don't yank on the lead to speed him up—it'll only make him like the idea less and less. Do run a few backward steps away from him, patting your legs and calling to him as you go. The same psychology that gets him to come to you if he's a runaway will speed him up when he's lagging. Make something of a game of it . . . run away from him, always going backwards. Run a few steps, but let him have plenty of line—don't yank as you run. Keep repeating the backward run until he speeds up to a run, or a respectable trot, himself. Then slow down gradually so that you come to a stop just as he is a pace or two from you. Don't stop suddenly just as he breaks into a lope or run, as that would tend to make him stop too. Still, insist that he come to a smart stop and sit in front of you, giving him a slight snap on the lead and a "Sit!" command if needed.

Use this same technique if he begins to sit crooked in front of you. Many dogs, having learned what's going on, will come in well but sit facing whichever direction they are going to go when they heel. And again it's just a labor-saving device he's invented which seems only too sensible to him. If, as he comes in, you see him about to sit crooked in anticipation of the heel, take a step or two backwards with another "come" command, and this time, when you stop, have the lead ready to snap his front into the proper position, sitting squarely.

Taking him off lead when he has reached the point of coming in smartly at a 30-foot distance is a process of tricking him past the stage of conversion from lead-control to voice-control. It is at this point in training that many dogs, if taken suddenly off lead, will decide to make a run for it, or will simply sit there and do nothing. If he's really off lead, there's nothing you can do about it but come back cursing under your breath for some repeat training. But you can fool him for the time it takes to establish the necessary control. First, have him come a few times with the long line lying on the ground between you and him, still attached to the collar, and you holding your end, but letting it drag as he comes in. Then, stretch it out over the 30 feet and take him to the snap end, putting the snap on his collar, and walk down the line until you come to your end, where you stand on it. If he comes at your call, fine. If not, you have the lead there to make your corrections. Then—and here is the deception—with the line stretched out on the ground, take him to the snap end and go through all the motions of snapping it on without actually doing so. Don't drop the snap to the ground with a great thunk or you'll destroy the illusion; rather leave a few spare feet of line at his end so you can set it down gently behind him. Then walk again to the end of the line exactly as before and call him. And there you have his first free recall from a distance.

Work on this a few times—after the first few times you won't have to bother with the pantomime snapping-on of the lead—and then, when you come to the end of the line step to the right or left a few paces. Call him in. He won't follow the line like a railroad track, but will come directly to you. Finally, you will be able to dispose of the deception entirely, and he will come in to you over any distance. Use the backing-away trick on the longer recalls to speed him up if necessary.

When he will do a long recall proficiently, you can start working him with distractions. Call him to come away from members of the family, or from friends, from food, or away from other dogs. Always put him back on lead for the first few lessons with each new distraction, and keep him on lead until you are satisfied that he will come immediately. Get him to come to you from any position—sit, stand or down. And teach him to come immediately even if he is running around at play—simply by using the long line on him when he is playing, and giving a sharp snap on it to get him coming in if he ignores the command.

You may feel, if your dog comes quite happily to you most of the time around the house and out in the open, that you really don't need this sort of training in the recall. But training must establish a response when you want it, not when he is in a good mood and feels like responding. It may save his life, and it will definitely save you frustration.

DISTANT CONTROL

Teaching the dog to sit or lie down while at a distance from you is, like the recall, an extension of the work you have been doing on leash. Up to now, you will have been sitting or downing him only at your side, on leash. As with the other exercises, the idea of the training is to get obedience to the command so firmly entrenched in his mind that it will make no difference where he is—"Down!" means just that, and the same with "Sit!" When your dog has shown that he will respond instantly to the commands, both on leash and off, at your side, move around directly in front of him (but not at the full length of the lead). Give him the command and be ready to correct with the leash. Progress to off-leash at a distance with both commands, slowly as always. You won't be able to give him any corrections from a distance, with or without a lead, so be sure he works very well close up and on lead before you move out. Work out any problems by moving right back to him and giving him a refresher course on lead. One principle to keep always before you in this work is that, once he has learned the exercise and has shown that he can and will do it without fear or resentment, he must always do it on the *first command*. Nothing is so detrimental to discipline and control as letting him get away with just sitting there while you rant at him. At whatever stage, when you tell him "Sit!" he must sit, without any further word from you. Don't make the mistake of waiting a moment to see if he'll do it, or urging him again and again. If he doesn't sit, get in a correction immediately, get back to a position where you can apply a correction simultaneous with the command, and work until he will respond at once. This sort of obedience and control on leash must be established before you can hope for control off leash. We repeat this to the point of boredom because it is so vitally important to successful training. In life around the house it is a mighty irritant to have to shout at your dog again and again to "Sit!" or "Down!" or "Come" or whatever—and in a show it is of course fatal if the dog has learned that he can daydream until your voice is raised in a second command. We have seen it happen time and again at shows; a dog will work quite well until he comes to an exercise of two or more parts. He will perform one part and, coming to the second, will wait and look at his handler expectantly. You can almost see him thinking, "Well, come on, give me the order." Don't let it happen to you.

TRAINING CLASSES

If you plan to enter your dog in the Novice classes at an AKC show, a training class can be a help. You will be able to teach your dog perfectly well without a class, to do all the exercises when the two of you are alone in your training area. What the training class supplies, aside from instruction, is the presence of other dogs and people, and the general noises and distractions that you will run into at a show.

In a show, your dog will have to perform the long sit and long down in line with up to 15 dogs, and the separation may be as little as three feet on each side. Besides which, you will no longer be standing alone 30 feet in front of him, but in a line of handlers with the judge and stewards walking about between you and the dog. However well he may have been trained alone, the possibility is very good that he will become unhappy and confused by all this nonsense, and will try to get back to you. He may, in fact, decide that now is the time for sex or warfare, depending on who happens to be sitting on either side of him, and you will not only fail the exercise but incur the undying enmity of the other handlers. There are few things so little calculated to begin a warm friendship as your dog sniffing or snapping another handler's dog into a move and failure.

If you have become fairly adept at training, and have your dog's confidence completely, you can of course train him well enough in the stay that he will not mind whatever new circumstances he finds himself in. In such a case there is no real need to go to a class, unless you want to see how other people are getting along with their dogs, and to get some of the feel of a show before actually going into one. If you are fortunate enough to have a few trained dogs in your neighborhood with accomodating owners, you can simulate the "other dog" atmosphere of the show stays without bothering with a class. Don't attempt it with untrained dogs, though—chaos is sure to result. One badly fouled-up stay with other dogs leaping at him or romping about can set your dog's progress back a long way.

Because in a show you may find your dog sitting next to almost any breed, it's a good idea to go to a training class that takes all breeds. The "specialty" classes, all of one breed, are in many cases excellent for general obedience work, but they suffer from an artificial situation in the group stays. This lesson was bitterly learned by one of the writers years ago at the beginning of his training experience. Having trained a Cocker Spaniel in an all-Cocker class, the first show was easily conquered by taking first place, and all was well in the stays. At the next show, however, the Cocker found himself sitting between a Great Dane and a St. Bernard. One look on either side convinced him that this was no place for a sensible Cocker Spaniel to be, and he lit out for hearth and home. His previous work in that show was such that he would have taken first place again, and the disappointment was considerable. So if you do find a specialty class most convenient to you, take the dog to a session or two of an all-breed class before entering a show, just to prevent unhappiness. Your dog *must* sit in the line according to the catalog listing—no judge will allow any exception, whatever the circumstances.

Training classes also offer benefits for the strictly home trainer. Unusual behavior problems can many times be worked out with ease by an experienced instructor, saving you hours of fruitless work and sweat. Again, the "other dogs and people" factor can be a valuable one, for a few sessions at least. Getting your dog to be obedient under all circumstances is the ultimate goal, and the presence of other dogs particularly is a circumstance that can best be met in a training class.

In most areas, there will be only one class (if any) within a reasonable distance, so the choice is not great. But if you have a choice, try to select the best class by inquiring among friends who have trained dogs. There are, as with anything else, good classes and bad, excellent training directors and almost criminally ignorant instructors. There are few tests of a good class we can offer you other than the feeling of the class you will get after looking on at a session. Avoid, if possible, the class in which the instructor insists on absolute quiet among handlers and spectators—noise and distractions may seem to shake the dog a bit at first, but he is not going to have respectful silence around all his life, so why try to train him under those circumstances? Various instructors do use different teaching methods, so don't cavil at departures from the methods outlined, but avoid instructors who radically violate some of the cardinal principles of successful training—using food as a reward, striking the dog with leash or newspapers, throwing leashes or chains to startle the dog into performing, using pinch or spike collars. Do look for an instructor who gives attention to your individual problems rather than running the class like a drill team.

The Gaines Dog Research Center, 250 Park Avenue, New York, N. Y., has compiled a list of training classes in various sections of the country, which they will send you on request. If they don't cover your area, try phoning or writing the secretary of the breed or obedience club in your area if there is one (see Pure Bred Dogs for list). The AKC will also try to be helpful to anyone interested in obedience.

SOME PRACTICAL APPLICATIONS

With or without show intentions, the dog who has received a thorough course in Basic and Novice training can be relied on to a great extent to conduct himself as a gentleman and a scholar. And even if the baser instincts at times seem to be getting the upper hand, his obedience training can be the tool whereby you give him further lessons in acceptable conduct.

One of the problems which almost always comes up with male dogs, that of mounting, can be easily controlled in the obedience trained dog. When he shows the first signs of trying to mount your leg, or try to molest guests, order him "Down!" and keep him there for a few moments. Repeat as necessary, and he will soon learn to control his impulses. Don't give him the order as a punishment, but issue the command simply as a command. Tell him calmly to lie down, and he'll go along with you. Use the same technique if he perchance has not learned yet not to jump up on you with muddy feet.

Yard boundaries in town and country can be taught by using the recall. Let him run until he comes to the limits of your yard, then call him, "Mike, Come!" Welcome him back with all due and appropriate praise and then let him run again. When he comes to the boundary call him again. Repeat this until he learns that he is not to go beyond a certain line without your express permission. If the recall lessons have been well ingrained, he will learn surprisingly fast.

The sit, stand or down stays can be used to control his aggressions when people come to the door. Instead of sending him to his bed, let him come with you when you answer the door. Sit or down him a few feet from the door with the order to "Stay!" If the caller is not a friend, let the dog stay there and watch what's going on. If it is a friend, keep the dog in position until coats are off and greetings made, or let him go at once to make greetings, if you like. The same treatment applies to the over-effusive dog—keep him at the down-stay if he tends to get too familiar with guests, or of course send him to bed if he persists.

One word of caution: don't ever use the recall as a practical way to get your dog to you for a correction. If he has done something quite beyond the pale, *always go to him* to correct him. Make it a rule absolutely without exception that whenever he comes to you, either on command or of his own volition, to welcome him with genuine friendliness and save the reprimand for next time, or until a few moments later when you can take him to the scene of the crime. It may be a bit difficult —you may have to say "Good Boy" through gritted teeth, but do it. Put yourself in his place and imagine how happily or readily you would come to someone if there were a very good chance you would get sworn at and slugged when you got there.

FURTHER TRAINING

Where do we go from here in training? If you are out for obedience degrees you will of course want to go on, but what is there in it for you and your dog if the ring doesn't interest you? A great deal, we believe. Through further training, even more control and cooperation are established, and the dog can learn a great many more practical skills.

In Open work, for example, he will learn to retrieve things, not just in play, but to retrieve what you tell him, when you tell him. He will learn to jump on command, over the equivalents of walls and ditches. He will learn the "drop on recall," an exercise that has saved the life of many a dog. And he will learn to sit and down at the stay for an even longer time, in this case with you out of sight. All these things are highly useful items to add to your dog's repertoire.

In Utility work, the post-graduate course in obedience, he will learn to work with you exclusively by signals, to find an article of yours that you have lost while walking, to pick out something of yours from among other articles by using his nose, to stand quietly while being examined by a judge—with you some distance away, and to elaborate his "jump on command" abilities.

Open and Utility work require a fairly sure understanding between you and your dog, complete mastery of all Novice and Basic work, and more patience, thought and control than you have had to exercise up to now. But believe us, the results—a really well trained dog who is a genuine companion, and a useful one—are well worth it.

CHAPTER V

OPEN

The purpose of Obedience Trials is to demonstrate the usefulness of the pure-bred dog as the companion and guardian of man, and not the ability of the dog to acquire facility in the performance of mere tricks." So says the AKC in its regulations for obedience trials. We might say the same about obedience training, and in fact we have from time to time in other chapters. Here we will say it again, with the added proviso that it applies to *all* pet dogs, mongrel, half-breed or pure-bred. The training that the dog acquires in the exercises comprising AKC Open work is such as to increase his usefulness to you, your pleasure in having him around, and his propaganda value as a dog. To explain that latter a bit—most dog owners feel that everyone else should have a dog, too, and are baffled by the people who either hate dogs, are afraid of dogs, or who feel it would be just too much bother and trouble to have a dog around. We have found that an obedience trained dog can make some astonishing conversions in any of these groups.

In following the work in this chapter, we again recommend that you train your dog up to show ring standards even if you never intend to go near a ring. None of the training will do you much good if you don't —a dog which does not drop on recall *every time,* not just when he feels like it, is little better than one which has never heard of the exercise. A dog which stays only most of the time is one which you can never feel fully confident in leaving outside a store off leash. Work for perfection and unfailing obedience.

HEEL OFF LEAD

This is simply an extension of heeling, and requires only more practice. In the show ring, you will do off-leash heeling in the figure eight for the first time, but there is no necessary difficulty in this. For practical use, off-leash heeling, including the figure eight, is a basic exercise. Well trained in this, your dog can accompany you through crowded streets and stores without the bother, to you, of holding onto a leash. The figure eight will give him practice in following at your side no matter how much pedestrian traffic you may have to duck around, and should be practiced. Work him, just as in Novice, through and around as many objects as you can think of, particularly people moving and people standing still. When he is this far along in training, try to heel him around other dogs (trained ones, of course) and even around cats, pigeons or whatever other livestock is available to you.

The trained dog, when heeling, should concentrate solely on staying at your side unless the preservation of life and limb becomes the greater consideration. He should not be distracted by other dogs, cats, horses, motorcycles, fires, floods or cyclones, unless they present an immediate danger to him or you. You can't of course ever keep him from noticing the distractions and looking at them, nor should you try, but a passing dog which merits a glance or perhaps a lip-curl from him should never budge him from your side. Work on heeling until he is absolutely steady off leash.

DROP ON RECALL

The practical usage idea behind this exercise is that your dog should respond to your command (or signal) to drop, or down, no matter where he is or what he is doing. He should, in particular, respond to the command or signal when he is running in to you on the recall—probably the most difficult of circumstances, as he wants to come in and be near to you. There have been many cases of dogs' lives being saved through the drop on recall—imagine for a moment your dog running to you from across a street and a car approaching at full speed. What would you do? Shout to him to go back? Or to look out? Not much good—but if you could shout or signal to him to drop in his tracks, you could avert the danger. And this is not the only practical application.

The first step in training is to introduce the "drop" signal. This is generally a raising of your right hand, open with fingers up and palm forward much like a traffic policeman's "stop" signal. When you make the signal, raise your hand directly up from a position at your side, without any swing either to the front or side—how high you raise it is up to you, just so long as it is higher than your head. Some trainers like to get the hand only that high, some like to extend it at arms length above the head. This particular way of making the signal is the one that has been found to be best, for it is easily recognizable by your dog at a distance (don't forget that most dogs are considerably near-sighted) and is hard to confuse with any of the other standard signals. See the utility chapter for illustrations of all the conventional hand signals. And remember—it is not the downswing of the palm that is the signal to the dog, but the upswing and the fact that your hand is sticking up there that should signal the dog to drop.

Teaching him to respond to the signal is simply the introduction of another secondary stimulus to get the action you want. By this time, he should drop instantly on your voice command, either at heel beside you, close in front of you, or some distance away. Now you will begin to give the hand signal simultaneous with the verbal command, and keep it up until he realizes that one means the same as the other.

Put him back on leash for the first lessons. With him sitting at your side, on leash, swing your hand up in the signal and at the same time command him "Down!" Swing your body around toward him as you give the signal, to be sure he sees it. If he does not go down instantly you have the leash and collar there to make the necessary correction. Be very patient, for the upswinging hand will confuse or even frighten some dogs. He may think you're about to swing at him, if you've done so in the past. Reassure him that all is well, but insist that he drop immediately, and then praise him. At the very start of training, you can keep your hand up in the air a few moments, and even wiggle it a bit to draw his attention, but the signal should quickly become a sharp raising and an immediate lowering of the hand. Repeat the command-and-signal training until you feel he has the idea, then try it without the voice command. If he does not drop immediately, get in a sharp leash correction. In most cases, the dog will have caught on quite well, but if you have difficulty, go back to the voice-and-signal a few times, then try it again with only the signal. Keep at it until he works well with the signal only—and insist on an *immediate* drop, not a slow and reluctant sinking to the ground. Be sure to use plenty of praise and patience. This is an entirely new idea for him, so bear with him if it takes time. And mix up the work. Don't drop him and then sit him back up many times in a row or he will quickly get as bored with the whole thing as you will be. Do half a dozen drops, then heel some, then do a stay, then return to the drop training. It'll keep you both from ennui.

When he will drop on signal at your side, have him sit-stay and move around to his front, close in front of him. Give the command-and-signal a few times, then progress to the signal alone just as you did above. With you in front of him, there is the possibility that he may become confused by the whole business and try to come to you when you signal, particularly if you have been using informal sweeps of your arm to get him to come in recall training. It is a natural enough confusion on his part, so deal with it firmly and gently. Stand quite close to him, and reach down with your left hand, taking hold of the training collar just under his chin. Then give the command-and-signal, plus a combined snap down and push backward on the collar and his chest to remind him that he is supposed to go down, and stay where he is while dropping. Work this a time or two until he has the idea, then go back to command-and-signal only. Mix up the way you get him out of the down position, one time giving him the command to sit directly from the down, the next time telling him to stay at the down, walking around him to heel position, then having him sit. This will make him feel a little better about the whole thing, for you return and are near him at the familiar heel position once in a while rather than standing formidably in front of him all the time.

When he drops on the signal only, in front of you, move back to about six feet away, the full length of the lead, and begin again with command-and-signal, working up to signal only. Then, leaving the lead·on, keep increasing your distance until he will respond at a distance of thirty feet.

Then, when he is reliable in his drop from a sitting position, go back to heel position, on leash, and repeat the entire procedure from the stand-stay. There should be no difficulty in this repeat exercise, but the fact that the dog is on his feet will sometimes bring up a problem of his trying to walk towards you rather than dropping in his tracks. If this happens, you will find it out while you are still close to him, and you can take immediate action. Go straight to him and take hold of his collar as before, with your palm against his chest, and push him firmly back and downward. Don't rush at him as you do this—simply get to him quickly and get in the correction. Any rushing or shouting or sudden grabbing at his collar will frighten and confuse him. Just be firm. Tell him "No!" quite sternly as he tries to step forward, then give him a sharp "Down!" as you apply the correction. Don't, whatever you do, try to keep him from walking toward you by shouting "Stay!" once you have given the down command and/or signal, or you will foul up things to a pretty pass, as you will see if you think about it.

With any of this preliminary drop-on-recall training, do not settle for wrestling your dog down to make him obey the command. If the addition of the signal confuses him or for whatever reason makes him fail to respond quickly, you cannot solve it by wrestling with him. Go right back to on-lead basic training in the down and work up again until he drops instantly on the verbal command, then progress again to the signal work. The collar corrections we have given you are simply to reinforce the primary "down" stimulus in his mind, not to drag him down resisting and howling.

When and if you have trained him to the point where he will drop on your signal from the sit or stand position at whatever distance, you have already passed over the major hurdle that causes trouble for many amateur trainers. Impatient to get on with things, many trainers will try to get a dog to drop while in motion before he is steady in the drop from the sit or stand. Naturally enough, the dog has at least as much trouble performing the exercise in motion as he does while sitting or standing still, and probably more. The inexperienced trainer then tries to make corrections while the dog is walking or running, despairs at the whole business, and at best ends up with a confused and unwilling dog who works imperfectly and wishes he had stayed in bed. At any Open class you watch, you will see one or more dogs fail this exercise—generally the dog slows down when he gets the signal and creeps tail down to the handler, looking afraid and sheepish about it. The reason, almost without fail, is that the handler rushed things too much. It is well worth it to be sure, completely sure, at every step.

The next step is back on lead. Walk with your dog at heel, then suddenly step back, calling him to come, just as you did in Basic Training. This time, however, keep walking backward until the dog is in full motion toward you. Then stop quickly and give the command-and-signal for the drop. Your stopping will stop him, and the command-and-signal should drop him. If not, get in a quick correction with the lead. Then, after he has been down a few moments, walk quickly backward again, telling him to come as you step back. Go backward until he is in full motion again, then stop and have him sit in front of you as in the normal recall. Keep the lead ready to force the sit this time, for he may have caught on too well and try to drop again as you stop. Then send him to heel and the step is completed.

In giving your "Down!" command, be sure not to use his name. As we have explained before, use of his name tends to alert him for action— probably coming to you. A good sharp "Down!" alone will get the desired results in training.

There is in this part of the training an area of easy confusion for the dog, and it must be watched for carefully and prevented. If you do the drop every time, he will quickly come to think that it is now a normal part of the recall, and will try to drop every time you call him to you. To prevent this, alternate the way you do it—one time dropping him, the next time having him come in to a normal recall, with a sit in front. Keep at this until you are sure that he is working on your command only and not anticipating on his own.

Don't at this time try to get him to drop on the recall with the signal only. It is enough that he learn to drop while coming in to you. That is the major part of the exercise. Wait until the next step, which is the drop on recall from the sit-stay.

After he is perfectly steady in the drop-on-recall from heeling, leave him at the sit-stay and walk to about ten feet in front of him. Call him in and when he is half-way give him the command-and-signal to drop. Let him stay down a few seconds, then call him again for a normal recall. If all has gone well up to this point there should be no trouble at all, for he has learned to drop while running in to you, and the slightly different circumstances should mean nothing to him. Otherwise go right back to the heeling drop to refresh him, then try it from the sit-stay again.

Work at the drop on recall until he will drop on a recall from at least thirty feet away. Drop him at varying distances from you rather than always half-way, and remember to alternate with straight recalls so that he works entirely on command. If, on straight recalls, or on what you intended to be a drop-on-recall, you notice him slowing down in preparation for a drop, start running backward and coax him to speed up and come in to you. Do not, ever, give him the command to drop unless he is coming in full tilt—it is a gilt-edged invitation to anticipation if you try to fool yourself or him. And he'll accept the invitation with pleasure. Don't blame him or remonstrate with him if he does try to drop without your command. He has learned that you want him to drop while coming in, and is only trying to do the right thing by you. It is to him just like the "sit" when you come to a stop in heeling—there he has learned to perform an action automatically, and he will try to do the drop without command. It is not bad work on his part, but actually too good an understanding of what training is about. If you realize this you will not be tempted to howl at him, but will simply continue patient training until he realizes that in this case he must act only on your specific command. Vary all drops with straight recalls until you are sure he works only at command. To be sure of it, try dropping him twice on a long recall. Keep mixing it up for steadiness. Also, mix up the drops and straight recalls with other work to keep it from becoming boring for both of you. Do a drop or two, then heel a bit, then do a straight recall, then a stay, another drop, and so on. Vary the length of time you keep him at the down, too, before you call him in. Otherwise he may get the idea that he is to stay down for just five seconds, then get up and come in to you. Do a drop and an immediate recall one time, then do a drop and keep him there thirty seconds the next time.

As you progressively increase your distance on the drop on recall, try it a few times with the signal alone. Work at it until he will drop by signal alone, and immediately. If he does not drop immediately, you can only go back a step or two in the training. It is absolutely essential that he learn to drop on one and only one command or signal—there is no effective correction we know of at the advanced stage. Certainly you should never rush at the dog and bash him or yank at him. There is only thorough preparation.

In a show you will be allowed to give him either the signal or command for the drop, not both, and he should work at either. In out-of-ring life, immediate response to either is invaluable for sometime you may want him to drop in noisy circumstances in which he might have difficulty hearing you.

THE RETRIEVE

The first consideration under the retrieve is that, like any other exercise, it must be performed every time, at command. You may hear, or read, comments that the "forced retrieve" is bad, a harsh thing to inflict on a dog. To us, "forced retrieve" means simply that the dog retrieves at command, every time, rather than as a playful act. As such, it is no more or less "forced" than any other aspect of obedience. Almost every dog from puppyhood on will enjoy chasing after anything thrown for him, and returning with it for another throw. His enjoyment of it is based in his prey-instinct, the urge to chase anything that is "running" away from him. This is all well and good, and can and should be used in the retrieve training, but in itself cannot be relied on. By steps, the dog must be trained to retrieve objects not particularly congenial to him, like metal, and to do so every time he is required to.

The standard method is that of using a wooden dumbbell in training. The dumbbell is a good device, being, if well chosen, easy for the dog to pick up and handy for him to carry. And here the operative phrase is, *if well chosen!* More dogs than we care to think of have been stalled permanently at this point in training, simply because the trainer gave no thought to the dumbbell and its selection. It may seem curious to you that we put so much emphasis on this, as the dog must eventually learn, in around-the-house life, to carry almost anything and everything, but at this touchy point in training, it is indeed vital. We have seen dogs, long in training, who balked totally at dumbbell training—and who learned to retrieve within days when the right dumbbell was substituted for a careless selection.

The proper dumbbell should be light in weight. It need not be of balsa, but there are balsa dumbbells, and good ones they are, too, for little dogs. But it should be of a light wood, for several reasons. One, the lighter it is, the easier it will be for the dog to carry at first, and the easier it will be to persuade him to carry it happily. For another, picking up and carrying a light dumbbell will teach your dog to grasp gently whatever he is to retrieve, whereas a heavy one in training will encourage him to bite down hard in order to hold it. Keep the weight in mind when you buy or make a dumbbell.

The next consideration, and the one that brings the most grief all unawares to many trainers, is the construction of the dumbbell. A great many of the commercially available dumbbells are made, and bought, with little thought except that the item have a roughly dumbbell shape. Actually, it should be specifically selected for two factors: the height of the bar from the ground, and the distance between the bells. The height of the bar, determined by the diameters of the bells and of the bar itself, should be great enough that your dog can grab it without having to rub his nose into the ground. Dogs don't like that a bit. What height this should be for your own dog only you can determine. Remembering that the dog will try to grab the bar and hold it just behind the long incisor teeth, calculate just how far the bar should be from the ground.

Next, and really foremost in importance, is the distance between the bells. As a rough rule, the bar should be as long as the distance between the outside corners of your dog's eyes, with one inch added. That way, when he is holding the dumbbell in his mouth, he can see where he is going, between the bells. This basically simple consideration has been the downfall of countless dogs in training, who have been provided with dumbbells so short in the bar that the bells sit squarely in front of their eyes when they hold it. A dog, much as anyone else, likes to see where he is going, and even if sitting still he doesn't like to have his vision obscured by two large blocks of wood right in front of his eyes. Try it yourself, holding your fists up dead in front of your eyes and about two inches in front—see how much you would like running and jumping like that. Then move your fists apart until they are about half an inch beyond the outside corners of your eyes. There's a great difference, no? And that's just the way your dog feels about things. We have found that this one factor—a change to a longer bar—will work wonders in solving retrieve problems in dogs who have been training with a poorly selected dumbbell.

Getting the right dumbbell for your dog may be a bit difficult, as the majority of commercial ones are made, at this writing, with no thought for the above considerations. The chances are somewhat better than 10-1 that your local pet-supply department will have nothing suitable (the right length and height of bar for your dog in the right size and weight for him) if it even has dumbbells at all. If you are a home craftsman you can turn one out on your lathe from a light wood, or a local carpenter should be able to make you one quite reasonably. Even without a lathe you can make a dumbbell from a dowel and two blocks of wood. Be sure, though, to glue the bar quite firmly into the blocks as constant throwing onto even soft ground can loosen a bar very quickly. Be sure that the bar is sanded very smooth, as nothing will discourage a dog quite so much as a splinter or two in the mouth. In fact, one layer of adhesive tape around the bar will insure against any splinter mishaps, and will make the bar a bit softer and more congenial to the dog at first. The bells should be about half as wide as they are high, and more or less square. If you want to plane off the corners and sharp edges, go ahead, but don't make the bells round or octagonal, as this will make the dumbbell roll when you don't want it to. As a general guide to construction look closely at the pictures in this book and follow the pattern.

As to appearance, we suggest that you paint the bells white for easier visibility in grass or anywhere else. Especially if you are working on bare ground, or if you enter an indoor show with wooden floors, a wooden dumbbell can become almost invisible to the dog unless it is painted a contrasting color. We have seen more than one dog fail because he simply didn't see the dumbbell. You may see, or hear of, dumbbells whose bells are decorated to resemble dice, and we would recommend these quite heartily for visibility's sake but for the fact that we have never seen any of this type properly built according to the specifications above. That degree of cuteness may repel you, however, and so you can settle for a good flat white—the paint will not bother the dog if you let it dry thoroughly before he uses it. But, paint only the bells, not the bar.

With the proper dumbbell in hand, you should introduce it to your dog with the greatest of care. Carry it around with you during a few training days while he is practicing heeling, or learning the last stages of the drop on recall. Let him sniff it and look at it and generally get used to it before you try to work with it. When you are resting during training, leave it on the ground or on a chair and let him sniff and investigate it as much as he will. But don't let him chew on it in play. If he does just pick it up, praise him highly, let him hold it a minute, and then take it from him with the "out" or "give" command. But never, now or later, let him think that the dumbbell is a toy to be played with or chewed up. It is strictly for business.

One day, during a rest period, hold the dumbbell in your hand and play with it yourself, rolling it around and tossing it up to get him interested in it. When he comes over inquisitively, offer it to him, saying "Take It" coaxingly. If he does take it, praise him to the cumulus layers, let him hold it a minute, then take it from him. Then after a minute, try it again, this time with him at the sit-stay. If that works, consider yourself thrice blessed, for this is one of the trickiest points in training. A few dogs will take the dumbbell from the beginning. Most won't. Some will shy away, some will clamp their mouths shut, some will just plain cut and run at the very thought. On the assumption that yours will be the difficult one, here is what to do.

Put him on leash at the sit-stay and loop the end of the leash around your wrist so that both hands are free to hold the dumbbell. Then, standing in front of him, reach down and push the bar gently against his lips, saying "Take It." Some few will give in at this point, and open up to take the bell. If your dog does, push the dumbbell gently into his mouth and say "Hold It." Leave it there a few seconds, then take it from him with the "out" command. Increase the length of time you have him hold it gradually, until he will keep it in his mouth for a minute or more, until you take it from him. If he tries to drop it before you take it, keep one hand under his chin and the other on top of his muzzle, pressing only hard enough so that he understands he is to hold onto it until com-

THE LEFT THUMB AND FOREFINGER FORCE THE MOUTH OPEN GENTLY, WHILE THE DUMBBELL IS INSERTED.

manded to give it to you. If you have a dog who accepts the dumbbell gracefully, you will have little or no trouble in getting him to hold onto it for as long as you want. The holding problems arise with the dogs who refuse to take it from the first.

If he has simply clamped his mouth shut from the beginning, then walk around him to heel position, letting your left leg touch him for reassurance. Then bend down, with your left arm around his neck and the left hand under his chin. Place the dumbbell gently against his lips with the right hand and command him to take it. If this gets no results, use the left thumb and fingers to press his lips against his back teeth, forcing his mouth open just as in the Pre-Training lessons in giving up an object. Say "Take It!" as you force his mouth open—and be as gentle as possible, applying only enough force to get the mouth wide enough to slip the bar in—and place the dumbbell in his mouth so that the bar rests just behind the long incisor teeth. Praise him quickly, and bring your left hand around and put the palm under his chin with just enough pressure to keep his mouth closed. When he has held onto it a few seconds, take hold of the bell and tell him to give it to you. Butter him up as though he had handed you a certified check. With much praise, you may see a great change come over him as he realizes that he has done something quite commendable in taking and holding the thing, and your problems may be largely over.

One of the major faults in training is the wrong attitude toward the dumbbell and the taking of it. Some people, knowing that the dog will most probably have to be forced to take the dumbbell, make a personal contest and triumph of it. This sort of trainer will cram the dumbbell roughly into the dog's mouth, grab his muzzle hard to keep it shut, and then yank out the bell with a cry of victory, saying in effect, "There, you obstinate beast, I made you do it, by gum!" Therewith is training loused up to a fare-thee-well, and the dog will have a reluctant attitude toward the bell for the rest of his life. It must be looked at as a triumph for the dog, for having learned a new idea, and he must be shown that you think highly of him indeed for his new accomplishment. The bar of the dumbbell is not so nasty an object as all that—he will happily pick up and carry dirty twigs and branches—but it is the idea that he will object to at first, the idea of anything at all being forced into his mouth. But if you let him know from the first that it is a great accomplishment to take and hold something when you tell him to, you're on the way.

Above all, no matter how reluctant he may be at first to take it, he must never be allowed to associate unpleasantness with the dumbbell. Never, for example, follow the method you may hear of—choking the dog with his chain until he throws open his mouth in a gasp for breath, then shoving the dumbbell in.

Incredible though it may seem, we once encountered a woman having difficulty with this phase of training who would offer the dumbbell to her dog, then when he refused to take it would hit him a smart crack on the head with it. She couldn't understand why her dog got hysterical every time she brought the dumbbell out. Other trainers, having trouble, will bang the bar against the dog's front teeth with considerable force, and with the same predictable results. Any of these procedures is repellent to any thinking person, and we doubt that you will ever try to use them—but keep them in mind as a reminder that the dumbbell must never become an object of unpleasantness for your dog.

One of the most extreme problems is the dog who cries and fights and tries to run away when the dumbbell is presented to him. This is almost always the result of a crude introduction, but it can happen occasionally with the best treatment. To cure it, take up the heel position again, this time kneeling with your left leg behind him to keep him from backing away, just as you did if you had a similar problem with the "down." Put your left arm around his neck again, this time holding the leash, quite close to his neck, between the third and fourth fingers of your left hand —leaving the thumb and first two fingers free to apply to the jaw. Then, keeping control of him with your left leg, your left arm around him and your left hand on the lead, give the command and put the dumbbell in, applying the gentle pressure to his jaw. Reassure him with your voice as you do this, for his reactions are purely from fright. Keep your left arm around the neck and use the left hand as before under the chin to keep his mouth closed, using your right hand on top of the muzzle, if necessary, to keep his head still and his mouth closed. Be as gentle as possible, use his name and praise as he holds it, and then take it from him.

In extremis, if for some reason you have a really serious problem with the dumbbell—if for example you have tried to teach him to take it by the wrong method—then you must examine your conscience and your training history for the trouble. No dog in the world will object to the dumbbell per se, or at least very, very few. Whatever the cause, if the problem is severe, you can only soft-pedal the training for a few days, then re-introduce the dumbbell slowly and gradually. Carry it with you while heeling, tucked under your left arm. Then after a while transfer it to your right hand and carry it with you for a day of training. Then carry it in your left hand while heeling. This may panic him and cause him to heel wide in order to get away from it, but this once pretend not to notice his bad heeling. He may sit wide when you stop, but ignore it —reach down and praise him, letting the dumbbell touch him lightly.

If he shies away, affect not to notice it, but keep up the heeling and the gentle touching until he realizes it won't hurt him. Then begin again with the training, being extra gentle this time. You may find it hard to believe, reading this, that it can ever be such a problem, but a dog really badly introduced to the dumbbell can panic in seven Oriental languages at the mere sight of one. Careful introduction will avoid the problem.

None of this really need be as grim as we may have made it sound— with the proper cautions and patience, teaching the dumbbell retrieve can go along quite smoothly. We have, however, seen so much trouble with this single exercise, through faulty training, that we feel the major problems need emphasis. Slow and steady wins the race, as someone must have said, and the same applies to dumbbell training.

The one remaining major problem is the dog who takes the dumbbell readily enough, but tries to spit it out quickly. If you run into this, first check his mouth and teeth to be sure there is no soreness there which makes it painful for him to hold anything hard. If all is well in his mouth, then you can concentrate on forcing the hold by simply holding his mouth shut. You will find that this problem is much more common in the smaller breeds, for the interesting reason that a small dog, to look at your face, has to raise his head nearly to the vertical. If there is a dumbbell in his mouth at the time, it will tend to roll back in his mouth and he will think he is about to be choked. Larger breeds need only to hold their heads level, and the problem does not occur so frequently. If yours is a small dog, you can solve that aspect of the problem by getting to your knees, or even sitting with him when first working with the dumbbell. Later, as he learns to hold it, you won't have to bother with this.

Whatever your problems, or lack of them, continue the "Take It" training until he will first open his mouth on command and accept and hold the dumbbell, then actually reach forward a few inches to take it from your hand. It won't take long if you work at it steadily.

With all the problems in the "take" and "hold" out of the way, you and he are ready for the next step—carrying the dumbbell while in motion. If he has been introduced properly to the dumbbell and now holds it without resentment, there will be no problems here. Give it to him, and from a position a few feet in front of him, tell him to come to you.

Reach out with your left hand and put your extended fingers gently under his chin to remind him to hold onto it and urge him forward with all praise and coaxing. Just one step is a victory. Take it from him and praise him extensively. Then continue until he comes to you with it, you walking backwards, for at least ten feet. Then go back to the beginning and have him sit-stay with the dumbbell while you walk a short distance in front of him. Call him in, make sure he sits properly in front of you, take the dumbbell, and send him to heel. Increase your distance until he is coming to you at least thirty feet, carrying the dumbbell and coming to a proper sit, giving it to you smartly, and going to heel.

The third step involves his taking the dumbbell while in motion at heel. Walk with him at heel, with the dumbbell in your right hand. Bring it around in front of you easily and naturally (don't just pop it suddenly into his face) and holding it an inch or so in front of his mouth as you both walk along, tell him to take it. When he opens his mouth, put the dumbbell in and let him hold it. Praise him highly, even if he didn't reach out for it. Then take it from him and come to a halt. Start up again and offer it to him again with the command while walking, this time holding it a few inches away and getting him to reach out for it. Keep at this, increasing the distance until you have it out in front of him as far as you can reach and he is almost jumping out to take it. Then, starting close to his nose again, offer it to him at a lower level. Get him reaching down for it, by easy stages, until you are holding it only an inch from the ground and he is reaching down quickly to grab it. This is not as hard as it may sound (except on your back), for if he has been trained well up to this point, grabbing for it will be automatic on your command.

Next, when he is reaching almost to the ground for it, actually touch it to the ground and come to a stop as you do so, commanding him to "Take It!" If there is any hesitation, guide his head down gently until he takes it. Then step backwards immediately and call him to come. When he comes in, take it from him, and send him to heel. Do this a few times, then actually drop it just in front of him as you stop, and repeat the take, come, and heel.

Finally, from the sit at your side, throw the dumbbell out in front of you a foot or two and tell him to take it. As he gets it into his mouth, tell him to come, and insist that he sit squarely in front of you and hold the dumbbell until you tell him to give it up. Don't, at this time, try to make him stay as you throw the dumbbell. Make it as much fun for him as you possibly can, with repeated coaxing and praise, until you see that he is going out eagerly to get it, and is enjoying the whole idea. Increase your distance until you are throwing it thirty or forty feet and he goes out rapidly to get it and runs back happily to you with it.

One thing you must insist on, even at this stage, is that when he goes out after the dumbbell, he must pick it up and return to you with it. As you get along in training, you will drop all extra commands until you have reached the point where a single "Take It!" as you throw is enough. If for some reason he doesn't take the dumbbell when he goes out, go right out with him and put it in his mouth, then run backwards calling him to come. But once you have reached the stage where he understands what to do, don't stand and plead with him to take it if he has run out and just stands there looking stupid. This double command situation is one of the great temptations—it seems so much easier to tell him just once again to take it, rather than going out and putting it in his mouth. Soon he will get the idea that he should go out after it and wait until you command him to pick it up—and it will show up in the ring. We will lay you eight to five that at any Open ring you watch, there will be at least one dog who goes out after the dumbbell, then stands there looking either at the dumbbell or at his owner, visibly waiting for the command to go ahead and take it. Don't let it happen to you—insist that he get it with only one command. If necessary, put him back on the old 30-foot clothesline so that you have him under control while solving this problem.

When he is going out to get it reliably, you can introduce the stay, thus establishing the final bit of control. Take hold of his training collar with your left hand and tell him to "Stay!," and throw the dumbbell out. As it hits the ground release him and tell him to get it. Next time hold him a few seconds longer, then longer the next time, taking your hand off the collar only when you are sure he is steady and won't break. Work on this until he will stay at least a minute after the throw, then race after it and bring it in to you. When he will do that, you have a dog well and fully trained in the basic retrieve.

To add practical value, and to get him used to taking, holding, carrying and retrieving whatever you want him to, you can graduate now to various items other than the dumbbell. Try a retrieve or two with a rolled-up newspaper held together with tape or string. Then get him to carry light paper bags or baskets. Before you know it, you will be able to send him to fetch your slippers. Try just that—point them out to him, telling him to "Get the Slippers!", and keep it up until he understands and will travel to wherever they are, locate them, and bear them back triumphantly to you.

There is one final word in this exercise, and that concerns throwing the dumbbell. A surprising number of competition obedience handlers don't know how to throw a dumbbell. And although this bit of esoterica is intended largely for ring-bound people, you will want to be able to control your throw in training too, so a little practice is in order. The best technique we have found is as follows: hold it by one of the bells, with your thumb on one side and the fingers on the other, holding it only tightly enough to keep it from sliding out of your fingers. Swing your arm back, then forward and up so that your thumb is on top when you release the bell, then let it simply slide out of your hand. This way it is difficult to put any backflip on the dumbbell, and backflip is undesirable as it will cause the dumbbell to bounce wildly when it lands. The perfect throw is the one in which the dumbbell travels through the air like an arrow, landing flat and sliding if at all only a few inches from where it hit. Try this a few times before you work with your dog, until you can make it land, and stay, where you want it.

THE HURDLE RETRIEVE

Jumping is in the realm of fun for any healthy dog. Combined with the already-learned retrieve, hurdle work, if approached properly, is something you can both enjoy. But, as much fun as jumping randomly may have been for him, the first step is to teach him to jump a standard hurdle, and on your command. The height of the hurdle used in obedience rings has been set by the AKC as follows: one and one half times the height of the dog at the shoulder, or three feet, whichever is less. The exceptions to this are the giant breeds (who have some trouble in getting off the ground)—Bull Mastiffs, Great Danes, Great Pyrenees,

Mastiffs, Newfoundlands and St. Bernards, who jump once their height or three feet, whichever is less. In training, use the proper height for your dog, plus two or three inches for insurance. But don't try it any higher than that—true, some breeds can jump considerably higher than the specifications, but don't strain your dog's abilities to show him off. One crash down onto the top of a too-high jump can hurt a dog seriously, and once hurt you may never, literally never, be able to persuade him to try it again.

In the Appendix you will find diagrams and instructions for building a standard ring-type hurdle. Basically, it consists of two braced uprights plus one six-inch board, one four-inch board, and enough eight-inch boards to make up the proper height for your dog. With these any height from four inches, by two inch steps, can be set up. If yours is a small breed you may need only two of the eight-inch boards. But even for the smallest, make your uprights the standard 4 feet, for that is what your dog will encounter at a show.

The home-training departure from the standard ring hurdle is that yours should be equipped to serve both as a solid hurdle (with the boards) and as a bar jump. There are several ways to make it serve as a bar jump—with the bar holder, spaced nails on the backs of the uprights, or a hole-and-pin arrangement on each upright. The details of all three are given in the Appendix under Obedience Equipment. The bar holder is easiest to use, being actually a pair of iron (or even wood) pieces roughly in the shape of an "h" which fit over the top board and support the bar. This combination jump will solve by itself two major training problems—teaching the bar jump (in Utility) and teaching your dog not to scramble over the hurdle—as we will explain as each problem comes up.

Whatever the size of your dog, you begin jump training by gradual steps, starting with what is not even a jump for him. Put the four-inch board into the uprights, and place the bar on the holder or nails so that the top of the bar is seven inches from the ground. Then, with the dog on leash and heeling beside you, walk up to the jump and step over it, giving your jump command as you do. "Jump," "hup" or "over" are widely used as commands for the jump, but choose what you will. A large breed will simply step over the obstacle, and even a small one will be able to

First step—WALKING OVER JUMP WITH THE DOG AT HEEL. LEAD GUIDES HIM OVER BUT IS NOT HAULING HIM.

Third step— ▶
DOG COMES STRAIGHT OVER JUMP TO YOU. NOTE LOOSE LEAD. THE BAR WAS OMITTED IN THESE PICTURES FOR CLARITY, BUT WE RECOMMEND THAT YOU USE IT FROM THE FIRST.

◀ *Second step*—DOG COMES OVER JUMP AS YOU WALK AROUND STANDARD.

WITH DUMBBELL, ▶
THE DOG COMES TO YOU OVER JUMP IN A RE-CALL. JUMP IS RAISED LATER.

négotiate it with a small hop. Praise him mildly once you are over, saying "Good Boy, Heel," but do not overdo the praise in this case, as you are trying to create the impression that the jump isn't much of a thing at all. Walk a short distance away, then turn and come back over the jump as before. Repeat until you see the dog thinks nothing of it. Then take out the four-inch board and put in the six-inch, raising the bar to suit. Go over this two or three times exactly as before, then raise the hurdle progressively to eight, ten and twelve inches.

At this point, size becomes a factor. Some of the tiny breeds are no more than eight inches at the shoulder and the twelve-inch jump (plus the bar for a total of fifteen) is as far as they need go. If yours is one of these, then follow only so long as we talk about twelve inches and then skip to the next step. In general, carry on with each step only so far as it applies to your dog's height.

At the twelve-inch level comes the first departure. After going over it with him a few times, the next time, as you walk up to it, aim yourself somewhat at the right-hand standard. When you reach the jump veer slightly to the right to go close around it, giving your dog the command to jump—and being very careful not to get the leash tangled with the upright or his legs. Swing your left hand, holding the leash, over the jump itself. There are several things that can happen here aside from his going over in good order. He may swerve with you and try to squeeze himself between your left leg and the upright, or simply follow you around to the right of the jump. If so you can't blame him a bit, as the idea of sticking at your side is much more firmly entrenched than this new business of jumping. If this happens, stop, and take him back and approach the jump again, this time pulling him gently to the left with the lead in your outstretched left hand, and try to guide him over. He may then, or even at the first try, simply stand there and look at the jump, or sit down. This is unlikely if you have gone over with him enough times, but if it does happen, go right back and go over with him half a dozen times more, then try again going around to the right as he jumps. Do not, very definitely, try to yank him over with the leash, as this will sabotage all your efforts to date as the jump becomes a hateful object to him. Simply keep at it until he realizes all by himself the jump is nothing to fear.

When he does it successfully (and most dogs will the first time), call him to heel and walk ahead a bit, then turn around to try it again. Because most dogs think the whole idea is a great lark, the quick command to "Mike, Heel!" as he hits the ground may be needed to get his mind back on the fact that you are working.

After he has done this well a few times, heel up to about three feet from the jump and stop, making him sit. After waiting a few seconds, start up again, with the command, "Mike, Heel! Over!" and then turn around to try again. The purpose of this is to let him know that he cannot just waltz up and jump, but that he must wait for your command every time. Then comes the final work on lead, and here you may have to use a longer lead of light clothesline for a large dog, as there must be enough length to allow him to go over, land, and return without interference from the lead, all while you remain on your side of the jump.

Start toward the jump with him, and as you get to it, give him the jump command, but this time stay on your side of it. As his feet hit on the opposite side, give him the command to come, and as he turns, the command to jump. Step back as he comes at you, giving him room to land and come in to a sit in front of you. Repeat this at least a dozen times, until you are sure he understands what you want and will do it with the lead completely loose.

A highly important cautionary word is in order at this point. *Do not, at this time or ever, allow him to walk around the jump.* Many of the tragedies of the show ring can be traced directly to this point. The trainer has, in moments of play and in pleasure that the dog is jumping well, sent him out over the jump and allowed him to circle around on his way back. Then months later in the ring, the dog, working well and enjoying it, will circle around the jump without even dreaming that he is doing wrong. And there goes the show for that dog and owner, kaput. You must impress on him, from the very first times, that he always goes over the jump. This is so important that even in the first times over the four-inch board you should go over, walk away and turn around, then come back over rather than circling around to approach it from the same side every time. It drills into the dog that over is the only way to negotiate that jump.

Once he has done the over-and-back several times without any correc-

tions, take the lead off and try him free. The chances are very good that
he will perform it perfectly. If so, repeat it a few times and you are ready
for the first jump with the dumbbell. If not, put him back immediately on
lead and make the necessary corrections as you retrace your training
steps. Do not try to make off-lead corrections, as you will end up in a
chasing and wrestling match all to no avail. The only exception to this is:
if he goes over correctly and then tries to run around on the way back,
get to the side of the jump he is heading for quickly and prevent him
from coming around if you can. Then take him back to the far side, on
lead, and jump back over with him. If you don't think you can head him
off, jump as fast as you can over the jump yourself and run straight ahead,
calling to him, to keep him from going around the jump. Then put him
on lead and jump back with him. Keep him on lead until he is doing it
well again, then try with it off.

With your dog doing the over-and-back steadily off lead, you can introduce the dumbbell. Set the jump back at four inches, plus bar. Sit him
at your side at an appropriate distance from the jump (you will know by
this time how much of a run he needs to clear it) and give him the
dumbbell. Tell him to stay and walk *over* the jump, then turn to stand
facing him as close as possible on the other side. Call him to you, and as
he approaches the jump step back quickly and give him the jump command. As he has been trained to come straight to you with the dumbbell,
and the seven inches is no more than a slight hop for even the smallest
dog, there should be no trouble. Have him come in, sit, deliver the dumbbell, and go to heel.

Watch especially here for a tendency to run around the jump to you,
even if it is only four inches high (seven inches in total with the bar) at
this point. If you see him swerve to go around, jump right over at him,
with a strong "No!" command, and intercept him. Take him back to the
starting point, leave him again, and try it all over.

Another possible problem, as the situation is a new one to him, is his
coming right up to the jump and then standing there looking confused
about the whole business. Don't laugh at him however funny it may seem,
but step right over to him and lead him back to the starting point, praising him heartily to take his mind off the fact that he may have done
something wrong. Give him all reassurances possible, then leave him to

try it again. This time, stand half-way over the jump with your right foot over and your left foot behind. Call him again, and as he approaches the jump swing your left foot over as a guide for him. This will give him the idea. After doing this three or four times, leave him, take up the same position, and as he starts at your "come" command, swing your left foot over right away. Repeat this a few times, and progress to simply standing close on the far side. By these easy stages you will build up his confidence and he will get the idea.

When he comes to you successfully, with you standing close to the jump, begin increasing your own distance from it until he will come over the jump, dumbbell in mouth, and into a recall with you standing about fifteen feet away from the jump. Then, build up the height of the jump by two-inch intervals until it is as close as possible to his height at the shoulder, but don't try to take it to full height yet. And remember that this is not a one-day affair. All the work we have described so far should be spread out through several training sessions, mixed up with other work for variety, getting a little improvement and progress each time. Don't try to push him too hard, as jumping is tiring for a dog, and if worn out he will just sit down on you.

Now comes the first try at an actual retrieve over the hurdle. Lower the height again, not all the way to four inches, except for the very small breeds. Eight inches plus bar is a good first-time height for most dogs. Do a few straight retrieves away from the jump to refresh his mind as to what he is supposed to do when the dumbbell is thrown. Then stand with him quite close to the jump, allowing only enough room for him to get up speed and make the jump, tell him to stay, and throw the dumb-bell over. Control your throw so that the dumbbell lands just about where he will, plus a few inches, so that when he goes over he will see the dumbbell right in front of him when he lands and be reminded of what he is supposed to do. Send him for it with your retrieve command, plus the jump command as he approaches the hurdle. When he lands on the other side, get in a quick retrieve command and then a "come" and "over" to get him back to you. Use all praise and encouragement necessary to get him to do the work, and praise him highly once he has come back with it, delivered, and heeled. Repeat this, gradually cutting down your extra commands and encouragement as indicated, until he will do the hurdle retrieve with only the original commands to stay and retrieve, and the final command to heel. Any problems you run into will be the ones you have already encountered in the straight retrieve or in simple jumping, and you can apply the necessary corrections to suit. But remember to insist, without exception, that every time he is sent out he must go over the jump both ways, and always come back with the dumbbell.

When he is doing good and reliable work over the eight inches, gradually increase your distance from the jump and the distance the dumbbell lands on the other side, until you are throwing from at least fifteen feet and the dumbbell is landing fifteen feet on the other side of the hurdle. Moving back from the jump for the throw is very important—he must learn to go over the jump even when he starts out at quite a distance from it. If he only knows to go over it when he starts out practically touching it—when its apparent size is such to make it almost the only thing he can see—then he will refuse it some time when you stand a bit further back.

As you increase your throwing distances, also increase the height of the jump (moving the bar along each time) until the boards equal his height at the shoulder. Then, start making your throws of the dumbbell a bit erratic—so that it lands to the left or right a few degrees rather than directly across the jump. This will teach him that no matter where it lands (and you will inevitably, due to nervousness or whatever, make a bad throw in at least one show) he must go over to get it and go over coming back. But be reasonable about how far off true your throws are— just somewhat to the right or left. Don't throw it 90° off to your right and expect your dog to go over, get it, and come back over with it.

When all this is under control you can start building up the height again until you have reached his maximum jumping height—with the boards equalling the specified height, and the bar making it about three inches higher. Now you will see the first problem-solving function of keeping the bar where it is during training. If you train your dog with the boards only, he will inevitably try to scramble over the top as the height gets up toward his maximum. He must, however, clear the jump, so how do you solve it? If the bar is there he will dislodge it in trying to scramble over and it will come clanking to the ground after him. The idea is not to scare him, but to supply a totally unsure footing at the top, thus encouraging him to go over clean rather than trying to climb. When it happens, at whatever height, reassure and comfort and encourage him to make light of it, pretending that it was all a most unfortunate accident, but that he shouldn't mind at all. Don't reprimand him. Let him figure out for himself that climbing isn't the right way. Then put the bar right back on and send him over again. He will put that little bit of extra effort into his spring and clear the whole apparatus. Later, once he has learned to clear his maximum height without touching, you can remove the bar and send him over a few times without it to get him used to the plain hurdle.

As a final caution, remember always that you are training a dog, not a jumping machine. He will inevitably make mistakes, especially in this exercise, as he is being asked to do a variety of parts of an exercise all without any but an original command. Be patient with him, correct the

At full height, a Weimaraner goes over 36 inches of jump, plus the bar.

mistakes when they come up, always as pleasantly as possible. Don't press too hard—jumping is tiring after a while. Keep it fun for him, no matter how "forced" the exercise may be.

THE BROAD JUMP

This exercise is considered by many inexperienced trainers to be the hardest of all to teach and perfect, yet it is actually one of the easiest if you go about it the right way. In a show, the dog is required to broad jump over a set of low jumps (see pictures), the total length of which is twice that of the height of the hurdle for the particular dog. Thus the greatest jump will be six feet for large breeds, and as little as two feet for a tiny dog. The great problem in most broad jump training is that the dog is pulled and lifted over the jumps to persuade him to get enough oomph into his spring to clear them—no dog likes this sort of thing, and the problems proliferate. We advocate the use of what we call a "crib," after its resemblance to the foot of a baby's crib. Attached properly to the second of the jumps this device forces the dog to get height and spring enough without any hauling about with the lead. You'll find in the Appendix complete instructions for making a crib. Using it, you never need more than "remind" with the lead—without it you may have to do a lot of hauling.

The practical background of the broad jump is that it teaches the dog to jump over such things as ditches and streams at command. As it is somewhat impractical to dig a series of ditches of graded sizes in the show ring, and equally improbable that you will want to spade up your lawn, the four-section wooden broad jump was developed for training and the ring. The construction of this, too, is described in the Appendix.

To begin training, set up the two lowest of the jumps close together, making a total width of about twenty inches. Set the crib on the second jump at a low angle, about 30° off the horizontal. Then, standing ten feet in front of the first jump with your dog at heel, begin running toward it with him still at heel. As you reach the jump, give him your jump command and sail over yourself. As you go over, bring your left hand, holding the lead, up and towards the front, but do not try to pull him over. The hand and arm movement is something of a signal to him, letting him know that he should go up and out just as your arm moves. Just as soon as you land, back around to the right until you are standing even with the middle of the jumps, about two feet to their right. As you back, call him to come to you just as in Basic Training recall from heeling. Finish by sending him to heel, and then circle away for another jump. Do this enough times that he realizes what is up, then you can progress to the stage of standing at the side of the jumps while he does the entire thing by himself.

If you should have really fundamental difficulty in his refusing to go over with you the first time you try it, don't try to haul him over. If he screeches to a halt, drop the leash and go on over the jumps yourself. Come around to him and reassure him that all is well. Remember that it is the unusual appearance of the broad jumps plus the crib that is holding him back. Take away the first jump, leaving only the second with the crib on it, and approach that with him. The remaining jump plus crib will then be no more than a low hurdle, and no dog who has mastered the high jump will have any problem. When he is used to going over that with you, add the first jump again, quite close, and go over both. Slowly separate them until there is a length element in the jump as well as height.

In a show you will leave your dog at a sit about ten feet in front of the jump, walk to a position at the side of the jumps, facing them, then call your dog to jump over and come around quickly to a sit in front of you (you having made a 90° right turn as he was going over). This procedure seems strange, but it is designed to give control of the jumping dog when he lands. Jumping excites a dog, and without some sort of established control, he might just go over a stream or ditch in the country and keep on going. But if he is firmly trained, ring-style, to stop afterwards, he'll do so outside the ring as well as in.

For the second step, get out your clothesline and use about ten feet of it as a lead. Leave him sitting ten feet in front of the jump, at the stay, then walk to the proper position beside the jumps. When you arrive, the lead should be just long enough to reach from him to your outstretched left arm without pulling on him. Then, as you face the jump, turn your head to him and tell him to jump. As you do so, move your left hand in a swing to your right and over the jump as you want him

GOING OVER WITH THE
DOG HELPS HIM GET
THE IDEA. THE LEAD
ACTS AS A GUIDE, BUT
NOTE THAT THERE IS NO
FORCE USED.

BACK QUICKLY TO THE
SIDE OF THE JUMPS
AND GUIDE HIM AROUND
INTO A STRAIGHT SIT IN
FRONT OF YOU.

STEPPING INTO THE JUMPS WILL KEEP HIM FROM JUMPING TO- WARD YOU.

THE FINISHED PROD- UCT—A CLEAN JUMP AS YOU STAND BESIDE THE JUMPS. NOTE "CRIB" IN POSITION.

King, the German shepherd in these pictures, was killed shortly after they were taken. Defending his owner's two-year-old child from a rattlesnake, King was fatally bitten.

to go. This will give him the signal he has become used to, and will also apply a light snap to his collar to remind him to get moving. As he comes to the jump, give him another jump command. As he goes over, turn to your right and call him in to you as soon as his feet touch the ground on the other side. Then send him to heel, praise him fulsomely, and circle around to try it all over again. If he tries to walk over the jumps—raise the angle of the crib until he is forced to jump to get over at all.

With the crib at its proper angle and height you have eliminated before it started one nasty tendency of dogs learning the broad jump—to try to walk over or between the jumps. He *must* jump to get over the crib and so has no chance to yield to the temptation to walk over the low boards. The problem you may run into is a tendency to jump at an angle from left to right, or even to try to sneak between you and the jumps rather than clearing them. If this comes up as he is learning, step right into the jump about a third of the way before you call him to come over. Then, as he does go over, step back out and into position to call him to you. This way he must jump straight, and obviously cannot do any sneaking-between. As the problem diminishes, step less and less into the jumps at each succeeding try, until he will do it well with you in your original position. When he has cleared the basic-size jump several times in good order, you are ready to try him off-lead.

Put him at the sit, off-lead, in front of the jumps. Walk away, this time jumping over the two-board jump, and stand across it, quite close. Call him to you and give the jump command as he nears the first board, then back away quickly to give him room to land. When he does land, keep calling him to you and circle around backward until you are in position at the side of the jumps. Stop there and have him sit in front of you. Then send him to heel and try it again. Work this a few times for steadiness. Then, one time, leave him as before, go over the jump, and this time stand just to his right of the center of the last jump, facing in the direction you would if you were standing in the proper beginning position for the jump. Turn your head to him, call to him to come and jump, and as he goes over, back around to your original position at the jumps' side, so that he can come in to you properly. Keep edging back and around on each successive jump until he is doing the exercise properly off lead—sitting until you command him, clearing the jump with only one original command, and quickly turning to come to you (without a command) in a proper recall and sit.

With this accomplished you can begin to increase the width of the jump gradually until it is up to the specifications for his height. Move the two boards apart until the total distance is about two feet, then introduce the third board and re-space them evenly to make about two-and-a-half feet, adjust the three until they total about four feet, bring the fourth board in to make four-and-a-half, and then move them all apart to total six feet, if your dog is that large. Use the raised crib again if he develops any tendency to walk over the boards as the distance increases. Depending on the size of your dog, stop this moving-apart process at the proper distance, but always make up the total with at least two boards. As a general rule: two boards for up to two feet, three boards for up to four feet, and all four for up to six feet. However, if your distance is at or near the border-line between a number of boards, train him to go over no matter how many boards (though at least two) make up the distance. At a show the judge may use three boards to make up, say, five feet. A dog rigidly trained with four boards just might balk. Dogs are funny creatures suspicious of new things. So get him used to the various possibilities, for the judge is under no obligation to change the number to what he's used to.

When he is jumping the specified distance with no trouble, and with the crib in optimum position, gradually lower the crib from one time to the next until it is lying flat on the jump. Keep him working at that distance, without the crib as an aid, until he is perfect in his performance.

LONG SIT AND DOWN

Here is an exercise of the greatest practicality, for it teaches your dog to stay where he is when you tell him to, even though you are out of sight for a few minutes. It will be very handy around the house, and when you are out of the house. If you are going into a store where you cannot take him you will be able to leave him outside the door while you shop, and there he will be when you come out again. Even if you only walk him on leash, it will be better for both him and you if he stays quietly in one position though he be securely tied to a tree or post.

The exact practicality of requiring him to hold one position, either the sit or down, rather than just staying in one spot, may escape you at first consideration. It would seem much more logical simply to require him to stay where he is, regardless of whether he changes his bodily position while you are away. Yet you will find that it is much easier, mentally, for a dog to stay in one spot if he must hold one position. Sitting up from a down position, or lying down from a sit, or standing, all are invitations to move about a bit while changing positions. These temptations lead from a slight straying to major movement, and the first thing you know he's off and gone. But if it is impressed on him that when he is left in a position he stays in that position until you come back, then all the temptations to movement are gone.

The major consideration in training the "handler away" sit and down is confidence. He must become confident that you will return. In the Novice stays he can see you all the time and knows you're not going to desert him. That he likes. But when you leave him at a stay and go out of sight his first thought will be, whoops, there he goes, better get after him and see what's up. This is entirely natural and is to be expected, for you two are after all companions and he wants to be near you. So proceed with care and patience in this training, remembering always that when he breaks he does it out of love for you and a desire not to be left alone.

The actual mechanisms of the sit-stay he has already learned, so the only addition is your being out of sight. Do the preliminary training in your house, where there are familiar surroundings for him. Pick a room where no one else is sitting around to distract him, put him at a sit in the middle of the room (facing a door) and leave him with a definite command to "Stay!" Make it an order, not a request, and walk away, stepping off on your right foot. Go through the doorway and out of sight for only a few seconds, then return to him and circle to heel position. Release him and praise him for the good work.

As soon as you are out of sight through the doorway he may get up and follow you. It's wrong, but the motives are clear enough, and you should not treat it as disobedience. If he comes after you, bring him to heel position and heel right back to where you left him. When he is at the sit again, take hold of his collar with your left hand behind his neck (don't try to use it as a choke) and just as you leave him, give him a sharp snap backwards with the collar as you tell him to stay. Tell him in no uncertain terms and swing your right hand around in a firm stay signal. Head out of the room again, but this time turn as you reach the doorway and return to him, praising him for a good stay. Repeat this three or four times, dropping the preliminary snap on his collar as it becomes unnecessary. Then, go just out of sight again, staying only a few seconds, and return to him. Keep increasing your time gradually until you are able to stay out of his sight for five minutes. You won't be able to do this in one or two sessions, or probably even in a dozen. Work at it slowly, and remember that you are not teaching him anything new, but slowly building his confidence that you will return to him.

Insist from the beginning that he remain not only where he is, but that he remain sitting. This will be a little difficult to handle in the observation end, but you should be able to work it with a small mirror, or through the help of an accomplice peering in at a window or around a corner (from behind the dog so that he doesn't know he's being observed) and signalling you if the dog breaks. When he breaks—and he will a few times, for it seems much more sensible to him to lie down and take it easy if you're going to be away for a while—return to him immediately and tell him quite harshly, "Sit!" with a sharp snap upward on the collar. Then leave him again immediately with a stern "Stay!"

After a few of these corrections he will grasp the thought that he is supposed to stay seated, as well as just stay.

When you can stay away five minutes in the house you are ready to try it outdoors. But be sure that in the house you have been well and truly out of not only his sight but of his ken in total. It will accomplish little if you sit in the next room and breathe heavily for the five minutes, for he will know full well that you are there. You must really be gone as far as he is concerned, out of sight and smell and hearing.

Outdoors, sit him in your yard or in a field or wherever you have to work. Leave him just as in the house and get out of sight somewhere. Behind a car is not much good, as he will see your legs underneath and will be tempted to come over and investigate this new game you've thought up. Nor is hiding behind a tree very efficient, for he will probably see a leg or whatever sticking out and succumb to the same temptation. Go around the corner of a building if possible. Do a complete repeat of the inside procedure, starting with only a few seconds out of sight and working up to about three minutes. Then start increasing the distance you go to get out of sight as you work the time up to five minutes. Work until you are walking about a hundred feet straight away from him before slipping around the corner, and can stay for five minutes with no breaks on his part.

All is well up to now and you can begin to tempt him with distractions as he sits there. After you have left and are out of sight have a friend or family member come into the training area and walk around, not too close to the dog, ignoring him. At this stage, don't make a break too tempting; just introduce the presence of someone he knows into the training area. As you progress, you can have your assistant walk closer and closer to the dog, and even brush right by him to test his steadiness. But work up to it slowly. Then try it with another dog or dogs. Try to get friends to bring their dogs over, even if untrained, and have them first walk around in his area after you are out of sight (but keep the dogs on leash unless they are trained!) and then try leaving him at the sit while the other dogs are already in the area and near him.

Every time you return to him, inside or out, insist that he stay until you have definitely released him. When you come back to him and have circled to heel position, praise him but insist that he stay. Make him wait a few seconds before you release him.

The long down is handled in much the same manner, except that you need not go back inside for the start of the training. Leave him at the down outside, and work up until he will stay at the down for at least six minutes with you out of sight. Be wary that he does not sit as you leave him or while you are out of sight. He has been taught that you want him to sit while you are out of sight, and may change his position to what he thinks is the proper one. Just let him know calmly and firmly that now you want him to stay down when you leave him in that position.

One additional point to keep in mind is that six minutes is a long time for your dog, and he should be in a comfortable down position when you leave him. Just what the most comfortable position is for him is something you will have to let him decide. If you have trained him correctly in the "down," with his rear slewed over, he will probably find that comfortable enough. But don't make the mistake you will see being made in the obedience ring, where handlers will down their dogs and then wrestle them into a position the handler thinks is comfortable. The handler doesn't really know anything about it, and is only imposing on the dog what he, the handler, thinks of as comfort. Let your dog determine his own most comfortable posture, and he'll stick with it.

Here again, as we suggested in Novice, a training class can be helpful in getting your dog accustomed to sitting or "downing" in line with other dogs—and getting used to noise and confusion and people moving about while he is at a stay. If you found a good class for your Novice stays, use it again for this Open work. You can teach the stays perfectly well all by yourself if you never plan to go into a ring, but if you do have ring ambitions, try him with other trained dogs before chancing your money on an entry.

FINAL THOUGHTS

Having gone through all the work in this chapter you will have a dog who can not only qualify for his C.D.X. (Companion Dog Excellent) in the show ring, but who can honestly be called trained. He will be much more than basically civilized, as he can jump, retrieve, stay, and even carry packages for you if you are so inclined. There are further steps, in the next chapters, and we hope you will continue with your training—by now you will have found out that training can be fun if done the right way. But, believe us, you can feel proud of yourself and of your dog once you have attained this level of obedience.

We must emphasize again, before closing this chapter, the extreme importance, the absolute necessity of progressing slowly and steadily rather than rushing through a skimpy training schedule. Every step must be built on the rock-solid foundation of perfect sureness of the ones preceding. If you do it this way, the path of training can be smooth and easy, and most of the problems we mention and give you solutions for will never come up. Without exaggeration, fully fifty percent of all training problems arise through haste and inadequate preparation before moving on to the next step. Don't fall into the trap of what seems the easy way out—a quick dab and a snatch of work. It is by far the hardest way of all. Training can and should be fun for you and your dog, and all the unpleasantness of sweating and snarling and shoving about is totally unnecessary. It should be, by this point, an act of cooperation and coordination between you and the dog, enjoyable to both and well done because you have learned together, the right way. Go to obedience shows even if you never intend to enter one. Watch the dogs. There you will see cringing dogs (although only a few any more), unwilling workers, sloppy workers, and happy and cheerful dogs who do everything right because they don't know any other way to do it. Decide for yourself which way you want to have your dog be. Then train him properly.

CHAPTER VI

UTILITY

U TILITY WORK, if you have seen it in a competition ring, looks frighteningly difficult. Taken cold, it could be. But as a further step in obedience training it follows with no more necessary difficulty than any of the exercises that have gone before. There are, of course, considerably fewer dogs trained at the Utility level than at the Basic or Novice levels, for the additional training takes time, and most of all, a successful technique. Novice training as we have given it to you is simple and rewarding, but it must be admitted that almost anyone can by cajoling, pounding, hauling about, cursing and sweating, get a dog to perform sufficiently well to just get by in a Novice ring. Many of them, unfortunately, do just get by as you will see in shows. But Utility work is another sort of thing entirely.

To quote the AKC again, "The classification which has been adopted is progressive, with the thought in mind that a dog which can be termed a Utility Dog has demonstrated his fitness to a place in our modern scheme of living." A trifle high-flown, perhaps, but the germ of truth is there. In utility work you will arrive at an entirely new concept of dog owning—as different from "Companion Dog" as that is different from simply having a dog around the house. Even as the highest AKC title is "Utility Dog" rather than something on the lines of "Companion Dog Super-Excellent," so is utility work of a different order altogether.

Even though you never plan to herd sheep with your dog, or use him in whatever other occupations might be considered as under "utility," you will see in this advanced work that your dog *could*, with a little work along the right lines, be trained to do just about anything except play chess. Even on that we wouldn't take bets. Some years ago one of the

157

writers met a dog who could distinguish between the pieces of a large-size chess set. By this time he may be beating his owner regularly.

In any case, utility work is as much a gateway as a goal—the utility trained dog is so much a working partner of his owner that it is no longer even a question of "obedience" as such. That is taken for granted. It is by this time cooperative learning for use and enjoyment.

SCENT DISCRIMINATION

At first look, scent discrimination may seem difficult, but it is, in concept and in practice, a very straightforward process. The actual use of the dog's nose is nothing unusual—you could do much the same yourself, taking into account the relative powers of your dog's nose and your own. If you were asked to pick out from among five identical objects the one which had been rubbed with Limburger, you would have little trouble. Your dog will have no more difficulty, for any article which has been touched by you carries, to him, just as strong and identifiable an odor. What you are doing, in this training, is not teaching him to smell, but getting across the idea that the object which smells of you is the one to be retrieved from among others.

In the obedience ring test of scent discrimination, each handler brings a set of fifteen similar small articles, five each of wood, metal and leather, each article numbered for identification. The box or carrying case is given to the judge, who picks out one of each type of article for the exercise. The remaining twelve are scattered within a roughly three-foot circle in the middle of the ring. With his dog at heel and facing away from the articles, the handler rubs one of the selected three to get his scent on it, and then it is placed by the judge in the circle with the others. Turning, the handler sends his dog to find and retrieve the article. It is a suspenseful moment, for the dog goes out and worries about among the articles, sniffing along at one after another until he finds the right one, grabs it, and runs back to his owner with it. Some examine each article quite carefully, even if they have happened to sniff the correct one first, making sure there is not another with a stronger and fresher smell on it. Some will pick up the right article immediately they come to it, ignoring the others. Either way, it is fascinating to watch a dog at this work, and even more so to know that your own can and will perform the exercise.

The "scent articles" used in the ring, as commercially available, come in a variety of sizes and shapes. Some are like miniature dumbbells in the three materials, some are simply small tubes or cylinders of wood, leather and metal. The best we have seen, and the type we recommend, are made in the shape of orange crates without sides and with ribs at opposite corners to hold the ends together. These as well as the other types can be bought in sets with attractive carrying boxes, or you can make them yourself from plywood, dowels, shoe leather and aluminum. If you are doing it yourself, make a total of six of each kind (one extra for training and practice) and number them with nail polish or paint.

Home-made or bought, the advantage of the "open orange crate" construction is that such an article will not roll about if walked on and/or kicked by the dog while working, and, more importantly, no matter how it falls, one of the bars is always in the air for easy grabbing and carrying. It is thus much easier for your dog while in training. We have had considerable discussion on this point with various manufacturers of obedience equipment, whose majority opinion is that "an article is an article" and so there. Their feeling, and we mention this because you may hear it from other sources, is that the trained dog must eventually learn to scent-discriminate among, and work with, almost any shape and so why should he be pampered with specially designed articles? The answer is simple enough—during this training as during any other, you must make it in the beginning as easy as possible for your dog. Let the hard work come later. It is rather like jump training—you can either face your dog from the beginning with a full size jump and tell him to flaming well jump it, or you can work him up gradually from the bottom. However relevant it may be to the above discussions, the type of article we recommend is not widely stocked, and you may have some trouble finding it. Instructions for its manufacture at home, with illustrations, are in the Appendix.

There are methods and methods of training in Scent Discrimination. Most involve one way or another of pulling the dog away every time he tries to pick up the wrong article from a pair or group, until he gets the idea. It seems much simpler to arrange the training situation so that the dog *cannot* pick up the wrong article even if he tries, thus eliminating corrections which can easily be interpreted by the dog as reprimands for having picked up anything at all. To this end we will ask you to construct one further piece of equipment—the article board.

From plywood, or an old piece of carpet, or even heavy cardboard if you can find a piece that large, cut a square three feet on each side. Then fasten four of the metal, four wood, and four leather articles to the "board," with the articles scattered randomly about six inches apart and well mixed up. The "orange crate" articles suit particularly well to the article board as they can be fastened by a loop of string or wire around the lower bar. And the old piece of carpet is an especially good material for the "board" if you are doing your preliminary training inside, for it will be less conspicuous visually to your dog, and when he walks on it, as he will, it will feel much the same as your regular rug. Whatever articles you use, and whatever your "board" material, fasten the articles so that they seem to be lying on the board. One trainer to whom this board was hastily described tried screwing broom-handle clips onto a board and then clipping the practice articles on. Naturally enough training faltered, for the articles were raised inches above the board in a forest of spiky miscellany and the whole affair had no resemblance whatever to a set of articles lying on the ground or floor. The article board does introduce an artificial note, but properly handled it is minimal and unimportant. When you have made your board and fastened your articles to it, let the whole apparatus air off for a day or two outside, and after that handle it only with pliers or tongs, but never with your hands, bare or gloved.

While the board is getting de-scented you can begin to accustom your dog to the three practice articles, one of each material, which you have not fastened to the board. Beginning with the wooden article, first give it to him to hold, then let him carry it at heel, then have him do a recall with it, then a short retrieve. In short, a repeat of your dumbbell training. The idea is to get him used to first carrying it and then retrieving it just as he did the dumbbell. When he retrieves the wooden article well, go through the same procedure with the leather article, and finally with the metal. This last may cause some difficulty, for many dogs object to the feel and taste of metal in the mouth. Some will go to quite ridiculous lengths to avoid picking up metal, as happened at one obedience show held in a chilly, drafty armory. A small Poodle in Utility found and retrieved the wood and leather articles in good order and then was sent after the metal one. Finding it, he picked it up and dropped it immediately—it had gotten cold in the chilly air—and pushed it all the way, with his nose, across the floor to his owner. You may, of course, encounter somewhat less picturesque trouble if your dog simply rebels at taking a metal article in his mouth. If he does, go patiently back over the entire ground with him, if necessary forcing his mouth open as at the beginning of dumbbell training and working up slowly to carrying and retrieving. The metal will not hurt him at all and you must patiently convince him of that, however he might object.

When he will do a short retrieve with any of the articles well in sight, find yourself a patch of moderately tall grass, just tall enough to hide the article when thrown, and do longer and longer retrieves with the article falling out of sight into the grass. If the first out-of-sight retrieve puzzles him—if he goes out but can't seem to find it—go right out to the article with him and stand close to it, encouraging him with your voice to find it. Don't actually point it out to him. Your standing there will make him look in close circles around you until he spies it. Then let him know he has passed a minor miracle, for the impression you want to give him is that you didn't really know where it was and that he did true and noble service in discovering the thing.

Somewhere along the line he will very likely start using his nose to locate it, and this is all to the good. But if he does all his searching by eye, don't try to think up some way to get him sniffing, for it will do more harm than good. That part comes later. Keep at this until he hunts and finds even a far thrown article, but keep things straightforward. Don't succumb to the temptation to make it nearly impossible for him, just to see if he can do it, or to try to make him use his nose to find a well hidden article. Discouragement comes easy at this stage, and he must never be allowed to become discouraged. After a few instances in which you have to go out and point or actually pick up the article, he is going to sit back and say, okay, smart guy, you're so much better at this than I am, you just do all the finding from now on.

If you are forced to work inside at first, the long throw into tall grass will have to be replaced by throwing the article so that it lands behind chairs or tables or any other inside obstacles. The work will go just as well inside as out but takes a bit more patience and ingenuity. Inside or out, work the routine with all three articles until you are satisfied that he fully understands that he is to look for, find and retrieve the article whatever the circumstances. Then you can begin to work with the article board to instill the idea that one article from among many is to be selected and retrieved, and he will figure out for himself that the correct one is the one with your smell on it.

Do not, whatever you do, fall prey to the temptation to try him out in a discrimination before you use the board. There you have all those articles, just sitting around if they haven't been put on the board yet. And it's terribly easy to think, well, I'll try it just once, to see if maybe he won't do it. Believe us, he won't, and you're in for trouble.

This is the function of the article board, to prevent trouble brought about by corrections after the fact. The unscented articles are fastened to the board and cannot be picked up. This is correction enough in itself to the dog—he will discover shortly that only the one *with* your scent can be picked up. Otherwise, not using the board, you will have to correct him time and again as he tries to return to you with wrong articles picked up. Such corrections are no good, and do definite harm, as we will point out later.

With the article board, the greatest care must be exercised in regard to scent. Your body smell gets around astonishingly easily, and before you begin to work with the board it might be a good idea to read over, in Chapter IX, Tracking, the discussion of scent. Just by stepping over the board enough of your scent will float down onto it for a trained tracking dog to tell the difference—so don't think that if you just hold it for a moment it won't make any difference. It *must* be handled with tongs or pliers once it has been put together. True, it's impossible to keep all your scent off it, but the less that gets on it the easier it will be for your dog during this training period.

Observing all the cautions, put the article board down in your training area and stand about fifteen feet away from it, with your dog at heel. Throw one of your practice articles so that it lands a few feet away from the board, and send the dog to retrieve it. All those other articles lying about on the board are a new factor for him and he may just go over to investigate them. Let him go, for this is the purpose of the thing. If he sniffs at the board articles, fine. Encourage him, as he sniffs, to "Find it." If he tries to pick up one of the articles at this point, give him a very gentle "No" and walk toward him, telling him again to "Find it."

The "No" that you give him at this point must not be a reprimand and must not sound even vaguely like one. It is a friendly advice from you to him that he's gotten the wrong thing. Here is where the article board has its use. When you tell him "No," if you time it right, he will discover that he can't pick up the article he is trying for. You do not have to go out and take it from him or order him to drop it. All of the physical correction has been accomplished for you by the fact that the article is fastened to the board—your "No" is just to explain to him why he can't pick it up. If you shout a reprimand he will think he is being corrected for having tried to pick up anything at all and will be understandably reluctant to pick up even the right one.

As you go to him, keep encouraging him to "Find it" and walk in the direction of the correct article. Do as before when you threw the article for a long retrieve—give him hints and clues until he understands what he is supposed to do. Then, when he gets it, praise him highly for doing it. If he becomes really discouraged by finding that he can't pick up the article he wants to, and some few will at this point, get the right article yourself and take him back to heel position and this time throw it quite a distance from the board so that there can be no misunderstanding. Then work your way around slowly to the board and he will have caught on.

If, on your first throw near the board, your dog goes directly out to the article and retrieves it, ignoring the article board, praise him as highly as if he had done some searching for it. The same applies, of course, if he investigated the other articles and then brought back the right one. Proceed with the same throw, using the other two practice articles of different materials, then do your next throw even closer to the board. Keep throwing closer and closer to the board, following the procedure outlined above if he attempts to pick up one of the board articles.

Finally, throw the article directly onto the board, working as before until he picks up the right one unerringly. If your throwing arm is good enough so that you can land it on the board every time, all well and good. If you miss, send him anyway. The practice is all to the good. When it does land on the board, he will have to use his nose definitely for the first time, as he may not have noticed exactly where it fell. Here again let him sniff to his heart's content, using only a gentle reprimand well timed if he tries to pick up anything but the right one.

You may encounter a mild discouragement in him at this point. You throw out the article, send him, and he goes out to find thirteen articles all sitting there. Which one to take? If he isn't really on to the idea of smelling it out yet, he may just stand there and look at the whole affair. If so, and your voice encouragements don't get him hunting, go out to him and keep up the encouragement. Nudge the correct article with your shoe to move it a little bit, and tell him to "Find it." Enough of this and he'll get the idea—you will have reassured him that, despite the confusing appearance of the situation, one of those articles is the right one and can be picked up and brought back to you, and he will learn all by himself that the right one is the one that smells of you. Be very careful when you are doing this bit of assistance not to touch anything on the board but the right article.

The next step, once he is retrieving the thrown article of any of the materials, is to leave him at heel facing the board, go out to the board with an article and place it on the board. Return to him and send him to get it. This first time may confuse him a bit, but if he hesitates to go to the board, swing your arm at it and take a step or two with him to get him in motion. What with the progression of this training, he will probably not hesitate a moment, for he has learned first to get the articles, then that what he is to get will be found on the board—so he will go to the board and begin hunting.

When he is actually at the board, let him sniff around as before, giving the correction if necessary, until he happens on the right one and grabs it. Keep a sharp eye yourself on the one you left there, and when his nose passes over it, redouble your encouragement and commands to find it. That will give him just the extra confidence he needs if, having found the familiar scent, he isn't quite sure whether or not to try to pick it up. When he brings it back to you this time, let out all the stops on the praise. Repeat with all three articles until he has a thorough understanding of what to do.

With all this in hand there comes your, and his, first true scent find. Get him in heel position facing directly away from the board, and leave him at the sit-stay while you go the board and place the practice article. Return to him, get both of you turned around to face the board, and put your palm over his nose for a moment to give him a refresher of your scent. Then send him to the board to find it. This is all exactly as before, except that he didn't see the article placed, and there should be no confusion whatever. Repeat with all three articles until he is sure of his smelling and finding.

Even at this advanced stage he may try to pick up a wrong article. If so, it is very likely your fault. Examine your aseptic procedures carefully, for you may have unwittingly scented one or more of the fastened articles. If so, no blame to him for trying to pick one of them up. If you can't imagine having done anything wrong, you probably did anyway, so don't fight it. Call off the training for a day and give the board a good airing overnight. Then begin again the next day and be even more careful than before. Scent discrimination training will take time in any case, so one lost day will make little difference.

Work at the board until he never makes a mistake in selecting the right article to bring to you, and shows complete confidence in going out, sniffing over the lot, and grabbing the right one. When you place the article, be sure to put it in different spots on the board—it will do precious little good to anyone if he has simply learned to pick up the article in the upper left hand corner. By this time you will be a fairly experienced trainer, and we probably don't have to tell you anything so simple as that, but the things some people do in training are a caution, to say the least. Always remember that this business of training isn't just a cut-and-dried, follow-the-rules proposition. You've got to think about it to get anywhere. And think the right way.

Once he is steady at board work, take the articles off the board and let them "cool off" a day or two, and give yourself and your dog a rest from the training. When you are ready, take the loose articles with tongs and scatter them around in a small circle, arranged much as they were on the board. Stand with him facing away from the articles, and rub one of your

THE DOG GETS THE SCENT. NOTE THE SCENTED ARTICLE LYING NEAR THE BOARD.

THE DOG GOES FIRST TO THE BOARD TO SMELL ALL THE ARTICLES.

He finds the scented article—the one he can pick up.

At a later stage in training—all articles are loose, but by now he will touch only the one with his handler's scent.

practice articles to get your scent well on it—this time it is for business. Leave him and place the article among the others, return, swing around, and send him to find it. Very probably he will do it just as before and will return to you with the proper article.

As he searches among the articles this first time, you must keep a very sharp eye out for a mistake. Be absolutely sure you know which one is the right article, for you can imagine the harm done if you gave him a correction while he was in the act of picking up that right one. But if he tries to pick up a wrong article, here is where your board training pays off again. Just as he reaches for it, give him exactly the same gentle "No" you would give for trying to take a wrong article from the board. He will have made mistakes before, and by now he will know full well that that "No," friendly though it may be, indicates that he is on the wrong track. If he desists, all well and good—encourage him to find the right one. If for any reason he continues with the wrong article, go out to him and let him know that it is the wrong one. Again, gentle and friendly, no harsh reprimands. Keep in mind that, no matter how wrong he may be, he thinks he is doing right in picking up whatever article he does select. If he thinks he is doing right, a strong, loud correction will give him a pretty poor opinion of everything about the training situation—here he went out and got the thing like you told him to and now you're hollering at him. What is he going to do?

Generally, if mistakes are made at all, one or two corrections will get him back on the right track and training can proceed. If not—if there seems to be real confusion in his mind as to what to do—the only thing you can do is go right back to the article board and work with him until he *never* tries to pick up the wrong article. Then return to off-board work and proceed as before. Work off-board until he can and will find and retrieve either the wood, the leather, or the metal article without error.

Now you are ready for the real test—a mockup of the show procedure in which you yourself do not know which is the right article. For this you need an assistant. Putting aside your practice articles, you will have five of each kind of article, all unscented, in some sort of box. Give your assistant the box of articles and ask him to take out one of each kind with the tongs, lay them aside, and spread the remaining twelve in a small circle in your training area. Give him a good lecture first about the necessity of being careful.

Then, facing away from the circle of articles, ask your assistant to give you one of the articles he put aside, carrying it to you in the tongs. Rub it well with your hands, but not too hard. The idea is to impart your scent to it, and if you rub too hard you will create friction and heat which will "burn" the scent off. True, your dog might find the right article by the "burned" smell, but this is not the point of scent discrimination. So rub well but gently. Then give the article to your assistant to place, using tongs, within the circle of the other articles. Turn with your dog, give him the scent briefly from your hand, and send him out. Then repeat the process with the other two articles.

If there are any mistakes, it is up to your assistant to catch them immediately and let you know so you can get in a correction. Along with your lecture on the dangers of careless handling of articles, impress on him that he must be very sure of which article is the right one, for here as before a correction at the wrong time is extremely harmful. Handle any mistakes as before, with a quiet "No" and further encouragement if it is necessary. Work at this practice until you can do the complete show routine—sending him out with no further commands or encouragement after the initial command to find it for each article.

If your dog makes a mistake or two even at this point, give him a chance to straighten out. You've made mistakes even in things you've been thoroughly trained to do, and he is no better than you are. But if the mistakes become many, the only solution is a return to the board and further intensive training until all is corrected. This may seem a tedious path to glory, and it won't be necessary if you have taken all the preliminary training slowly and carefully. But it is an unfortunate truth that the temptations to rush training, particularly at this advanced level, are mighty. You may have done so, and now you'll suffer for it. But buckle down and go back and start all over at the board. The second time will do it, and then it will be done.

DIRECTED JUMPING

This is one of the most impressive things to be seen in obedience work, for in it the dog goes away from his handler and then comes back over one or another jump, widely spaced, as specified. It is a considerable advance over the hurdle retrieve where the dog sits directly in front of a solid hurdle and has the simple task of going over it and back. For the first time your dog must go away from you with nothing specific to do other than simply going away until he hears your command to stop. Then he must do, not always the same thing, but first one and then another, in response to one of two signals. Because it is impressive when done well it has acquired the reputation of being one of the hardest exercises to teach. It isn't. Perhaps we should say it is only as hard as you imagine it or make it. It is rather like the calculus, appalling to contemplate without preparation, but easy enough providing you have the proper mathematical background.

The training in directed jumping breaks down into three stages: teaching the bar jump, teaching the "go" and teaching the directed return. Of these, the easiest and procedurally the first is the bar jump. For this you will need the jump, which is easily made of two four-foot standards and a two-inch-thick bar. The bar you will already have if you were with us through Open, and by the same token your dog will be accustomed, from Open training, to going over the bar on top of the solid hurdle.

The procedure with the bar is almost exactly the same as with Open training for the solid hurdle. Start your dog out, on leash, with the bar set very low (about half his shoulder height) and go over it with him at heel. Then progress to stepping around as he goes over. Then send him over-and-back on lead and finally off-lead. Work up the height until you have reached one and a half times his shoulder height as with the solid hurdle. For the details of the training and corrections, re-read the Open chapter on jumping—even if you trained in Open with our chapter, go back and read it again and follow the methods step by step. It is all too easy to forget details of procedure if you went through them months ago.

Having become accustomed, in Open training, to going over the bar, it may never occur to him to go under. At the very least the concept of going over the bar will not be new to him—all that will be new is the fact that the space underneath is not now blocked by the boards. If he does try to go under any of the times he is on leash you can instantly restrain him and there is no problem. If, as the height goes up and he is off leash, he tries to go under, the problem is minor. The solution is the same old one we have given you for every exercise—go back to on-lead work and concentrate on that until the idea of going under the bar is as foreign to him as walking fences at night and screeching at the moon. The chances of this coming up are really quite small, but if it does, go right back. It's no reflection on anyone.

Step number two is the "go" or "sendaway" in which, at your command, the dog is to go in a straight line away from you until you instruct him to turn and sit. Put him on leash again, at your side, and hold the leash by the loop at its end, letting the remainder hang free. Then, so that he does not think he is to heel, take a step away from him, face him—in general get him to understand that this, at the beginning, is an informal situation and that he need not stick to your side as in heeling. Give him the command, "Mike, Go!" in as happy a voice as you can summon up, at the same time flinging out your right hand and arm in the direction he is facing. Begin running in that direction yourself, encouraging him to run along with you. In play, he will begin to get ahead of you, and now you must time things carefully. Just as he gets to the end of the leash ahead of you, stop and call his name. Just his name. If your timing is right his name will hit his ears just as the leash pulls him up short, and this combination will not only stop him but he will turn around to see why you are calling and what has happened. When he turns, give the command "Sit!" If your previous distant control training was good, he will sit without asking any questions and wait for what comes next. If he doesn't sit (and here again, to the point of monotony, we will repeat that each exercise is built on what comes before; he *should* be thoroughly trained to sit at a distance under all circumstances, and you have no business starting Utility training unless he will) the problem is relatively minor. He might just stand there, or he might try to come to you. In either case, go to him quickly, repeating the sit command more forcibly, and, if necessary, apply the lead and hand corrections to get him to sit. Then praise him for sitting.

When he has the idea well in mind, try it without any moving on your part. Sit him at heel at your side, on leash, and give the command to go along with the arm signal for the direction. If he hesitates, take a step or two with him, urging him to get going, snapping him lightly with the lead in the right direction. But be patient and understanding. To him at this point it will seem entirely senseless that you tell him to go away from you, then just stop and sit with nothing to do but do it all over again. After each sendaway and sit, go to him for praise and return to heel position. Do not, repeat, do not at any time send him away and then call him in straight to you. If you do you will give him the idea that he can come straight in to you, which will cause you endless trouble once you have gotten to the jumps part of the exercise.

When he will go, turn and sit at your commands on the regular leash you can graduate to the thirty-foot clothesline. Work with this, slowly increasing the length of the sendaway until he is going out the full thirty feet before turning and sitting on command. You will have to work a little on your timing of the commands. It is not, "Mike, Sit" all at once, but "Mike" as he reaches the point where you want him to turn, and then "Sit" just as he completes his turn and is facing you.

Watch carefully that he does not try to anticipate, particularly now that you are on the thirty-foot line. If, when getting six feet away from you he tries to turn and sit, go to him at once, repeating the "Go" along with the arm signal to get him moving again. Keep at it until he keeps going until you call him. It may take a bit of sweat, for you will probably have to walk out with him a good many times, even as you approach the thirty foot distance, to keep him going. But don't resort to any labor-saving devices like a pulley fastened to a tree so that you can pull him away from you via a block and tackle arrangement. If you have ever had the common experience of getting a lamp post or street sign between you and him while walking on leash, you will know just how bitterly he resents any attempt to pull him around with the lead. Any attempt at this sort of thing in the sendaway training will end up in a battle, and your entente cordiale may be severely strained as a result. Much the same applies to having a confederate concealed somewhere, tugging on the dog to pull him away from you when you give the command to go. Your dog isn't so stupid as not to realize that the confederate is there—ropes just don't pull one about with no one at the other end—and the first time you try it sans rope and assistant he is just likely to sit there and smirk at you.

After each sendaway, go to him and praise him where he sits. At whatever stage, don't call him back to you as another labor-saving device. As we said above, this will cause large amounts of sweat and agony when you suddenly want him not to come straight in, but over the jumps. Also, if you send him away, then call him in to praise him, he is going to get the very logical impression that it was the coming in that was praiseworthy, and will concentrate on that rather than the going.

The final step, of sending him over the jumps, will require that you have a fair amount of space in which to set up the training situation. Your hurdle and your bar jump should be set up about thirty feet apart and in line with each other end to end. There should be at least forty feet of clear working space on a line between the jumps and at right angles to them. For the city dweller this may amount to a bit of a problem, for it dictates a training area of about forty by forty feet, but there is simply no way around it—there is no abbreviated way you can do the exercise. If you are really strapped for space, look into the facilities of any training classes in your area. Most training directors will let you use their facilities during training sessions if you pay the regular class fee.

With your jumps set up, place yourself and your dog about twenty feet from the front of one of the jumps and six feet to one side of it. Send your dog from you so that he passes beside the jump as he goes, and turn and sit him twenty feet beyond it. Call to him, "Mike, Over" and point vigorously at the jump with the nearest arm and hand. As you move your arm and give the command, run to your side of the jump and encourage him to come to you over it. As he comes, back up enough so that he has room to land and come in to a sit, then send him to heel. There should be no difficulty, with this part of it, for he knows the jumping idea quite well, and he has come to you over the jump many times. But if for some private reason he just sits there you will have to back a half step. Send him in exactly the same way, then move before you call him so that you are directly across the jump from him. Call him to you just as in Open training. Then work your way slowly over until you are calling him from the sendaway position. Work this procedure with both jumps, alternating them. Do not get him used to going over one jump more frequently, or you may have trouble, for on the sendaway he will tend to turn and face that jump.

When he is doing this well, cut down your movement gradually after

THE DOG IS COMMANDED AND SIGNALLED TO "GO."

THE HANDLER RUNS PART WAY OUT TO SHOW THE DOG WHAT SHE WANTS HIM
TO DO

He is sent on his own for the last part of his run.

◣ At the command, the dog turns and sits.

Having walked back, the handler commands and signals the dog to take one of the jumps.

the original jump command until you can stand where you were when he left you and he will go to the jump, over it, and come in to you. As he jumps, turn in position to face the jump so that he can come straight to you and sit straight.

In the show ring, you are allowed to give him another command to jump as he approaches the hurdle or bar, provided it is different from your original command to go over the designated jump. Just why that curious specification exists we don't know, but if you are going to use another command to get him to jump, make it different from the original one of "Mike, Over" or whatever you use. Some handlers like to use this second command, some feel that it merely distracts the dog as he is approaching the jump with the full intention of jumping anyway. Whether or not you use it is up to you—you'll find out in working with your dog whether it helps or hinders him.

From your position only six feet to one side of the jump, now progress until you are standing directly between the jumps (and twenty feet in front) when you send him away. Work from the beginning with both jumps, sending him a few times over the solid hurdle, then a few times over the bar, so that he doesn't get the idea that one is more important than the other. Also, when you have reached this point in training, change ends from time to time, to have the bar jump on the right sometimes, and sometimes on the left. There is nothing in the rules that states which side which jump shall be on, and although the great majority of judges place the solid hurdle to the dog's right, you may run into one who doesn't. So mix it up.

When the dog will go out between the jumps and come back in to you over either jump on your command and signal, you have finished the training, and need only practice to get him and you sharpened up. Try the ring procedure several times. Get an assistant to act as judge, and stand with your dog beside you in position in front of the jumps. At your assistant's command to "Send Him," send the dog away. Then have him come in over whichever jump your assistant designates. Get yourselves facing straight again, then send him again, and at your assistant's order, have your dog come in to you over the other jump. Then rest for a bit and try it again. In practice by yourself mix up the work so that the dog does not come to expect a pattern of alternation. Send him out and have him come back over the bar jump three times in a row. Then do it over the solid hurdle twice. And do the same sort of thing with the assistant giving you orders—a dog is quick to realize differences in situations, and it is quite possible that he will work perfectly when you and he are alone, and then will expect an alternation when a "judge" is present. Don't let him get "ring wise" or you will run into trouble when you do go into the ring.

The one remaining problem you may run into is an erratic sendaway once you have started working regularly with the jumps. Almost without fail this will be your fault, the result of having sent him out to come back over one jump or the other most of the time. At shows you will see the result of this—the dog who goes out and circles halfway back to sit directly in front of one jump, usually the solid hurdle. And the judge inevitably instructs the handler to send the dog over the other jump. Result? Failure, probably, although we have seen dogs recover from the situation. You need never run into it if you insist on a straight sendaway from the first, and mix up your jumps from the first. But if you do, for whatever reason, have the trouble, it requires only your insistence that he go out straight every time.

SEEK BACK

In this, your dog learns to find something that you have dropped while walking along. The ring version of it is necessarily formalized, but in itself the seek back is an exercise of great practicality, being as it is an exercise in finding lost articles. It brings together the retrieve and elements of scent discrimination, both important in the seek back. We have separated it in training from scent discrimination for several reasons—to let him get a rest from this type of work, and to separate it for him from the different scent discrimination work. On this latter point, it would be wise to have an entirely different command for the seek back, different from your command to find and retrieve the article in scent discrimination. If you use "find it" in one case, use something like "seek" in the other to make a clear distinction in his mind. We have seen many times in the ring dogs who weren't at all sure when to look for an article and when to do the seek back, until they actually saw the scent discrimination articles laid out, or failed to find them. So make it easy for him.

The best article to use in this training is an old leather glove, one well impregnated with your scent. Turn it halfway inside out so that it will stand above ground no matter how dropped and be somewhat visible. Prepare him first by having him take it, then carry it, then come to you with it. Then, with glove in right hand, heel with your dog a few moments, stop, and throw the glove out a few feet in front of you. Send him for it in a straight retrieve. Then throw it further on successive times until he has the idea well in mind of getting the glove and bringing it back to you.

Next time as you are heeling with him, drop it at your side, continue a few steps, then do an about turn and halt. Send him for it and pile on the praise, for this is the first time he hasn't seen it go flying out in front of him. Then do the same with right and left turns. All of this is to get across to him that the glove might be anywhere in relation to your line of travel, and that he may have to go in any direction to find it.

Finally, drop it behind you and stop without turning. Send him for it and turn as he goes so that you are facing him when he returns. There will probably be no trouble, but if he seems confused about where to start looking, turn and point in the right direction for him. Work at this until he has the idea that the glove is going to be found somewhere along the line of your travel, then, one time, as you are heeling along, quietly drop it from your right hand (don't toss it in any direction, just let it drop) and walk along for another ten or so steps. Turn and send him back along your path, pointing out for him the direction to take. Progress from this to walking farther and farther after you have dropped the glove, until he will go back thirty or forty yards to find it. Then take one turn between the drop and the send, then take two and more turns, until you can walk in a complicated course after having dropped the glove, and he will be able to retrace your path and find the article and return to you with it.

There are actually very few problems that can come up in this work. If he has trouble getting onto the trail of the glove, you must simply lead him along the trail until he catches on to the fact that if he just looks and sniffs a bit, he will come across it all by himself. In finding it, he will very probably begin by himself to use his nose, but if he works by sight alone don't try to change him. He knows best how he works best, so don't try to impose on him your ideas of what to do. In an obedience ring he is allowed to search for it in any way he pleases, and in practical life outside the ring you won't much care how he goes about finding a lost article, so long as he does find it. And when he does find it, make as much fuss over him as though it were a well packed wallet. He may get the idea that you're a fit subject for commitment, what with being so careless about your belongings, but make him think every time that he has saved the family jewels from uninsured loss. He'll work all the better if it is made to seem less like a formal exercise.

Finally, work with him in your practice ring in the training area. Heel around and between the two jumps left over from directed jumping training, and drop the article in various spots, sometimes quite near the jumps. You will find, in shows, that judges very frequently ask you to drop your article by one side of the solid hurdle, then heel you to the other side before having you send him. But don't make an exclusive practice of this in training or it will backfire on you. A dog has his own curious idea of what is going on in training, and if you always drop the article behind the jump he will expect to find it there. When he doesn't one time, he may get more than a little confused and just give it up as a bad job.

SIGNAL WORK

Working in response to signals is another accomplishment which impresses the unitiated onlooker a great deal, and for no good reason. It is as easy for the dog to learn as working at verbal command, if not actually easier. Signals, after all, are a more basic means of communication than words. It is, when you think about it, more surprising that a dog can learn to work on spoken commands than on signals. If you keep this in mind and forget how impressive it looks, you will have no trouble at all in training your dog in signal responses.

The signals you will use in the Signal Exercises as performed in the obedience ring are: heel, stand, stay, sit, down, come, and go-to-heel.

Heel—a sharp forward motion of the left hand and forearm over or beside the dog's head, depending on his size.

Stand—the standard stay signal, now used while he is in motion: the right or left hand brought sharply to a few inches in front of the dog's muzzle, with palm facing him and fingers extended.

Stay—either the right-hand stay signal again, or the left hand placed sharply in front of the dog's muzzle, palm to him and fingers extended.

Down—right hand and arm extended above the head.

Sit—a forward scooping motion of the right or left hand and arm from a normal hanging position at the side, the hand moving in a quarter-circle with palm forward at the beginning of the sweep.

Come—swing right or left hand out from side to shoulder height, then around to left shoulder.

Go-to-heel—depending on which way your dog goes to heel, the signal is a quick motion of the right or left hand around in the proper direction.

The first step in training is the signal for heeling. In this case you do not progress from command-and-signal to signal alone, but begin again on leash and work with the signal from the first. Here you will see one of the great benefits of the system we have been asking you to follow all along—starting off at heel always with the left foot, leaving your dog at the stay always on the right foot. When you begin your heeling signals, starting off with only a signal, your dog will be so accustomed to moving off when he sees your left foot go that he will in all probability start right up the first time.

Put him at heel at your left side, leash on and in your right hand, and step off, giving the heel signal as you do. If there is any hesitation on his part, give him a gentle snap with the lead to get him in motion. He is no longer a novice at this business, and the slightest snap on the lead, if necessary at all, will get him going. Heel him a way, halt, start up again, halt, and continue working until he fully understands the heel signal, then work with him off lead until he is steady at it.

The next step is a review of your "drop" training on signal. Leave him at a sit, walk out in front of him, and drop him on your signal. Return to him, have him sit, heel forward a bit, give him the command-and-signal to stand, then to stay, and walk out in front of him and drop him ˙on your signal. All this is training done before, and any problems should be corrected by the methods outlined in the appropriate chapters.

When the drop from either position is learned, begin to train him to stand on signal alone from heeling, and also to stay on your signal alone. Begin with command-and-signal on each part, and gradually abandon the command as he begins to understand what the signal means. It is up to you whether you want to use your right or left hand for the final signal to stay; we have a slight preference for the left hand just because it is a different signal. Be careful with it, though, for if you swing your left hand forward to get it in front of his face he could very easily think it a heel signal and start off walking. When he stops at the stand, your left hand should be hanging directly over or in front of his head, so just drop it sharply in front of his face for the stay signal.

There is a variation in the "stand" procedure which you can teach at this time. It involves a different signal, and a different way of getting to the stand position—this time directly from the sit. With the dog at heel position beside you, on leash, place your left hand with the palm in front of his nose as if you were making a stay signal. Move your left hand forward and slightly up at the full length of your arm, and give him a "Stand!" command, at the same time snapping him forward with the leash in your right hand. As soon as he is on his feet, give him a "Stay!" command and keep your left hand in front of his muzzle momentarily. In first training you may have to take a forward step with your right foot to get your weight forward for a snap and easier handling. Later you can drop this step.

As he learns, drop the leash snap first, and then the verbal command, until he will move to a stand on the signal alone, and stay at the stand with no further signal. We give you this method of the stand-stay because, within the AKC rules as presently written, a judge can ask you to stand your dog from a sitting position. As the rules require one signal only, you may be disqualified for giving first a heel signal, then a stand-stay signal. Very few judges will use this lack of precision in the statement of the rules to try to confuse you, but some do, so it might be better to be prepared.

The final steps are the recall and the go-to-heel signals, and both are worked from a command-and-signal status to signal only. In both cases, the signal will remind him of the motion of your hand in using the

THE "HEEL" SIGNAL—
AT THE FORWARD
MOTION OF THE HAND,
THE DOG STARTS FOR-
WARD. NOTE THAT
HANDLER STARTED WITH
LEFT FOOT.

THE "DOWN" SIGNAL
—HAND WELL UP. FROM
ANY DISTANCE, THE DOG
CANNOT MISS OR
MISTAKE THIS.

THE "SIT" SIGNAL—
HERE WITH LEFT HAND,
AT THE HIGHEST POINT
OF THE SIGNAL.

THE "COME" SIGNAL—
THE HAND IS BROUGHT
AROUND HORIZONTALLY
TO THIS POSITION.

leash in your original training, so the transition should be very easy for him. Then you are ready to try the complete exercise. Sit him at heel beside you, start up with the heel signal, and heel around with turns, about turns, fast and slow and a halt or two. Then, on one straightaway, give him the stand signal and stand beside him a few seconds. Then give him the stay signal and walk about thirty feet away from him and turn to face him. Give him the down signal, then after a few seconds the sit signal, then the recall signal, and finally the go-to-heel. And there you have it, as simple as that.

If possible, go through the routine a few times with an assistant signalling the parts of the exercise to you (and read the AKC rules on this quite closely so that you and your assistant understand which parts the judge gives verbal orders for and which parts he signals to you). Be very sure that your dog ignores the signals and commands of the "judge" and is working only at your signals.

Through the point of leaving him at the stand and walking away there should be no problems in the final exercise, except of course the ever strong temptation to give him a "heel" command as you start up each time. Trouble can come in with the succeeding signals, and it will all be your fault—sloppy signals which confuse your dog. He may, unless you execute it carefully, mistake the raising of your hand for the "down," and sit, so differentiate clearly between these. Be sure that your down signal is a quick raising of the hand without any outward motion, and that your sit signal is a definite forward scooping motion. And in the sit signal, watch that your hand starts immediately forward and up. Do not swing it back a few inches to get momentum, as is natural and as you will see quite often in the ring. At that distance it isn't likely, but your dog just could see that preliminary backward motion as a signal to go-to-heel. He might just try it, and then all would be up with you. Also be careful of confusion between the sit and the beginning of the come signal. Improperly executed, the movement of your right hand up to the beginning position for the recall signal can look quite a bit like the sit signal, and he might just stay there confusedly at the sit instead of coming in to you. Make all your signals clear and distinct, and be sure that he knows every one and never mistakes them.

When he will do the show routine perfectly, work in variations so that he does not come to expect the same sequence every time. Although it is always done in exactly the same order in the show, and you could pass if your dog knew only that order, that is not the point of the thing. The idea is to have a trained dog who works at specific signals—not just one who has learned a circus routine and will proceed from one part to the next at any old signal from you.

LONG STAND FOR EXAMINATION

As a further exercise in control, the stand for examination as practiced in the Utility obedience ring is excellent. When your dog will do this well—stand still for three minutes while you are twenty feet away, and allow himself to be thoroughly gone over by a judge—you can be quite sure that there will never be any unpleasant incidents along the line of aggression, in the ring or out. And remember that what he is doing, he does strictly on command. It will have no effect on his use as a watchdog around the house or as a protector of your person or property.

He already knows the one minute stand for examination on lead, and the progression to four minutes off lead (one minute longer than is required in the ring), with you twenty or thirty feet away, is a simple one. Give him some on lead work as a refresher, then, off lead, move farther and farther away each time, staying longer as you move out, until he will stand there for four minutes without moving. Correct any breaks or movements just as you did with the Novice work in stand-for-examination.

The examination you must do, at the beginning, yourself. Leave him at the stand-stay in your training area, and stay twenty feet in front of him for about two minutes. Then walk rapidly toward him, and as you approach him repeat "Stay!" to keep him steady. Take hold of his head and move it gently from side to side, then open his lips on both sides and look at his teeth. Run both hands down his shoulders and down his front legs, inside and out. Repeat all this standing on both sides. Test his steadiness by bouncing your hand on his rear in a half-attempt to make him sit, but repeating "Stay, Stay" and "Good boy" to him as you do it. Then walk away from him and return to your position in front. Stay there for another minute, then return to him, going around to heel position, wait a moment, then release him and praise him highly.

After putting him through an ordeal of this sort, and it is a strain, give him a rest before you try it again. Do not do the full stand for examination more than two or three times during any training session. Then, when he will submit to your examination without your having to repeat "stay" to him as you do it, take the final step to examination by another person. Put him at the stand-stay off leash and this time step out only six feet away and watch closely for any sign of a break as your assistant approaches the dog and goes over him thoroughly. Then increase your distance until you can stand the full thirty feet away while your dog is being examined. Have your assistant approach the dog from any direction, coming up to him both fast and slow, and vary the time of the examination—have him examined almost immediately after you leave him and then keep him standing for more than three minutes, next time have him stand for at least three minutes prior to the examination, plus variations in between. In the ring, all the Utility entries will be lined up and left at the stand at the same time, and the judge begins at one end of the line and works his way down, examining as he goes. If your dog should be first in line, he would have an examination and then the long wait—if last in line the long wait would come first. So be prepared for any combination of wait and examination.

Again, be particularly careful on this that you do not strain the dog's patience and strength. Standing still for four minutes is very tiring. Try it yourself once, standing at solid attention without so much as moving your eyes for four minutes. Then you'll have more sympathy for your dog.

HOW TO BE HAPPY THOUGH PERFECT

It has been the particular pleasure of the authors, when showing their own dogs in obedience, to be stopped by spectators outside the ring after a competition with comments on how happily the dog worked, how much he seemed to enjoy being in the ring and doing the exercises. Win ribbons or not, qualify or not (and, Lord knows, we have been in more than once and not qualified, so don't despair when it happens to you), the dog has worked happily and willingly. This, we maintain, is the goal to be worked for. If you've read through these chapters, the way to that goal should be plain enough—it rests mainly on thoughtful handling, and mainly on praise. Your dog will forgive you almost anything if you are kind and gentle with him, and if you praise him for what he has done, even if all the work was yours. In this chapter on advanced work we have not emphasized it at every turn as we have in others, for you are by this time an experienced trainer, or at least we hope you are. It should come to you naturally at this point.

Remember that always—praise him, understand him, make excuses for him, and he will love you for it and work his heart out. Treat him harshly and the game is up. Particularly in this advanced work, when the frustrations can be immense, keep a tight control over your temper, think out everything from his angle, give him always the benefit of the doubt, and remember that any mistakes he makes are mistakes you taught him to make. Do that, and you will have a happy working dog who will bring you not only private joy but compliments at ringside—a far greater reward than any ribbon, prize or trophy ever devised.

THE OBEDIENCE RING

COMPETITION in the show ring is the ultimate proof of the training of your dog, and of your ability to work together. For successful work in the ring, the AKC awards the degrees C.D., C.D.X. and U.D., which the dog then wears after his official name in the records. He may be "Slugger" to you, but on the books he'll be Rajah von Scharnhorst, U.D., a scholar and a gentleman, with all the rights and privileges appertaining thereto. Ideally, the degrees are awards signifying a certain level of training, even as a college degree is nothing of itself, but an indication that you have supposedly learned a few things. Unfortunately, even as in human affairs, the pursuit of degrees at times becomes an end in itself to some dog owners and handlers. Dogs are brought into the ring when the handler hopes and prays that the dog may sneak by with a barely qualifying score. As a result, we have seen some shockingly bad dogs "working" in the ring, a procedure that reflects little credit on the handler and in fact justly merits seething looks from other handlers whose dogs are going to have to sit next to the flighty pooch. We hope, if you go into the ring, that yours will be there just to show how well trained he is in comparison to all those other louts.

Shows come in two varieties, point and match, and these too each come two ways. Point shows are the ones at which degrees are won and match shows are more or less just for practice. An obedience trial may be held of itself, usually sponsored by an obedience club, or as a part of either an all-breed or specialty breed show. In either case the show may be benched or unbenched. "Benched" means that there is at the show a specific stall for each dog, in which he is kept when he is not in the ring. At an unbenched show you keep the dog with you wherever you go about the grounds. Depending largely on the season, a show may be indoors or outdoors—if benched outdoors, the benches will be under tents and the whole affair looks at times like a medieval fair with banners flapping from the tent roofs.

Match shows also come in all the varieties found in the point show, except that rarely will a match show be benched. The two special divisions of match shows are "OA" and "OB", AKC designations which tell you something about what will go on at the show. An OA show is one held by a club trying to get AKC permission to hold a point show, and the procedure will be exactly that of a point show, except that the results won't count toward a degree. OB matches, on the other hand, are held strictly for the fun of it, under only loose AKC supervision, and may have additional classes such as "Beginners" and "Graduate Novice." For your practice, experience and fun, one kind is just as good as another. And we do recommend that you enter a match show or two before trying for a degree—it will give you and your dog invaluable experience in ring procedure and handling.

ENTRIES

Most shows are handled by one of the several superintendents who operate in the various areas of the U. S. It is from them that you will get your "premium list" and to them send fees and filled-out entry forms. "Premium" is the dog jargon for a small booklet which gives the date and place of a show, the classes offered, judges, entry forms, and various miscellaneous information. To get them, write to the superintendent in your area (write to the AKC for names of superintendents in your area). When you have decided to enter a given show, fill out the form and ship it off with your check. The entry fee may be from $3 to $8, which covers everything, your admission, the bench if there is one, and the dog's appearance in the ring. If your dog is not registered with the AKC or is in the process of being registered, there is an additional "listing fee," always 25 cents. The provision for dogs not listed or registered with the AKC doesn't open Obedience Trials to cross-breds, though. Every entry must be obviously a purebred dog.

Most shows "close" two weeks in advance, which means that no entries can be accepted or canceled after two weeks before the show—giving the superintendent time to get the catalog printed, organize the rings, tents, benches and a myriad other details. During the week before the show you will receive your entry ticket in the mail, and you're ready to go.

When you make out your entry, the question is—which class division to enter, whether Novice A or B, Open A or B. The distinction between A and B in Novice is that in A only the owner of the dog, or a member of his immediate family, may handle the dog in the ring. In B, anyone may handle, including professional handlers and/or trainers. But despite the first-glance appearance of that, we have found that Novice B is the best place to enter if you're trying for one of the four first places (and who isn't?). The way it actually works is that dogs being handled by their owners often work better than those handled by a professional who has no close contact with the dog. So you have a better chance for a ribbon and a prize in B.

In Open, the A and B distinction is the same, with the addition that dogs already having either a CDX or a UD may still compete in Open B. All of which will throw the beginning Open dog up against stiff competition. Here our recommendation is definitely for Open A as the best chance of coming in among the winners. Also, in either Novice or Open, your choice may be dictated by who is judging, but more on this later.

If you have two dogs and are reluctant to leave one home all day while you take the other to the show, there is an entry category called "Exhibition Only" which you can take advantage of. The entry fee is generally the same as for a regular entry, but the dog is not shown in any ring, although given a regular bench and entry ticket. Don't, if you want to take along a non-performing dog, enter him in an obedience class and then just not show up with him at the ring. Once a regularly entered dog has been received at the show he must be shown unless you have the show veterinarian's excuse on the grounds of sickness or injury—the AKC is very strict about this. Any entered dog which doesn't appear at all at the grounds is presumed to be absent for some good reason, and no one will bother you about it—it's your loss of an entry fee.

Match shows are something else again. Very rarely if ever will a superintendent run one of these. The sponsoring club will be in charge of all arrangements, and entries will be made when you bring your dog to the show. Entry fees are substantially lower at match shows, and the entire atmosphere is one of informality. Finding out the where and when of matches can be a difficult procedure. Among dog people there seems to be a sort of jungle tom-tom system inaudible to the uninitiated—word of match shows appears quite mysteriously out of the air. Sometimes the managers of match shows mail notices to people known to be seriously interested in obedience, sometimes culling names from recent show catalogs. Otherwise, it always seems to the tyro to be "Joe told me about it." Until and unless you get wired into the circuit, check with doggy friends, with local breed and obedience clubs or with the AKC to find out what matches are going.

AT THE SHOW

Before you even get to the show, make sure you know the hours of admission and of your particular ring. Admissions stop at a certain hour, and you won't get in after then, even if your dog doesn't go into the ring for several hours afterwards. Check carefully the advertised hours of your class, and try to be there on time. And note especially the "closing hour" of the show—many shows require that all dogs remain on the grounds until a certain hour of the afternoon (generally 3 p.m.) even if the dog has finished completely with all judging much earlier. Don't try to sneak your dog out early, hidden under a blanket in the back seat, for many shows take up the entry stub when you leave. If you've snuck out early and your slip is among those missing when the roll is counted at the AKC, you are in for some sharp questions and possible suspension. The best policy to follow with this, as with all AKC and show regulations, is compliance with the rules, however unjust and pointless they might seem. The AKC's rules are made for a reason, and, believe us, they have a great deal of experience in detecting evasions. After having overseen several hundreds of thousands of show entries, they know every dodge you or we might think up, and then some. They are an eminently fair bunch of people, but when they have reason to crack down, they do so, and hard.

If you're at a benched show, you'll need a couple of items of equipment for your dog. First is a bench chain, a handy device about three feet long with a snap at each end and two loops, each about a third of the way from each end. At the back of each of the wooden stalls (for the bigger and middle-sized breeds at shows), on the "floor," there is a sort of ring-bolt that you fasten the end of the bench chain to, usually by slipping an end through and fastening the snap onto one of the loops. Some pet-supply departments have them, but they will be sold at a booth at almost any benched shows. Don't worry about getting the right length—just tell the salesman what breed you have and he'll supply you with the right one and instructions on its use. And don't use your leather or canvas leash as a bench chain; it is much too easily chewed through by a lonely dog. Something in the way of padding for the bottom of the bench is not a strict necessity, but it's nice for the dog to have an old blanket or something to lie on.

Dogs are benched by group and breed—all Cocker Spaniels together and so forth. When you get to the show, ask the way to the section of your breed—obedience dogs are benched right in with the "beauty" speci-mens of the same breed—and find your bench number. Put him on the chain, make him comfortable, and leave him in peace until just before you're ready to go into the ring. He may be lonely and upset the first few times he's benched and you go away, but leave him be. It's time he got to be a man, and he'll get used to it. Nobody will mind his howls (just wait until you get an earful of your first benched show!) and probably nobody will bother him. If he's an especially trusting and friendly type, various children and strangers may pet and fondle him, but there's nothing you can do about it unless you sit right with him and fend off social climbers. It's just one of the perils of the benched show. No mat-ter how friendly he really is, if he's one of the larger breeds he'll be left alone—few people, other than masochists and those suicidally-inclined, go along sticking their hands into the large dogs' benches.

Benching arrangements for the really tiny dogs are somewhat different.

For one reason or another, including that of preventing grubby poking fingers, the little dogs are benched in small metal enclosures, completely closed in by a sort of heavy metal mesh. There you don't need a bench chain, and you can snap the catch of your bench and go off sure that he won't be bothered by anything but stares and pre-ring nerves.

At a benched show, dogs must be "on their benches, in their show rings or exercising rings, or enroute thereto or therefrom, during the advertised hours of the show's duration" according to the AKC. For obedience dogs the "enroute thereto" can be stretched to include some preliminary practice work before you go into the ring and nobody will mind. But in general, keep him on the bench. At unbenched shows the dog stays with you on leash. For outdoor unbenched shows there is a handy gadget on the market, looking much like an overgrown corkscrew. This you can sink quite firmly into the ground and attach the leash to. It's more of a convenience than anything else; to keep you from having to hang onto the leash all day. It's definitely not a good idea to hook him to a stake and leave him alone, for anything that happens during your absence will be entirely your own fault for leaving a dog unattended. People at unbenched shows are sometimes quite careless about walking about with their dogs on loose leashes, and conflict might easily result.

Many outdoor shows, and all indoor ones, provide fenced-in areas where your dog can relieve himself without littering up the grounds. There'll be an area for males and one for females. Water is always supplied at shows, with a spigot somewhere or other with arrows directing you to it. You may want to bring your own bowl—but at larger shows one or more of the dog-food companies will supply composition bowls. The dog-food people also supply at many shows buckets of their brand of food, and you are free to take along a bowl or two for your dog.

THE RING

Your obedience number, as distinct from your bench number, will determine when you "go on" in the obedience ring. Soon after you get to the show and get your dog settled and benched, check with the steward of your ring to let him know your dog is present and to get your armband with your number on it. The judge and stewards will try to take the dogs in catalog order as far as possible, but if the dog and handler don't appear at the ring when their number comes up the judge is not going to hold things up for them. While they will appreciate it if you are there when you're supposed to be, there's nothing to prevent your coming along later—your number may come up just as you've gotten to the show and your dog may be tired from a long ride, or you may have had no chance to give him a little workout. Stewards are very understanding about this sort of thing, usually being obedience handlers themselves. Nobody will insist that you march straight in on arrival. But once your number has been passed don't expect any special concessions from the steward as far as time of showing goes—the people who are ready on time have priority over you. If the class is large enough to be broken up into several sections for the sits and downs (AKC rules allow no more than 15 dogs in each section) you may even be in a completely different section from the handlers with numbers directly before and after yours. Except for the actual placing of the dogs (in strict catalog order insofar as they are available) for the sits and downs, things are pretty flexible regarding order of appearance.

When you are ready to go in and the steward gives you the okay to enter the ring, march in, get your dog settled at heel by your side on a loose lead, and wait patiently for the judge. When he has finished marking down the scores of the last dog, he'll come up to you and ask if you understand the rules of obedience. You should be able to give him an unequivocal yes (be sure to read and understand *all* the AKC rules as printed in the Appendix). If not, now is the time to ask questions. Don't be afraid to speak up if there's anything at all you don't understand about ring procedure or the regulations. If you think anything is wrong, now is the time to sound off about it. Once you've started off there should be no further comment to the judge unless you haven't been able to hear a command or have misunderstood one. And be sure you understand that, once in the ring, you *must* go through all the exercises, no matter how badly you may do in the opening ones. You might want to go hide, and the judge might wish he could boot you and your unready dog far out of the ring, but you've got to finish what you started. And that includes the later sit and down.

We assume that you've brought your dog to the ring completely trained and ready to display his prowess under any circumstances. If so, and you're shooting for a prize, there are a good many tricks of handling that can help you improve your score, things that are not really so much tricks as principles of good handling. One of the first of these is observation at ring-side before you go in. By watching the routine the judge puts the dogs through, you will be more prepared for the turns and halts in heeling, for where the stewards will stand for the figure-eight, for which direction the judge will ask the dog to go on the recall. Almost all judges will run every dog through exactly the same pattern—and your preparation for the parts of the pattern will help allay your nervousness, which in turn will make the dog feel better about things in general. With this in mind, here is a detailed description of what happens in the ring in Novice, along with some handling pointers.

NOVICE

Heeling: As soon as you've answered the judge's "Are you ready?" he'll start you off, commanding "Forward." From this point the routine is up to the judge, but as we've said he will usually follow the same pattern for all dogs. There will be a few right and left turns, about turns, one fast, one slow. Be prepared for the judge who asks you to stop directly from the fast—some do. And watch for a stop only two or three paces after you've started—some do this, too. Give your dog plenty of lead, enough so that you won't pull on him inadvertently on right or about turns. Many judges will take off for that as "guiding the dog." Hold the leash so that it hangs almost to the ground. There are several schools of thought about what to do with the left hand while heeling in the ring. The right is always held either at your waist or chest, holding the leash. You can stick your left hand behind your back or hold it at your waist or just let it swing free, but don't touch the leash with it. Keep your head up and don't watch to see if your dog is there. If he is, he is; if he isn't there's nothing you can do about it. Have confidence in him. Nothing in the rules requires you not to look at your dog but if you are unsure of him and keep looking for him it may upset him. The judge can in fact deduct points for too much anxiety, as the rules hold the ideal performance to be "working as a team," and in this, continued anxious checking on your dog's position has no part.

Keep moving at a smart pace except in the "slow." A creeping pace won't help the dog a bit. It will in fact tend to make him unsteady and not sure whether you're about to stop or not. We've seen more than one handler moving so slowly at supposedly "normal" pace that when the command came to "slow" it wasn't possible to go any slower without stopping. Usually this sort of handler goes through an elaborate pantomine of going more slowly, but in fact doesn't slow at all. It means a certain deduction in the judge's book.

Float into and out of the fast and slow, increasing and decreasing your speed over three or four steps. And float to a halt, from either normal or fast. Sudden, sharp changes of pace or halts will throw your dog off and cause him to lag or overshoot. Put yourself in his place for a moment— imagine yourself walking at the left of a friend at a good pace. Suddenly he stops. How much chance do you have, without any warning, of stopping dead beside him? And you, we like to believe, are smarter than the dog. True, some dogs have been able to master a sudden stop, but their heeling is uncertain, hesitant, because they are constantly watching their handlers for some small clue that a screeching halt is coming.

Remember to swing your right leg around on left turns, and your left on right turns. Make your corners exactly square, and walk around the about turn—don't spin on your heel. The first few times in the ring you'll be so nervous you'll forget you ever read these paragraphs, but practice the pointers at home and they'll become habit. Remember that you are allowed a "Mike, Heel!" each time you start up from a halt, but at no other time. Don't use any other command or signal or encouragement. And don't praise the dog until the judge has said "Exercise finished"— then give him plenty.

Figure Eight: The two stewards will come into the ring and place themselves eight feet apart, facing each other. With the judge standing at one side of their axis, bring your dog around to the other, facing him, about two feet from the center of the axis. Don't set yourself and wait for the judge and stewards to accommodate you—wait until they're in place and then position yourself. Some judges will tell you to start around either to the right or left first, some leave it up to you. It makes little difference to the final result if you've practiced it both ways. As you're going around the stewards, give them enough clearance so that neither you nor the dog have to brush against them. The judge may ask you to halt anywhere in the circuit, in the middle, or behind one of the stewards, so be prepared for it.

Stand for Examination: When the stewards have left the ring, the judge will ask you to stand your dog. Wait until he, the judge, is placed and ready, then bring the dog around so that he is facing the judge, about eight or ten feet away. Stand him there, give him the stand-stay without further orders from the judge, and move away to the front almost to the lead's length. You can take as much time as you want, within reason, to get the dog settled and comfortable in his position, but be sure to give only one stand-stay command. When the judge has finished going over the dog he'll tell you "Return to your dog" whereupon you walk around to heel, being careful that the leash, here held in the left hand, doesn't drag across the dog's face and head. Stand at heel until the judge gives you the "Exercise finished," then finish whichever way you like, by heeling the dog forward a few paces, or letting him sit.

Heel Off Leash: At the finish of the stand, hand your leash to the steward who will come out to get it. Then, from the same starting point as before, you'll be started off in probably exactly the same routine you followed on lead. Do everything as carefully as you did on lead. Here is where the problem of the disinterested or runaway dog can come up. It's a sure sign of shoddy training and unreadiness for the ring, but it does happen, so here's what to do (but if it happens to you after training by this book you're on *our* list forever). If the dog lags and wanders a bit, keep right on going where the judge tells you. Don't lag yourself in hopes he'll catch up, or pat your leg, or talk to him. That's an automatic failure for the exercise. Don't even look down or around for him—if you're handling properly you won't know until some ring-side friend tells you whether or not your dog was with you all the time. If he really lights out for the far country, the judge will let you know that he's running out of the ring, so call him back and wait for the judge to decide whether to boot you out of the ring or just flunk you. A second time is sure disqualification, so don't worry about what to do on repeats. Our advice, if your dog repeatedly runs out of the ring while heeling, is to turn in your uniform and take up needlepoint.

Recall: Get your dog sitting at heel where the judge tells you. He'll ask if you're ready (and be sure you are), then tell you to leave your dog and walk to the other end of the ring. Tell the dog to stay (this is one time you may, and should, use both command *and* signal) and walk away confidently without looking back. Looking back won't help a bit if he isn't sitting there quietly, and if he is it's tantamount to an engraved invitation for him to break and follow you. When you get to the spot to call him, turn around and face him. Be careful with your arms. Don't swing them around or suddenly fold or unfold them as you're turning or once you've turned. The dog could interpret that as a signal to come, and it would serve you right.

When the judge tells you to call him, wait a few moments if necessary to be sure you have the dog's attention, then sing out loud and clear. We've seen too many people lose this exercise simply because the dog didn't hear the command in a noisy armory. Make it plenty loud. Nobody's going to take off points for a loud command even if it wakes the chickens three counties away. Just don't shriek harshly enough to scare the wits out of the dog. Make it loud but confident and coaxing. Don't make any inadvertent signals as you call—quite a few people unconsciously lean forward as they give the command. Some judges don't mind but some will count that as a signal and lacerate your score, even if in your own heart you know it was unthinking "body English."

If by some horrid mischance he *doesn't* come when you call him, it's all up with the two of you. Don't call him again until the judge directs you to—there's always the change the dog is thinking about other things and the command will sink in after a moment or two. If after, say, five seconds the dog shows no signs of coming, look over to the judge and wait for some word or signal from him. He won't let it go on too long.

When the dog has come and heeled, and the judge has said "Exercise finished" the steward will give you your leash and you then leave the ring to wait for the long sit and down. Don't make any comments or ask any questions of the judge then, unless of course he stops you to make a point or two. Many thoughtful judges will take time then to give you pointers on handling, or to tell you how your dog did, but let him take the initiative. As you leave the ring check with the steward on how many dogs there are to go before the long sit and down so that you can be at ringside when you are called.

Long Sit: When you come into the ring the steward will show where your place is in line. Get the dog seated, then take off his leash and stuff it into your armband and place the works about three feet directly behind your dog. The armband at the rear is so the judge and stewards can tell quickly which dog it was that goofed, and the leash stuffing helps keep the armband upright. You may have to wait a minute or two until all the dogs are assembled—there always seems to be one laggard. If so, you'll know best how to handle your dog. If he's very steady, just let him sit there and wait until things begin. If he tends to be nervous, heel him forward a few paces, and then back around to position to keep him from getting bored or flighty from sitting there too long. It's quite legal, as long as you're set and ready when the judge asks "Are you ready?" of all the handlers in the line. When he says "Leave your dogs!," give your dog the usual command and signal (this is another place in Novice where *both* command and signal are permitted), and walk across the ring to the line the judge has designated for handlers. Again, don't look back, and watch your arms as you turn. Unless you have exceptionally good rapport with your dog (in which case you shouldn't need to stare at him) don't glare across the ring throughout the minute he's sitting there. It may make him nervous and all your silent urgings and cursing won't keep him sat a moment longer than he feels like. If you can keep him upright by pure will alone, you should be managing boxers, human variety, not training dogs. Stand as still as you can, but play it cool and casual. When the judge says "Return to your dogs" walk back with all the other handlers at a normal pace, and don't get ahead of the crowd. If you are ahead it just means that much longer you will have to stand at heel waiting for the end of the exercise, tempting your dog to get up, or lie down, or whatever. Wait until the "exercise finished" before you so much as look at the dog, then give him plenty of praise.

If your dog has gone down during the sit there's nothing you can do; if he gets up and comes toward you, let him come. A steward may take hold of him, or he may be allowed to come all the way to you. In either case, stand quietly until the exercise is finished, then go back to position for the long down. Let the stewards handle any misdemeanors such as wandering or sniffing another dog, unless of course an all-out fight develops. We've never seen that happen, so don't worry about it.

Long Down: Get him settled in the down position when the judge orders "Down your dogs," and follow all the procedures for the sit. The three minutes you stand across from the dog will seem the longest in your life, but once you've got back to him it's all over. If you've done well, it's a leg, one of three you need for your degree. And maybe even a ribbon.

Once out of the ring it won't be long until you know your score if it's a one-section class. Otherwise you'll have to wait until all the sections are finished. After the last long sit and down, the judge and stewards will tot up all the scores and call the four winners into the ring for presentation of ribbons and prizes. If you're one of the four you won't have to worry about finding out your score—the judge will announce it to the spectators. Otherwise, after the ribbon presentation is over, ask either the steward or judge. Don't try to discuss anything else—everybody will be busy giving out scores—but you are justified in asking: 1) what was my dog's score, and 2) is that a qualifying score. It's possible to get a score well over 170 without qualifying, but see the later section on scoring and degrees for details on this. Some judges will give out the individual score sheets they've kept on each dog, some won't. Ask for yours anyway because it will give you a good analysis of where you and the dog went wrong.

Problems and Pointers: If you don't hear what the judge is telling you, in a noisy armory or on a windy field, let him know about it quickly. He'll speak up. And if you mistake right for left, or something else, bear up. All judges are former handlers and have been in your position once. They know you're probably nervous and will do their best to help you along within the rules.

One of the major problems that can arise in the ring is anticipation. The dog comes when he hears the judge say "call him" or starts up to heel when the judge says "forward." There's little you can do about it on the spot—if he anticipates any command even before the judge gives it, there's literally nothing you can do. You can forestall it, or cure it, by having a friend act as judge when you're practicing, giving the judge's commands loud and clear and in as commanding a tone as he can. Wait for varying lengths of time between the "judge's" commands and your own, until you are sure the dog is working on your command alone.

Between exercises in the ring, heel your dog around with you without pulling on the leash or his collar. Although it is permissible to lead him from one exercise to another, it is a sign of bad training if you have so little control over him that you do have to use the collar or leash. By the time you get to Utility it will be forbidden by the rules, so get used to controlling him without the lead.

OPEN

Up to now we have been writing for the complete novice who has either never been to a show or who is having handling problems in Novice class. By the time you're ready for this section on Open, you will have been in at least three shows and will have watched Open procedure in the other rings. So we'll leave out the detailed description of what goes on in the ring and concentrate on handling and behavior pointers.

Heeling: All off leash, including the figure eight. The same principles apply as in Novice off-lead work.

Drop on Recall: Use either command or signal, following our explanations in Chapter V (signal when it's noisy, command if visibility is bad). If you use the command, watch for unconscious body motions—some judges will mark you off for them. And in using the signal, be sure that your arm goes up and comes right back down in a sharply-defined signal. Some judges will look leniently on a long-drawn-out hand waving, wherein the signaling hand stays up in the air for several seconds until the dog reluctantly complies. Some will mark you complete failure for this, calling it a double command if your hand stays up in the air. Be sure you understand whether the judge wants you to drop the dog opposite him, or on a signal from him. If it's opposite him, determine from your knowledge of the dog when to give the command or signal. If the dog takes a step or two before dropping, time your command so that he does down directly in front of the judge. Watch this point in training—he should drop immediately. Some judges will count several steps between command and drop as complete failure. For the reasons behind this, see again the practical applications of the Drop on Recall as set out in Chapter V.

Retrieve on Flat: Be sure the dog is settled and given a firm "Stay!" before throwing the dumbbell. When you throw, throw carefully and well with a technique developed by the practice outlined in Chapter V. Be careful with your hands when the dog comes in with the dumbbell; anticipatory motions on your part might cause him to drop it before the judge says "Take it." If your throw has gone really wild, as out of the ring, let the judge move it if he sees fit. He may not, and if he tells you to send your dog after a bad throw, it's nobody's fault but your own. Don't ask him for a second throw; if he thinks it's in a very bad position he'll either move it or give it to you to throw again.

Retrieve over High Jump: Again, settle your dog well, and be *very* careful of your throw. If it lands where the dog can see it from where he sits, he has every good reason to go around the jump to get it. Try to get it just a few feet ahead of where he will land when he goes over. In case he gets the dumbbell and stands looking at you across the jump, wait for the judge's instruction before giving a second command.

Be sure you know the correct height of the jump for your dog as specified in the regulations—the steward will probably ask you for it as you enter the ring. It will be set up before you begin heeling, so be sure that it is set up right. The numbers painted on the high jump boards will tell you if there are the right number of inches. If there seems to be anything wrong, ask the judge to have it corrected when he asks you if there are any questions. Don't save it until you come to the jump, and above all don't hesitate to ask if there's any doubt at all in your mind.

Broad Jump: Be sure you know the proper measurement here, too. It's not too easy to tell the width of the jump just by looking, but you'll be able to see if it seems radically out of order. If so, speak up loud and clear. Remember, it's "a distance twice the height of the high jump as set for the particular dog." That may not need re-emphasis for you, but we've seen more than one handler come into the ring thinking it was twice the height of the dog at the shoulder. You can get that impression if you read the regulations too quickly.

In fact, a close re-reading of the regulations for this exercise might be in order; we've seen misunderstandings over almost every sentence of the AKC's rules for the broad jump. One of the most common is about the handler's turn while the dog is jumping. First of all, the turn must be made while the dog is *in mid-air,* not before he takes off or after he lands. This is very specifically spelled out in the regulations. Just why the insistence on turning while he is in mid-air we don't know, but there it is, it's the rule.

The turn must be a right face. Here is a point open to the interpretation of the judge, some holding that a right face means just that, exactly 90°. Others will allow you to turn more than 90° to face your dog whichever way he comes in to you. Our advice is that you make an exact right face in training and train your dog to come in to you properly. You're almost sure to run up against one or more "90° right face" judges in Open showing. Our feeling is that they're closer to the letter and spirit of the rules than the lenient judges, so you have no squawk if you're marked off for over-turning.

Long Sit and Down: Here everything from Novice applies, except of course that you will be out of sight of the dog. Don't let your curiosity get the better of you when you're away with the other handlers. The dog knows pretty well where you've gone and he may be straining his head around watching the place where you were last seen. If he catches a glimpse of you peeking around a corner it'll give him every encouragement to come to you as if it were a game. Stay out of sight.

UTILITY

It is surprising, but even on this high plateau of obedience there are still serious and basic handling mistakes made, and evidences shown of grossly improper training methods. Check over your own handling carefully to see if any of these apply to you.

Scent Discrimination: One very curious thing about scent discrimination is that, although the regulations call for five articles of each kind, some handlers use six. In the commonly available article sets there are usually six of each kind, but in these cases the sixth article is intended as a spare and practice article for training. Yet some handlers bring this one, too, into the ring and make things just that little bit harder for their dogs. True, it's a small point, and the well-trained dog should be able to find the proper article from among a hundred, but every article less out there on the ground will make life easier for him.

Watch how you scent the article. Holding and squeezing it and rubbing it gently will apply plenty of smell, but rubbing it vigorously will heat the surface by friction and change the character of the scent. Of course, if your dog has learned to find a briskly-rubbed article in training don't change your scenting method in the ring. See Chapter VI for a discussion of scenting methods.

When you send him, we recommend that you do not follow the procedure you will see in many rings, of whirling with the dog at heel and sending him straight out without a preliminary sniff of your hand. The rules allow you to hold your hand briefly over his nose, so why not do it just to have your scent really fresh in his nostrils as he goes out. It's just that extra little margin of help for the dog that might make the difference one time.

Seek Back: Be careful here that you keep in mind the practical aspects of this exercise, that the dog here is demonstrating his ability to find an article that you have unknowingly dropped in the course of a walk. Almost without exception the judge will direct you to drop the article "behind" the high jump and ask you to send your dog from somewhere on the other side. If you point when you send him, don't point at the article, but point back along the line you have just come in heeling. Some judges will mark you zero for the exercise if you point to the article, and with good reason. Best not to point at all. Don't try to improve your chances by always dropping it behind a jump in practice, for sure as fate you will run into one of the judges who will tell you to drop it in a far corner of the ring. Your dog, not finding it behind the jump where it has always been, may just give up and come back to you empty-handed, or— mouthed.

Signal Exercise: Make your heeling signals sharp and clear. At the end of the exercise you are allowed by a sort of unwritten agreement to wait a moment or two between the judge's signals for each part and your own signal, to be sure you have your dog's attention. Don't stretch it out too long or you may be marked off rather heavily on general principles. Again, make your signals as sharp and clear as possible, and make them brief, just as in the drop on recall. The AKC specifies that the finishing parts of the exercise, the stand, leave, drop, sit, recall and finish must be done in exactly that order, so you can profitably rehearse that sequence in your ring preparations.

Directed Jumping: We have seen more dogs come to grief in this exercise than in almost any other. And the reason is without fail thoughtless training. At the ring you will have seen it yourself—dog after dog will, when sent out, either edge toward the high jump or actually circle around and sit squarely in front of it. And we'll bet you've never seen a dog circle to sit in front of the bar jump. The reason is simply that through faulty training the dog has come to expect always, or most of the time, to be sent over the solid jump first. This is less a handling problem than one of training, but we mention it again here as in Chapter VI because of its importance. *Always* mix up the sequence of the jumps in training, and insist that the dog go out straight to the sit. If he sits squarely in front of the solid jump, most judges will ask you to send him over the bar jump, and then it's up the spout. Even if you run into a lenient judge, what happens when you send the dog out the second time?

Group Examination: Handling errors are few and far between in this simple exercise. Be sure only that the dog is well set and comfortable before you leave. Take your time about it. For some reason dogs break far less often in the seemingly more difficult stand than in the sits and downs.

RUN-OFFS

If you really have an outstanding dog whose work is such that you finish in the ribbons, you may become involved in a run-off for one of the placings. If so, your dog and the other dog or dogs who have tied in score will be put through one of the exercises in your class to break the tie. In Novice it is almost always the Recall, in Open it is the Drop on Recall, and in Utility the rules specify the Signal Exercise. If you're really feeling competitive and want to sharpen one exercise to a fine edge, work on these.

Here incidentally, at least in Open and Novice, is where loud and clear commands are highly useful—in the Novice and Open run-offs all the tied dogs do the exercise simultaneously. If your command happens to be drowned out by the handler standing next to you, you've had it. We know one handler who has never lost a run-off because he drowns out the opposition, although quite without intent to. His normal commands are such as would shatter the eardrums of a hog-caller—in a run-off, with the extra tension, his "Come!" rings out fit to shatter windows, and the other dogs never even hear their handlers. We don't recommend you develop quite such a bellow but do make sure your dog will be able to hear you.

HANDLING IN GENERAL

The operative word here is: relax. Far easier said than done, but try at any rate. Time and again dogs who have worked perfectly in practice will cover themselves with inglory in the ring and their handlers never seem to understand why. Largely it is because in practice the handlers are relaxed, but once in the ring they tighten up and make mistakes themselves. Nervousness and tension are transmitted to a dog somewhat faster than light speed, and the dog's work suffers as a result.

Be very careful about one thing—motions that might be interpreted by a strict judge as extra signals to the dog. As an example of this take the handler we know who was once knocked out of first place in a very tight class because he came to a very military halt when heeling in Novice. Every time he halted, his heels came together with a bang, and the judge took off a point or two each time because of the possibility that these bangings of the heels might have been signals to the dog to stop and sit. They weren't, but the judge has to mark on appearances. He obviously can't go up to the handler and ask, "Were you trying to cheat, or was all that stuff unconscious?" Watch especially for a forward lean when calling the dog either in Novice or Open, and for a sideways jerk of the head or body when telling him to heel from a sit in front of you. True, none of these will fail you, but you may lose points.

One word which we hope is unnecessary: don't try to cheat. Cheating is reprehensible in any sport, and there's the additional thought that in obedience one very seldom gets away with it. Judges as a whole are a lynx-eyed lot, and their ears are finely tuned to the softest of whispered extra commands even at the far end of the ring. Additionally, there are quite often plain-clothes AKC types loitering about at ringside keeping an unobtrusive eye on things. Don't risk a life-time suspension for an extra point or two.

In the ring you are not allowed to correct or discipline the dog in any way. If you do, the judge may fail you or even throw you out of the ring. If your dog has fouled up really badly, all you can do is take it with a smile and resolve to work on that point in further training. And although nothing is said about it in the rules, remember your training and praise the dog when the exercise is finished, even if he shamed you and your descendents for three generations to come. Displays of temper towards the dog are one of the most unpleasant things you can see in a ring, and they make no sense at all. The dog won't learn anything if you yank him about spitefully, and you'll lose points in the eyes of the spectators—they know full well whose fault it is if your training hasn't been good enough.

Match shows are something else again as far as correction goes. Because they are largely for practice and are much more informal, many times the judge will let you go through an exercise again if the dog has made any serious mistake. The second time will be strictly for your benefit though; you'll be scored on the first try. Don't hesitate to ask the judge for a second practice-try. Unless he has a heavy schedule of dogs to get through he'll probably okay it. Here again, though, serious corrections or disciplining are frowned on. Just take the dog through the exercise again so that he doesn't get ring-wise and realize that he can never be corrected while in a show ring.

SCORING AND DEGREES

In each of the three classes, you must qualify at three shows, under a different judge in each, with a score of 170 or more, having received more than 50% of the points for each exercise. The "more than 50%" is an important point, and the reason you should ask the judge, when you receive your score, if the dog has qualified. It is technically possible to get a total score as high as 185 in Novice or 190 in either Open or Utility and still not qualify. It's not likely, but it can happen—say in Novice you get 15 on the recall, or in Open 10 on the broad jump or in Utility 10 on one of the scent articles. Be sure of this, for it would be a bitter disappointment if you made scores in the 180's in three shows and then sat back to wait for the certificate that never came.

Presumably the judge's "yes" to your question about qualification will take into account the number of dogs present, but some people are rather hazy about the exact number required. Check on it for your section of the country—see the AKC rules in the Appendix.

Because of the fact that each of your "legs" as qualifications are called must be under a different judge, watch the premiums carefully to be sure you don't enter under a judge who has passed you. Usually show-giving clubs will stagger the assignments of judges in a show if possible. One judge will have Novice A and Open B, another Novice B and Open A, unless of course there is a separate judge for each division of each class. If you've worked successfully under one judge at another show you generally will be able to enter the other section—this consideration will outweigh other reasons for a choice between A and B within a class.

When you have made your three legs, just sit back and wait for the certificate to come through from the AKC. It's an automatic process and calls or letters to the AKC won't help at all. They have hundreds of registrations and championships and degrees to contend with every day of the week, and though it may take a little time yours will come.

JUDGES AND JUDGING

Judges come in all shapes and varieties—male and female, old and young, helpful and grumpy, strict and lenient. Exactly the same work may get you a leg under one judge and a failure under another. This however can be applied only to marginal performance, a pass in one case with 171 and a failure under another judge with 168. It can be safely said that if you and your dog do your work well you will pass and with good scores. If the judge is hyper-strict he will be so with every dog in the ring, and it won't affect your chances of winning a placing. For the most part judges are eminently fair and helpful, and the score you get will be the score you deserve. Remember always that the judge is the absolute authority within the ring; argument with his decisions will do you not a whit of good. If you think you've been done wrong there's nothing in the world you can do but swallow it and vow never to show under that judge again. Human nature being what it is, there are the rare few judges who have forgotten that they themselves were ever handlers, and if they've had a bad breakfast that day you'll be marked off for blinking your eyes. We say this not as a slam at judges, but to prepare you for the facts of ring life—you may run into one of them. If so, take it as best you can for there's nothing you can do about it. The AKC regularly reviews the qualifications of its judges, and word gets around with lightning rapidity in the dog world if a judge seems really out of line. It will catch up with him, and it's just unfortunate that you had to be in the way before the ax fell. But until the day of judgment, the AKC gives its judges the widest possible latitude within the regulations and there's little use in trying to appeal a decision. You can, if things really rankle, write to the AKC about it. They will take note and investigate.

Don't however, take these statements and turn them against the many strict but fair judges you will run into. We know many judges who judge by the letter of the law, who are as helpful as possible to handlers, extremely considerate, but who insist that your performance be what is required in the rule book. These, we feel, are the real backbone of obedience—the too-lenient judge is not really helping anyone.

Remember, in all obedience, that dog shows are a sport. Exercise sportsmanship at all times, and go into it for the fun of it. Obedience should after all be enjoyable for you, for the dog, and for the spectators at ringside. Have fun.

CHAPTER VIII

BRACE AND TEAM

A DEFINITION strictly for two-dog people, brace work is primarily a ring competition endeavor. Even if you have two entirely noncompeting dogs, parts of brace work are handy as practical training, in particular the heeling and figure-eight work. Too many times people with two dogs have problems with them on the street—one goes one way, one goes the other, and leashes, arms and legs get tangled about until the owner looks like a multi-limbed East Indian idol with the hiccups.

In the ring (and there are no degrees awarded for brace, only prizes and ribbons) the exercises are almost exactly the same as in Novice class, with both dogs performing each exercise at the same time. The dogs walk shoulder-to-shoulder at heel, they stand for examination side-by-side, both come in at the same time on the recall, and they sit-stay and down-stay together. In order to begin brace work, both dogs must be fully trained in Novice work (though they need not have degrees), and brace training consists simply of teaching them to do the work together.

As heeling together is the first exercise to learn, you must determine which of the two dogs is to heel close beside you and which is to take the outside position. This can best be done by observation—walking along with them, get them both at your left side with one in close to your left leg. If the other constantly crowds and tries to get closer, try them with positions reversed to see if they are happier that way. If both want to walk close to you, you will have to make an arbitrary decision on the matter. Perhaps you will want your older dog to work closer to you, or if one works just a little better and is a mite sharper, perhaps you will want him to work on the outside. It is the outside dog who will have to make the most adjustments to the new situation—walking faster on right and about turns, slower on left turns. Probably the sharper dog will be able to learn this better.

The second consideration is the matter of what to call your dogs. If you want only to do a bit of brace heeling for street use, the problem of names won't arise, but in the ring you will find that their own names may not serve. "Asafoetida, Blankinsop, Heel!" is an awkward command, and even with shorter names, the one called first may react to his name and start off a beat or two before the second dog. About the best solution is to use an accommodation name for both, one that they will learn to recognize as the attention-getter in brace work. If both are males you can simply use "Boys" and your command will be "Boys, Heel!" or "Boys, Come!" If this strikes you as a bit cute you can use anything at all that appeals to you, just so it is distinctive—a word they can come to recognize as applying to them.

The third item is the tandem chain, used quite commonly in ring competition. This is a chain with a snap at both ends and a ring in the middle, the chain being just long enough to keep the two dogs together without making them crowd each other. When each end is snapped to a training collar and the leash is snapped to the middle ring both dogs can be guided by one hand and leash, but the tandem is not used until later in training.

With names and positions decided, you can begin to work on the brace heeling. The tandem chain should very definitely not be used at this point, for with it, it is very nearly impossible to correct one dog without also snapping the other, a circumstance which will lead only to confusion compounded. Start out with a leash in your left hand to control the outside dog, and one in your right for the inside dog. Either can thus be corrected separately in the heeling. It will take some getting used to, this working with either or both hands, and there is no way in the world you can practice except on the dogs, so concentrate on your coordination and you will soon learn to control two almost as easily as one.

Get the two of them sitting side by side, and put yourself in the proper place to the right of the right-hand dog. With leashes in hand (your right hand held to the left so that any corrections on the inside dog come from the proper direction, not from across your body) give them the heel

command and start off. Use your leads for whatever corrections need be
given—gentle snaps to urge either one forward or back to keep them
even with each other and with you. Such verbal corrections as you may
have to give, give gently. Here is where control of the voice and emotions
are absolutely essential, for if you shout a correction for something at one
dog, the other will hear it too and wonder what he did wrong, even if
the correction was prefaced by the name of the erring dog.

Go through the entire Novice heeling routine, with fast and slow, turns
and about turns and halts. Remember on the turns that the outside dog
will have to move either faster or slower to keep the line straight. Give
most of your attention to him, as the inside dog will have to do little
more than what he has been doing in individual Novice work. Such corrections as are necessary for the inside dog will generally be in the
nature of holding him back slightly if you slow a bit on turns to make the
work easier for the outside dog. Keep at the work until you can go through
the entire heeling routine, including the figure-eight, and both will work
perfectly.

Now is the time to introduce the tandem chain—keeping the dogs both
on their separate leashes, hook the tandem between their collars and do
some heeling that way until you are sure the idea of the chain between
them, tugging on them occasionally, does not bother them. Then take
off the leashes, snap one onto the ring at the center of the tandem and
try heeling that way. Remember that a leash on the tandem cannot be
used for correcting an individual dog, but can be used only for gentle
guidance of both. When they work well that way, take the leash off entirely and work them through the heeling routine off leash.

The go-to-heel is again taught at first with two leashes. In this exercise,
the "around" heel is far easier for them, but if individually they know the
"left" heel, they need only learn that they must accommodate each other
as they make a wider swing to your left to get into position without
fouling each other. Work on them with the two leashes until they do it
well, then go to tandem and one leash, and then tandem alone.

In teaching the brace stand-for-examination, you can either pose them
both or let them walk into the stand, whichever they have done in individual Novice. The one thing to be careful about in handling two dogs is
the leash—when you return to the heel position watch that the leash does

THE TANDEM CHAIN. WITH THE LEASH SNAPPED TO THE CENTER RING, BOTH DOGS CAN BE GENTLY GUIDED.

not pass over either dog's head or brush his face. This is more tricky than you might think, for the leash is snapped onto the ring of the tandem chain between them. As with the other exercises, start this one with two leashes, and progress to one leash on the tandem.

The brace recall is taught with the tandem on from the first, for by this time they will be used to working with it. Put them at the sit-stay and stand about ten feet in front of them. Give them the recall command and as they approach you, begin to run backward just in front of them. This way neither will forge ahead of the other and both will come to you on an even keel. Keep moving backward, even if only a few steps, until they are even, then stop for them to come in to a sit in front of you. The original ten feet does not give them enough room to become seriously entangled even if they are clumsy about it at first—the greater probability is that they will come in fairly well the first time. As they get used to it and work together, increase the distance you stand in front of them until they will do a thirty-foot recall in proper order, without your having to go backward to straighten them out.

The long sit and long down require hardly any extra training. The only difference in the situation is that they will be sitting or lying closer together than would be the case in the Novice ring. Be sure that your tandem chain is long enough so that they can sit without getting in each other's way too much. In some rings, as Brace rules are somewhat flexible, the sit will be three minutes and the down five, so train them to sit-stay and down-stay for one minute longer in each case.

For any serious corrections in any of the exercises, at whatever time, go back to individual leashes. Any tugging on the tandem will be felt by both dogs, and the dog who is doing right at the time will become confused if he feels snaps on his collar. And with that you have it. Brace work can be a great deal of fun, and it is impressive to watch in the ring, for two dogs working well together are somehow more than twice as appealing as one. It is, true, hard and extra work, and you'll never have a nice engraved certificate to show for it, but the enjoyment can more than make up the difference.

TEAM

Team obedience is strictly for demonstration and ring competition, having no application to everyday life unless you happen to be one of four inseparable friends who take their dogs everywhere with them. In team work, four handlers and their dogs go through a variety of exercises from Novice and Open, all in line and all working much like a drill team. Here again there are no degrees, but there are sometimes quite attractive prizes in the ring. At this writing the majority of dog shows do not have team competition, but interest in it is growing. It may come to be, if not an every-show affair, quite common.

The ideal team would consist of four handlers of the same sex, hair coloring and general build, with four very similar dogs of the same breed.

NOT A BRACE OR TEAM EXERCISE—BUT AN EXAMPLE OF WHAT OBEDIENCE TRAIN-ING CAN ACCOMPLISH.

As these circumstances are a bit hard to come by, there are teams of very nearly every nature, with varying sexes and sizes among the handlers, and four different breeds of dog. If you contemplate organizing a team, try to have the dogs of the same breed, but even that is secondary—although a team comprising a Great Dane, a Chihuahua, a Poodle and a Doberman might strike a more comical note than would seem proper.

Ideally, in getting a group together to practice team work, you should have five people with their dogs—an extra in case of sickness or other inability to make a show. In practice and performance each of the five members of the team should work each of the four positions—thus in case of enforced absence any four can make up the team without the necessity of extra practice. If all five are able and willing to make all the shows, there will have to be a rotation of the "off" man. Team work can of course be done with only four people and their dogs, but the fifth member is a good idea as insurance.

When you choose your team members, if you have much of any choice at all, you will have to consider personalities, but this is no different from any other line of human endeavor. The team members will have to work together in close cooperation, they must be able to learn the equivalent of close-order drill, and they must be able to work amicably with each other and under the orders of the captain of the team. Actually, team work is far more a matter of training the human participants to work together than it is of work with the dogs—everything the dogs do they will have done already in individual training. All they have to do is learn to follow their handlers' instructions while working in a group. For the dogs it isn't difficult—almost all the team troubles and problems are human.

The first training is done entirely without your dogs. Once you have gotten the team together, appoint a captain. Then, under the direction of the captain, the team will begin to learn to do the field movements all by themselves. The first steps are difficult, for unless you have four veterans of ROTC or army service or something of the sort, you will have to start out instructing your members in the basics of close-order drill, walking in a straight line, turning in unison and column, and all the other niceties of common or garden-variety drilling.

The first order of business is to get everyone into line, as at a review or inspection. The proper spacing for the line, with or without dogs, is one arm's length. So, working from the left-hand man, the one on his right should raise his left arm and adjust his position until his finger tips just touch the left-hand man's right shoulder. Then the third man does the same, and so does the fourth. For purposes of drill and identification, the man at the left of the line is No. 1, and the others 2, 3, and 4 to the right. However the line is facing, left-hand is No. 1. This will be a bit hard for your team members to grasp at once, but if you about-face the line a few times and explain it, all will become clear. When the line becomes a file, one man behind another, the man in front is No. 1 in every case. In the course of a few turns the No. 1 position will switch back and forth rapidly from one end to the other, but this way works out best, we have found.

All this preliminary drilling and lining up will be simple enough. If you do it in your back yard, the neighbors will think you have either gone quite mad or are drilling up a small army for an insurrection. But bear with it, there's worse to come.

When your team is in line at the proper spacing, and you have decided who is to act as captain (the captain may work in any position) you can begin your first marching. At the captain's command, "Forward" everyone steps off, left foot first, and moves forward until the command "Halt." People totally inexperienced in the idea of drilling will wander off course, lag behind, or forge ahead. But these matters must be straightened out at the beginning, and the team must work until it can walk as a line across the yard, keeping a straight line. Instruct everyone that the left-hand man, No. 1, will set the pace, and that each other team member is to guide on him—look to their left to make sure the line is straight as they are walking, and when they halt. At each halt, have the members raise their left arms to check spacing. Do this, as a matter of fact, at each halt for quite a while. After some practice everyone will be working together and each man need only check the straightness of the line and the spacing by looking out of the corner of his eye at the man on his left, and will be able to maintain proper pace and space without giving it too much thought.

At first there may be more trouble than you might imagine, unless you were a drill instructor in your early days. People who have spent all their adult lives walking quite comfortably and competently will suddenly develop severe cases of non-control when asked to walk in line with others. Also, some people are incurably right or left-footed—they simply cannot walk a straight line to save themselves. Keep at it, though, and do not try to progress to more complex maneuvers until your four members can walk abreast across your training area in good order.

With this in hand you can introduce the about turn. As all four walk across the field, the captain commands "About Turn" and all members turn in their places and walk in the opposite direction, again maintaining the straight line and spacing. If you want to work out a regular bit of footwork on the order of army drill procedure, fine, but any sort of thing will do as long as everyone turns at the command "Turn," not on the "About." It is a good idea to work on that a bit—the captain giving the

"About" part of the command several times to catch the unwary, before giving the complete command, "About Turn."

Then more complicated movements come in. Here it is a very good idea to have your fifth member act as drill master, issuing the commands as a judge would. If you have only four, the captain will initiate all commands. In the ring, the judge gives commands to the team just as he would to an individual handler in Novice—forward, slow, halt, fast, about turn, right turn, left turn and so forth—and the fifth-member drill master is a help in getting the team used to working to external orders.

The left and right turns are easy—at the command "Right Turn" each member turns to the right in place and steps off in the new direction. From walking abreast, the team is then walking in file. At the command "Left Turn" each member then turns to his left and steps off, and the team is back in line, walking abreast. To get some semblance of order in these movements, you can only practice and practice again until your members work together.

All of these maneuvers can be a great deal simpler if everyone keeps in step, but this is sometimes too much to ask. They can be done if everyone is walking normally, but if you are interested in real snap and precision, get a copy of any army, ROTC or other close-order drill manual and study in it the proper way of executing each movement. From it you will learn how to control things to a fare-thee-well, with commands given on the proper foot and turns much simplified and more orderly. Or recruit an army veteran friend from your neighborhood to show you the basics.

As your team develops competence in the drill, switch positions so that all five, or four, of you can work in each position. The captain should of course be able to work in any of the positions—and the captaincy should remain in the same hands except when the usual captain is the "off" man in the five-man set-up. Everyone, though, should learn to call the commands and act as captain.

Having gotten your team working smoothly together, you can now bring the dogs into the act for the first time. But, caution—don't succumb to the temptation to bring them in earlier. If you bring your dogs into things when the humans are still stumbling over their feet it will make for great difficulties. Bringing the dogs in will be the easiest part of all, for all they have to do is follow their handlers at heel, just as they have always done. Work at first on lead, for the dogs are accustomed to working alone. There will be a little confusion when each dog finds himself not only at heel but with another handler practically at heel beside him, but a very little work will cure this—soon the dogs will come to accept the novelty of the situation.

With the dogs at heel, go through all the routine the team has practiced up to this point. If each dog is a good and steady worker, there should be no problems, except of course with the handlers. Drilling alone and drilling with a dog at your side are different things, although not all that different. By the time the handlers get used to it, the dogs will be veterans of the game, and you can go through all the routines again, off-lead, switching places from time to time so that each dog gets used to working in each position.

If one dog member of the team is a little lacking in his training, or if one suddenly begins to get his feet mixed up, the whole team must go back on lead until the one dog is straightened out. For some curious reason, the other dogs have a tendency to repeat any mistakes made by one dog, and so all should go back on lead to prevent this contagiousness until the erring dog has been straightened out by lead corrections.

When dogs and handlers have gone through the drill to this point, leave the dogs aside again. The next maneuver, the Column Right and Column Left, is easy in the watching but more difficult in the doing. It is performed when the team is walking in file, and at the command "Column Right" the No. 1 man turns right and steps off. No. 2 follows in his path, forward until he comes to the spot where No. 1 turned, then turning himself, and so on for No. 3 and No. 4. Then the file is moving off to the right, still in file. The overall mechanics of the thing are not difficult—it is the timing that takes a bit of work. When No. 1 is making his turn, he necessarily slows his forward motion a bit, and No. 2 is strongly tempted to slow down before he hits the turn to avoid running into No. 1. Trying to keep things neat, he piles up No. 3 and No. 4 behind like freight cars in a collision. When the entire file has turned the spacing has stretched all out of hand. No. 2, and each man behind him, must practice going into the turn at full speed—nobody will step on any one else's heels.

Put all the members through this exercise in each position, and mix up the work as you go along until everyone can perform without trouble. Run a full routine in practice (this is not a show routine, just for practice): forward, about turn, left turn, column left, right turn, about turn, column right, right turn, halt. That will bring you about back where you started, and if everyone has gone through it well, you can get your dogs at heel and go through the whole thing again.

By the time you have gone through all this and stumbled over your own feet and everybody else's and turned left when you should have turned right and committed all the other basic sins of drilling, you should be in a properly humble mood and sympathetic to any mistakes your dog may make. Insist, though, that he heel properly all the while you are going through the drill—that he keep his mind on his work. Particularly while walking in file, watch for attempts to sniff the dog in front of him. Another dog walking only three or four feet ahead may be interesting in the extreme, but he must pay attention only to keeping strictly at your side. But go easy on the corrections, just as you have done all through training. It may be a bit easier for you now when you just might find him working better than you.

The figure eight in team work is. a fairly complicated and grandiose affair, and for a clear picture of what happens, see the diagram of team formations in this chapter. In brief, eight stewards are needed, which may be a bit difficult for you to organize for training. In practice, eight stakes in the ground will work well enough, but we will refer to them as stewards for simplicity.

Two of the stewards stand eight feet apart, facing each other. Another pair stand eight feet to one side of them and eight feet apart, and so on with each pair of stewards. Then the arrangement looks like two facing ranks of four stewards each, with eight-foot spacing all round. To get into position for the team figure eight, the team approaches one end of this double rank of stewards, in file, and walks between the ranks— No. 1 continuing until he is in a position between the far pair of stewards, and each other member of the team stopping when he is in position. With each member in position, the captain gives the command "Forward" and each member proceeds around his pair of stewards in the standard figure eight, taking the left turn first. During the exercise it is up to each member to keep in position with the others. This can be tricky, and can only be learned by practice—No. 2 should keep his place by watching No. 1, No. 3 watches No. 2, No. 4 watches No. 3. Once everyone is working well, the dogs can be brought into it. Start in line somewhere in the field, and by turns and column approach the stewards and get into position. Then perform the figure eight, ending with each member and dog roughly in the starting position. From there, file out in the same direction you entered, closing up your ranks as you go.

The stand for examination can be done by a team either on-lead or off, depending on the rules of the show, so you will have to practice it both ways. Either way, all the dogs in the team must be stood by the same method—the stand from the sit, the stand from heeling, or posing. We have explained all three in other chapters, and if the four team dogs are dissimilarly trained, you will have to put in some time deciding which method best suits all four and then train all the dogs to do it the same way. We will say that the stand from the sit is by far the most impressive when done by a team—it is unusual enough in itself, and the

A Keeshond team, ready to go, in uniform.

sight of the four dogs rising in unison from the sit to a stand is something to see.

When you have decided on your team method for the stand, the on-lead procedure consists of the captain giving the command to stand the dogs, whereupon all four members get their dogs into position. Then at the order to leave, all members step out at the same time and walk to the lead's length away. If you use the posing method, you will have to check on each other to make sure all are ready, as your walkaway must be done together. Then all return at the same time and walk around to heel position—and all members should practice the same method of release from the stand, either a direct sit or a short heel forward to the sit.

The off-lead stand is somewhat more complicated, looking somewhat like the Changing of the Guard at Buckingham Palace. The captain orders the various parts of the routine, and everyone takes his cue from the No. 1 man. First everyone unsnaps leads, in unison. Then, No. 1 gives his dog the signal to stay, takes a step out front, does a right turn and goes down the line collecting leads. These he hands to the steward who will be waiting at the end of the line. Then he does an about face, walks back down the line and around his dog to heel.

When No. 1 is back in place, the captain commands "Stand" and all team members stand their dogs. At the order "Leave Your Dogs" each handler gives his dog the command-and-signal to stay and all members walk away, keeping in line, until they are about twenty feet away. Taking the cue from No. 1, all turn and halt, facing their dogs. After the examination, at the judges' command "Return to Your Dogs," all return in line, circle to heel, and wait for the judge to give the "Exercise Finished."

The straight recall and drop-on-recall are the only exercises done separately by each dog. Each could be done in unison, but the best team going would have trouble getting all four dogs to come running in at the same pace, and a ragged bit of business would result. Therefore, in the ring, each dog is called separately, beginning with No. 1, and all sit in front of their handlers until the go-to-heel is done in unison.

The training involved is almost entirely in getting the dogs accustomed to working the recall near other dogs. At the beginning, space the dogs and handlers about ten feet apart, then slowly reduce the space until the regulation arms' length is achieved. One problem that may come up is the dog who responds to another handler's command to come. It shouldn't happen with a well trained dog, but the newness of the situation sometimes causes it—the problem is easily enough solved, though, by practice and concentration.

The drop on recall is worked similarly. At some shows the dogs are left in the down position, so practice leaving them either at the sit or the down. At the judge's command to call the first dog, his handler calls him and drops him halfway. Then the second dog is called and dropped halfway, and so on for the third and fourth. Command or signal can be used for the drop, but each team member should use the same. Remember, too, that each dog will drop in a slightly different fashion—some dead in their tracks, some after one step, some after more. Each member must judge the timing of his "down" command or signal accordingly, to make the line of dropped dogs as straight as possible.

When all dogs are down, the judge will give the command to call the dogs, and all are called at the same time. The distance is now so short that differences in pace will make little difference. All dogs are then sent to heel simultaneously.

The long sit and down exercises are, even with the team, identical with individual work. The only practice involved is timing on the part of the team members, so that they give their command-and-signal at the same time, leave their dogs and walk across the ring in line, stop and turn at the same time, and return to their dogs again in line and circle to heel together.

And there you have team work. It takes, as we have said, long and hard work, most of it on the part of the handlers in learning to work together as a team even before the dogs are brought into it. Team work is, however, rewarding and fascinating to watch—some breed teams have even gone to the lengths of having special uniforms made up to add to the picture. Others simply decide on, say, dark pants or skirts and white shirts to give an appearance of uniformity. Others dress as they please. It is, however, the precision and work that count, so don't hesitate to try making up a team even if the thought of informal uniforms leaves you cold. It's fun.

Exercises for Team Competition

ASSOCIATION OF OBEDIENCE CLUBS & JUDGES, INC.
NEW YORK, N.Y.

I & III HEELING	II FIGURE EIGHT (8)
(On Leash and Free)	(On Leash)

This exercise will be done on leash and repeated off leash after the figure eight exercise.

In addition to calling the turns the judge will give the commands "FAST, SLOW, NORMAL and HALT."

On command "Prepare for Figure 8" handlers and dogs will take position as shown in diagram At command "FORWARD" do the figure 8, making first turn to left and proceding as indicated below, working around the stewards who were at your right and left at the start of the exercise.

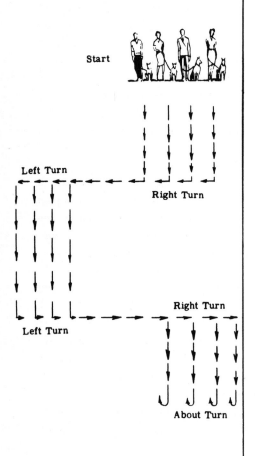

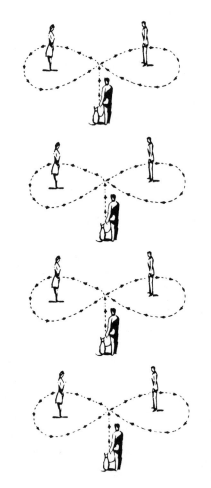

IV   RECALL

On command "Prepare for Recall" handlers will prepare to leave dogs in sitting position and on command "Leave your dogs" will do so and proceed forward until the judge gives the commands "Halt" and "About Turn". The judge will then command "Call the first dog". The first dog on the handlers' right will be called and when it is sitting in front of its handler the next dog will be called and this will be repeated until all four dogs are sitting in front of their handlers. On command "Exercise Finished" all four dogs will go smartly to heel.

Handlers forward - leave your dogs.

Halt - About Turn

V   DROP ON RECALL

The drop on Recall will be done the same as the Recall except that the dogs will be left in the Down position and when the command "Call the First Dog" is given the first dog on the handlers' right will be called and the handler will drop his dog (without command from the judge) midway between the dogs and the handlers. The dog will remain in the Down position until all four dogs have been called and dropped.

On command "Call All Dogs" all dogs will be called in together and sit in front of handlers until the judge gives the command "Exercise Finished", when all four dogs will go smartly to heel.

VI   STAND STAY

The "Stand Stay" exercise will be done as above except dogs will be left in a standing position.

After the judge has circled the dogs the command "Return to Your Dogs" will be given.

Return as in Utility Exercise.

On command "Exercise Finished" all four dogs will sit.

VII   LONG SIT AND DOWN

The long sit (1 minute) and the long down (3 minutes) will be done with no more than 4 teams (16 dogs) in the ring at one time.

CHAPTER IX

TRACKING

Tracking, in a brief definition, means that the dog uses his nose to follow an invisible path of scent to find an object or person. For most people, tracking is at once simplicity personified and the greatest of mysteries. Actually it is neither of these. Almost any dog can be trained to track quite respectably (and mind you, we said *almost* any dog). Once you have mastered the principles, it is easily understood. The training and the work are enjoyable, both for master and dog, and it can be of practical use. They may laugh when your Toy Poodle sits down at the trail of that lost child, but oh when he starts to track!

For the most part, though, tracking is an end in itself. It is a source of considerable pride if your dog can use his natural born nose the way it was designed. Also, a pure-bred can get a T.D. (Tracking Dog) degree at AKC trials, which is a nice thing to have around the house.

Done the right way, teaching your dog to track can be easy enough, even if time consuming. If he already has done U.D. work or its equivalent he has the idea of smelling things out from Scent Discrimination and the Seek Back. Even without these, there's hardly a dog in the world who hasn't used his nose for his own purposes, one way or another. He should know retrieving fairly well, and be under good obedience control before you start, as you will see when we get into the instruction. Aside from that it's wide open.

Above all, tracking is enjoyable. You and your dog of necessity get out into the fields, and are exposed to sunshine and fresh air. You both get exercise whether you like it or not—and a great feeling of accomplishment when things begin to click. There are few greater thrills in dog owning than the first time you see him actually loping along a track, nose down —and he'll get a kick out of it too.

THE THEORY OF TRACKING

Just exactly what happens when a dog follows a scent trail no one really knows. There are many theories, among them one which holds that the dog is able to follow a track by holding his nose half in and half out of a path of scent in the air—getting his directions at turns in the track by the way his nose slides out of the scent path. This sort of thing would imply a sharp border to a scent path, which, as far as anyone can tell, doesn't exist. Yet a dog *will* tend to follow one "edge" of a wind-blown scent, so far as we can tell. We don't really know.

For that matter, no one really knows even what smell itself is and how it works. Some scientific experiments have been done which would indicate that odor and its transmission operate on a wave-length principle. This theory too leaves a great deal to be accounted for. The other senses we know a good deal about, but smell, in humans, dogs, or whatever, remains obscure.

With our own relatively weak human noses we smell. We get good smells and bad ones. After a fashion we, too, can locate the sources of strong odors. Thus far we can see into what goes on when a dog follows a track, but really little farther. Our smell-location is almost entirely on a trial-and-error basis. Comes a good smell of steak, we know it comes from the kitchen. Comes a smell of escaping gas and we check the stove, the heater, and all the likely sources until we hit a strong patch. Sometimes, by poking about a bit, we can even track down an elusive smell, good or bad, by casting about with our noses until we stumble on the source. But following the path taken by an odor source is largely beyond our comprehension.

Imagine, if you will, some strong smell that appeals to you particularly. Steak, or fried fish, or whatever. Then imagine again that someone has gone ahead of you in an open field with a platter of whatever it is, walking at random, making turns and twists for a quarter of a mile. Then, half an hour later, it's your job to follow the path that person took and end up wherever he laid the platter down. Pretty difficult to imagine even how to start. And that's the job that faces a dog in tracking.

Without knowing exactly what smell is, we have found out quite a bit about how it operates, and how a track is laid. When a person walks across a field, some of his personal smell is left on the ground by his shoes. More of it descends from his body (this smell-stuff, whatever it is, seems to be heavier than air) and is left on the ground and in the air where he has passed. It stays there or thereabouts for a surprisingly long time. Really good tracking dogs have been known to follow a track as much as a week old under good conditions.

On a still, calm day, the scent stays pretty much where it was laid, getting fainter and more dispersed as time goes on. Heavy rain will wash it away, but a light shower may actually freshen it. Winds will push it this way and that. Later in this chapter we will go more thoroughly into the effects of winds and terrain on a track. For the moment, though, suffice it to say that a track, once laid, is astonishingly permanent and can be followed by a trained dog even if half a dozen different tracks and scents have been laid over it more recently.

This power of distinguishing is one of the most interesting and baffling factors in tracking. The dog without question follows a specific, to him identifiable, scent—and not just a strong smell of indeterminate nature. Not only that, but he can distinguish readily between two tracks, one older than the other, laid by the same person. He even seems able to detect the difference in strength of smell between one footstep and the following, for a tracking dog seldom backtracks. Put a dog on the middle of a trail, and he will head in the direction the tracklayer went, rather than where he came from.

The falling air-scent of a person comprises the greater part of the track, contrary to popular mythology. A trained dog can follow a track laid by a person wearing rubber-soled shoes, galoshes, or rubber hip-boots for that matter. Leather shoes, well impregnated with a personal smell, will leave a slightly stronger track by their contact with the ground, but leather shoes are far from a necessity, except in early training. Some dogs even track with their heads quite high in the air, giving the appearance of going for a casual stroll, with none of the B-movie business of snuffling along the ground and baying hideously. They work on the higher body smell left hanging in the air. Others do work with noses close to the ground, but here it is less the influence of the smell of the shoe leather than the fact that the heavier odor tends to collect at ground level and leaves a stronger track. So if you plan to work the other end of this business, don't bother to include gum-soled shoes in your escape budget. It doesn't do a bit of good.

One item that popular opinion and the Sunday Supplements have largely right is the effect of water on a track. If a tracklayer crosses a fast-running stream he will confuse a tracking dog, but only momentarily. The air currents above moving water tend to carry scent and everything right along with them. If the dog comes along a few hours later, the scent that was left above the water may be in the next county by that time. There is also the fact that anyone crossing more than a minor stream without a boat handy swims across, leaving little or no scent. But if the tracklayer exits from a stream directly across from where he entered, he might as well not have bothered. The dog and his handler, when faced with a track that ends at a stream, simply go across and see if a track is to be picked up on the other side. In a serious case, as with a lost person involved, the dog and handler will cast up and down the far side of the stream for a mile or more to find the spot where the tracklayer came out.

When a dog is about to begin a track, for business, pleasure or competition, he has to get the scent he is to follow. The stock scene of giving the dog a shoe or other article of the tracklayer is quite valid in the business cases. It tells him what to look for, and then he is shown where the track begins, or set to looking for a track. In pleasure and competition tracking, the tracklayer scuffles around a bit at the start of the track, leaving an area well impregnated with his scent, and the dog is given this area as his clue. From then on he is on his own. If he knows what he's about, and you've trained him well, he'll get to the end of the track through sleet and snow. All the theory in the world won't do him or you a bit of good. Let him have his head and be ready to move fast behind him.

TRACKING EQUIPMENT

The special equipment required for tracking training is quite inexpensive. You need, first of all, a tracking harness. This is much like a regular walking harness. The main idea of the tracking harness is to put the strain of pulling at the tracking line on the dog's chest. A walking harness will do this to some extent, but a real tracking harness is better, if it is at all possible for you to lay your hands on one, or have one made.

Second, you should have a tracking line—a light leash 30 to 60 feet long. This sounds like a great deal, but 60 feet is the ideal length. There are on the market standard light webbing leashes for the purpose, or you can get a light length of nylon clothesline and put a snap on one end. However you acquire your tracking line, tie a knot in it 30 feet from the snap. This is to let you know by feel when the dog is working 30 feet away from you—not only a good optimum distance when tracking, but also an AKC regulation if you happen to try for an official tracking degree.

Next, two track flags, which are easy enough to make. They should be of quarter to half inch dowel, approximately four feet long and sharpened on one end for ramming into the ground. Onto the other end fasten a square of some material—the bigger the better up to 18 inches square. These two flags are used to mark out the beginning of your practice tracks. They are important for two reasons—it is highly important that you remember exactly where the track goes, and they will get the dog used to working next to flapping flags if he ever tracks in competition.

Half a dozen "turn stakes" also come in handy. These are easily made from green bamboo garden sticks, three to four feet long, available at any garden store. Again, sharpened at one end—and on the other a small bit of bright material wrapped around tightly (not flapping loose, as in the starting flags) so that you can see them at a distance in a green field. These stakes are used to mark the turning points in practice tracks—visible to you, but to the dog looking just like something growing there. Fortunately for training in this case, dogs are color blind, and are not likely to notice the colored material at the top, be it even blinding red. But the stakes themselves should be green, or close thereto. Color-blind or not, the dog does see varying shades of white, gray and black, and a white dowel used as a turn stake will attract his attention.

Finally, you need an "article" for the dog to find at the end of the track. Generally, this is an old glove. A glove is ideal; it is small, hard to see lying in grass, and probably has been soaking for years in your scent.

Other articles are all right if you've given all your old gloves to the Salvation Army. An old sock rolled up isn't bad—some use an old wallet, or even a cheap new one from the dime store, thoroughly scented before using.

In the final analysis, none of these things, except for the article, is drastically necessary for the early stages of tracking training—the dog could be trained at first using a normal collar and a lead, no flags at all and not a stake in sight. But we wouldn't guarantee it. The first day or two out in the field you might want to try it with just a collar and short lead to see how things go before putting money into harness and tracking line. We don't recommend it, but if you want to try it that way, go ahead. Where we say "harness" in the first stages, read "collar"— but if it's a choke collar, be sure to fasten your snap on the "dead" ring so your dog isn't choking himself when he strains to pull along the track.

TRACKING EQUIPMENT—TWO FLAGS, TRACKING LEAD AND HARNESS, AND TURN STAKES (YOU MAY NEED ONLY TWO OF THESE).

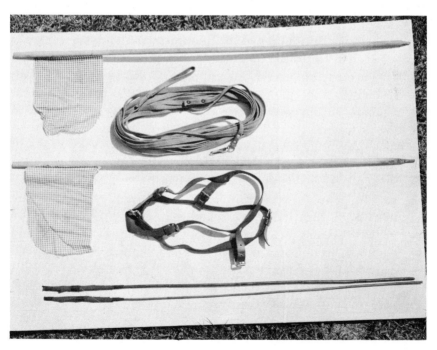

THE FIRST STAGES

The harness and line will be new factors to the dog. If he's well trained, and pretty well resigned to various kinds of foolishness from you, he may not react to them at all. Find out first, though, before you start to work. Operate just as if he were a puppy with his first collar, letting him get used to the thing before you strap it on him. And then let him romp and play a bit with the harness on, to get accustomed to it. Next step—fasten on the tracking line, and let him drag that around for a little. When you're actually tracking you'll find it impossible to keep 30 to 60 feet of line off the ground, and in fact you shouldn't try to. So let him get used to the idea of all that line dragging behind him and at times snagging on things. Here we don't anticipate any trouble, as most dogs work quite happily as soon as a harness is put on. But if you have one of the rare problem cases, just stick with it, slow and easy and cajolingly until he gets used to it.

Once he has gotten used to it, the harness should be kept strictly for business. Put it on him when you are ready to start work, take it off when you take a break, and take it off as soon as you have finished working for the day. To him the harness should mean that the time for tracking has come—when he has it on he is to work, and no nonsense.

As soon as the dog doesn't mind the harness and line, you are ready for the first step. This is the point which to most people seems hardest of all, but is actually the easiest. All his life your dog has been using his nose for his own divers purposes, to identify friend and foe, to see where you've been by sniffing your clothes and shoes when you come in. Now you're going to almost trick him into using it to follow a trail. Perhaps we can best explain it by using you as an example.

Whenever, in the past, you've wanted to find a bakery, you've gotten there by means of addresses and signs in the window. And at the same time you've undoubtedly mouth-watered at the wonderful and unmistakable smell of fresh bread, cakes and rolls. Suppose, now, that you were blindfolded and led down a strange street in which there was a bakery with an open door. Think you could find it? You could, and without straining a bit—yet you've probably never thought of trying to find a bakery by smell alone.

This is pretty much what you're going to do with your dog now. From visual finding of something with your smell on it, along a strong trail of your own odor, you're going to nudge him into scent finding. Remember, you're not teaching your dog to smell—you're just teaching him a new way to use the talent he's had all his life.

At the beginning, it's a big help if you have someone else along with you in the field to lay out the flags and stakes you'll use for the track you'll lay, but it isn't essential. If you can manage to start training along with another handler, the two of you can reciprocate in stake-planting. If an assistant does all the handling and placing of stakes, they won't have your scent on them and the dog won't be tempted to try to retrieve them. But again, it's not strictly necessary, so if you have to do your initial training alone, go to it.

Select an open field somewhere—as big as you can find. This will be a problem for urbanites, but a little judicious investigation should turn up a promising area not too far from where you live. Ask at farmhouses and the like—if you can establish your bonafides and make an interesting story of tracking training you should be able to get permission to use an empty field. But whatever you do, and this we cannot emphasize too strongly, take care of that field like a putting green. Any littering or damage will end your use of it, and ruin it and the entire neighborhood for anyone else who may want to use fields for tracking, picnicking or anything else.

If you have any choice at all, pick a flat field with no trees and bushes, and with grass about ankle high. At least avoid as many obstacles as possible, and keep an eye out for such natural hazards as low-lying brambles, poison ivy and other bucolic flotsam. Before you go out field hunting, we recommend a reading of the section on "Scent and Tracks" so that you'll be able to avoid some of the worst barriers to tracking success.

When you have the field in hand, take a good reading of the prevailing wind. This is best done, not with the traditional wetted forefinger raised, but by dropping some dried grass and chaff to see which way it blows. This bit of advice may seem superfluous if you're an old woodsman, but you'd be surprised how many city dwellers can't tell which way the wind is blowing until their hats go rolling down the street to leeward.

Set up shop in the downwind side of the field, about thirty feet from the edge—and don't let your dog play about in the field before you settle down to work. Plant your first flag in the ground. Walk thirty feet straight into the wind and plant the second flag (in a Tracking Test, the flags will always be 30 yards apart). Then walk back straight along the line to the first flag and the dog. Get your article ready and you're off.

This day, and all through your beginning, we recommend that you wear leather shoes, despite our introductory remarks about leather vs. rubber. True, to a trained tracking dog it makes little never mind whether the tracklayer has been shod in rubber or leather. But a leather sole does leave a slightly stronger scent along the ground, and you want to throw every advantage to the dog in the beginning. So stick to leather at first.

With the dog at heel beside you—you on his right and the starting flag on his left—throw the glove about halfway to the second flag. Send him for it, harness and all, and shower him with praise when he retrieves it for you. Then throw it out a little farther and send him again. Keep this up until he has retrieved it a time or two from as far away as you can throw it.

All this, of course, presupposes the dog to be trained in the retrieve. If for any reason you are trying to teach a dog tracking who does not have the basic obedience training preceding this chapter, we can only refer you to the appropriate section of this book, in this case "Open," and tell you to go back a step and teach him to retrieve, starting with the dumbbell. And of course learning the retrieve depends on the dog knowing the sit-stay, so if yours is completely untrained at this point, back you'll go right to "Basic Training." Rare indeed is the handler who will try to train his dog in tracking before anything else, but if it happens to be you, this is as good a place as any else to point out again that all training, including tracking, is built up pyramidally on the foundations of the work that has gone before. We don't mean to say that he must be ring trained, or even obedience trained as we define it—but to follow our method of tracking training he must be able to do a controlled retrieve of one kind or another.

If the dog is well up on his retrieve, you may at this point run into a momentary problem with the flags. Some few dogs, of almost any size, will be put off by the flapping. If it happens to you, don't try to force him to retrieve by the flags until you've heeled him in a figure-eight around the flags to get him used to them. Then, give him a few retrieves away from the flags, slowly working him back until he is going out right by them without minding. Of course, after this, change your flags to a new location before starting work again, as this area will be well churned up with scent in all directions.

As soon as the dog has done the few retrieves as far as you can throw the article along the line of the flags, you are ready for the second step—beginning to lay a heavy path of your own scent leading to the article. Have him sit and stay just back of the first flag. Walk directly past the second flag about ten feet, drop the glove (and be sure he's watching you do it—make a production of it if necessary) and walk back directly to him. Snap on the line and be sure it is lying free and unkinked on the ground behind him. Don't try to carry it coiled up, cowboy style, in your hand. Then give him a command to lie down— having placed him first so that when he goes down his nose will be close by the first flag. This means little in actual practice at this time, but it is the pattern for future tracking and you may as well start establishing it now.

Putting him down at the start of the track is done to get his nose close to the beginning of the scent. Some trainers and handlers advocate going further—actually holding the dog's head down so that his nose is millimeters from the ground. We don't like this procedure largely because it is totally unnecessary. There is plenty of odor a few inches from the ground where the dog's head will normally be at the down— and forcing his head down for, say, thirty seconds is an imposition on the dog just at the time when you want his wholehearted cooperation.

When he has been at the down for a few seconds, take hold of the line about six inches from the harness, and as you give him the command to get the glove, urge him along in the right direction. The command you use here should be different from any other obedience command— "Seek" or "Track" are both good. Do anything within reason to get him moving out after the glove. Fling out your free arm in the proper direction—begin yourself along the route—give him the command again and again coaxingly—guide him a few feet by the harness. Generally, after having gone through the free retrieve along the track and having seen you go out to drop the glove, he will charge right off to get it this time.

Once he's going, let the line slip through your hand and stand still while he gets the glove and returns to you with it. Next time, clamp down on the line just slightly so that he has to pull a very little as he's going. If he's so well leash trained that a slight pressure stops him, encourage him to go on—and on successive tries increase the pressure as he goes out until you have control of the situation. But don't make it too hard for him, and don't force him to a dead stop just yet. Just get him used to the idea of pulling against the harness as he goes after the article.

Increase the distance by ten-foot steps until you are going out 70 to 80 feet to drop the glove. Stop calling his attention to the fact that you are dropping it. At that distance a dog's sight is not too good anyway, and at 80 feet about all he will know is that you went out with the glove and came back empty handed. When he goes out on these longer retrieves, let the line slip through your hand until you feel the 30-foot knot, then begin to apply light pressure and go along behind the dog. Vary the distance between you from 30 feet to the end of the line, depending on how fast he is going out. When he gets the article and runs back to you with it, praise him highly each time, of course, then take it and go along with him back to the starting flag—being careful yourself to walk back along the straight-line track, no matter if he wanders beside you off the track.

By the time he's going out 80 feet for the article, he may already have started using his nose to find it. In most cases he will have, so you must be careful about your handling of him and the line. Important: don't restrain him or call him back to you if he does not go out exactly along the line of the track as you've laid it. Even into the wind, and particularly if there's any cross wind at all, the dog may be working a scent that has blown a good distance away from where you walked. As long as he's going approximately in the right direction, let him go. He may in fact travel in a wide semi-circle from starting point to the article. If so, let him go. It is of the greatest importance at this point that the dog not become discouraged about tracking—and nothing will discourage him more, than you pulling him off a track that he was happily and correctly following.

At this point, too, it would be well to re-emphasize the essential fact that no dog in the world can be coerced into learning tracking. Tracking is, more than any other thing he does, a gesture of good will from the dog to you, and he'll only learn it on a foundation of obedience and respect. Aside from that, it's fun for him when he's handled correctly—as witness the fact that every puppy in the world loves nothing better than to chase things and find them. But the dog absolutely cannot be forced into tracking. Just about the first time you scream at him, or belt him, he's going to turn in his uniform and head for the showers. And if anyone thinks they can make a dog track by gritting at him, "Smell, dammit, smell"—well, we hope they never offer their dog's services when we get lost in the woods.

Therefore—if your dog seems to be having difficulties on these first easy retrieves, the only solution is patience, praise and a willingness to think out the difficulties and to go back over each step until the dog has the idea down. When and if you run into trouble, sit down and ponder on where it was that you made the mistake—*he* hasn't made any mistakes in training. And whatever you do, don't try to rush tracking training. Take each step slowly and don't go on to the next until you are absolutely sure that your dog has mastered the one in hand. Too fast progression may only confuse him, and then you've had it.

If the dog is beginning to use his nose on the longer straight runs—and as we've said, most of them will have—you'll run into a few minor points in handling aside from the temptation to pull him off when he's not searching dead in your footsteps. Among them is the problem of what to do with all that line. One of the most common mistakes of the beginning handler is trying to keep the line too short, and in the air. If the dog is loping along after the article, you should be working 30 feet or more behind him. Unless he's pulling quite hard, part of the line will be on the ground. Then, suddenly, he will seem to lose the scent, and will circle around trying to find it again. He will in all probability come right back up to you as he searches for the scent. When he does this, don't try to keep the line straight between you and him. Just hold onto it wherever you were holding when he stopped going straight ahead and let it lie on the ground. He'll walk over it and won't get tangled up. Then, when he's off on the trail again you can either let him take up the slack himself or close it up a bit yourself. If you try to keep pulling it in as he wanders it will almost inevitably get fouled up in his legs, and then the panic is on for fair. Just let it lie. This takes a bit of practice and self-control, but you'll catch on almost as quickly as he does.

The other greatest beginner's mistake is a feeling of horror when he does circle back to you in looking for a lost scent. The immediate reaction is: lordy, here he comes—he'll get a great big fresh whiff of me and then the track I laid will seem like nothing to him. It isn't so, for some reason we can't fully explain. Even if he brushes right by you, getting a really ripe nosefull of just the scent he's looking for on the ground, it won't confuse him. He'll just ignore it. Probably it's because he knows full well *you* don't have the glove—and he knows that the glove does lie at the end of that older scent trail. Whatever it is, coming near you or passing behind you on the track won't bother him at all. He'll hunt until he finds the original track, put his nose down, and off he'll go until he finds the glove.

When he does do this circling to re-find the track, stand right where you were when he lost it. Play out the lead if necessary, and let him cast around until he comes across it again. If you yourself move about with him, chances are you will both wander away from the track, and you will lose it. In the early stages, it is vital that you remember where it is, and give him help and encouragement in finding it again. With you standing still and letting him cast around you in a circle, he is sure to cross the track again at two points, and will pick it up more surely.

What you've been doing all this time, walking back and forth over the same path, is laying down a really powerful path of your own odor. Each time you walk over it you reinforce it until it has become the dominant impression the dog receives as he runs out along that line to get the glove. Every time he goes out along the right line his nose is filled with your scent. Then, the first time he's not sure by sight of where the glove is—and wanders off the true trying to find it—the great light will dawn. By that time the two factors, the glove and your scent along the ground, will be closely joined in his mind. He'll hunt back until he finds the scent trail, follow it, and lo—there is the glove, giving off a slightly stronger scent of you to lead him on the last few feet.

The moment he first makes the connection is monumental—when he first puts his nose down and begins sniffing the trail. It is one of the greatest thrills of dog owning and training. And from that moment on, the procedure of tracking training is simply one of extension of that discovery of his, and practice under increasing amounts of difficulty.

THE FIRST TURN

Provided you have the space in your training field, you should continue your straight line tracks until the dog will go out 200 feet to find the article dropped there by you, working with his nose all the time, and retrieve it without fail. When he can do that to your satisfaction (and that is probably as far as you will get on your first training day) you are ready for a turn in the track.

Here is where the turn stakes come into use. If possible, have an assistant go out about 210 feet beyond the starting flags and place a turn stake there. Wait 20 or 30 minutes to let his track cool off a bit. Then, with your article in hand and the dog waiting by the first flag, walk out along the line until you are 10 feet or so from the stake and make a turn to the right or left. Try to make this turn beyond the last spot you left the glove in the straight line tracks—otherwise there'll be some leftover scent carrying him past the turn and he'll get confused even more than necessary. Walk about 15 feet in the new direction, drop the article, then walk back directly over your path to the dog.

If you're working alone, go out the 200 feet carrying both article and stake. Sink the stake and make your turn right there. Unless you have to place them yourself, though, make all your turns well away from the stakes—keeps the dog from catching on that turns are to be made at stakes.

Down your dog at the beginning of the scent, right by the first flag, then give him the command to get the article. He'll go sniffing along the path until he comes to where you made your turn and probably keep right on going a few feet before he realizes that the scent has stopped dead. Then comes your first real handling in tracking, for now you must control him via the line while he learns that all tracks do not invariably go in a straight line in this best of all possible worlds.

This takes a bit of skill and practice. When he comes to where you made the turn (and this is the purpose of the stakes—so you'll know exactly where the turn is) you should be 40 or 50 feet behind him on the line. He will be pulling hard on the harness, and when you see him overshoot the turn you can bring him to a halt with not much extra pressure on the line. However, and heed this most carefully, be *absolutely sure* that he is well beyond the turn and off the track before you bring him to a stop. A vagary of the wind may have blown your scent 10 or 20 feet ahead of where you actually turned, and he may still be working a legitimate scent even if he is that far past the turning spot.

When he finally has run out of scent, either directly at the turn or beyond it, he will appear confused for a moment, or he may immediately begin to circle, or "cast," to find out where the scent went. If he appears confused it is because he didn't find the article at what, to him, is the end of the track. Be sure to urge him on encouragingly here—coax him with the "Find It" command. This keeps him working, and lets him know that it's perfectly all right that he didn't find it where he expected to. Otherwise, if he walks out to the end of that straight line, finds nothing, and you just let him stand there, he may think he's gotten a bad shuffle this time around.

Most dogs, running out of scent, *will* begin to cast for the track. Whether he moves in a circle toward or away from where you know the new "leg" to be, stand where you are and let him cast, acting as the center of the circle he can move in by not letting any more line out. In casting, the dog will do one of two things. He may go around a half circle the wrong way, come across the original straight line track and follow it again to the turning point. If he does this, let him go right along, not moving yourself unless you are standing right where he wants to go. When he comes to the end of the scent again he will probably stop a little sooner in his overshoot and may even repeat the whole performance. Keep letting him have his head and eventually he will try a circle in the other direction and hit upon the second leg. He may of course turn the right way in the first place and get right onto the track again. In either case, remember that the scent of the second leg may have been blown about a bit, so don't be too adamant about where he should or should not get onto the track. He'll pick it up, or the edge of it, and follow that along until it runs out, this time at the article. As he searches for the second leg keep encouraging him with the command, his name,

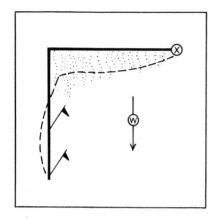

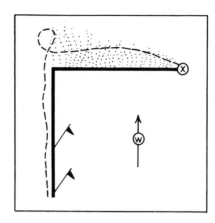

DOG (DASHED LINE) MAKING TURN WITH FIRST LEG INTO WIND.

DOG CASTING FOR TURN WITH FIRST LEG DOWN WIND.

DOG'S PATH WITH DIAGONAL WIND ACROSS TRACK.

DOG CASTING FOR TURN, WITH NO WIND.

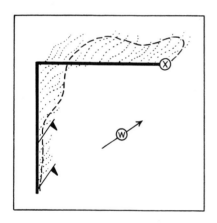

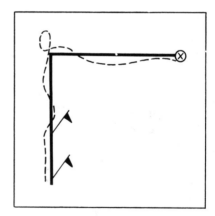

THESE POSSIBLE PATHS INDICATE HOW A DOG MAY WORK APPARENTLY FAR OFF THE ACTUAL LINE OF THE TRACK UNDER VARYING CONDITIONS. IT IS VITALLY IMPORTANT *not* TO TRY TO INSIST ON HIS FOLLOWING RIGHT IN THE FOOTSTEPS OF THE TRACKLAYER. HE CAN'T AND WON'T DO IT.

and an occasional "Good Boy" to keep him happy and working. And of course when he comes across the article and brings it to you, smother him with effusive praise.

Again, there is the rare dog who simply can't seem to grasp the idea at first that there can be a turn in the track. If he passes right over the new leg several times without realizing that it is the track, or if he simply gives up when the first leg runs out on him, go right up to him and gently lead him to the turn and then off in the right direction until you both happen upon the article. Point it out to him if necessary, tell him to retrieve it, and then make a gigantic fuss over him as though he'd done the whole thing all by himself. If you have gone slowly and carefully in your training up to the first turn, being sure that he is actually using his nose, your chances of running into such serious first-turn trouble are small indeed. And if you do run into it, leading him through the turn a few times will solve it.

Having gotten over this second major hurdle in tracking, you then proceed to make the second leg longer and longer until he can infallibly negotiate the turn at 200 feet and go along the new leg another 200 feet. But be absolutely sure he has the turn well mastered—do the "turn plus 15 feet" several times before starting to increase the distance. He may overshoot and cast about for the scent every time, but you will know when he has the idea well in hand.

Surprisingly enough, no matter how often you have done it, your dog will probably not automatically turn in the direction you've been turning unless his nose tells him to. By this point in training he will be well convinced that you're a pretty sly character, albeit lovable, and he wouldn't put it past you to make the turn in the opposite direction one of these times, just to confuse him. So don't worry about him cheating. Even if he comes, within a time or two, to take the turn easily, count only your blessings and look not the gift tracking dog in the mouth. It means only that he's getting good at the business quickly.

He may even shortcut the turn quite sharply, changing direction toward the glove well before he comes to where you've been making the turn. Again, it's his nose that's dictating his actions, not any real foreknowledge that thither lies the article. If he does do this, check your wind direction to see if perhaps the scent from the second leg mightn't have blown back along the first leg, allowing the dog to find the turn many feet before you actually made it. The wind, in fact, may be blowing the stronger scent of the article right along to the first leg. If so the dog will of course take off in a direct line for it. The only solution for this is a careful check of wind direction to make sure that it is not blowing diagonally from the article back across the first leg.

As the dog goes along the straight second leg, or even in the middle of the first, he may lose the scent even without a turn. Just why this happens to a dog we don't really know, but it does happen. Here again, the handler should allow the dog to circle at the end of the line, encouraging him with commands and praise to cast until he finds it again. Here you can be specially helpful because you know when he has come across approximately the right place to pick up the scent again. When he reaches the spot increase your praise and make your commands more urgent so that he will know there is something of significance about that area. He'll probably pick it right up again and be off. It may happen several times on the straightaway, but keep him at it, and have patience.

Sometimes, right in the middle of a hot track, the dog may stop cold and appear to forget not only what he is doing but even why in the world he's out in the middle of a big field wearing a harness and a 60-foot line. Right in the middle of a training session he may go cold at the very beginning of a track. In either case, try taking hold of the harness and leading him along the track for 10 or 20 feet, urging him and commanding him to "Find It." This may snap him out of it. If not, take him back to the start, take a break, lay a fresh track out to the article, and try to get him started off again. If that doesn't get him going, the only solution is to give it up for the day. He may be just plain beat. There may be something in the wind that bothers him—perhaps a nasty odor blowing in from the next field. There's no way to know, so take his word for it that he can't or won't track any more that day and pack it in. Come back next day to another field, if possible, or a few days later to the same place. But think about it in the interim—especially about whether you may have been overworking him. Overtraining can be fatal in tracking. If he gets bored with the whole thing, you're finished, so only keep him working as long as he seems happy about finding that glove.

There are two disciplinary problems that crop up not infrequently in the field. In the middle of a track, he may see an appetizing bird or rabbit or other denizen of the woods and take off after it. The answer to this is a fairly sharp correction with the line and your voice. No tantrums, though. Yank him back, then smilingly put him back on the track and encourage him to pick up where he left off. The other, and minor, problem is that of the dog relieving himself while on a track. These natural functions can't be controlled to any extent when the dog is exposed to succulent bushes just made for leg-lifting, so let him finish and then put him back on the track. Insist on this—some dogs will want to halloo around the field in triumph after so wondrously complicated an accomplishment as wetting a bush, but bring him up short with the line and put him right back to work.

MORE TURNS

When you've progressed to finding the article 200 feet beyond the turn and the dog is doing a steady and sure job of it, you are ready for the second turn. The procedure here is exactly the same as with the first turn. Again, if you can have someone else place the stake for the turn, well and good, but do it yourself if necessary.

Again, drop your article about 15 feet beyond the turn. If your first turn was to the right, make the second to the left. When he comes to the second running-out of scent he'll have had experience of turns, so won't be confused. Use your handling experience and let him cast until he has found the way, and he'll get to the article. When he's sure of his second turn, keep increasing the distance until you're dropping it 200 feet beyond. This will make a total track of 600 feet—and you'll get strong legs in the process. Twelve hundred feet out and back with the article, then another 1200 behind the dog as he goes out and back. What with a total of 800 yards (nearly half a mile) of walking on each two-turn track you do, there's not too much danger of your overworking the dog. You'll probably be willing to call it quits before he is.

At this point we might insert a cautionary word about progress and overworking. As we do not attempt to give you a day-by-day schedule of steps and work, it is easy to get the idea that tracking is something that can be learned in a week-end or two. It isn't so. Particularly if you live in the city and can only work at it on weekends, it will take you several months before he is tracking well. The rule here, perhaps even more than in any other work, is: slow and easy. He cannot learn more than a little each day, and it is far better to get that little well established than trying to push on to new things. Work with him an hour at a time, at most. If it is a cool and pleasant day and you are in the country anyway, it won't hurt to put in two one-hour sessions, well separated. But give him plenty of rest, and try not to work steadily for the hour—take a break at the half hour. That way he will be fresh and willing, and your progress will be good. But, again, don't expect it to be sudden and easy. It takes time and work, and nothing else will do it.

On all the tracks, from the very first one hardly farther than the second flag to the 600-foot two-turn tracks, always keep in mind the vitally important fact that the dog's nose is better than yours. This may seem ridiculous, but it's something that even experienced handlers forget at times. Either they do know just where the track is and can't believe that the dog is really working way off there—or they don't know and can't quite believe that the track was laid that way. In the beginning, even when you know where the track is and your dog seems to be way, way off, let him have his head until and unless he has gone a long way in a completely wrong direction and obviously isn't working a track. Later, when you're following a track that you haven't seen laid, you have to be completely dependent on your dog's nose, and not at all on your own common sense.

At one AKC Tracking Trial we watched a really heartbreaking example of the pitfalls of knowing more than the dog about the track. One handler, who had trained for months and had an excellent dog, was put on a track. The starting flags made a line pointing directly between two large, close-together trees about 50 feet in front of the flags. Sure enough, the dog put his nose down and started loping directly out toward the gap between the trees. His handler, however, was convinced that the track couldn't have been laid between those trees. As the dog headed toward the trees, the handler held him back via the line and urged him to cast for a turn. The dog cast around a bit, then headed straight for the trees again. Once more his handler pulled him off and told him to cast. Again it happened and when he was pulled off for the

◀ ARRANGING THE LEAD
BEFORE THE START.
DOG IS DOWN AT THE
STARTING FLAG,
GETTING THE SCENT.

THE DOG MAKES THE ▶
FIRST TURN, SHORT OF
THE TURN STAKE. THE
MODEL HERE IS THE
COUNTRY'S FIRST
U.D.T. GREAT DANE.

◀ THE DOG STARTS, WHILE
THE HANDLER PAYS
OUT THE LINE. THESE
SNOW PICTURES ILLUS-
TRATE THAT TRACKING
IS NOT CONFINED TO
SPRING DAYS.

VICTORY. THE DOG RE- ▶
TURNS WITH GLOVE IN
MOUTH.

third time the unhappy dog said, in effect, okay boss, I'll go somewhere else. He turned to the right and made off in that direction. All of which made his handler very happy with his astute handling until the judge's whistle shrilled to let him know that he was far off the track and had failed.

When he got back to the judges' table, one of the judges asked him, "Why in the devil didn't you let that dog go between those trees?" The awful truth dawned, and great oaths were heard in the land. It was hard on him, but it was an object lesson never to be forgotten by the spectators. When you're working with your dog, keep this story in mind—and remember that the dog's nose is a good deal better than yours.

THE STRANGE TRACK

The third and final hurdle in tracking is the switch from your own long-familiar scent to a track laid by someone else. We call this latter the "strange" track simply to differentiate it from all those going before that were laid and relaid by you. Here it is of course absolutely essential to have an assistant who is willing to work with you and your dog—and also helpful to have a third person to place the flags and stakes if possible.

You will be ready for the strange track when your dog can follow your own track at least 600 feet, through a minimum of two turns, and do a very respectable job each time. If you have room in the field, practice with even longer "self" tracks and more turns to be sure your dog knows his job before going to the strange track. A little later in this chapter there are sample diagrams of tracks laid to get the maximum distance out of a moderate sized field—you may be able to lay a longer track in your field than you think. You can, of course, go through gates into adjoining fields. For the effects of gates on wind-blown scent, see the later discussion of "Scent and Tracks."

Once you are ready, the switch of tracks is a simple extension of all your training to date. Keep the dog in the car, or at least somewhere well away so that he can't see what's going on. Then, after determining the best area to work in, ask your third party to lay out a long track, starting with the flags and marking the turns with stakes. He should be wearing rubbers or rubber-soled shoes for this to cut his track down slightly, but it isn't strictly necessary. If you have no third party to work with, your tracklayer himself will have to go out to plant the stakes as he makes the turns.

Your tracklayer, be it wife, husband or friend, is going to have to work with you all through the training session—and is going to have to know something about tracking himself to be of maximum help. Before you send anyone out to lay track for you, be sure you have explained carefully what you want. Better yet, let him read this chapter for background. One of the unfortunately true maxims of tracking is, "It's harder to train a tracklayer than a dog." Be sure your tracklayer understands what's going on.

With the track plotted, flags and stakes in place, you begin on the strange scent almost exactly as you did with your own. Your tracklayer goes out into the wind about 25 feet beyond the second flag to drop the article, holding the article in his hand as he goes to apply his scent to it. To begin the track, he should walk around within a two-foot circle around the first flag, to leave a strong patch of his odor there as the dog's first clue. Then, walking between the flags, he should walk along slowly to leave a strong track there. From the second flag to the dropping point, ask him to walk slowly, taking small steps. Then, when he has dropped the article, he should put on rubbers and, if feasible, run with long strides at least 50 feet downwind from the article, and then make a wide circle around to the cars.

Wearing the rubbers once he has dropped the article will lighten his track somewhat, and running with long strides will also lessen it a bit. Thus, after he has dropped the article the track will immediately weaken considerably, and the in-training dog will hesitate there, even if he hasn't grabbed the article by then.

The major divergence you will have noticed is that for the first time a track has been made without anyone retracing his steps back to the flags. This is done now to introduce the dog to the idea of direction in a track —to teach him that a scent gets stronger and fresher as he approaches a find. Actually, this first strange track will be the first true track he will do—the times before having been not so much tracking as following an overpowering path of heavily laid odor.

As soon as the tracklayer has gotten off the field (and be careful that he doesn't come near the dog afterwards), take the dog to the starting flag and down him so that his nose is in the middle of the heavy patch of scent made by the shuffling around the flag. Start him off with the usual command, and help him by leading him by the harness toward the second flag if necessary. If he seems to have the idea right away, start paying out the line and let him go. If he is puzzled at not finding a strong trail of your scent, encourage him forward by commands, pointing and leading with the harness—right up to the article if required. Ninety-nine percent of all dogs who have been carefully trained up to this point will catch on with little trouble. By this time he has gotten used to the fact that the article he is to find lies somewhere out along the line of the flags. Even if your scent isn't there, and tricky as he knows you to be, he'll take a sporting chance and start out along that line. Then, somewhere along the line he realizes that this new scent filling his nose is going right along with him, and the second great light will dawn. Lo— other scents than yours can lead to the article!

We have never seen a dog, trained up to this point, who cannot make the switch. If yours is slow to get the idea, lead him all the way to the article several times until it gets through to him. In a way, you're tricking him again when you do this, as you're laying down a mixture of your scent and that of the tracklayer's along the line—and the dog will follow first the mixture, then get the idea of the new scent also leading to the article.

When he makes the first unassisted find on the strange track, make a great deal of fuss over him. Even if you've had to lead him right up to the article and build a large sign over it with neon arrows, praise him each time he gets it. Then the first time he gets it all by himself, really let out all the stops. Give him to understand that he is the most loyal, intelligent, trustworthy, kind, considerate, noble, talented dog in the surrounding seven counties. He'll get the message. Then give everybody a rest.

It is possible that with a really acute dog you may run into an overshoot problem. After all, there is for the first time a track, however much lighter, leading right past the article. In the excitement of following this new scent he may try to lope right past the article and follow the track the tracklayer left when circling out of the field. It does happen. If it happens to you (and you're luckier than you realize if it does) then you can use the lead to snub him up just as he passes the article, and call his attention to it. If he's stopped cold by the lead, and you give him the "Find It" command, he'll stumble on the article in casting. Continue to apply this correction as often as necessary, for it is essential that the dog find the article rather than follow the track to its end.

When you are sure that your dog has a thorough understanding of the new circumstances, you can have the tracklayer go out progressively to 100 feet beyond the flag. Then introduce one turn with a short second leg —then longer second legs, then on to two turns and more. Don't try to go too fast, but be sure the dog is doing a very good job before adding more distance or another turn.

In tracking the strange scent, you will use the same handling techniques you used on your "self" tracks. If he loses the track momentarily at a turn or on a straightaway, snub him gently with the line and encourage him to cast until he has picked it up again. And always keep in mind the prime dictum about his nose being better than yours.

THE BLIND TRACK

Though this will be the first "real" track for you as the handler, it is no harder for the dog than the ones directly before. For a blind track, ask your tracklayer to go out into a fresh field, put down the starting flags, and proceed to lay a long (600 feet or more) track with at least two turns, and without putting down any turn stakes. Here, of course, is where you must have an understanding tracklayer, for he must himself plot a good track that will not confuse your dog with too-close turns, overlapping scents or scents splashed along walls or bushes. The tracklayer should proceed as before, leaving a strong patch of scent around the starting flag, a strong track to the second flag, and then step out along the track. You yourself must not have any idea where the track goes, so sit in the car with your dog until the tracklayer signals from a distance that all is in readiness.

When you bring your dog up to the first flag for this track, do everything just as you have done it before. Take your time, make sure the harness is on properly, talk to the dog encouragingly and try to keep his enthusiasm up. Then down him at the first flag, give him a minute to get the scent well in his nose while you're straightening out the line, and start him off.

Stand beside the first flag paying out the line until he is past the second flag and obviously on the track. If he seems confused before getting to the second flag, let him cast for the scent at the end of your line, but don't let him get beyond the second flag until he obviously is working the track. It is very nearly impossible for us to tell you how to know when your dog is really working—by this time you will certainly know. Once he is beyond that second flag, do your utmost only to keep going along with him, without trying to guide him with the line. From there on out the track may go 100 yards straight or it may take a turn 25 feet beyond the flag, or do almost anything. Only the tracklayer knows. If at any time the dog seems to have lost it, stand still and let him cast at the end of the line but don't try to encourage him in any particular direction from that point. The track may take a turn there, or go straight ahead. And don't, because you saw the tracklayer coming from the left as he returned to the car, assume that a turn must be to the left. The article may be there, but there may be any number of curious turns before you get there. We keep repeating this advice to the point of monotony only because it is such a common mistake, even with experienced handlers. You won't really understand how easy it is to try to guide the dog until you're out in the field yourself, but once there you'll find the temptation at times near irresistible. Don't do it.

If the field you are working is a particularly bushy one, or even if not, the line may become tangled and snagged somewhere as the dog is casting for the scent. When and if it happens, go to the snag and work it loose, calling encouragement to the dog as you do so. If you've been keeping an eye on things properly, you'll know which way he was headed when he was stopped by the snag. This is one of the few times you can somewhat guide the dog—when he starts up on being freed you can encourage him with the line to continue in the same direction. But don't insist if he wants to go another way. He may have been at a turn just then.

When he passes this test, do another one with a colder track. Wait 20 minutes after the tracklayer finishes before putting your dog on. Then try one half an hour old. Work him up until he can pick up and follow a blind strange track that is at least two hours old. Once the dog has followed several such tracks successfully with the same tracklayer, switch again to someone else. Put him on two or three tracks of varying degrees of coldness laid by various other people—men, women or children. When he will follow any strange track laid for him you've very nearly got a tracking dog.

ADVANCED WORK

Up to this point the dog, however well he has been working, has followed only what are essentially simple, straightforward tracks. They have started at a well defined point, gone in a stated direction, and traversed only ordinary ground. Before a dog can truly be called a tracking dog, he must be able to work under considerably poorer circumstances. He should, for example, be able to find and pick up a track in a field, all unmarked. He should be able to follow one person's track even when it has been crossed, before and after, by other people. He should be able to track across a stream, and along and across a road.

Difficult as these things may sound, they are only a few of the conditions that might easily be met in a "professional" track—one in which you used your dog to find a lost person. A lost child or adult may wander aimlessly in circles in a field, crossing and recrossing his own track. He may stumble through thick undergrowth, crawl over a stone fence, flounder through a marsh or hundreds of yards down the middle of a shallow stream. A fully trained tracking dog could handle all of those contingencies, and would have to be able to if he were to be of any practical use.

Even if you are learning tracking only for the fun of it, you should not be satisfied with simple tracks in an open field. Mastering most of the difficulties we've listed is, again, only a matter of working at them sensibly.

To teach "tracksureness"—sticking with one track even when others cross it—start out with an older crossing track. Have one friend walk across a field, then half an hour later have your tracklayer lay a simple track which crosses that. Put the dog on and watch carefully when he comes to the crossing. If he ignores the older second track, fine. If he casts and tries to follow it, stand where you are and snub him with the lead. Let him keep casting until he finds what you know to be the right track, then urge him on that one with your voice. If he really becomes confused, lead him by the harness past the crossing until he is well on the right track again.

When he will confidently pass an older track, reverse the procedure and have someone lay a cross track after your tracklayer has laid his. The fresher scent may well confuse the dog, but proceed as with the older crossing. Don't make the mistake of pulling your dog off immediately if he tries to follow any cross track. Let him investigate it for about 30 feet, just to get the scent of it. If after a few yards he rejects it and casts back for the original scent, that problem is over. He has learned that there is a specific scent to follow—not just the freshest scent going. Otherwise, keep at it, letting him cast and investigate the cross tracks, or leading him right, until he has learned the lesson.

To teach stream crossing, find if possible a shallow stream about ten feet across. Have your tracklayer wade through it and proceed ahead directly he gets ashore. (By this time you will have realized that your tracklayer must be someone willing, patient and durable—preferably a wife or other indentured person). When the dog comes to the edge of the stream, he will try to cast in both directions along the bank to find a turning short of the edge. Not finding it will confuse him, so you must lead him across the stream to where the track begins anew and put him on it with encouragement and commands. Don't insist that he plunge right in when a track comes to an end at a stream—if he learns to do that he will ignore the very good possibility that a tracklayer may have turned off without crossing.

When he will confidently pick up a track leading straight across a stream, have the tracklayer walk 10 or 20 feet down or upstream before going ashore again. When the dog gets to the far bank and finds no track, encourage him, or lead him, to cast upstream and down until he finds it again. It is a surprisingly good general rule that lost individuals, if they do not go directly across a stream, will wander downstream rather than up. Whatever the reason for this—perhaps it is the path of least resistance—you can concentrate on tracks picking up downstream from the entry point without prejudicing the dogs training—with only an occasional upstream restart.

The various other difficulties you may encounter—roads, stone walls, heavy thickets, crossing animal tracks—we leave to you to work out. If you have reached this point in training your dog to track, you will have acquired in the field a good knowledge of how the dog works and how best to carry him through any further difficulties. It remains for us only to suggest that you do definitely work on two further variations—a pickup in the middle of a track, and the track in which the dog finds a person at the end rather than an article.

In both these cases an article of the tracklayer's is needed to give the dog the beginning scent. Have your tracklayer leave with you a glove or shoe or any other item of clothing of his, then have him enter a field at one edge and leave a straight track across it, leaving at the other edge. Bring your dog to yet a third edge of the field and give him the article to smell, then command him to "Find It." This may shake him up a bit, for here you have the article right in your hand and you're telling him to find it. But by this time he will be a pretty wise dog about this whole business and he may just gallumph across the field until he hits the track. If he seems puzzled, lead him to where you know the track is (and you might have the tracklayer put in a few stakes so you'll be sure) and put the dog on the track with encouragement and commands.

You can, if you wish, combine the two variations by having the dog find the tracklayer at the end of this track. It will be particularly effective if the tracklayer proceeds to a field with fairly high grass and lies down halfway across. When the dog stumbles across him it will come as a considerable surprise and he will in all likelihood set up a considerable commotion at this curious turn of events. Encourage him to make a racket when he has found the tracklayer. If it should happen to be a large dog and a small tracklayer, we recommend that you discourage the dog from trying to retrieve in this case. Whatever happens, the dog will certainly not stroll unconcernedly past a body lying in his path, and will let you know that he has made a world-shaking discovery. On the next track of this sort, though, make sure that he finds only an article and does not try to go on to find the tracklayer. He must not be allowed to get the impression that he has graduated from articles to people. Mix it up for him, using the "lost person" find only occasionally.

At the beginning of these last variations, you should set him searching for the track while it is very fresh, but put him on older and older tracks until he can pick up one that is at least two hours old. When he has reached this point in tracking, and can pick up a two-hour-old scent, either from the beginning or middle, and follow it unvaryingly to the article, he is a veteran tracking dog and there is little more you can teach him. He is now ready, if you're interested, for AKC competition and a crack at a T.D. (Tracking Dog degree.) For details of what to do, see the last section of this chapter.

SCENT AND TRACKS

When you have worked at tracking for a while, the behavior of scent will become clear to you through experience. What we know about it has been learned in just that way—by watching dogs work tracks under every possible condition, and adding a little theorizing.

You can best visualize the actions of scent if you think of it as being a slightly heavier-than-air gas, very easily blown about by the wind, yet sticking tenaciously in part to everything it touches. Imagining, or describing, the actions of something invisible (scent) in something else invisible (air) is tricky, but we can outline very generally some of the actions of scent under various wind and terrain conditions.

Scent of course travels with the wind. This is not meant to say that it travels wholly and bodily with the wind—rather that a breeze will stretch it out from its starting point over considerable ground. In a crosswind there will be a diffused broad path of the tracklayer's scent stretching between where he walked and the limit of the windblown area. Dogs generally work the downwind "edge" of such a diffuse scent —perhaps the "front" is slightly stronger; perhaps because they do, as the theory holds, like to work half in and half out of a scent path.

If a track is laid close to a downwind tree the scent will blow onto the tree and plaster it with odor. The scent accumulating there may confuse a dog badly in the early stages—therefore it is best not to lay beginning tracks too close to trees. The same thing will happen if a track is laid too close to a downwind fence. The fence will be plastered with the scent all along that leg of the track. The dog, trying to find the downwind edge of the scent will run into the wall and may want to give up there and then if he hasn't had enough experience. This holds true, also, with thick bushes. A track laid near them will, wind willing, blow scent all along the front of the bushes, and even into them, and this will unsettle your dog more than somewhat if he's just catching onto things. Test your wind carefully and avoid laying a track near any close-downwind objects of any considerable size. And, in the beginning, try to avoid them even if they are upwind, for the wind may shift at any moment and plaster them with smell.

Gates in such solid fences as stone have a curious effect if a track is laid through them. A cross wind will plaster first one side of the fence, downwind, with scent, and then curl the scent along the other downwind side as the tracklayer passes. The dog may spend quite a time investigating along the sides of the fence before he gets back onto the track. Let him investigate to his satisfaction, for where he is working there will be scent, and he has to work it out all by himself if he is to learn anything about gates.

Hills have a sometimes devastating effect on a track. If the wind is coming at all into the hill, across the track, it tends to lift the whole track up and blow it uphill and even across the top and into nothingness. Hitting a hillside seems to accelerate a wind, and an angle somehow lets it "dig under" a scent and obliterate it for the novice dog. So avoid this condition if possible.

The corresponding valleys, however minute, also can work havoc. Scent tends to collect quite heavily in a small valley (and here we mean even only a few feet deep) and roll around like mist. If a track several hours old crosses a small dip like this, you may see the dog casting about quite confusedly within the dip as he explores the extent of the rolling scent. After a bit he will find the slightly stronger track and go off again.

Even the time of day will affect a track. In the morning, when the ground is cooler than the air, a track will lie very low to the ground as the ground absorbs heat and almost sucks up the scent too. Conversely, in the evening when the ground is giving off heat to the air, a track

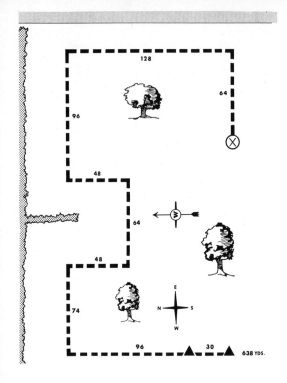

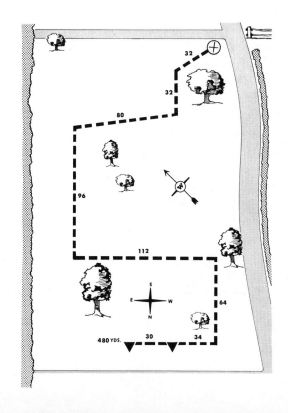

Four examples of good tracks laid in different fields under varying wind conditions.

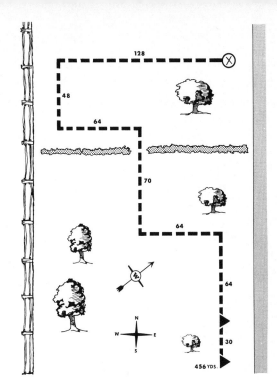

EACH TRACK IS AKC REGULA-
TION LENGTH OR MORE, AND
MAKES EXCELLENT USE OF THE
AVAILABLE FIELDS.

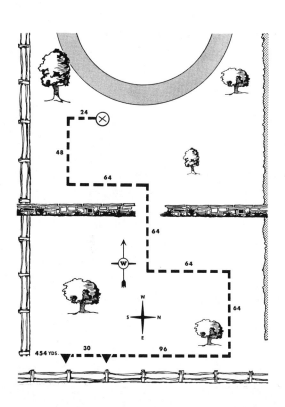

will tend to rise as it gets older, and you may find a dog which normally works with his nose right to the ground will be tracking high, head in the air as he follows the track.

Keep all these factors well in mind when you are laying tracks for your in-training dog, and even when he is more advanced. The central idea is never to try to confuse the dog. Make it as easy as possible for him as long as possible. Only when he is fully in command of the situation and you are sure he could track the Devil himself over burning coals should you deliberately introduce confusing factors of wind and terrain. And be sure that your assistant-cum-tracklayer has a good working knowledge of this section before he goes out to lay track for you.

The diagrams of tracks under varying circumstances should be of help to you and your tracklayer. Study them carefully before you lay your tracks, and adapt the principles to your own chosen fields.

AKC TRACKING TESTS

These are hard things to find. About the only way to find out when and where a Test is to be held in your vicinity is through the AKC— either by a mail request or through the current issue of The Kennel Gazette. As Tracking Tests are hardly ever run by professional obedience superintendents, and never at shows, notices are rarely sent out. It's up to you to find out when and where.

Even when you manage to locate one you've only started. To enter a Test, you must have a letter from an AKC tracking judge certifying that he has examined your dog and considers him ready for a Test. This, of course, involves finding such a judge. Here again, the AKC is the only answer. They will give you, on request, the names of tracking judges in your area. Then it is up to you to contact the judge, persuade him to come out in the fields with you, and put your dog through a tough track. If you pass his inspection, and there's no reason you shouldn't if you've followed this chapter and don't try to jump the gun with a partly-trained dog, he will give you that precious letter, and you're ready for a Test.

Armed with the letter, you apply for entry to a Test you've found, and if it isn't full, you're ready to go. As for the Test itself, there's little we can tell you except: relax. Most dogs fail their first Test, even very well trained dogs. This, we are convinced, is because 95% of all handlers freeze up into unmanageable masses of raw nerves when they step out onto that fatal field for the first time. It can easily happen to you, too, so don't sneer until you've given it a try.

A Test track will be considerably easier than the hardest tracks you've encountered in this chapter. It will be quite a straightforward one, over generally simple terrain—440 yards long at least and not more than 500 yards, with at least two turns. If you keep cool and let your dog use his educated nose, you'll breeze right through. But don't count the prize money yet. That T.D. is the most coveted degree in obedience, and for a very good reason. It's damnably hard to get. By a rough calculation (from the number of TD's won in a sample year) we get a figure of about 300 Tracking Dogs in the entire country. And if that figure errs at all, it is on the high side.

We've included the complete Tracking Trial rules in the Appendix along with all the other rules, so be sure to read them well. At the field you'll find the two old familiar flags—and you'll be told to go find the article. All we can say, if you've gotten to this point, is a heartfelt—good luck!

CHAPTER X

TRAINING PROBLEMS

BECAUSE every dog is an individual, and especially because every trainer is an individual, problems in training will inevitably arise. The major cause of problems, as we hope you have seen from reading the other chapters of this book, is the trainer. It is an easy thing indeed to go wrong in one phase or another of training, as well we know from our own beginnings in training. Despite all the cautions we have given you, all the admonitions to go slow, to take each exercise carefully step by step, the temptations are great to skip a thing or two, to think "Oh, nonsense—my dog just doesn't work that way," or "I can skip that bit of work, for my dog's much smarter than average." If you have followed every step in every exercise in every chapter, you are the exception among human beings. If you haven't, then the problems you have with your dog are highly likely to be due to your deviations.

This is not to say that training is as rigid as all that. We should be the last to advocate a mechanical approach to training, because your dog is not a machine, and can't be trained by one-two-three rules and regulations. What we do say is that the variations from good procedure that the great majority of amateur trainers make are those that complicate training. Your variations may have worked out extremely well. But the fact that you are reading this chapter on problems indicates that at least some of them didn't. It is those we are concerned with.

You may also be coming to this chapter with problems originating in your own training methods, or in methods of friends or other trainers which have not worked entirely well with your dog. In such a case, we recommend that before going any further you turn back to the chapter covering the particular exercise you are having trouble with. Read over our method and explanations regarding that exercise, compare them with what you have been doing, and you may well find a solution right there. In a great many problem cases, complete retraining is the only satisfactory answer, and you may find that it is the answer in your case.

In the examination of problems which follows, we will repeat much of what we have said in other sections of this book, and for good reason. Most of training involves learning to think about your dog in a new way. The more times we indicate to you the right way to think about him, the more likely you are to accept it, and to put it to practical use. We know from personal experience that a student trainer can not only hear an explanation, but even see the proper method work on his dog— and turn around a few minutes later to repeat his own private method which has resulted in weeks of failure. Much too often, training problems degenerate into a contest of wills, with the trainer thinking, "This is the way I've been doing it, and my dog is bloody well going to learn it my way, because *I* say so!" If this can happen, and it can, then a mere exposition of method in a book will be far easier to either ignore or wrongly adapt.

To the point—if you are having problems in a specific exercise, it is simply and flatly because you have been doing something wrong in your training procedure. Somehow, you have done it wrong. What you must do now, rather than look for a specific answer in this chapter, is to take a look at exactly how your dog is doing things wrong, and then sit back for a long think about it—about why he does what he does, or doesn't do what he doesn't. And leave out answers like "He's stubborn" or "He's stupid." The only acceptable answers are ones which point to faults in your teaching.

Under each of the following sections, we will discuss the probable reasons for the major problems that arise, the way you may have been thinking wrong about the exercise, and some general pointers on correcting the problems. But from there on it is up to you to apply your own mind in a constructive way.

HEELING

The major difficulties encountered in heeling are those of position—total failure to get the dog walking more or less alongside in some sort of fashion is almost beyond the bounds of possibility. Thus we will assume that your dog heels to some extent. The first thing to examine, if your dog heels out of proper position, is why. Here there is usually a good and simple reason. If he lags, for example, there is a very good chance that he does so in order to be able to make the turns and about turns without being constantly corrected. And behind that lies the very good possibility that you have been making your turns without any warning to him. You should slow slightly before any turn or halt, to let your dog know something is going to happen. If you haven't been doing this, then he will have trouble making the turns sharply, and will have been getting correction after correction to no good avail. So now he lags behind to be able to see what's going to happen.

Much the same, of course, applies to general problems on the turns—inability to make them with you. If you've been giving him no warning, you can't expect him to move smartly with you. Slow down slightly before any turn. If he has trouble even then, corrective measures are in order. Crowding on the left turn can be corrected by bumping him with your right knee as you come around the turn. Swinging wide on left and about turns means that you should guide him around the turns in practice. You have probably been trying to get him around using the full length of the leash. This allows him to swing wide like an aerocar at an amusement park. But if you take hold of the leash close to his collar and bend down to guide him around, he will have to stay close. On the about turn, be sure first that you aren't doing some sort of fancy footwork or kicking up your heels, which he is trying to avoid by going wide.

Pulling on lead, forging ahead—do a quick about turn when he gets ahead, with a good snap on the lead to bring him around. After a few times he will begin to stay back in better position to be ready for a turn and avoid the snap correction. An older dog who falls into the habit of forging ahead can quite often be brought out of it by a sudden stop, even off leash, when he gets ahead. When he sits he will be far out of position. For some reason, a trained dog will realize instantly that he is out of position at the halt where in motion he may ignore it.

Heeling wide—look for the reason he wants to walk at a distance from you. A woman trainer's swirling skirts will often make a dog heel wide. You may have been too harsh with left-turn corrections and he's trying to escape your prodding knee. When you've found the reason, eliminate it and apply gentle snaps of the lead to get him back in. Don't keep up a pressure on the leash. Also, try sudden stops as he heads to the left after you start heeling.

Crowding—reason may be over-insistence on your part, too harsh corrections on wide heeling, or even a timid nature. Don't try to pull him away from you. Bump him gently with your left knee at each step. Don't overdo, or he may begin to heel wide.

Snapping at heels—generally done in spirit of play, but needs fairly severe leash corrections, followed by praise. Don't kick at him with your heels, for you may either hurt him, or even convince him further that it is a game.

Biting at hand or leash—this is active rebellion, and for some good reason. May have been a harsh or too-sudden introduction to collar and lead, or your whole training attitude may be too harsh. Lay off for a while, then try gentle reintroduction. If the habit persists, apply a strong rebellion correction (see Basic Training) but don't be vindictive. Let him know you won't stand for it, then continue calmly with the training.

Refusal to change gait— generally means you give him no warning by slight anticipatory slowing for the "slow," slight anticipatory speeding for the "fast." Always "float" into a change of pace. This may solve it. Otherwise, insist with constant snaps on the leash, don't haul or tug him.

Refusal to move after halt—you may have emphasized "stay" training too much. You may be moving off on the wrong foot. Be sure there is no confusion in his mind, then snap him forward sharply when you start up.

Trying to get at other dogs, sniffing ground, sniffing stewards on figure eight—probably no reason but inattention. Insist quite firmly on work-with continued snaps on leash, plus praise.

Good work on lead, bad work off—a rerun through leash work is indicated. It is very possible you have been tugging on him on lead, rather than snapping for corrections. You may have gone off leash too soon.

Re-do your leash work until he will do all work with the leash hanging slack. Then work for a while with the leash hanging loose at your left side to let him know it is still there. Then try him off lead again.

Good work off lead, sloppy work on—this problem occurs not infrequently with city dogs. To them, the leash means going outside for a walk or a romp, while heeling off leash is always work. One solution is to do some on-leash heeling practice in the street every time you take him out. Another one is to snap the leash on the "dead" ring of his training collar when you do on-leash heeling in the Novice ring. You can't use the leash for corrections anyway in the ring, and so it makes little difference to you which ring it is snapped onto. But to the dog there is an entirely different feeling about the collar, even when the leash is slack. A third possible solution is the use of an entirely different type of collar for street walks. It is less desirable than simple insistence through practice on good work when you want it, but if the problem is severe, the dog will readily learn that one collar, a leather one, means freedom, while putting on the training collar means strict work, on lead or off.

In general—the major overall error in training which leads to bad heeling work is tugging on the dog to get or keep him in position. A constant pressure on his neck will teach him nothing but resistance. Make every correction a quick snap and an immediate release, plus praise, and he will soon learn that there is nothing to pull against, and that it is far more comfortable to stay in the right place.

THE SIT

Sitting is an easy enough thing for a dog to do. He certainly does not have to learn any new skills in order to sit, so you can be quite sure that problems in the sit can be traced back to faulty training.

Refusal to sit—probably not enough on-lead work. If on-lead he resists strongly, bracing his feet against you, and you cannot get his rear down without a fight, try surprising him. Heel along, and as you slow to a stop, give a sharp "Sit!" command. Get your left hand down hard on his haunches and bring your right hand up with the lead, before he has stopped moving. Thus he does not have time to brace himself at the stand.

Sits wide, ahead, behind, in back or in front—very likely he is trying to escape too harsh corrections. Start teaching the sit all over again, using the surprise technique outlined above. Be gentle in your corrections and be sure to praise him each time. The essence of the idea of teaching a straight, close sit is to get him down right in his line of travel, close at your left side, before he has a chance to make a mistake.

Sits and then stands—not enough emphasis on staying where he is. Also, anticipation of starting up again, if you have been a little too harsh on forward yanks when you start. Insist that he stay sitting at your side, and counteract his anticipation by staying at the halt for as much as a minute before you start up again.

Keeps moving after handler halts, then sits—probably no warning from you that you are about to halt. "Float" into the halt, taking one or two slightly slower steps before halting. To correct, hold the leash close to his collar and be prepared to give a sharp backward snap as you halt —don't use the full length of the leash.

Refusal to sit after halt from slow—you may have been overcorrecting on his attempts to sit when your pace is slow. Also, your practice "slow" may be too slow—it need only be a slow stroll as contrasted to the brisk pace of "normal." Don't make your "slow" a funeral step. Correct the refusal to sit with the short-lead snap.

Refusal to sit, or crooked sit in front on recall—generally means that he is anticipating the go-to-heel. Each time he refuses to sit, or sits crooked, begin walking backward. When he is straightened out, stop with a sharp sit command. Don't attempt to correct with hands or feet. Do the backward step as many times as necessary until he straightens himself out, or sits of his own accord.

Swings rear away on the heeling sit—this generally results from trying to correct the sit, or force the sit, with the right foot brought around in back. He is trying to get his rear away from you for some good reason. Correct this by using your left hand on the outside of his haunches as you come in to the halt. Don't try to correct it after he is down—start up again and this time get him straight on the way down.

Refusal to stay sitting on the long sit—generally due to inadequate preparation, and nothing else. Go back to the beginning, have him stay sitting a minute or two at your side, then longer while you stand directly in front of him, then move away slowly. If you establish the habit thoroughly close to him and on leash, the problem will not occur when you're off leash. Long before you go off leash and/or any distance away, he must thoroughly understand that he cannot leave the sitting position under any circumstances until you release him. Don't progress in the training when he will just barely, with luck, stay for the required time. Be sure there is no question of it.

THE DOWN

Because of widespread misunderstanding of how to teach a dog the down, this causes quite a few problems. We suggest that before looking at the specific difficulties, you read the section on "teaching the down" in the Basic Training chapter.

Refusal to go down—results from trying to force him down with a leash or your hand. Try the idea of "lifting" him down as outlined in Basic Training. That way he has nothing to fight.

Cries or panics when forced down—the answer lies in the definition of the problem. "Lifting" him down involves no force, and he will not dislike it. Try that method.

Refusal to down unless at heel—when he has learned the down with you at his side, the new situation—you in front—may confuse him. Go back to the side, then slowly move around to the front on each successive try, still crouching and helping him down by lifting his legs. When you are in front, one hand on his back and one holding both legs will get him down without a fight, if you have worked enough at his side.

Refusal to stay down without your hand on him—probably you have taken your hand away too fast. When he is down and your hand on his shoulder is holding him there, take it off for only a second. Next time take it off for a few seconds. Work slowly to longer times. Also, you may be making the mistake of straightening up too soon—your rising will tempt him to rise. Straighten up only when he will stay down unassisted, and then do it by gradual stages, don't just shoot up.

Goes down only with collar and lead—you have probably been depending on the collar and lead to hold him or force him down. Use your hands and body as described in teaching the down. Once he has learned it, you can dispense with the collar and lead, and do more downs using hands and body only. Then he will not differentiate between collar on and collar off.

STAND FOR EXAMINATION

Almost all the problems in the stand-for-examination occur in the examination segment. Some few dogs are so very timid by nature that they require hours of careful, slow exposure to other people, some have unfortunate aggressive streaks and require hours, too, of slow re-education. For the most part, though, problems in the examination result from a too-hurried introduction to the idea.

If you have trouble with any of the facets of the examination, start your stand training all over again. Go back to the first stand-stay, and work through standing in front of him while he stays, standing at his side, and standing in back of him. Be absolutely sure before you try an examination, even by yourself, that he is firm in the stand. This may take weeks, but it is essential. Then proceed again to examining him yourself. When he is perfectly steady under your own examination, have a friend stand by as you examine your dog. Have the friend stand quite close after a time or two, and make a casual business of showing your friend how to go over the dog. Then, have the friend put his hand gently on your dog at the same time you have your hand on him. Gradually, work up to the point where the friend can examine him gently while you stand at the dog's head without touching him. Then move slowly away from the dog, farther on each succeeding examination. The idea is to make it casual and easy—a good many of the problems found in the examination result from a too formal approach to the situation, wherein a handler expects his dog to undergo a full examination as soon as he has learned to stand and stay. Go about it slow and easy.

Moving as you walk around to heel—this can be tricky, for the dog will almost always try to watch you as you walk around. It can be solved by a re-training in the stand-stay, wherein you get him to stay as you stand at lead's length away in any direction. After a while he will come to ignore you as you stand away, and will stand steady as you come around. Another angle is that you may be brushing him with your body as you come around, or dragging the leash across his head or face. If caution in this does not solve the problem, we suggest that you go back yet again for some intensive retraining. Begin with the sit-stay and walk around him several times, holding the leash beside his head as your axis. When you can do that, do the same at the down-stay, not only going around but stepping over him as we described in Basic Training. Keep at it, repeating your "stay" commands as you move around him or over him, until he is steady no matter what you do. Then begin again on stand-stay work, and he should be confident that he can stand still as you go around without coming to any harm.

Sits as you return to heel—this is generally confusion on his part, and needs only patience to clear. He is accustomed to the idea of sitting at your side when you are standing still, and is simply trying to do the right thing by sitting when you get to heel position. As you come around, block his sit by putting your left hand just in front of his rear leg. Another possible reason—if you have been teaching him to sit directly as a release from the stand, he may be anticipating. Make him work at command only, by standing for as much as a minute after you return to heel, and before you let him sit.

THE RECALL

Some of the most maddening problems of all can arise in the recall. It seems a simple enough thing for a dog to run to his owner, yet in the ring you will see every possible variation of foul-up. Perhaps one of the most common is the lagging dog, the one who stays where he is left and then comes when he is called, but at roughly the rate of reluctant molasses. Almost without exception, this can be traced to that cardinal sin, calling the dog to make a correction. As we have explained before, one can hardly expect a dog to come in gaily and fast if there is a chance he will be hit or shouted at when he gets there. The minority cause is tugging and hauling on the leash to get him to come in the original recall training. This is one of the "common-sense" ways of training that are terribly wrong, for if you give a dog something to pull against, he will pull against it. If you try to tug and haul him to you, he will tug and haul in the opposite direction for all he's worth. It all goes back to the very basic philosophy of training with the leash and training collar—using snaps on the leash. A quick snap and a release gives the dog nothing to fight, and several snaps will accomplish far more than a steady tug. However, in recall training, even the snaps are to be left as a last resort.

If you have been doing either (and be honest with yourself), then there is nothing you can do about it but resolve never again to call him in for a correction and never again to haul him in with the leash. The damage is done, and it will take time and patience to correct it. You must now sit down with your dog and re-establish happy relations. Put him at a sit-stay, go to the other end of the leash and crouch there facing him. Call him to you in the friendliest voice you can muster up. If he doesn't move, don't touch that leash! Call him, cajole him, sweet-talk him, roll on the ground, clap your hands—anything at all to get him to come to you of his own accord. When he gets there, praise him as you've never praised him before. Don't insist on a sit, or a go-to-heel—just get him to come to you. Keep working at that, day after day, never giving him a correction, but cajoling until he will come to you happily on your first call. When he has done that a dozen times, begin to use the leash as a guide, not as a correcting device. Guide him in straight, and after a few times tell him to sit as he gets in front of you—but make all your moves gentle and friendly. Persuade him to sit, as one friend to another. When he will do that with no help from you, progress to the go-to-heel to finish the exercise. But go slowly, praise him at every step, and do not try to insist on precision and accuracy for quite a while.

When he is coming in well, and if he still does not do it at a full run, speed him up by running backward away from him. Call him, and if he does not begin to run immediately, run backward as fast as you can, running in a crouch and calling to him to hurry up as you do so. The sight of you receding will make him step up his pace to get to you before you fade into the distance, and he will start to run. Keep that up until he runs from the first.

Refusal to stay—there are many variations on this theme, from walking after you as you leave through getting up just before you call. All reflect sloppiness in the stay training, and the solution is a redoing of that. Go back over it step by careful step, not rushing it this time. Be sure there is no question of his staying when you are three feet away before you try going four feet away. It is the only solution. One further problem may be in your handling if he always breaks, say, just when you turn around after leaving him. Check carefully to see that you are not swinging your arms as you turn, or after you turn, for such motions can look to him like signals to come.

If this problem occurs mainly in the show ring and not outside it, look into the possibility of confusion with the heeling which he has just completed in the ring. In Novice, you have heeled first on leash, and then off leash, and from that you go right into the recall. Every time you have started off, he has been supposed to go with you. Now you start off quickly again, and he may be confused, even if you have given him a firm "stay" command. After you have finished heeling and are in a position to leave him for the recall, make a little break for him. Within reason, you don't have to slam right into the exercise. The judge will ask if you are ready, and only when you say "Yes" will the exercise begin. So before he asks crouch beside your dog for a moment, and talk to him quietly. Tell him in a low voice, "Stay. Good boy. Stay now. Stay." That will take only a few seconds, but it will serve to get his mind off the heeling and onto staying. Then straighten up and give him the firm "Stay!" as you leave him and the problem may be solved.

As a last resort, if the problem is of serious proportions, you can try a retraining to establish a difference between the "stay" stay and the "recall" stay. Some dogs, having gotten the idea of staying when told until you come back, refuse to come when called, and others have the problem in reverse—finding that sometimes they are called from a stay they never learn fully to stay at all. As a desperation step, teach him to stay permanently (until you return to heel position) at the command "Stay!" and to stay until called at the command "Wait!" Thus he will be spared confusion about the meaning of "Stay!" Thus when you leave him to walk away for the recall, you tell him "Wait!" and he knows he is to stay only until called.

We do not recommend this idea in original training, for we feel that the dog should learn to work at command—that he should stay simply until something new happens, either being released by your return or by a call from you. Teaching him to stay at the "Stay!" command regardless of your subsequent commands might be an inconvenience. And his stay when told to "Wait!" may be jumpy and unsteady. But if you are unable to solve it by simple retraining in staying at command, this distinguishing between "Stay" and "Wait" may solve your problem. Better this than a constant problem with the stays.

Refusal to come, or break and run—here again the reason is that he does not want to come to you. Examine your training to find out why, and then go through the procedures outlined above for slow recall.

Running straight to heel—a natural enough thing for him to try, for it is a sensible shortcut. Why bother to sit in front for a moment if he is going to end up at heel every time? You may have been sending him to heel too quickly on the recall—try, on leash, having him sit in front of you for as much as a minute before he goes to heel. If he tries to go straight to heel even on leash, you must snap him back quickly as he heads around to the side, but praise him just after you snap! It is essential that he think of it as a regrettable accident, not as a correction coming from you.

Curving on recall—a frustrating problem for which we cannot offer much of an explanation. Most dogs come in, at whatever speed, straight. Some, for reasons known only to themselves, will take a curved path as if they were avoiding an obstacle. Any number of methods of correcting this have been tried, including practice recalls in narrow alleyways or passages, and using a fishing reel to take up line fast enough to haul the dog in straight. These have very little success, if they work at all, for as soon as the dog is called without them, he curves again. Some very few dogs never do lose this curious habit, but many can be cured by the backward running method. If you stand still and call him, he will almost seem to plot a curved course that will bring him to you. But if, as soon as you call him, you begin to run backward away from him, this calculated course doesn't work out, and he will tend to straighten out and make directly for you, for he doesn't know where you will be when you stop. Try that if you have a curve problem—chances are it will straighten him out.

The many other recall problems—stand in front, refusal to go to heel, crooked sit at heel, and others—are almost all the result of confusion on the dog's part. He is not sure what you want, and you must show him patiently with the leash, guiding and snapping him around and into proper position. Most of these minor problems require only a firm but gentle insistence on your part that he does what you want him to.

DROP ON RECALL

Most of the problems in this exercise result from inadequate training in the plain drop, or down. Refusal to drop, slow drop, sit instead of drop—these can only be worked out by going back to your "down" training. Do it all over again until your dog will drop on your command from any position, at any distance, and in any direction from you. Only when he will drop promptly *every time* while he is stationary in any position (see earlier chapter for drop training) should you try to drop him in motion. Then start again with the drop on the recall from heeling, and work up to the drop on the straight recall. We have found that this is the only way to correct the drop problems, for these problems are invariably the result of hurried and inadequate preliminary training.

Drops before command or signal—you have probably been training him too rigidly in dropping at a certain distance from you. If you always drop him ten feet after he starts coming, he will quickly learn that that is the place you want him to drop, and will try to accomodate you by going down without a command. Retrain on the drop, this time dropping him sometimes immediately after he starts coming, sometimes only just before he gets to you. And of course mix it up with non-drop recalls to teach him that he must not go down except on command or signal. Whatever you do, don't try to fool him by slipping in a quick command as he slows for an unordered drop. It fools nobody. If he has started to drop by himself, always call him in to you and finish that recall without a drop. Don't chastise or correct him. Just keep doing it until he will come all the way without trying to drop, then restart the dropping at various places. A variant of this problem is the dog who has become accustomed to the idea of dropping in front of the judge in a ring. Train him out of this by having a friend stand close to the line of the recall, and insisting that your dog come past the "judge" either with no drop at all, or dropping him well after he has passed. Only by recreating the actual situation can you solve this one.

Signal problems—this may result from faulty training in one of two ways. If your dog will drop on your signal only if your hand is held in the air, chances are that you timed your corrective command wrong when you were doing the original training. If you gave a signal, then shouted a command when he did not go down, you should not be surprised that he has learned that he is to go down after the signal hand has been in the air a few moments. Retrain him on the signal, this time giving the command simultaneously with the signal several times. Then try the signal alone, and if he does not respond immediately, go right back to the simultaneous command and signal half a dozen times, and then try the signal alone again.

The other possible mistraining involves simply holding the signal too long. If in training you have taught him that your hand going up in the air and staying there means to drop, then he will have learned just that. You must retrain, using simultaneous command and signal, this time shooting your hand up and bringing it right back down. Work until he will respond to that—don't try to make a visual correction by keeping your hand up in the air, perhaps even wiggling it, if he doesn't drop at once. At any failure to drop when your hand flashes up, go back to the command-and-signal a few times, then back to quick signal alone, and so on until he responds to the quick raising of the hand rather than its presence above your head.

THE RETRIEVE

Running after and bringing back a wooden dumbbell is not a thing which should logically put a strain on any healthy dog. Yet something which is so natural for a dog causes endless problems for trainers. Largely, the reason is a faulty and over-formal approach to the situation, an approach which does not allow the dog to enjoy things.

First, though, we will refer you back to the Open chapter for the discussion of the proper construction of the dumbbell for your dog. If you have been training with the wrong dumbbell, using the right one will work wonders. Take care of that first. But assuming that you have been working with a properly constructed dumbbell all along and are having the most serious common problem—refusal to take, hold or carry the dumbbell—our suggestion is that you go right back to the basics of retrieving for a complete retraining.

If your dog is frightened of the dumbbell, if he runs at the sight of it, or just stares dumbly when you tell him to get it, or goes out to it and just stands there, something has gone radically wrong somewhere, and applying patchwork corrections will probably not do much good. Instead, put the dumbbell aside for the moment. Your first job now is to establish the fact, for him, that simply going after something, anything, is fun and won't hurt him. Take a favorite toy of his, a ball, a stick, anything at all, and play with him. Throw it to him, at him, from him, urging him to chase it and get it and bring it back to you. This must be done entirely in play, with no atmosphere of formal training or compulsion. You must simply romp with him and slowly get him to the point of retrieving things you throw. Don't make any attempt to make him stay as you throw it, or come in to a sit when he brings it back, or anything of that sort. Just get him retrieving again.

Next step, reintroduce the dumbbell. As you play with him, throw it from you and urge him to get it. If he is still unhappy about it because of his past experience with it, chase it yourself. This may take hours of patience and running, but in the end it will work. Throw the dumbbell, and say to him in an excited tone, "Get It!" and then take off after it yourself at a run, urging him to come along with you. Make a contest and a game of it. If the problem is serious, you will reach it first and get it yourself a discouraging number of times. He may in fact just sit and watch you apathetically. But if you persevere, calling to him and competing with him for the privilege of retrieving the dumbbell, he will break down finally and try to get it first. Then you have won a great victory and you must praise him highly for it.

When you have done this for a while, after he has relented and is chasing it with you, slack down your own attempts to get it. Don't do it suddenly, but one time run just a little slower so that it is an easy victory for him. Slowly work down until he is going out all by himself to get it. Don't expect to get to this stage in one day, or two, or even three. Take it very slowly.

Now that you have shown him that retrieving is fun after all—that you are not going to be an ogre about it any more—and that the dumbbell is nothing to be afraid of, you can begin to reintroduce the "forced" part of the retrieve, but gently. With him at a sit, put the dumbbell in front of his mouth and tell him to take it. If he doesn't, get his mouth open in the manner we have described, and put the dumbbell in, but do this as gently as you possibly can, praising him and talking to him all the while, and then take it from him promptly. When you've done this, throw the dumbbell and get him to go get it, to keep in his mind the fact that everything is still okay. Then with him back beside you, repeat the "take it" lesson. Do it again, then throw the dumbbell for him in play. Keep up this alternation of work and play with the dumbbell, never correcting him or doing anything but very gently forcing him to take the dumbbell, until he will open his mouth for it. That, of course, calls for even higher praise.

From this point, go right through dumbbell training as we have outlined it in the Open chapter, progressing from a "take" in the air to a "take" on the ground and to the final retrieve. You must, however, and we will say this yet again—you must go about it slowly and gently and make it as much fun for him as possible.

You may, of course, have far less serious problems in the retrieve, but difficult ones nonetheless:

Waiting for second command—the problem is just that, as we have described it in the Open chapter. The dog goes out fast to the dumbbell and stands there, waiting. What he is waiting for is a command to go ahead and pick it up—the only reason he does that is that he has learned to do so in training. In training, when he goes to the dumbbell and stands looking at it, you must go out to him, put it in his mouth, then get him back with you to the original position to deliver it to you. Then go back to the shortest possible retrieve, just a few feet in front of you. There he will either pick it up immediately or at least you are in a position to make the correction without moving your feet much. Then throw it only a very little bit farther. And then only a very little bit farther again. Progress very slowly to a long throw. The mistake that is commonly made is that of doing the long throw too fast. The trainer will say, "Ah, he does it fine when I throw it only three feet in front, so now he must understand." Then he throws it as far as his arm will serve, and the dog goes out to stand and look at the dumbbell again. Increase your distance only a foot at a time—the idea is to put it over on the dog. If you increase the distance slowly enough, he will be retrieving successfully at thirty feet before he realizes it. But whatever you do, don't give him a second command, or you'll be right back where you started. The foot-by-foot progress seems tedious, and is, but going a foot at a time it will take only thirty throws until you are at the thirty foot distance, and that's not so wearing.

Sudden unwillingness to take dumbbell—this does not happen often, but it can be terribly frustrating if it happens to you and you don't know what has happened. Check to make sure that the dumbbell has not become fouled in throwing and rolling along the ground. A fouled dumbbell is repulsive to a dog. It may be so slightly tainted that it is only apparent to his nose, but sufficient to make him reluctant to pick it up. Just in case, wipe it well with a damp rag and let it air a day or two before trying again. In any case, suspect at once some change in the dumbbell, don't chalk it up to sudden stubbornness in your dog.

Dropping or playing with dumbbell—this traces back to insufficient practice in simply holding it. Take him back over the ground, giving it to him to hold, and then having him hold it for several minutes as he sits by you and heels with you, ending with a short recall so that he can deliver it to you. Simply holding a properly constructed dumbbell in his mouth for several minutes absolutely cannot hurt your dog—he is able to breathe and swallow and everything else, so you must simply convince him, by working up slowly from a short hold to several minutes, that he must hold it until he delivers it to you.

Overeagerness, refusal to stay—if you have this problem, you may consider yourself lucky, for there are legions of trainers who wish only that their dog would be so eager to go after the dumbbell that they would have trouble restraining him. This problem sometimes results from a playful retraining, in which the dog comes to like the idea of retrieving so much that it is difficult to make him stay when you have thrown it. The best solution is putting him back on leash. Take a short hold on the leash, and throw the dumbbell. If he charges after it, you can snap him back into position. Then release the leash from his collar and send him for the dumbbell. Go from that to holding lightly onto his collar at the back of his neck to restrain him—but be careful in both cases not to be harsh about it. If you do he may lose interest in retrieving altogether, and there you'll be, ready for the third round. Another method is to interpose other exercises. Put him on leash and throw the dumbbell not far—about six or seven feet—and then start up at heel, making a quick turn in either direction, then another turn and another until you have come around quickly back to position. Then release him and send him for it. This will get across to him that he is to work only at command—the short throw in this case is to make it easy for him to see the dumbbell and remember, once you are back in position, that he is to get it. Then try the same thing off lead, holding lightly onto his collar until you begin to heel. Another time you can give him a down command, and then a sit, before you send him. Finally, send him only after a wait of as much as a minute—without any other exercises in between—to keep him in mind of the fact that he is to work only at your orders.

THE HURDLE RETRIEVE

One of the most serious problems in this is going around the jump. It results almost without fail from having allowed the dog to go around it in early training, and in play. It is, however, an almost universal error of training, and extremely easy to do, and once done difficult to undo. But it is important that you realize, when you are trying to solve the problem, that he is going around the jump not out of spite, or stubbornness, or stupidity, or any unwillingness to take the jump in both directions—but simply because he doesn't know any better. In early training, when jumping was great fun, he went cantering around it with your full permission. Now, when you are throwing the dumbbell and all relations are warm and friendly, he goes around it again. Whatever you do, don't shout or scream at him or chastize him for it. What you must do now is convince him that under no circumstances can he go around the thing. The answer is retraining, but first investigate the idea that differing circumstances may be causing it. Not infrequently, a dog who has been working extremely well on the home training grounds will, at a show, suddenly go around the hurdle. This is the result of the dog's failure to generalize his training from the specific (your training hurdle) to the general (any hurdle he is faced with). If this seems to be the situation, don't go back over all the training, but do do some practice work in several different situations—and if possible with a different hurdle. Take your own hurdle from the back yard and set it up in a park if you can, or in a country field. Set it up inside somewhere where there is room. If possible, work with a training class hurdle. The dog who has had the idea that his instructions to jump apply only to a hurdle set up in your back yard will soon learn after practice work in different locales that he is to go over any hurdle you point at, no matter where he finds it.

If the problem occurs in your training area, too, then retraining is the only way out. You can never completely erase from his mind the fact that he can go and has gone around it, but an intensive new course will help a great deal. Foolish though it may seem, the dog who can jump full height must be taken, on leash, back to the basic step of jumping over the single eight-inch board with you, then over and back, and from there up to full height and regular work again. This time, on leash or off, never allow him to go around.

Climbing over jump—for some dogs it's simply easier under normal circumstances, and you have to convince him that it really isn't. Set up the bar according to the instructions in Open, either with nails or the iron holders. Then when he tries to scramble over he will knock the bar off and soon learn to clear it. Remember, though, that the idea is not to frighten him with the falling of the bar, but to convince him that the footing is not so good up there. If the falling bar should frighten him, go back for a quick refresher course by lowering the hurdle-plus-bar and letting him clear it a few times, then build it up slowly. When he is clearing everything at full height, remove the bar.

Refusal to jump at all—look for a good reason. His feet may be sore, or his legs. You may be working on too hard a surface, or one that is too slippery—change or pad it somehow. Another thing to check is what he can see as he sits in front of the jump. If his view over the top consists of nothing but sky, he may just possibly be worried about what's on the other side of the jump—pit or precipice or solid ground. We've seen it happen. No matter how many times you've gone over it with him, he may be much happier if he can see trees, or a wall, from his spot. Try repositioning the jump. If none of these app.y, it may mean that you have been trying to drag him over the jump with the leash—a not un-common training method which leads to many difficulties. The only real solution is again retraining the right way. Take him right back to the first steps and slowly follow the procedure in our Open chapter.

Refusal to jump with dumbbell—check first that it is not too heavy for him, and then that it is otherwise properly constructed for him. Quite often a dog who can be trained to retrieve and carry a wrongly-designed dumbbell will refuse to jump with it—the bells in front of his eyes make jumping difficult if not impossible. If this has nothing to do with it, go through a quick jumping retraining while he is carrying the dumbbell—walking over the jump with him as he holds it, progressing to over-and-back holding it, and to a recall over a low hurdle holding it. Then start off again doing a retrieve over a low hurdle, and work the height up slowly.

Jumps over, refuses to retrieve—first of all, it may mean that he does not see it when he lands. Practice your throw until you have it well under control, then in training throw the dumbbell so that it lands just a foot or two in front of where the dog lands in going over. Keep doing that until he retrieves well, and only then throw farther. If this is not the problem, examine the possibility that here, too, the dumbbell may be wrongly constructed for him. Otherwise, the solution may be strong drilling in the retrieve on the flat. Work at this until he retrieves without fail, then begin hurdle work with a very low jump—hardly more than a flat retrieve. Work your distance up very slowly.

Picks up dumbbell, does not return—this may be caused by a fear of jumping with it, in which case check the construction of the dumbbell and go through the retraining outlined above under "refusal to jump with dumbbell." It may also indicate severe corrections on your part concern-ing the return—you may have been too harsh with him about sitting straight, or about dropping the dumbbell. If so, do a retraining from the beginning, with gentle handling. Otherwise, the chances are his work in the flat retrieve is not steady enough. Go back over that thoroughly, then begin work again with a very low jump.

THE BROAD JUMP

Broad jump problems are often quite severe, for the situation is a highly artificial one, and the long jump is nowhere nearly as natural for a dog as a high hurdle. If you have trained, or tried to train, your dog without the "crib" described in the Open chapter, we strongly recommend that you make yourself one and then retrain with it, for its use almost automatically solves most problems involving clearing the jumps.

Inability to clear jumps—check first on your dog's physical condition, and then on the surface he has to land on. Here particularly a slippery surface will throw a dog off. Then go back to the beginnings and work with the crib and only two jumps making up a short broad jump. The crib will force your dog to get height into his jump, and then he will be able to clear the required length.

Refusal to jump off lead—this probably means you have been using the lead to pull him over, a common mistake. Go back through a proper retraining, then try him off-lead again when he will do the jump with no lead corrections at all. If this does not help, work up from a short jump, going over the jump yourself with him at your side, on lead. You should try as long a running jump as necessary up to six feet. From that you can go to jumping with him off-lead, and then letting him jump by himself.

Running to left of jump—a fairly rare problem, but easily solved with leash control. Use a longer clothesline on the full jump, and keep it short enough to be able to control him.

Jumping toward handler—step into the jumps before calling him to jump. Step in about a third of the way the first time, then gradually step in less until you can stay outside of them and he is jumping straight.

Refusal to stay until command—this comes from overtraining in the jump. Leave it alone a few days, and concentrate on firm "stay" training. Then start again with a very short jump, which allows you to be close to him while he is staying, in position for a quick correction if he breaks. Work up to the full jump and leaving him ten feet away, only very slowly.

Goes to jump, then stands—this is another "second command" problem. It almost always means that in training you have been giving him a second command to jump as he gets to the first board. The only solution is retraining, leaving out the extra command. Never expect your dog to do anything in performance that he hasn't been doing in training—and always expect him to do in performance what he *has* been doing in training.

Does not come around quickly after jump—a very common problem, traceable to the fact that it is simply easier for him to keep on running in a straight line after landing, rather than swinging around quickly. If he is jumping well and confidently, put him back on lead and insist that he comes around to you fast and sits straight. It is almost always as simple as that. Don't be ashamed to go back on leash even if he is a fantastically good jumper—it is the only way you will teach him to come around fast. The first few times, send him over—and just as he lands give him a sharp "come" command, timing it nicely with a mild snap on the long lead to bring him around. Then leave out the command and give him the lead snap—remember, a snap, not a tug and a haul. Then work him on leash for a while without the snap when it has become unnecessary, finally going off lead again.

DIRECTED JUMPING

The problems here involved can be divided roughly into three parts— the sendaway, the bar jump, and the direction signals. Of these, the send- away offers the most trouble, for it involves a totally unnatural concept for the dog—going away from you at command. Also, because of its diffi- culty, and the patience needed, it offers the greatest chance for a lost temper, which will founder the training quite effectively.

Refusal to go out—if when you send him your dog simply looks con- fused or takes a step or two and then stops, it is due to insufficient instruc- tion on your part. Remember always, when he looks confused, he is confused. Put the leash back on, give him the "go" command, and then run along with him thirty or forty feet, then call him and step backwards to bring him around. Give him the sit command when he has turned him- self around, then praise him and go to heel position to try it again. Only by patient repetition of this will he get the idea. It may seem difficult to get across to him the idea that you do not want him, at the command, to run alongside you, but rather to go out himself. But if you work at it and watch his reactions and encourage his being out in front, you will be able to make him differentiate. Some dogs have been taught the send-away by throwing an article for them to retrieve, then calling them to halt before getting there, and by being pulled away on a long rope—around a pulley or in the hands of a confederate. These methods are sometimes effective, but we have found that they are no substitute for basic insistence on the dog going out unassisted, and for no reason except that you tell him to. Going out with him again and again and yet again may get to be a colossal bore, and seem to be getting you nowhere, but it will eventually show results, and good ones. Keep at it, urging him to keep going in front of you. As he begins to take the first tentative steps away, don't be afraid to keep repeating the "go" command and pointing with your arm. Later you can cut down on the extra commands. But whatever you do, don't try to keep him moving by running at him to scare him away—that will destroy your friendly relations to a fare-thee-well and ruin your other work.

Refusal to go out straight—often, this is a result of the rope-and-pulley training. It gets him there, but in his attempts to resist the pull of the rope he pulls to one side or the other and follows a semi-circular course on the way out. Retrain by going with him, time and again, and urge him on to a faster pace. This will counteract the circular trend. It can also result from training in a limited space, in which he always ends up the sendaway in a specific spot. Much as in the curving recall, he learns to plot a curved path to the ultimate destination. Somehow find a larger space to work in, and send him farther and farther, until he realizes that a straight line is the easiest way to do it.

Turning to sit in front of a jump—this can be the result of sending him over one jump too often. Frequently, a trainer will begin directed jumping with only one jump, the solid hurdle, already built. He works with that one, figuring to build the bar jump later when and if the dog masters the idea of the sendaway. Thus the dog always tends to circle to face the solid hurdle. If the dog has learned his mistaken lesson too well, it can be solved by working again with the jumps—sending him between the jumps and then very far beyond, fifty or sixty feet, without having him return over the jumps, but going to him and then sending him back between them. If he never knows whether he is going to be stopped near the jumps, or in fact if he is going to be sent over at all, he will lose the tendency to circle to face one of them. One caution, though—do not ever call him back to you between the jumps to save the labor of walking to him and sending him again—always go to him or he will get the idea that coming back between them is okay.

Tries to jump going out—this is a logical thing for a dog to do, for in Utility training he will have strong memories of being sent out over the hurdle after the dumbbell. Even if you have laid a firm foundation of straight sendaway work, he may try it the first times you work between the jumps. To curb this tendency, stand with him squarely between the jumps and send him away, then walk back to a normal position to call him over either jump. Next time, stand with him only a few feet in front of the midline of the jumps, and send him, then walking back to call him over. Work back slowly to a normal sendaway position, and he will have become gradually accustomed to going out between them, and the problem should be solved.

Walking under bar jump—the slight change of situation, from being sent over and back on the bar jump, to being directed over it, sometimes causes confusion. Try sending him out and directing him over the bar set very low. Gradually work it up to regulation height, and he will have relearned the bar-clearing idea in the new circumstance.

Inability to clear bar—if he can clear the solid hurdle at the regulation height, he can clear the bar. Some dogs, though, have a hard time learning to make as much effort. Some even change jumping styles for the bar. This will rarely occur with a dog who has learned the solid hurdle with the bar on top, but the dog who has been introduced cold to the bar sometimes finds it hard to realize that the bar is as high as it is. In most cases, the problem can be overcome by slow and patient retraining on the bar. Take it down low again and work up slowly, never raising the bar until he has no trouble at all gauging the distance and clearing it. Too sudden raising will throw him off, for he has been used to taking the spring required for a lower position, and the different height of the bar is not as apparent to him as is raising the solid hurdle. You must almost fool him into making the extra effort, by successive raises of no more than two inches at a time. If you want to go to the trouble of fixing your jump standards so that the bar can be raised one inch at a time, so much the better. What you must do is create in his mind the idea that the bar hasn't really been moved up, but that he has mistakenly jumped a little too low—then he will put out the slight extra effort needed to clear it easily. It may seem improbable that you can fool him that way, but you can.

Another minor possibility is that he simply can't see the bar well. If in training you haven't bothered to paint the bar in the regulation black and white stripes, do so at once. That specification is not to make the bar attractive, but to make it as visible to the dog as possible. And be sure the bar is as thick as the regulations call for—at least two inches in diameter—again for easy visibility. Don't try to use an old broomstick cut off, or anything like that, or he may have trouble seeing it, and consequent difficulty in gauging his effort.

A third possibility is a misconception on your part of the function of the jump command. Some trainers have the idea that the command "Hup" or "Over" or whatever they use is a command to the dog to jump right then. With that idea in mind, you *can* train your dog to take off as he hears the word. Unfortunately, some dogs are trained that way. Thus, you may be mis-timing the command and making him take his spring too early or too late. The idea of the jump command is that when he hears it he is to go over either the obstacle directly in front of him (as in the hurdle retrieve) or over the one you point out, no matter how many steps he takes before he gets to it. If you have trained your dog, either consciously or unconsciously, to leap when he hears the word, go back and untrain him in that particular. Get him to go over jumps with only the original command given when you send him—let him decide by himself how to gauge his leap. In fact, we recommend in directed jumping that you do not use the second command to jump as allowed in the rules, for that second command leads to just the problem we have been discussing.

Ignoring directional signals—generally stems from a too-quick introduction to the idea. Go right back to basics. Send him out, then walk to one side until you are facing him across one jump. Call him to you across that jump, pointing vigorously outside it. Then heel with him back to the center position and send him out again. Walk over to face him across the other jump, calling him over that as you point outside it. Gradually cut down your walking, but very gradually, until you need only take a few steps toward the desired jump as you direct him. Then cut it down to a very vigorous signal, and only after he is completely sure of what he is doing should you cut it down to the arm signal alone. Taking an arm direction is an entirely new concept, and you must explain it to him clearly and patiently.

SCENT DISCRIMINATION

The most common problem in scent discrimination is a simple general confusion on the part of the dog. Because of mistaken idea on how to teach discrimination, the handler often creates in the dog's mind the impression that nothing he does is right, and so the dog just gives up trying. The specific villain in this case is a correction for picking up the wrong article. You must keep uppermost in your mind in this training that *whatever* article the dog picks up, he thinks that is the right one—when you correct him you give him the idea that even picking anything up is wrong, and deep confusion sets in.

If you have been training him by any other method and are having trouble, we recommend strongly that you stop, make yourself an article board as described in the Utility chapter, and begin again with that. It is the only way he can be prevented from picking up a wrong article without strong corrections from you.

Assuming, though, that you have trained with the article board and are having trouble once off the board, the probable fault is that you went off the board too soon. One or two mistakes in the articles are natural, but continued mistakes off the board after good work on it indicate that you should make another board and go right back over the training. There are any number of specific ways the dog may demonstrate the fact that he is confused about the idea—he may simply stand near the articles, circle them without going near them, kick at them, refuse to go out at all, go out and run away, or even wet on the articles. Anything of that nature means that he is not sure what to do, and the only solution is to go right back to throwing the scented articles near the board, then progress to the board, to get the idea well in his mind.

One special caution: when you begin to work off the board, be extremely careful that you are sure of which article it is that has the scent. It is far easier than you might think to place an article in the group and then lose track of it when you are back in position to send him. Even assistants who place an article and whose eyes never leave the circle can become confused. It needs only one correction when the dog has picked up the right article to set training back a great distance. So watch it with great care.

Picking up article next to proper one—this happens fairly often, and results from having your articles too close together. Even if your dog understands fully what to do, he may pass his nose over a wrong article, and just as it is passing over he may get the scent from the right article only an inch or two away. If he grabs, he grabs the article right under his nose, which is the wrong one. It is not his fault at all—so work with sufficient distance between articles.

Refusal to walk between articles—usually results again from too close placement of the articles. If only two or three inches separate the articles, he won't be able to walk among them without stepping on them and perhaps stumbling. Have a minimum of six inches between articles. To cure the tendency to be afraid of stepping on them, try working for a while with the articles well spread out—a distance of two feet between articles is not too much until he learns that it is all right to walk between them. Then reduce the distance.

Insists on picking up one or more specific wrong articles—suspect immediately that scent has somehow gotten onto them. If it is only one, remove it for that training session. If more than one, leave all articles to air a day or two, outside if possible, before trying again. Remember that scent moves in mysterious ways, and give your dog the benefit of the doubt. A strong correction on a wrong article that does have your scent is just as bad as a correction on a right article.

Refusal to pick up one type of article—this generally requires only patient insistence on your part. Put the article in his mouth, time and again, and insist that he hold it and then walk with it. Almost always the problem is with the metal article, and this may require more patience, but persistence and praise will solve it. With metal articles, one thing to watch is temperature. If you are working outside in cool weather or inside where there is a cold draft along the floor, the metal articles will be colder to the touch than the others—and cold metal in the mouth is not pleasant. When teaching him to carry the metal article, warm it by holding it and rubbing it before giving it to him. This will make him less reluctant to take it. In the ring, the metal article you have scented will be warmed from contact with your hands, and he will take it then, too.

Dropping article—this may simply be inattention on your part to sufficient "hold it" training with each type of article, or it may be a reflection of wrong corrections. If he has been corrected frequently after picking up an article, he will be reluctant to hold onto any article, and will tend to drop it. The solution for either problem follows from the cause.

Smelling in wide circle around articles—this may not even be a problem, although you may think of it as one. If he goes out to work at the articles, and first, or even in the middle of working, strays away to sniff the ground, stones, the jumps or anything else, he may simply be working extra hard to be sure the right article is not somewhere outside the circle. If this extra sniffing is within certain limits, don't do anything about it— it might just save the exercise if one time the article is placed a little away from the circle of other articles—extra sniffing is much preferable to giving up if the article is not right in the circle. But if he goes too far afield, retrain by going back a step or two, letting him watch you place the article in the circle, and give him the idea that it will always be found near to or in the circle.

Ignoring some of the articles—this will result if you have been placing your article, in practice, always in one section of the circle. Go back a bit and work in practice with the scented article placed in various parts of the circle.

Sudden confusion after good work—not infrequently, a dog who has been doing faultless work in scent discrimination will seem to lose confidence in his ability. Often, this confusion can be traced to another exercise you are working on. If, for example, you are having trouble with directed jumping and have had to give him continued corrections, he will lose confidence in his ability to do anything right. Human though that sounds, it does at times happen to dogs. The answer is to build up his confidence in his scent work by going back a step, although you need not go back to the board. Set out the articles, and throw your scented article only a short way, then send him for it. Throw it farther on successive tries, until you throw it among the other articles. Then proceed to placing it with him watching, and with him facing away. A brief refresher will rebuild his confidence. And incidentally, this occurrence should give you pause about whatever other exercise you are teaching at the time— if your corrections in it have been so severe and frequent, and your praise so lacking, as to cause him to lose confidence in his ability, you had better sit down and think things out. Something is going wrong somewhere in your training.

THE SEEK BACK

Surprisingly few dogs have trouble with the seek back, perhaps because chasing after or looking for something is a very natural thing to do, and perhaps because the leather glove or article is a congenial object. Such problems as are encountered result, we will repeat, from faulty or hurried training.

Even if he has a natural bent for the work, a dog can become discouraged and lose interest if it is made too hard for him in training. A handler will sometimes see good and rapid progress in his dog, and drop or hide the article in a quite difficult spot. The dog, unable to find it, will lose confidence in his ability, and lose sight of the object of all this, and give up trying if it happens several times. Whatever the genesis of the problem (and spend a little time thinking about possible causes), the best remedy is, once again, retraining. This second time around, progress very slowly. Put special emphasis on the early straight retrieves of the article, with generous praise to make him really want to get it and bring it to you. Go to the advanced steps only when you are sure of his performance—and give him plenty of encouragement the first times the article is out of sight. No matter how much he may like finding things for you, too much work at any one time will bore him. Particularly as you reach the advanced stages, do only two or three seek backs in one session, to keep him alert and willing.

Playing with article—this may indicate that you have allowed him to play with it, chew on it, throw it in the air in training or during your training rest periods. Throw away that particular article and begin work with another, going rapidly over the basic steps and insisting that he hold the article without chewing or playing. It also may result from laxity in insisting on a prompt return of the article, especially if tracking training is involved. In your pleasure that he has found the article at all, in training, you may have been allowing him to toss it, chew it, or otherwise play with it as a sort of reward and incentive. Go back a step or two and always insist that, once found, he bring the article to you at a run.

SIGNALS

About problems in the signal exercise we can actually say very little, for almost any signal problem you can name results from the same old vice of insufficient training and too-rapid advance. Slow reactions to signals follow the pattern of slow reaction to the drop signal as discussed earlier. Absolute non-reaction results from either insufficient preparation or too-hurried progress from command-and-signal to signal alone. If there is confusion between signals, we can only advise you to practice your signals until they are sharp and very distinct—concentrating on distinguishing between the sit, down and recall.

One thing to watch for in particular is heel signals if you have a small dog. It is entirely permissible to bend slightly to swing your hand near his face when you give the "forward" signal, so do this if he has been having trouble seeing it.

Inattention on the latter part of the exercise is sometimes troublesome. If his gaze and attention wander around as he stands, or sits, or lies at some distance from you, he can't see your signals. And sometimes this can be blamed on nothing but a basically scatter-brained nature. Whatever the case, don't call to him, or whistle at him, or otherwise make noises to get him to look at you, and don't wave at him. Noises and motions are far more likely to make him break from his position than anything else. As soon as his attention wanders, run away from him. That may seem a curious thing to do, but not only is your movement away going to catch even a wandering eye, but your slipping away as soon as his head is turned will make him want to keep an eye on you. If the cause is just boredom, it is only when he is sure you will stay put, hooting and waving, that he will look around for diversion. If you make him uncertain of your whereabouts when he looks away, you'll find that his attention will stay riveted on you.

PROBLEMS IN GENERAL

There are, naturally and unfortunately, many more minor problems than those we have mentioned and covered in this chapter. To cover all problems in detail, and even to give detailed attention to all the major ones, would quite literally require an entire book on problems alone. So what we have done is give specific advice on those problems which we have found occuring most frequently.

It may well be that the particular problem that is driving you to the brink of distraction has not even been touched upon. If this is so, we can only ask that you read carefully the section of the book devoted to the exercise that is causing you trouble. Compare the methods given there with what you have been doing. Try to isolate the problem—put in words just what it is that he doesn't do, or doesn't do well enough. Then sit back and think hard about it along the lines we have indicated throughout this book. Sometimes, the reason for a problem may not occur to you for days—it has happened to us enough times. Confronted with a particularly tricky problem you may cudgel your brains for hours trying to find a logical explanation, then two or three days later the solution may spring into your mind like a lightning flash of revelation. Thus we counsel patience and a lay-off of several days if something is really going wrong. Put yourself in his place as much as you can, and ask yourself what your reaction would be if you were being treated as you have been treating him.

Above all, in cases of non-performance, ask yourself if you have really been demonstrating to him what you want done. If you have been simply telling him to do something and then trying to correct him into doing it, you'll have had very little success. Remember that the dog won't even know there's a lesson going on if you are not teaching him—if you are just standing on your ego and insisting that he do something he doesn't understand.

Whatever you do, use as your guides to analysis and retraining the basic psychology of the dog and the philosophy of training as we have outlined it, and the psychology of your own individual dog as you know it. The dog has feelings, he has dignity, and he is capable of infinite response to the proper inducements. He is not a machine, but a living, breathing, responsive creature. He remembers, and remembers things for a long time, but keep always in mind that he does not have a "connective" memory—you cannot correct him today for what he did yesterday, nor can you correct him now for what he did two minutes ago. Unless an action of his carries either a penalty result or a pleasure result, it will have no meaning for him. And the penalty or the pleasure must be immediate. All corrections must be made at the time of the fault, and they *must be followed by praise.*

On that note we will end this chapter, for there is no one thing in obedience which even approaches the importance of praise. We cannot say it too often. Praise him when he does right, and praise him when he does wrong and has been corrected. Praise him to keep him happy. Praise him to keep him working. We know how hard it can be to fully grasp the idea of praise after a correction, to accept it as something basic. But there it is, the one and only way to have a happy working dog, and for that matter, a working dog of almost any nature. Do it.

CHAPTER XI

FEEDING AND HEALTH

T HE FEEDING and health problems of puppies and grown dogs are areas in which you will encounter a great deal of pontification and nonsense. Feeding, particularly, is rife with old wives' tales. Both fields, however, need only the application of a little common sense, backed by some of the facts we will give you, for easy understanding.

We firmly believe that your dog should be fed according to a sound nutrition-diet plan, for his health and development. The diets and schedules you will find later in this chapter are what we, and many dog owners, have found best for our own dogs. But none of this is to say that you can't do it differently and have a perfectly fine and happy dog around the house. Uncounted millions of dogs lived, grew and prospered for thousands of years before the advent of scientific feeding and balanced diets, and many thousands now alive and healthy have never known any diet but table scraps and leavings. Lest we seem to paint too rosy a picture of the results of thoughtless feeding, we must also point out that millions of dogs have suffered shortened and unhappy lives through neglected feeding. However that may be, it has been our experience that a dog whose feeding is planned with a modicum of care has a definite edge in health, vitality and longevity over the dog haphazardly fed. We feel that edge is well worth the small trouble involved.

PUPPY FEEDING

The first rule applicable to puppy feeding is that you can give him solid foods as soon as he will take them. The average age of acquisition is three months—at that age puppies will happily eat, and should get, solid food. If you should happen to get a pup two months old, he can eat solid food too. Much younger than that it becomes a special case beyond the scope of this chapter, but you are not likely to encounter the problem.

When you do get the puppy, find out from the breeder or former owner what he has been feeding. If the pup comes to you in good condition—as indeed he must, or you shouldn't have taken him—the diet he has been getting will keep him that way. Follow the breeder's diet, but with a cautious eye to padding of the list. With only the best interests of the pup at heart, many breeders will supply the buyer with a fabulous list of condiments the like of which the pup has never seen. Some feeding lists will include, for example, baby foods. Such canned foods are if anything too rich in vegetables and other human-nutrition items, and short on plain meat. Baby foods are fine if you can afford them and if you supplement them with meat, but it is an unnecessary expense.

Rather than take you through a maze of possible diets—and there are many—here is one we can recommend for the young puppy. First meal, milk and Pablum or dried cereal; second meal, milk and any good canned soft dog food; third meal, canned food plus a small amount of starchy filler (dried bread or kibbled biscuit, moistened with milk, water or meat broth); fourth meal, fresh meat with fat.

You can also take your veterinarian's advice on the puppy's diet, and we strongly recommend this. If his advice on what to feed is different from ours, your best bet is to stick with him. Especially if your puppy has any specific problems, follow the vet's advice quite religiously. There are, as we will later point out, good vets and poor vets. It is unlikely that you will ever get actually harmful advice on feeding from any veterinarian, but then again you might just have bad luck. Just keep your eye out for patent nonsense. General rule: trust your veterinarian as you would your own doctor, because he knows a good deal more about it than you will learn from this book or any other.

The prepared dog foods which we recommend for feeding, the soft canned foods, are almost all scientifically compounded by experts. In general, you are safe in buying canned foods distributed by major packers and companies. This is not to say that many of the canned foods put out by small specialty companies are not excellent—but you are on the safer side, until you know more about it, if you stick with the companies of known reputation. And this, incidentally, does not mean just companies with large advertising budgets. Among the reasons we recommend the prepared foods is that they are an economical feeding for the puppy and grown dog. The table scraps idea may seem the cheapest way out, but it is, in a good many cases, simply false economy. Particularly if you have a medium or large dog, you will find yourself not just giving him the true left-overs, but sneaking in extra amounts at cooking time, so there'll be any adequate amount left over for scrap feeding. And bingo, there goes the food budget—you're feeding him at human costs.

The prepared foods may seem to you like fairly unappetizing messes, but to the dog they are generally tasty. Don't make the mistake of anthropomorphism, which is a nice word covering most of the aspects of thinking of your dog as a person. Dogs just simply don't have the same tastes, preferences or food prejudices as humans. Aside from that, their senses function differently, and to the dog a can of dog food is a mixture of a dozen different smells and tastes. You get one smell, dog food; he gets a dozen smells from the components and thinks of it differently. This may seem improbable to you, but consider for a moment that humans, at least some of them, can be trained to do almost as well. The famed "noses" of the perfume industry can tell at a whiff all the ingredients of a perfume, plus the approximate amounts of each—and many organic chemists have trained themselves to do almost as well with malodorous chemical compounds. The dog has a long head start on them. To him that smell of hash is actually an interesting blend of food odors, and he'll pitch in.

Along this line, we might say also that some of the "meal" dog foods are also excellent for general feeding. We generally recommend that you don't feed them too young, but when the pup has reached, say, 3 months, he can quite profitably eat the meal foods, moistened with water, milk or meat broth. Here again, what to you is just dry-looking gravel will be to him a melange of quite attractive things.

This is not to say that dogs don't have preferences in foods. They do. One dog will, for no reason known to man, court starvation rather than eat some foods. Some will adamantly refuse to touch one particular brand of prepared food which thousands of others guzzle with gusto.

There is, in fact, a famous television incident involving a prepared dog food—on a local show the producers somehow neglected to try the advertised food on the actor dog before the commercial. When he was led on camera, the dog sniffed it once, circled it, and then pointedly lifted his leg on the bowl. This reaction is hardly a common one, occurring, we suppose, only with the more demonstrative television dogs, but it does illustrate the fact of definite likes and dislikes. If your puppy really takes a strong dislike to one particular type of food, don't force it on him. Try another brand, and then another until you hit one he likes. If he turns up his nose at all prepared foods, and the vet certifies him as well, then he is just being finicky about it. Put one brand in front of him at several meals, until he gets good and ravenously hungry. He'll eat.

In addition to his milk, meat, starchy filler and prepared food, give him dietary supplements. Bone meal is good for the puppy and will help his growth. Any good commercial mineral supplement will also help, as will vitamin supplements emphasizing the A and D vitamins. We recommend these supplements even if you are following our recommended diet for your pup, and especially if you are planning to feed him scraps, or all canned food, or any other diet. In using the supplements, follow the label regarding amount to be administered according to the size of the pup. Better to overdo slightly if anything—it is difficult to overdose as the body tends to throw off superfluous minerals and vitamins.

Most puppies seem ravenously hungry all the time. They gobble their food as though it might be the last meal in the world. But some few present eating problems that can be worrisome to the owner. If you are faced with a puppy who simply doesn't eat, or eats listlessly—and you have established through trying that it isn't just that he doesn't like some particular food—you should suspect illness of some sort. Judge what to do by the pup's general behavior. If he is otherwise happy, alert and active, it may just be a phase. Pups have them just like human children. If he mopes around the house and is generally unhappy about things, then non-eating is likely to be an indicator of one illness or another. Not eating in itself won't do any harm to a puppy, but if he has fasted for 36 hours, take him to your vet for an examination. Once the vet has examined him and given you advice on the situation, follow that advice about periods of non-eating. But the first time it is indeed far better to be safe.

A good general approach to number of feedings for a puppy is to assume that he needs four feedings a day at the age of two or three months. The puppy's stomach is small and cannot accomodate the large quantities eaten by an adult, and to insure good growth and health he should have food coming into his system regularly. Puppies, like children, are growing literally every minute and must have the materials available. It is a well accepted maxim that "if you don't get it into them the first year, you won't get it into them," meaning that the pattern of growth, health and development is laid firmly then and little you can do afterward has much effect. And within that first year, the first few months are again predominantly important. So feed your pup right up to the eyeballs with everything nutritious you can, and watch him sprout.

As he gets along in age, the number of feedings per day can be gradually reduced until he is eating just one meal, probably the late evening meal. Another very general rule, assuming you are starting at three months, is to knock off one daily feeding every three months until at one year he is eating once a day. This is, however, only a very general rule, and treat it as such. If he seems lackadaisical about any of the four early feedings, and consistently refuses or only nibbles at one, cut him down to three right away. Feed him, in fact, only as often as he wants to eat. This is good physically, and also psychologically—for if you allow him to turn up his nose at a feeding every day of his early life he can easily get into a finicky mood about the whole business of eating.

Approaching it from the other end—his feedings definitely should be cut down at about the stated intervals. Even if he relishes and gobbles four a day at six months, cut him down to three (with more in each), and so on. Many dogs, of course, stay at two meals all their lives, getting table scraps as they are available. But the balanced feeding plan of one meal a day is preferable. Among the reasons for this is that it establishes a good pattern of once-a-day elimination at a fairly regular time, which is considerably more convenient for you as the owner. Another is that this is the pattern of the wild dog, or any wild carnivore, and the dog is built to operate best that way. The wild animal makes a kill, wolfs his stomach bulging with food and then rests and sleeps until it is time to get up and prowl again. Often, of course, the wild carnivore eats at much longer intervals than one day, but the once-a-day schedule of your civilized pet is a concession to your convenience and his small degree of removal from the wild state.

The amount to give at each feeding is something which only you can judge. What with wildly varying sizes of breeds, different basic appetites, and different puppy sizes within a breed, any fixed schedule of amounts is an illusory thing at best. The best rule is to feed him what he will eat. With your puppy, once you have decided what his diet is going to be, try him with an overlarge amount the first few times—more than you can imagine him eating at one sitting. He will eat his fill and then waddle away. Take note of how much he put away and judge the next feeding accordingly, giving him that much plus a little more until you have a good idea of how much he will hold each time. Continue this practice, in fact, throughout his life, adjusting the amount given to the amount taken, except in special cases of sickness or treatment of obesity.

Tid-bits and between-meal snacks for the puppy should be avoided if you have the will power. The temptation, as we know full well, is great —to offer the cute little pup just a nibble of cracker, or a piece of dough-nut, or any snack, just to see if he likes it. He will, never fear, and once the habit is established he will be on the cadge all the rest of his life. It can get to be an annoyance to you and your guests, and it can and will foul up his diet and quite possibly make him unpleasantly fat. What he puts away in the form of snacks leaves less room for his calculated diet— and human snacks are generally of the fattening variety. But if you hold an iron hand over yourself from the first, and give it to be known that he eats only at mealtimes, he'll never get to know what he's missing. It's hard, but try. A little restraint at first can pay off large dividends in his later life.

ADULT FEEDING

Under normal circumstances your dog will be able, as an adult, to in-gest and profit from almost anything you give him, including almost all of the items forbidden by rumor and custom. Milk, for example, will most definitely not cause worms in him, any more than it does in you. Raw meat will not cause worms any more than cooked (which is not at all) nor will it make him savage or vicious. If you feed him nothing but raw meat he will thereby suffer from an unbalanced diet, consequent malnutrition, and may get irritable and touchy about things as a whole. One item we do recommend against is pork in quantity. Pork, and particularly pork fat, is an extremely rich meat, and if fed in large amounts can easily overburden a dog's system. If you feed it, use moderation. There is also the minor danger that humans tend at times to be somewhat less careful about cooking meat for a dog than for themselves (although this won't apply if you just feed pork scraps from your table). Thus the familiar spectre of trichinosis raises its multiple head, along with a highly unpleasant condition known as toxoplasmosis, both resulting from underdone, infected, pork.

One highly prevalent superstition concerns raw eggs and the dog's coat. People will go to considerable expense to feed the pup or the grown dog raw eggs, sometimes two or three a day, in the vain hope that a glossy coat will result. There is, unfortunately, nothing to it. If there were, you and we would be swallowing raw eggs ourselves and could throw away the brilliantine. It just doesn't work. Neither will garlic or onions have any effect on intestinal worms. A garlic a day may keep the vampire away, but intestinal worms yield only to specific medication. A sulfur block in the drinking water does nothing at all for the dog's health, adding only a dubious decorative note to the drinking bowl, no matter what "scientific" claims you may read on the boxes of sulfur blocks in pet shops. In short, what you feed him simply nourishes him. If he needs medical treatment, give him medicines.

On the positive side of the ledger, beef and more fresh beef can do him nothing but good. Beef is the best source of protein, and good beef muscle cuts can be bought relatively cheaply if you shop for the sections low in human demand. Horse meat is also a good protein source, but rising relative prices of horse meat have lost for it the protein-per-dollar advantage it once had. Organ meats are also very nutritious. Some of them tend to be considerably cheaper than table cuts for humans, and dogs love them. You may be repelled at such items as hearts, lungs and the like, but your dog will probably love the variety and taste, and he couldn't care less where it comes from.

Beef bones are almost without exception good for dogs, especially the heavy long and knuckle bones. They will chew all the meat scraps and gristle off the bones with great pleasure, and then chew some more for fun and mouth exercise. Sometimes, the bone will disappear bit by bit. Once in the stomach, bones of whatever variety are rapidly dissolved and digested. The dog's stomach acids work things over with a gothic ferocity, rapidly reducing almost anything to digestibility. This, incidentally, is why you should not worry if your dog wolfs his food without seeming to chew at all. From the hereditary necessity to eat and run, the dog has developed the habit of gulping things in large chunks, chewing only enough to make a given mouthful somewhat manageable and to lubricate it with saliva. All the digestion goes on in his highly durable and efficient stomach.

PUPPY HEALTH

The health of a puppy is at times a baffling business. A pup's life seems fraught with a multitude of dangers, very easily lost, and contradictorily, puppies seem to have an incredible hardihood and resistance to human and bacterial mistreatment. The major areas that will concern you in caring for your puppy are: feeding, preventive shots, worming, and a sharp eye for disease. As this is not intended to be anything like a handbook of veterinary care, what we will give you in each area are simply good general rules to go by.

The first major question you will have to attend to in the consideration of your puppy's welfare is: which vet to take him to? It is a difficult one to answer. There are, as we have said before, veterinarians ranging from excellent to downright poor. The balance is fortunately quite far to the high side, but this does you little good when it comes to choosing your man. You may live in an area where there is only one vet, and there you have it—no choice. But in larger communities there are likely to be several within a small radius of your home, or you may be willing to travel quite a distance if you can find an exceptionally good vet.

The best possible answer, albeit the obvious one, is personal references. The breeder of your pup will tell you vociferously enough who he thinks is the best vet in your area. Other dog owners will be glad to give you advice. And from there out, quite frankly, we can tell you little enough. Use pretty much the same criteria you would in choosing your own family doctor—a good manner (with dogs), a willingness to discuss symptoms and treatment without mumbo-jumbo and retreat into lofty professional hauteur, a gentle touch with his patients. You can make some sort of evaluation from the veterinarian's premises—anything really run down and shabby hardly speaks well for the owner. Even if he treats only animals, the premises are a reflection of the man. But don't rely on gleaming tile and shiny instruments. Some of the best veterinarians we know function in totally unimpressive (but not run-down) offices and small clinics, and some ensconced in glittering array we wouldn't trust to treat a mild headache. But whatever you do, look into the matter beforehand—don't wait until the last minute to phone frantically around the city with a sick puppy on your hands.

The next major matter is that of preventive shots against distemper, hepatitis, rabies and leptospirosis. Distemper is a prevalent disease of dogs, and many thousands of unprotected puppies are lost each year in heart-rending circumstances due to this ailment. Fortunately, persistent work by veterinarians and veterinary researchers plus a wide-spread vaccination program, has reduced the once general menace of distemper. Still, it is a substantial danger, and we cannot too strongly recommend protection, for your susceptible young puppy can get distemper without even being near an infected dog. There are half a dozen methods of protection your veterinarian may prescribe, consisting of anywhere from one to a series of four injections, which establish life-long immunity.

There is also available now a combined distemper-hepatitis series which may be recommended to you. By all means have it administered. If it should be unavailable in your area, ask for the specific hepatitis vaccine in addition to the distemper series. Hepatitis is an insidious disease in that a puppy may suddenly die of it without his owner having even known that he was sick.

About rabies, little need be said. This horrifying disease is still very much with us—to the extent that any person bitten by an unknown dog must suffer through the painful and expensive Pasteur treatment rather than risk the utter and irreversible ferocity of a rabies infection. In certain areas of the country the rabies problem is much less serious than in others. If you live in one of these areas (the nearest Public Health Officer can advise you on this) and your dog literally never comes into contact with strange dogs, the danger is minute. But even in this case we recommend vaccination. The rabies shot for your puppy will give protection for one to three years, depending on the type of vaccine, and should be repeated at regular intervals for full protection.

Leptospirosis directly affects the kidneys, and can result in crippling uremia, or death through uremic poisoning. A recently developed vaccine seems to give good protection—previously penicillin was the only hope—and this vaccine can be given along with the shots for distemper, rabies and hepatitis in a regular program of prevention.

These four diseases are major threats to your puppy's life—and all are preventable. The preventive shots usually are given in a certain order, at specified times in the pup's growth—and this should be left in the hands of the vet, for only he can judge whether your puppy is old enough to begin the course of treatment, and whether he is in the proper physical condition. Again, as we have said about every aspect of dog care, it is possible that your dog would live to creaking old age without ever coming near a vaccination needle. Millions have. But we feel the chance is not worth taking. The time and expense involved in protection seem very small as against possible pain and death of a well-loved animal.

Worms of various varieties are also a particular problem of puppies. There are roundworms, hookworms, whipworms, tapeworms and others —the most common being the first two. Diagnosis of worm infestation in your puppy is something which should be left strictly to your veterinarian, as should worm treatment. We recommend against the commercial worming preparations you will find on the market, for two very good reasons: you are completely unqualified to diagnose the presence of worms in your dog's system, and you as a layman are quite likely to give either the wrong preparation or in the wrong way. Most veterinarians will do a stool examination of any young puppy under their care as a matter of course, and are of course equipped to do the right thing if worms are found.

A serious infestation of roundworms, the most common variety, will generally show itself in the puppy through a distended abdomen (regardless of feeding), occasional diarrhea, dull coat and general listless-ness. You may even see tiny white worms in the stool, or occasional vomiting of worms. If these signs appear, take the pup to the vet. If possible, consult him on the phone before bringing the pup in, for the vet may want you to starve the puppy for 12 hours or more before he sees him. This will allow the vet, if he finds worms, to begin treatment right away—otherwise you would have to bring the puppy back after a starvation period. The reason behind this is that various of the worming chemicals can react fatally on the pup if he has any food at all in his stomach or intestines, and he must be brought to the vet totally empty.

In general, the healthy puppy is characterized by all the familiar outward signs of playfulness, alertness, bright eyes, good appetite and healthy coat. The first signs of illness you will see in your pup are the reversals of these. If his appetite falls off sharply, suspect illness. If he becomes listless, if his eyes are dull, or if his coat seems coarse and dry, something is wrong. Continued whimpering or moans of pain are obvious trouble signs. In addition, there are two very reliable indicators which require only a little more watchfulness—the puppy's temperature and the condition of his stool.

A normal puppy's temperature will vary between 101° and 102.7°. A cold and wet nose means nothing, incidentally, nor do cold ears. A cold nose does not indicate health, nor does a warm nose indicate the presence of fever. You will, in fact, notice that your pup's nose will be warm when he has been sleeping. So discount ears and nose as temperature indicators. We recommend that you keep in the house a good rectal thermometer and use it as an additional check if you suspect illness. It will help you, and will help the vet to know if the pup's temperature has been high. Using a rectal thermometer appeals to some people not at all, but it is a simple matter and one that can be gotten used to with little difficulty. The major problem, really, is getting a puppy to hold still for the necessary minute. Shake the thermometer down (you must have seen doctors or nurses do it—it's the flip of the wrist that does the trick), lubricate the business end with salve or butter (and be sure you have the rectal model thermometer) and insert it a little more than half way into the anus. Be sure to keep hold of the protruding end throughout, as a wiggly pup might get away and smash even a strongly built thermometer. Keep it in for a minute, then wipe the end off with cotton or tissue and read off the temperature. This part seems to baffle large numbers of people, but if you settle down to it you'll find you can read any thermometer with a very small amount of practice.

The condition of the puppy's stool is also a very good general indicator of health. Keeping a check on this will be easy enough during the first paper-cum-housebreaking days, and later on you will just have to watch. A firm, normal-colored stool indicates, but does not assure, good intestinal health—variations are the signs of trouble. The character and color of the stool will vary with diet—the main thing to watch for is any radical change while the dog's diet remains the same. Persistent diarrhea and loose stools indicate that something is wrong. Constipation is important to watch for, as it may indicate illness or may be caused by a blockage of the puppy's stomach by something he has swallowed when you weren't looking. Blood in the stool will warn you that something is wrong. While none of these conditions will indicate anything specific to you, a good description, along with a temperature check, will go a long way in helping your vet with his diagnosis.

TEETHING

At approximately four months (slightly later for the smaller breeds) the puppy will begin to lose his milk teeth and grow a permanent set. This process causes a puppy's gums to become sore, and he may show other symptoms. There may be a slight fever, occasional vomiting or diarrhea. He may cut down on his eating during this period. It is advisable to have your vet check him at this time, even if you strongly suspect all the symptoms point only to teething troubles. Unless there is a growth abnormality (failure to lose a milk tooth and resultant crowding of the growing permanent tooth) there is little indeed you can do for the puppy at this time. He will chew on things in an instinctive attempt to loosen the milk teeth, so it is a good idea to let him have something to chew on other than your shoes and furniture. An uncooked beef bone is fine for this. Don't tug him about in tug-of-wars in an attempt to help the process—he'll do what's necessary all by himself. Just keep an occasional eye on his gums to see that all is going well and that there are no double-tooth situations. Don't be alarmed, incidentally, if a pup's erect ears flop down at this stage, or at any ear curiosities. Teething affects ears in a curious way. It's only temporary.

THE FEMALE PUPPY

There comes a time, in every female puppy's life, when she shows conclusively that she is indeed female. The average age of the first season is eight months, but it may occur anywhere from six months to a year, or even later. Thereafter she will probably have a season quite regularly at six-month intervals, each period lasting about three weeks.

From the age of six months on you should keep a careful eye on her for indications. Sometimes she will show it by an increased activity and affection, but this may be hard to judge in a happy and already affectionate pet. A preliminary swelling of the vulva area can often be seen, and more frequent urination is another common sign. If she is outside among other dogs much of the time you will be tipped off by a sudden increase of interest in her by male dogs—interest not only in her but persistent and noticeable intense interest in wherever she has been, especially where she has urinated. Otherwise, you may not know it is upon you until she first begins to discharge and spots rugs and floors.

The primary action you can, and indeed must, take, once she has come into season is protection against males. If her habit is to run free outdoors, she must be kept behind a good high fence during her season—and be sure the fence is a good one; the leaping abilities of an amorous male are marvelous to behold. If possible, or if it is your usual habit, let her outside only on leash, and be prepared to fend off precipitous advances from males. In a large city apartment you will have little trouble with males trailing her to her lair, but in a house you will find that the news gets surprisingly far around the neighborhood and you will be beseiged by unwelcome and noisy dogs from the surrounding counties. There is nothing so attractive to the male nose as the scent of a female in heat, and they can track her from far away by such abstruse means as her in-season smell carried away from your house on the feet of another male. So be prepared.

To keep the inside of the house from being spotted and soiled by her vaginal discharge you can either confine her or use one of the commercial sanitary pads and harnesses. Confinement is probably the best answer if you have a room to spare, but the commercial pads with harness or dog-panty, will do the job quite adequately. They're a bother, both to you and her—and to some people highly ridiculous—but they work. Don't despair—it will be over in a week or two, and then you are safe for another six months.

If, by some unpleasant happenstance she is caught by a male either before you know she is in season, or during a known heat, you have fairly well had it. Your veterinarian may be able to induce chemical abortion if he gets her early enough, but the method is far from reliable. You may just have to resign yourself to puppies of half-unknown ancestry, to be handled in the best way possible. If yours is a mongrel, you may even have pups better looking than their mother, and you may like them. But if yours is a pure-bred and she is caught out by a different breed or a mongrel, don't despair. The old wives tale about a mixed litter ruining her for future breeding is total nonsense. Each and every litter she has is a thing unto itself and has positively no effect on future litters.

Spaying is, of course, one way out. A "whole" female will be subject to seasons and the need for cleanliness and protection every six months, and some people find this bothersome in the extreme. If you find it so, and have no plans for breeding her, spaying may appeal to you. But we generally recommend that you wait until after the first season, for two reasons—first, the heat problem may be very slight with her; second, as you get to know her better you may change your mind about wanting to have a pup of hers. One thing you should disregard completely about spaying, however, is the possibility that it will make her fat, vicious or disaffected, or whatever you may hear. Most of the folklore about spaying is based on false cause-and-effect. If an unspayed bitch gets fat, nobody remarks on it, but if it happens to a spayed bitch, spaying is assigned the blame. Many vets prefer to do the spaying operation at the age of six months, because the operation is relatively simple at that age. An older bitch, particularly an obese bitch, runs considerable risk, but if your bitch is up to two years old, and in good physical condition, you can quite safely have the job done by your vet. The fact that she will no longer go through the minor physical changes, and no longer experience the mating urges may have some slight effect on her weight and disposition, but it would be a chancy thing indeed to attribute any particular characteristic to spaying—she might well have got that way unspayed.

ADULT CARE

Once your dog has reached adulthood his health, aside from continued good feeding, is a matter of incidents, even as with the adult human. The adult dog falls heir to many of the ills and minor sieges of man. To guard against these you can only exercise the same cautions you would with yourself—feed him sensibly, allow him to get plenty of rest, keep him clean, and watch for danger signs of illness. Look for any change of disposition, lack of energy, pain symptoms, dull eyes, dull coat, radical change in eating habits. Aside from incidents of illness or accident, your main concerns in his care will consist of grooming and attention to his ears, teeth, skin and nails.

Under grooming, perhaps the major item is bathing. This, though surrounded by its own lore, is simple enough. We recommend that you do not bathe your dog until he is a year old, for a variety of reasons, central among which is the high susceptibility of puppies to bad colds and possible pneumonia. If he gets dirty as a pup, wet a towel with witch hazel or rubbing alcohol and clean him off that way, being careful to keep it out of his eyes. But after a year, bathe away. You may hear that any bathing at all is bad for a dog's coat, and to some extent that is true. A good soap-and-water scrubbing will wash away some of the vital oils of his coat, but it will do no more permanent harm than sensible washing of your own hair. The rule here is moderation. If he is bathed at reasonable intervals, the oils will replace themselves. Bathe him when he really needs it, and between times wipe the occasional mud off his feet with a rag and use the witch hazel or rubbing alcohol to clean up minor dirt on the coat.

When you do get to the actual bath, we recommend that you do it just as you would for yourself—with warm water and a gentle soap. The standing cartoon subject of the household dog avoiding baths like bubonic plague is based very little on any necessary truth. That comes from senseless plunking, wiggling and howling, into a tub of water. If your dog is well obedience trained, you will have no trouble getting him into or making him stay in the tub or pail. Introduce him to the idea just as you would to a new obedience exercise—gently and with praise and coaxing. Make him stand or sit and stay while you wash him. Soon he'll get to think quite favorably of the whole business. When you're through, dry him thoroughly with a rough towel. That he'll like without reservation—to him it's just one prolonged petting.

With a short-haired dog, you will never have the bother of clipping, and with most long-haired breeds, clipping is seldom necessary. The exception to this latter is very hot weather, when some long-haired dog can benefit from the removal of part of their coat. This sort of thing is taken care of, ordinarily, by the natural process of seasonal shedding, but civilized and house dogs get their shedding cycles fouled up by living much of the time under artificial lights. So if he seems to suffer a great deal in the heat, have him clipped. "Sculpture clipped" breeds such as Poodles, Bedlingtons, Kerry Blues and Sealyhams are real problems unless you give it a good deal of study and become handy with the clippers. All of these breeds can and do live quite happily without ever seeing a clipper—artistic clipping is done solely for esthetic values. If you plan to go in for that sort of thing, and it does make for a more attractive dog in most cases, we recommend strongly that you have the original clipping done by a professional and learn how to do it by watching. Charts and instructions such as you will encounter more often than not result in a botched job and a literal shaggy dog in the hands of a rank amateur. But once having seen what to do, and with clippers in hand, most people can handle things quite well. Warning, though—don't try to do it with scissors. If you're going to go to all that trouble anyway, invest in either electric or manual clippers.

All dogs, long-haired or short, benefit from regular brushing. Any hairbrush or special dog brush will work well. The long-haired breeds need brushing and combing on a regular basis, to control mattings and "rats" in their hair, and to keep them comfortable and neat. It requires no more technique than taking care of your own hair. And even though the shorthairs don't often develop mats and rats, regular brushing will keep the coat sleek and healthy. In addition, it keeps your house a lot cleaner, for the loose hair of normal shedding ends up on the newspaper instead of all over the house.

For the dog, brushing becomes a very enjoyable experience. Just as in towel drying after a bath, it is like prolonged rubbing and petting. Teach a small dog to stand quietly on a table, or a large dog on the floor, while you brush him, and the job will be that much easier.

Care of the teeth is a subject of some contention. You may hear or read recommendations that you brush your dog's teeth at some regular interval, but we cannot hold with this particular bit of anthropomorphism. The major menace to dog teeth is tartar, a hard brownish deposit which may build up, particularly around the base of the teeth. Tartar in itself is no particular danger, but it often causes objectionable mouth odor in the dog, and increases the possibility of cavities and decay. It is easily removed by your vet with a tartar scraper—and although you can acquire one of these yourself, we don't recommend that you work on your dog's teeth with one unless you're a dentist. It takes a knack and practice. What we do recommend is that you check your dog's mouth at least once a month for heavy tartar deposits, and for loose or broken teeth. These latter of course require professional attention, but the chances are very high that he will never have any tooth trouble. If he has bones to chew on, he will help keep his teeth free of tartar.

The care of your dog's nails is something you may very well never have to bother with. City dogs who are constantly running and walking on pavement tend to keep their own filed by contact with the rough cement. Country dogs who are largely outdoors grow long and strong nails and, in fact, need and use them in getting around. It is the house dog, city or country—the one who spends most of his life on floors and rugs or sleeping in the corner—who needs nail care. Having no opportunity to wear them off, and no earthly need for them—he will in fact lose traction on floors and linoleum if his nails are too long—he must have them kept short. Keep an eye on his nails, or better, an ear. If, as he walks around the house, you hear a continual clicking, his nails may be too long. In serious cases of neglect, where no attention at all has been given them, the nails may even grow around and bend under the pads, causing pain and unwillingness to walk and run. The latter case is strictly a job for the veterinarian, who may have to anaesthetize the dog while he does some fairly major surgery on the nails. But normal care can easily be handled at home with a special nail clipper. There are two very good kinds of clipper—one a heavy nipper operating somewhat like pliers, the other a sort of guillotine arrangement with a sliding blade. You can learn to use either quite readily.

When you do the clipping, proceed with caution. Within every nail there is a quick, and it may extend farther down into the nail than you think. This quick is visible but extremely hard to describe—once again we will have to refer you to the vet, if only for an instructional session in the recognition of the extent of the quick so you can avoid cutting into it when you clip. If you can't get this instruction, the best way to go about it is to clip each nail very cautiously, taking off only the very tip, and do it regularly. If you clip too far in, you will hit the quick, which is a very painful experience for the dog. You may even cause the nail to bleed. This in itself is not dangerous, unless you have whacked off a mighty chunk and the bleeding is copious. In such cases a styptic pencil is of some use, or you can control bleeding with a bit of cotton soaked in hydrogen peroxide. Most minor nail bleeding will take care of itself through capillary closure—just be sure to keep the dog off his feet for a few minutes, and off rough surfaces for a few hours, to let the healing take place.

No matter how carefully you do it, your dog will probably never accept nail clipping as part of his normal life in this best of all possible (for him) worlds. It is a mildly traumatic experience, and you and he will just have to make the best of it. Be gentle, and firm, and clip away with a firm hold on the leg being worked on. Though traumatic, the experience will not damage his psyche permanently if you go about it the right way, with great caution and snipping off only the smallest bit of the tip at a time.

One of the major problems you may encounter, this one somewhere on the borderline between grooming and basic health, is that of the old familiar fleas and other skin parasites. The symptoms of these hardly need explanation—excessive scratching and biting at the skin. As far as we know, almost every dog in the world has fleas at one time or another. It's just one of those things and no sign of slovenly care on your part.

Lice are a little less prevalent, and the same goes for ticks. When you see him scratching and biting at himself, it may of course be a skin rash, but investigation will either establish that or rule it out. More likely it will be the parasites, and treatment is in order. There are anti-parasitic dips and rinses that can be used in conjunction with a bath, and many of the commercial flea and louse powders are highly efficient if worked well into the coat and onto the skin. Follow the label instructions carefully when using either dips or powders, especially keeping the stuff out of the dog's eyes. And be very careful when buying powder or dip for your dog. Be absolutely sure from the label that it is intended for dogs and other animals that lick themselves—otherwise he might just lick up a lethal quantity of something poisonous. That's one sure way to end the flea problem, but not the best.

Ticks you will have to look for. Every week or so, and in particular after a run in the woods or high grass, go over his entire skin surface carefully in a strong light. Even if you've never seen a tick before, you'll know what it is when you've found it—a smallish bean-shaped item stuck firmly to the dog's hide. The old saw about holding a lighted match near it is not a very effective method of tick removal. The best method is dousing the tick well with alcohol from a cotton swab, then removing it with tweezers. The alcohol treatment dazes the tick and makes it lose its hold in the skin, whereupon it can be extracted whole. Grasp it as close as possible to the dog's skin with tweezers, and work it out slowly. If you simply pull it off you may leave the head in the skin, where it can cause infection or even a nasty cyst.

Attention to all of these things—and they take little enough time—will result in a healthy, happy and attractive animal to have around the house and call your own. Regular inspection of teeth, nails and skin takes little of your time, bathing is a short process when necessary, and regular brushing is more of a gesture of affection for the dog than a chore. Keep at it, and you'll have a pet and companion you're proud to own and claim, and not just another scratching, shaggy, messy dog.

HOME NURSING AND FIRST AID

A sick or injured dog is far harder to care for than a human, largely because of lack of understanding and cooperation on his part. You can't tell him that he must take his medicine, or hold still, or rest for a while. At best, home care for your dog will be a compromise with what should be done, but fortunately dogs are so resistant to such things as infections that it generally works out all right.

When you have a sick dog at home who has been prescribed for by your veterinarian, you will probably have to give him pills or liquid medicines. This can be difficult. For liquid medicines, there are two ways to go about it, depending on the temper of your dog. The first, and best, is to have a member of the family hold the dog's mouth open while you pitch a spoonful of the medicine in. Then close the mouth and hold the muzzle high while you gently stroke the dog's throat. This keeps the medicine in, and the stroking promotes swallowing, and then its all over. If he's really obstinate about it, determined to keep his mouth shut come flood or fire, you can still get the liquid into him. In this method, with his mouth firmly closed, pull out his lower lip until you have made a small flesh pouch and dump the medicine into that. Then close it up quick and concentrate on keeping the mouth shut, the muzzle high, and stroke the throat. The medicine will go right in through his teeth and he can't help swallowing it. It can turn into an almighty struggle, even if you have help, but here again your basic obedience training will pay off if he will sit and stay at your command.

Pills are something else again. For these you will have to get his mouth open somehow. Try using the lip squeezing trick described in the chapter on Open work, for making him take a dumbbell. When you have the mouth open, put the pill in as far back on the tongue as you can get it, and then raise the muzzle and stroke the throat. If you get it far enough back on the tongue he won't be able to help swallowing it. But keep his mouth closed for a minute or two, and watch carefully that he doesn't hold it and later spit it out. As an alternative, you can try poking the pill or pills into his food. Chances are very good that he will, in the course of eating, take them right down without ever knowing they were there.

First aid treatment may be called for in the case of accidents, and for this we recommend the following be kept in a handy box or your medicine cabinet: gauze, iodine (or any other good antiseptic), mustard powder, a good commercial burn ointment, witch hazel, and cotton. Also, keep handy a bottle of Milk of Magnesia as a mild cathartic, although this is for general and not emergency use. Anything else you keep around as a standard remedy should be on the advice of your veterinarian, as his will be the responsibilty for your dog's health and care.

The major roster of serious things that can happen to your dog includes: broken bones, serious cuts or bites, burns, poisoning, car accidents, heat stroke, electric shock and foreign object swallowing. Here is a brief course on what to do until the veterinarian comes.

Broken bones—when you suspect a break, put a restraining gauze muzzle on the dog before you handle or attempt to move him. This is for your protection, as a dog who is injured and in pain may snap at anything that moves near him, and may blindly bite you when you attempt to move him. To put on a gauze muzzle, take a strip of gauze about two feet long (and two or three inches wide) and pass it around the middle of the dog's muzzle, making a single half-knot under the muzzle. Then pass the ends around in back of the dog's neck, there making a bow knot, firm but easily released by you. Be sure it is a bow that can be released in a hurry. In an injury case, he may want to throw up—you'll have to keep a close eye on him all the time he is wearing a tight gauze muzzle. Otherwise he could quite conceivably strangle with his mouth clamped shut. Make the loop around the muzzle tight enough so that he cannot get his mouth open, and the loop around the neck just tight enough to insure that he cannot paw or slip the muzzle loop off over his nose. He won't like it a bit, but it won't hurt him—the gauze muzzle is standard veterinary practice when treating a dog who may bite—and may save you both a great deal of trouble.

If the broken bone is in the leg, which it will be in 95% of the cases, he will take care of keeping it off the ground all by himself once he has recovered from the initial shock of the mishap. It is all right to carry him away from the scene if there is any good reason to. Otherwise leave him there until he recovers enough to limp away himself. Then get to the vet. Once he has recovered and is on his feet, remove the gauze muzzle, as the danger of fear and pain biting is almost entirely over, and he will feel better with it off.

Car accidents—here you may not have gauze handy, so use a necktie, or a strip torn from a shirt or skirt. Apply the muzzle immediately, before you attempt to move the dog. One added value of the muzzle in this case is that it will remove any temptation on your part to give him water —and you should never give water after an accident, in case of internal injuries. Always suspect internal injuries and bleeding until you know different, and treat him with according gentleness. If at all possible, leave the dog where he is, but if you have to move him try to find something flat to slide him onto. A wide plank will serve for a small dog; a piece of plywood for a larger one. Usually, though, nothing of any use is ready to hand in such cases, so even your coat or a blanket or car robe will help. Somehow, as gently as possible, get the dog onto it, and use it as a litter. The idea behind this is that he should be moved, internally, as little as possible. The safest position is the one in which he falls—broken bones can easily gash flesh and rupture veins and arteries if they are moved about within him, and movement will aggravate internal injuries. Keep the movement down as much as possible, consistent with getting him to the vet as quickly as possible. In case of serious bleeding, see the discussion in the next section.

Cuts and bites—the major danger here is bleeding, and not infection, although this can be guarded against too by the application of a mild antiseptic. Serious bleeding on the head, neck or body can only be stopped by the direct application of a pressure bandage. On the body or head, strap on a pad of gauze as tightly as you can—make the pad thick so that the pressure of the strap of gauze around the body or head will press the pad well into the wound. It will be painful for him, but control of blood loss is more important. On the neck, use your good judgment about pressure to be used on the pad. Major cuts or openings in the legs can be treated with a tourniquet if bleeding is serious. A slow flow should be pressure-bandaged, but a serious spurting of blood, meaning that a major vein or artery has been cut, is more easily controlled with the tourniquet. To make the tourniquet, take a strong strip of anything— gauze, shirt or whatever, and wrap it around the leg, then after making a half-knot tie the loose ends around a stick. Twist the stick until the band around the leg is tight enough to stop the bleeding, or cut it down from a spurt to a slow flow. Be very careful with a tourniquet—loosen it every ten or fifteen minutes to allow the blood to flow a little, then tighten again. Otherwise, with all blood shut off from the limb, serious complications can set in. If, for some reason, the tourniquet doesn't control the bleeding satisfactorily, then apply a direct pressure bandage. On the leg you can strap it very tight, and should be able to diminish the flow of blood sufficiently to save his life.

Poisoning—this spectre which haunts every dog owner admits of no concise symptoms to look for. But if you suspect for any reason that your dog may have been poisoned, through spoiled food, accident or deliberate action—he may vomit, exhibit nausea and stomach pain—immediately give him mustard and water as an emetic, and once he has thrown up, give him as much milk as you can get into him. To make the emetic solution, mix three tablespoons of mustard powder (not bottled mustard) in half a standard glass of warm water, and pour it into him. It may be a real struggle, but it might mean your dog's life, so force it in until he vomits. That will help get some of the poisonous material out of his stomach, and the following milk will help dilute it and generally soothe the system. Then, of course, get him to your vet.

Burns—the treatment for minor or serious burns is much the same as for humans. Apply a good commercial burn ointment to the affected area, and do not cover it with any bandages. Keep a close eye on him to see that he does not attempt to lick the ointment off. If there is considerable pain, apply the gauze muzzle before you begin to treat him—this will also prevent him from licking off the ointment.

Electric shock—this is almost entirely a hazard of house dogs, particularly younger ones. It usually results from chewing on a lampcord or other electrical wire. With any luck, the only result will be a burned mouth, bad enough in itself—and this should be left strictly alone and for the veterinarian to handle. House current will rarely knock a dog completely out, but if it does, remove him with caution from the wire and cover him with a blanket to keep him warm. If he seems not to be breathing, by all means try artificial respiration. Such cases are rare, though, for the biting that gave him the shock and burn usually causes a short circuit, blowing the house fuse and saving his life.

If you happen not to have read the section on electric cords in the chapter on raising the puppy, we will repeat our advice here. You simply can't keep a watchful enough eye all the time to keep him away from lampcords, so coat every light cord in your house with something bitter tasting that will discourage chewing. Musterole, citronella or any of the commercial "keeps dogs away" items will do the trick. It is well worth the trouble, for we have seen puppies and older dogs with badly burned mouths from chewing on light cords. It isn't pleasant to see.

Swallowing foreign objects—most dogs, particularly young ones, swallow a few solid objects that aren't good for them. If you see something going down, apply the mustard-and-water emetic immediately—but only if what you saw didn't have any sharp edges. He might get a sharp object down successfully, but coming up it could rip his throat. If the emetic doesn't get it, only the vet can, and anything he swallows probably won't do him any harm once in the stomach. It'll just sit there, and may even pass out through the intestines—but a vet's care is advised. As an example of the quite incredible things a dog can swallow and get away with, consider the case of a Doberman belonging to one of the writers. Over a period of nine months, unbeknownst to anyone, he managed to swallow five 22-inch chrome choke chains. He showed no sign of it, being as happy and active as any dog can be—and was only discovered in his secret vice when he was actually seen to take the fifth one down. Several weeks later, after some fruitless attempts to get the chain regurgitated (during this time no one knew the other four had gone in the same way), he was operated on and out the five chains came from his stomach, weighing a total of a pound and a half. Today the dog is just as healthy and happy as ever.

Heat prostration—in the summer, this happens to quite a surprisingly large number of dogs. Mostly, they are city dogs who are out of condition and slightly overweight, and who suffer through a city heat spell. If it happens to yours, bathe his head with cool water, keep him quiet and feed him very lightly until he recovers. And from then on out keep him quieter, and in general cut his feeding down until the heat is over. In particular, don't allow him to exercise just after a meal—it works much on the same principle as the human rule about not swimming for an hour after eating. He must rest while he is digesting his food. If you have a really serious case dump him up to his neck in a tub of cold water, as cold as you can get it, and keep him there until his breathing improves. You can also give him two or three drops of aromatic spirits of ammonia in a teaspoon of water to bring him around. Then keep him cool and quiet.

As a last thought, and as a good general rule in all these emergency situations: don't panic. Easy to say, and sometimes hard to do, true. But keep your head in case of accidents, and move swiftly and gently. Except for the muzzle, treat the dog as you would an injured human, and you stand a good chance of pulling him through.

CHAPTER XII

TRAVEL AND MISCELLANEOUS

Sᴏᴍᴇᴏɴᴇ once said (probably quite a few someones, for that matter), "You can either travel comfortably, or with children." The business of traveling with a dog, or dogs, is not altogether different. Dogs are a little easier to travel with in that they do not have to be amused with license number games and similar diversions, and a little harder in that plane, train and overnight arrangements are more difficult. With suitable preplanning, some basic training for your dog, and a few facts, however, taking your dog along can be quite a smooth operation.

BY CAR

If you plan a long trip with overnight stops, your first problem will be that of a place to stay. Fortunately, this problem has been partially solved by a booklet entitled "Touring With Towser," compiled and distributed by the Gaines Dog Research Center. The booklet lists several thousand hotels and motels across the country, covering most communities of any size in every state—all establishments which will accept dogs. Write to the Center (250 Park Avenue, New York 17, N. Y.) enclosing 25¢ to help cover their handling and first-class mailing costs, and they will send you a copy of the latest edition.

"Touring With Towser" is periodically revised to include new establishments, and to delete listings which have changed their policies on dogs. This latter is unfortunate, but hotels and motels are constantly dropping off the "Dogs Accepted" list because of unpleasant experiences with dog-owning travelers. On these lines, here is a pertinent paragraph from the Gaines booklet:

"It is significant that almost every hotel and motor court we questioned had at one time or another accepted guests with dogs. In many cases, where a hotel or motor court has a 'No Dogs Allowed' policy, the management explained that they had been forced to take this stand because of their unfortunate experiences with badly-behaved dogs and irresponsible dog owners. It seems only sporting for the dog owner who is traveling with his pet to see to it that his dog causes no damage or disturbance that may in the future close the doors of a hotel or court to other dog owners. Fewer managers would object to canine guests if traveling dog owners observed the following rules: 1. Dogs should be kept on leash when in public rooms and hallways. 2. Dogs ('Seeing Eye' dogs excepted) should not be taken into dining rooms. 3. Owners should exercise and care for their own dogs and not make kennel-men of the bellboys. 4. Dogs should not be left alone in rooms if they are likely to bark and disturb other guests or be destructive. 5. Guests should expect to pay for any damage done by their dogs. 6. Untrained dogs should be confined to a crate or sleeping box while in motor courts or hotel rooms."

All excellent points, to which we will add one further. If you are planning a definite itinerary and writing ahead for reservations, you will find your answer considerably more cordial if you include the information that your dog is obedience trained. Hotel and motel managers are perhaps more alert to the advantages of obedience training than any other group of people in this country, having had experience with trained and untrained dogs. If the manager knows in advance that your dog is obedience trained, it can easily make the difference in acceptance or rejection of reservations when he thinks his place just might be filled anyway.

Additionally, the fact that the establishment accepts dogs does not in any way mean that you will be condemned to a series of run-down shoddy flea-bags. We have stayed, with dogs, in motels that boasted wall-to-wall carpeting, free television and radio, tiled baths and all the amenities. As to hotels, little more need be said than that the Waldorf-Astoria in New York accepts dogs. True, there are also poor places which accept dogs, but you will find that you will be able to stay in hotels and motels that are as good, or as bad, as the one down the road that can't abide dogs.

Even having found a place that will take your dog, there are still minor problems. In hotel or motel, what do you do with the dog when you go out to eat? Only you can answer that, depending on whether your dog will get lonely and raise a great commotion if left alone for hours in a strange room. Remember, though, that even a dog who is well adjusted at home may surprise you in a hotel room. There are people constantly going by, voices from the corridor and the adjoining rooms, and things that go boomp in the night. If being left alone will make him vocally unhappy, you can only take him along and leave him locked in the car while you eat—being sure to leave the windows open a crack for air.

We have found that motels are better for traveling with a dog, largely because of the convenience in exercising. In a hotel you will have to get him down in the elevator (and some hotels ask you to use a special service elevator with a dog), through the lobby and out into the street when he has to relieve himself. At a motel, on the other hand, the outside is just beyond the door. In addition, some motels have grounds for limited free running and exercise. If your dog is well enough trained that he will not run out of bounds (and be very, very sure of this before releasing him in strange territory) this can be a considerable advantage—always provided the management doesn't mind.

Some few dog owners, for lack of dog-accepting establishments, will blithely put up any place and leave the dog locked in the car for the night. We cannot condemn this sort of thing too highly as senseless cruelty. Leaving a dog alone in a car for eight or more hours is cruel enough in itself, but you run the constant risk of trouble. If the windows are open to any great amount, he may get out, no matter how well trained he is. If the windows are closed, he'll suffocate. Drunks, for some reason, seem to gravitate to cars with dogs in them, and if one sticks his arm through the window to pet the "nishe little doggie" and gets a chunk taken out of him, you alone are to blame for the damage. Otherwise sober but mentally retarded louts sometimes take their evening pleasure by poking sticks through even the slimmest window opening to torment a dog who cannot get at them. Other stalwart citizens will pound on the car and shout at a locked-in dog for the diversion of seeing him bark and race around in frustrated anger. True, there is a minor risk of this sort of thing even when you leave your dog in the car for a half-hour's shopping in broad daylight even in your own home town, but it is as nothing compared to an overnight stay in strange territory. In short, don't. There are enough places around the country which will take dogs that you will always be able to find one reasonably near.

Enroute, a large cardboard box lined with papers at the bottom is a good idea for a puppy or an un-housebroken dog. It prevents damage to your car when he has to relieve himself or if he gets sick, and can be used in the hotel or motel room at night. For the older dog, you should have a regular small kit of supplies, which can be carried in a canvas flight-accessory bag, small suitcase or even a fibre-board dime store doll's suitcase. Put in a few cans of his regular food, cans of evaporated milk if he gets milk in the mornings, a pan for his food and one for water, and a favorite toy or bone for him to play with at night. Include also a blanket or something for him to sleep on if he is accustomed to it at home—the familiar smell of his own blanket will make things easier for him, and will make the management much happier than if you used their sheets or pillows.

No matter how well trained he may be, it is an excellent idea to have a tag on his collar at all times in case he wanders or runs off and is lost. A stamped metal tag is best, but you can make your own from a leather or imitation-leather luggage tag. A good form for the tag is: "Rover"—If Found, Please Telephone or Telegraph Collect. Reward." Give your name, phone number, and full address, including the state. If you are on a long trip, it is a good idea to give, instead of your name, the name and address of a friend or relative at either end of the trip. That way anyone who finds your dog will be able to get in touch with someone immediately—and you will be able to check with occasional calls to find out if someone has located him.

Further, your dog should have a certain minimum of training for travel. Housebreaking is essential. Novice level training in heeling, coming and staying are very handy in this as in other aspects of dog owning. Beyond these, there are two special things he should learn—to stay quietly in the car until he is released, and always to sit and stay just outside the car when you let him out. A dog who wants badly to get out of a car, as you may have learned, is a force to be reckoned with. If he scrambles and leaps out of the car as soon as the door is opened at a stop, you may yourself be hurt or at least shaken up, and he just might get himself badly hurt by running out into traffic. Train him quite firmly that he must sit quietly until given permission to leave. Also, with leash on it is simple to train him to sit quietly after leaving the car, until he is released. This too may save his life. Insist on it at all times, traveling or at home, and riding with your dog will be more pleasant, not to say safer.

Car sickness can be a difficult matter, for some few dogs never seem to get over an aversion to long trips in cars. If you are starting out on a trip with a dog who has never ridden much, we suggest you introduce him to the idea in stages, as we have outlined in the chapter on Pretraining. In addition, if he is fed only at night he will have less chance of throwing up in the car. If the problem is serious, see your veterinarian, who may be able to give you something in the way of medicine—don't try dosing him yourself with aspirin, tranquilizers or sea-sick remedies. Keeping him in a cardboard box will minimize the mess in the car if he is small enough—but if yours is a large breed and the problem is serious, you can only arm yourself with rags and fortitude. Some dogs just get sick in cars.

Traveling through various states, counties and cities you will run into a bewildering variety of dog regulations and laws. In the car you will have little or no trouble, but once you step outside you will find that some localities are highly restrictive about dogs. Whatever the state of affairs in your own community, many cities and towns are very strict about allowing dogs off leash, and in stores and restaurants and groceries. Keep him on leash whenever he is out of the car, and find out first before you try to take him in any store. Also, for general convenience, take along a health certificate signed by your vet, and if possible a rabies certificate.

BY TRAIN

Railroads vary considerably in their regulations regarding dogs accompanying passengers, so be sure to check the line you will be traveling on. As a general rule, dogs are allowed to accompany owners in private Pullman space such as compartments. Getting on and off the train in these cases, the regulation generally is that the dog must be either in a carrying case, or on leash and muzzled. Even in the private space, the rule sometimes is that a muzzle be worn, for the protection of porters, trainmen and conductors. It is pretty much up to the conductor whether this rule is enforced, but the rule is there, so always carry a muzzle with you. We have found conductors and trainmen almost always cooperative and helpful about dogs on trains if you give them half a chance, and you will probably have no trouble at all if your dog is well-mannered about things.

If you and another person are planning to travel first-class anyway, you will find that it is surprisingly inexpensive to take private space. The extra charge above the cost of two ordinary Pullman seats is small, particularly if you travel by day. Look into it if yours is a family trip, for the convenience of private space in traveling by train with a dog is considerable.

In non-private space, some lines allow certain dogs to accompany owners on coaches but not in first-class space. The reasons behind this curious distinction we have never been able to fathom, but be that as it may, such is the general rule. By "certain dogs" we mean that it is up to the conductor whether or not your dog gets on the coach with you. Dogs in carrying cases are seldom barred, providing they don't make a great fuss, and dogs on leash up to a reasonable size may be welcomed. But the larger varieties are almost always relegated to the baggage compartment, unless it should be one of those lines where the back end of the rear car is set aside for large dogs, bicycles and other impedimenta. The conductor may himself be a dog-lover, but the passenger across the aisle may be one of those people who are frightened out of their wits by anything bigger than a Pekingese, and the conductor has to operate by the rule of the greatest good for the greatest number.

If you are relegated to the baggage compartment, or just put your dog there in the first place, a leash and muzzle are very necessary. Some lines will allow you to ride right with him on short hauls, or to come into the baggage car to feed and comfort him at stops. Some, however, insist that passengers stay completely out of baggage cars, and you will have to leave him under the care of the baggage man. Here again, we have found that baggage handlers are almost universally pleasant and helpful about dogs, and quite good at their care. So deliver him to the baggage man, leash and muzzle on, and you will find all well at the end of the trip.

The final alternative is putting your dog in a crate for shipment along with you as baggage. If he has a large and comfortable crate, there will be no problems. In fact the baggage man will in all probability give him water occasionally if the trip is a lengthy one, and you will be able to stick your head in from time to time to see that all goes well. But check these arrangements with the baggage agent at your station before starting out.

Unless he travels at your side, and perhaps even then, you will need a special ticket for him. In years of traveling with dogs, we have had tickets describing the dog as "vehicle," "bicycle," "baggage," "livestock," "special baggage" and just plain "dog." Whatever the description, the charge for him will be relatively small.

BY PLANE

In carriers or not, dogs (with the exception of guide dogs) are never allowed in the passenger compartments of airliners. On an air trip your dog will go along in a special crate in the baggage comprtment. Some major airlines, especially United which commissioned its development, will rent you an item called the "Tuttle Kennel." This is an aluminum shipping crate especially designed for air shipment, and comes in two sizes. The small size measures 24" long, 15" wide and 17½" high on the inside; the large model measures 36" long, 21" wide and 30" high.

It is a very solidly constructed portable kennel, with more than sufficient ventilation. The bottom is of fine aluminum mesh which the dog can comfortably stand or lie on, and beneath each kennel there is a "sanitary" tray filled with a deodorizing and antiseptic solution. The solution used by the airlines is a very efficient one, and does not, so far as anyone knows, offend the dog's nose.

The total empty weight of the kennels is 28 pounds for the small and 50 pounds for the large model. This weight, plus the weight of your dog, will be charged to you as excess baggage on your flight, and the charges for a large dog can get quite considerable. In addition to the weight charge, each airline supplying these kennels makes a small rental charge —why there is this double charge is another travel fact that rather escapes us, but perhaps the airlines use the rental charge to defray cleaning and extra handling costs. If you plan to travel extensively with your dog, you can have your own shipping crate made. But be sure it is a sturdy one and big enough so that your dog can travel comfortably. He should be able to stand erect comfortably in the crate, and turn around. The airlines people have full discretionary powers to reject any shipping case which they feel is not well-built, or which is too small for the dog concerned.

They will reject them, too, for they are not only humane but concerned about damage suits and damage to their reputation in cases of dogs injured or killed in flight as a result of badly-built or cramping crates. In a conversation with one airline's baggage agent during the writing of this chapter, the authors were told of some appalling instances of dogs being presented for shipment in a wierd assortment of totally unacceptable and actually inhumane carriers—including one woman who had presented herself that same day at the baggage office with a two-month-old Boxer puppy literally crammed into a tiny cardboard box. The puppy had already evacuated in the box, and couldn't even move his legs, but the woman was greatly affronted when she was told the line wouldn't think of accepting the dog that way.

If you should happen to have one of the short-nosed breeds, check with the airline before trying to take him along on the plane. There have been occasional unfortunate incidents, in particular with Bulldogs, in which a dog has suffocated in flight. The lines take every precaution in putting the crates in the baggage compartments, but the compartment is after all a restricted space. It is also, though pressurized, not maintained at a pressure equal to that at ground level, and a dog which has even slight trouble breathing on the ground may find the thinner air fatal.

Just as with the railroads, the airlines baggage people will go out of their way to help you in everything relating to carrying your dog, so check with them well before your flight. Most lines will want you to be at the airport at least an hour ahead of flight time to take care of getting your dog comfortably settled in his kennel or crate. From the time you leave him, he will be well cared for and will ride comfortably in the pressurized baggage compartment. Some few airlines and liners do not have pressurized baggage compartments, and as a result cannot accept dogs—some just simply don't take dogs, so if your town is served exclusively by one of these, there is just no way out. If you want your dog along with you, he'll have to be shipped ahead by train.

TRAIN AND PLANE SHIPMENT

If you are sending your dog on ahead, or shipping him anywhere by himself, much the same rules apply. Unaccompanied, he will have to be in a strong shipping crate with some provision for sanitation. By train or plane he will generally be charged for at the regular freight rates, and you will have to make arrangements for him as such. Enroute, baggage-men will follow reasonable instructions for feeding and watering if you attach them to his crate and supply the material. As there are few flights of longer than eight hours within the U. S., there is no trouble, for any dog can go that length of time without food or water without danger.

FOREIGN TRAVEL

If you plan to take your dog with you into Canada or Mexico for a trip or a stay, there are certain health regulations of those countries that will have to be taken care of. Canada requires that you have one of two things—a certificate from a "Veterinary Inspector of the United States Bureau of Animal Industry" certifying that your dog has no signs of dis-ease and that no case of rabies has occured within a fifty-mile radius of your home within the last six months; or a certificate from your vet that the dog has been vaccinated against rabies within the last six months. As you can imagine, the former might be a bit difficult to arrange, so the solution is the shot and the vet's certificate, plus another stating that the dog is in good general health.

Mexico requires the health and rabies vaccination certificates also, and a Mexican consul must visa the papers before you present them at the border. If there is no consul in your city, you will probably be able to find one in any of the larger cities of Texas along the way. Reentry into the U. S. from Mexico requires no further papers if you have stayed less than thirty days—if longer your certificate of vaccination must indicate that the rabies shot was given within six months of the date of reentry.

For further travel, check with the nearest consul of the country or countries involved. Some few countries, England especially, will admit no dogs whatever except after a six months' quarantine. There is no rabies in England, for example, and they are scared silly that an infected dog

might get in and start it up there. You could have a vaccination a day for
six months, plus a certificate signed by the President stating that the dog
was pure and healthy and it wouldn't make the slightest difference to the
British authorities. They're very stuffy about that sort of thing, and make
no exceptions—even Seeing Eye dogs, among whom the incidence of
rabies is somewhat small, are refused unless they are quarantined.

KENNELS AND BOARDING

When the trip requires, or your personal preferences dictate, that you
leave your dog behind for days or weeks, the problem of what to do with
him can be bothersome. Friends or relatives are of course one solution.
But willing friends or relatives are a breed apart—even if willing at the
outset you may find relations somewhat strained when you return after a
week or more. People who do not have dogs often have no real concep-
tion of how much attention a dog requires, in feeding and exercising
and such. Beyond that, a lonely dog can often make a wreck of the lives
of his temporary keepers, so think long and choose well—remembering
too that some people, no matter how pleasant personally, have no concept of how to care for a dog properly.

The other alternative is a boarding kennel which will keep him at a
flat per diem charge for room and board. There are kennels and kennels,
some with no more than a fairly roomy cage for your dog, some with an
elaborate hut plus fenced run for him. Just which kennel you pick is a
matter only you can decide, for there are no rules we can give you. If
it's clean, and the owner or owners seem to know and love dogs, your
chances of having found a good one are high. Try to investigate any local
kennels long before your trip by getting opinions of other dog owners or
from the local humane society.

We have reproduced here a sample boarding contract form, and the
one you will sign for your dog will probably not be too much unlike it.
You will notice that the small print legally releases the owner from any
responsibility for a great number of things. This is only right, and don't
think you have walked into something unsuitable if the kennel owner
points this out to you when you appear with your dog. You cannot expect
to find a kennel owner who will accept total responsibility for sickness,

BOARDING CONTRACT

RECEIVED on this date, ——————————————— 195——, from:

Name ——————————————————————— 'phone ——————

Address ———————————————————————————————

ONE DOG: Breed ———————————————, Sex ——————, Age ——————

Color ——————————— ☐ for BOARDING.   ☐ for TRAINING and BOARDING.

For other purposes ———————————————————————————

State yes or no, Has had distemper: —— Inoculated against distemper—— Against rabies ——

Veterinarian to be called in case of illness ————————————— 'phone ——————

CHARGES are to be ———————————————————————————

payable IN ADVANCE on the first day of each —— week —— each month —— until owner calls for dog or gives other instructions for disposal.

I have received this date $———as advance payment to and including——————195——

The next payment of $————— will be due on ————————— 195——, and a

similar amount —— weekly —— monthly——— ——————————thereafter.

The dog is to be fed properly and regularly, and to be housed in clean, safe quarters. Dogs are boarded or trained, or otherwise handled or cared for by me without liability on my part for loss or damage from disease, death, running away, theft, fire, injury to persons, other dogs, or other unavoidable causes. At least once weekly the dog is to be brushed, cleaned and groomed. The dog is not to be taken off the premises except by consent of the owner. If dog becomes seriously ill, the owner shall be notified at once in case no particular veterinarian has been designated. If the owner does not inform immediately regarding measures to be taken, or if the state of the dogs health reasonably demands quick action, I reserve the right to call a veterinarian or administer or give other advisable attention, within my discretion and judgment, and such expenses, being reasonable in amount, shall be paid promptly by the owner of the dog.

If any charges for boarding, training, medicines, or veterinary services are not paid within thirty days after they are due or if dog is not called for within thirty days after time for return of dog, the dog will be sold by me publicly, privately or otherwise for the best price available. Notice in writing of such intended sale shall be mailed by registered mail to the owner of the dog at the address given hereon, not less than ten days before such date of intended sale, and no further notice shall be deemed necessary. Any excess amount over charges will be given to the owner; any deficiency is to paid by the owner.

The owner represents that he is the legal owner of said dog, that title to said dog is not mortgaged in any way, and that said dog has not been exposed to distemper or rabies within the last thirty days, and that the required annual license has been obtained.

This agreement is signed in duplicate by both parties, each party having a copy.

Signed ————————————— Signed ————————————

Owner of dog   Owner of Kennel

Kennel address ——————————————————————————

Received back in good condition the foregoing dog on ————————— 195——

Signed————————————————————————

accidents, damage or death. Although he knows dogs, he cannot know whether your dog is harboring some germ, or whether he will pine away from loneliness, or what. The great majority of kennelmen take every possible precaution, for although they may not be legally responsible for mishaps, their reputations and business are at stake. A few vocally unhappy former customers can bankrupt a boarding kennel, and the owners well know it.

Feeding is up to the kennel owner unless you specify otherwise. He will feed your dog the kennel's standard food in sufficient quantities, and that is included in the basic charge. If your dog cannot or will not eat anything but his special diet, be sure to give the kennel people full instructions and if possible supply a quantity of the food—you will otherwise have to pay for special diets supplied by the kennel.

Some people are able to put a dog in a kennel and walk away without so much as a backward look, some have a hard time even thinking of the poor dog closed away in a cage or a run with no one to pet or play with him. If you have to travel, though, and can't find an accommodating friend it's got to be the kennel. The loneliness and confinement probably won't hurt him, and he will be in good hands. Kennel owners are "dog people" or they wouldn't be in the business, they know dogs and how to care for them, and will take every reasonable precaution to see that your dog is well and happy when you return.

DOG IDENTIFICATION

Despite all the highly organized facilities of the AKC for registration and certification of pure-bred dogs, there does not exist in the U. S., so far as we know, any organized system of identification of dogs. True, cases of dog substituion or theft are rare, but such cases do exist. If a lost dog has been picked up by another person and kept for some period of time, it is a difficult thing to establish true ownership in the eyes of the law. Such devices as having the contending parties call the dog and awarding him to whomever he goes to are not the most satisfactory, and even a fairly detailed description of markings may not work.

If you want to have your dog permanently identified as yours, one curious but effective way is nose-printing. The lines on the front of a dog's nose are as distinctive and individual as human fingerprints. All it involves is getting some finger-printing ink, or similar ink, and pressing your dog's nose on a card, which you can then file away for possible future use. It takes a bit of practice on scrap sheets to get a good print, but a good nose-print, once taken, is a positive means of identification. To do a really good job, you can even get special nose-printing ink and forms from the Canadian Kennel Club for a very modest price—in Canada all registered dogs are identified by either this method or a tattoo system.

If yours is an AKC registered dog, you can even go to the length of registering him in Canada by mail—that way his prints and your ownership are kept safely in the files of the CKC. At this writing the CKC charge for registration of an American dog is a total of $6.00. Very few people in this country bother with nose-printing or registration with the CKC, but if you're interested in such a thing, write to the Canadian Kennel Club, 667 Yonge Street, Toronto 5, Canada.

DOG INSURANCE

Comical though the idea may appear to some, you can actually insure your dog's life, and some owners of valuable dogs do so. It is a difficult thing to arrange through a general insurance company—their rates and conditions are generally such as to make the idea prohibitive to anyone but the owner of a tremendously valuable show dog. But there is, at this writing, at least one company specializing in animal insurance, which advertises that it will insure pedigreed dogs against death from any cause but poisoning. We know nothing of any of the companies directly, and so cannot say whether their rates and conditions are within reason, but it is a reasonable assumption that you would have to have a veterinary certificate of health as at least one preliminary, and that the rates would tend to the high side. If you're interested, we suggest that you write to the advertising manager of the American Kennel Gazette of the AKC for information on companies known to him to be doing business at the time of your inquiry.

You can also get insurance against your dog's biting anyone. Sometimes this can be included in a general "homeowner's" liability policy. It's not a bad idea, for one bite can lead to some nasty lawsuits and damages, and a policy just might save your bank account. Along this line, incidentally, we definitely recommend against bruiting it about that your dog is a nasty one, or having "Beware of the Dog" signs on your premises as warnings. There is in some areas a "doctrine of the first bite" which involves the feeling that every dog is assumed to be not vicious and that one bite may be accidental and even provoked. Under this reasoning, the first time your dog bites someone you may get off easy, but the second time, look out! The same reasoning leads to the conclusion that if you have posted signs about your dog you are aware of a tendency on his part to bite and that you assume responsibility for keeping such a dog around—thus the first bite might be an expensive one for you.

THE DOG'S SENSES

Throughout this book we have spoken, in one light or another, of the dog's senses and capacities—his sight, hearing, smell and memory as they are different from those of the human. To expand a bit on these mentions, and in a way to justify ourselves in case you have been thinking, "Oh, come now, how do *you* know how a dog sees?," we will try to explain what is known about the dog and the way he receives his impressions of the world around him.

The fact that dogs are near-sighted, at least by human standards, is not only a matter of continued observation but of laboratory experiment. Any number of studies of dog eyesight have been run in various laboratories interested in such things. Generally the procedure is to train a dog to respond differently to certain shapes. He is taught, say, to sit up when he sees one figure and to lie down when he sees another. Then the figures are shown to him at increasing distances. The dog will begin to encounter confusion at distances far short of those at which humans can still easily differentiate. Thus the dog's near-sightedness is established. You may say, of course, that this simply means that after a while the dog just didn't care, but this is only a minor example of the type of experiment used to establish the fact—others, for example, use recognition or non-recognition of objects at a distance as a food signal.

Just as with humans, there are considerable variations in natural sight from one dog to another. There are severely near-sighted dogs and "far-sighted" dogs whose vision approximates that of a normal human. Some breeds, in fact, have better distance vision than others, and these "sight hounds" will tend to hunt visually rather than by smell. They are generally the taller dogs, which, incidentally, points to one of the possible reasons for the general difference between the dog's sight and man's. An animal which normally travels and stands on all fours will have a much smaller horizon than the one you are accustomed to—from that low position dogs and other quadrupeds simply cannot see as far as you can, near-sighted or not. Just as the seeing is better from the crows nest than from the deck, so is the seeing from five or more feet in the air better than from only a foot or two up. For the hunting quadruped, distance vision was not too important, but when animals began to stand erect the horizon broadened and "human" normal vision was an advantage. Ergo, it developed, or was sustained in the race by natural selection.

This is a point, incidentally, which is good to keep in mind when training or otherwise working with a dog. The object which you see at a distance may be totally invisible to him, your signals or motions from a distance may be, to him, blurred and indistinguishable one from the other. You should not expect him either to see the object nor to learn to distinguish between signals when it is physically impossible for him.

Even though near-sighted, dogs seem to be far more alert to movement than humans. Anything running or moving jerkily or rustling in the bushes will catch a dog's eye even though it is beyond the range of his accurate vision. This too is probably a throw-back to hunting, the dog being considerably nearer to the savage hunting state than most humans—and in hunting prey an acute awareness of even the smallest movement in the bush was and is a distinct advantage.

The color-blindness of dogs and most other animals has also been established in experiments similar to those mentioned above. The actual effects of color blindness are almost as difficult to describe and imagine as is describing color to a totally color blind person. It is a little easier, because you have seen black-and-white pictures of colored objects all your life. To a dog the world looks much like one long black-and-white movie. Just as in a picture you can tell the difference between light and dark colored objects, so can a dog—he can distinguish bright red from deep

blue, for example. But between two colors of the same shade and bright-
ness, he simply cannot differentiate.

The dog's reaction to pictures is a curious aspect of things—whether
of vision or of perception no one really quite knows. We do know that
dogs do not recognize pictures of things as the things themselves. A
picture, no matter how large, of another dog will not interest a dog in
the slightest. Neither will he react to even a photo-mural of his beloved
master. Perhaps it is the two-dimensional quality of pictures—meaning
nothing at all to a dog except as marks on a piece of paper. This seems
to be borne out by the fact that a dog will react to things he sees in
a mirror. There what he sees has a three-dimensional quality.

The subject of mirrors is another source of puzzlement as far as the
dog is concerned. Young dogs and those who have never seen mirrors
before will growl and challenge their reflections in a mirror, or even
want to frisk and play with them. But with the passing of time and
experience, a dog soon learns to ignore his reflection. It is hard to believe
that he comes to realize that it is his reflection—and it seems more likely
that he eventually learns that that other dog is no menace and can't
be reached and has no smell, and so he loses interest. Yet a dog who
has learned to ignore his own image will often react throughout his
life to seeing his master in a mirror. The exact nature of that particular
mechanism is quite beyond us.

Along the line of pictures, there is the matter of dogs and television.
Although there is an occasional dog who is said by his owners to enjoy
watching the television screen (and a few who are even reputed to
have favorite programs such as "Lassie"), the explanation is probably
that the dog is fascinated by the light and movement on the screen.
Just as with still pictures, the actual pictures on the screen mean nothing
at all to a dog, other than as patterns and shapes of light and dark. There
is another reason for a dog's seeming interest in the television set, but
that is a matter of hearing.

It is a widely known fact that dogs can hear sounds far higher in the
frequency range than we can. It is generally accepted that dogs are
able to hear sounds up to approximately 30,000 cycles per second, while
the average human can hear only 15,000 cycles, with the exceptional
individual just making out 20,000. (As a reference point, the highest

note on a piano is 4,186 cycles; the lowest 27½.) Russian scientists, who seem to spend a good deal of their time trying things on dogs, claim to have established canine hearing as far as the 75,000-100,000 cycle range, but there has been no substantiating evidence on this.

The "silent" dog whistles you will see in pet shops are one sure proof of a higher hearing range. Although you will seem to be just blowing to no good effect, a dog can hear one of these whistles at distances up to a half a mile. As with humans, a dog's hearing begins to fall off as the frequency gets higher, and so these whistles are designed to operate not far above the range of human perception. If you have exceptionally sensitive ears you may hear just a faint shrilling when you blow one. In any case, such a whistle is a handy thing to have around if you want to call your dog without shouting up a storm and disturbing the neighbors. Train him to come when he hears the whistle and you can blast away at bedtime with no complaints from an aroused citizenry. The only drawback is that such whistles have no distinctive sound other than being in the high range—if several neighborhood dogs are trained to come at the blast of one, you may be inundated with dogs when you tootle away.

Hearing of this nature may explain the occasional case you hear of in which dogs seemingly respond to mental commands. We have never seen these exhibitions (for some reason, Indians seem to have a corner on this sort of thing) but there are fairly well authenticated stories of such. It may be just that the handler in question has trickily mastered the art of ultrasonic whistling and has trained his dog to respond to whistled signals. We don't really know, but it's a thought.

Back on the subject of television, this higher hearing will cause some dogs to exhibit an unseemly interest in the set when it is turned on. In many sets, perhaps in all, there is an inaudible (to humans) frequency generated which performs certain vital functions. This tone, somewhere in the neighborhood of 25,000 cycles, is perfectly audible to dogs. Whether it is an attractive sound to them or an irritating one, it is true that many dogs will perk up their ears when the set goes on, and perhaps even sit and listen attentively for some time with every appearance of enjoying the program.

About music we can say little, for lack of effective communication limits our knowledge rather sharply in this sphere. Animals do respond to certain types of music—dairymen have found that soothing classics or background music will tranquilize cows, while jazz has the opposite effect. The dog howling while you play the piano may or may not be a critic, but dogs do seem to recognize music or musical attempts as being somehow different from other noises. Dogs can be trained to respond differently to different tones in a laboratory, but it has been found that they generally cannot distinguish intervals of less than a whole tone (or at least they can't be persuaded to react to less) while the average untrained human can hear quarter-tone intervals or less.

As with sensitivity to movement, dogs seem to have very selective hearing—the ability to catch a familiar or expected sound through or above a veritible cataract of noise. A Doberman belonging to one of the authors demonstrates this constantly. Living in a New York apartment the dog is subjected to constant blasts of traffic and street noises and suffers the affliction of an efficient hi-fi loudspeaker. Yet with a crashing symphonic number roaring from the machine and competing with heavy trucks outside, he can detect the faint noises of the elevator rising to the floor and will bristle protectively even before the car has arrived at the floor and the door opened. It may be that in this case the elevator gives off a loud, to him, noise in the ultrasonic range which rises above hi-fi and traffic. Other dogs, though, have demonstrated incredibly selective hearing under circumstances which do not seem to offer the ultrasonic explanation.

The extended range of hearing, or perhaps even of smell, may be an explanation for the often-heard stories of dogs being aware of ghosts and other psychic phenomena. We have had the experience of having a household dog suddenly stare fixedly at an ordinary corner of the room, and even bristle and snarl at it. In one case it was found that the dog was reacting to reflections in a window—to him it looked as though there were people moving about close outside the house. In other cases we have assumed that there was simply something earthly there that we couldn't detect, perhaps a peculiar reflection of sound waves beyond our hearing range. It may be that we are haunted, but the dogs extended senses offer a more logical way out. We must admit, though, that it is a chilling thing to see a sudden bristling at empty air

—it is easy to see how the thought of ghosts and other shiveries arose when dogs manifested this behavior.

Smell is the particular province of the dog. His sensitivity and analytical ability in the odor field are so widely known and appreciated as hardly to require comment. Partially it is the result of a considerably extended nasal range—the average large dog has four or five inches of nose passages—and partially it is greater sensitivity. Even very short-nosed dogs such as pugs and bulldogs, who have hardly greater nasal length than humans, far exceed humans in smelling ability, even though they may rank in this talent far below their long-nosed colleagues.

A dog is able to break down a smell into its component parts, just as a music lover can distinguish all the simultaneous instrumental sounds in a symphony. He can detect minute quantities of a liked or disliked constituent in a hash of mixed food, and he can detect and isolate a familiar smell from among a great range of other and stronger odors. It is in fact nearly impossible for us to imagine just how a dog smells and what the smells convey to him. Experiment is difficult because dogs can and do detect odors of which we are not even aware, and which we could not begin to reproduce.

Smell may be responsible for some otherwise unexplained reactions of dogs—for example the curious business of dogs being somehow aware of fear in a human. It is our theory that dogs can smell fear. It is well enough known that fear causes an increase of adrenalin flow in the body, and that there are other minor physical changes involved in a fear reaction—cold sweat is only one of them. It follows that it is highly probable that a dog can smell the results of these physical changes; can for example smell even a minute amount of "cold sweat" that the fearful person himself cannot detect on his skin.

The standard lie-detector, the Keeler Polygraph, operates along much the same lines, detecting electrically the increased conductivity of the skin as a result of fear or anxiety sweating. And even as the polygraph also measures involuntary increases in muscular tensions when a subject is lying, the dog may also be able to detect physical signs that we ourselves are unaware of.

It is certain enough that dogs can and do recognize moods in humans, even above and beyond obvious anger, happiness or depression. It is within the bounds of possibility that dogs actually smell moods. Or that they may be able to detect the tiny and unconscious movements and muscle-tightenings which the psychologists speak of as "subliminal cues," indications normally below the threshold of consciousness and the average perception. Whatever the mechanism of this in particular, it is certain that with their extended perceptions, dogs do react to many things we are not aware of—and this again is a point of importance to the trainer. When your dog reacts peculiarly in training, always examine the possibility that he sees, or hears, or smells, or otherwise detects something that is quite beyond your range of perception. Give him, when he balks or seems frightened or refuses to work in a certain place, the benefit of the doubt. You can't possibly know what he does, and attempts to "straighten him out" will be more useless than helpful.

TRICKS

Training of the "trick" variety is a thing quite apart from obedience training for companionship, control and convenience. Tricks are strictly for fun and display, obedience training is for practical purposes and sometimes for competition. Both, however, are taught by the same basic method of demonstration, correction and praise. Tricks can be taught to a dog who has had no obedience training, although a trained dog who has acquired the habit of obedience and learning will pick up any trick you desire faster than his untrained colleague.

There are, of course, thousands and perhaps millions of dogs in this country and around the world who can sit up, roll over and shake hands who wouldn't know a training collar if it bit them—far more, certainly, than there are obedience trained dogs. Tricks are, in fact, the entire meaning of training to a very large segment of the population who have never seen or heard of an obedience trained dog—this situation can at times be trying in the extreme to the proud owner of an obedience dog. You modestly aver to an acquaintance that you have a well-trained dog, and he immediately reaches down to Rover and says, shake hands, boy. When you manage to stammer out that, oh no, training doesn't mean just silly tricks, then your acquaintance says, well, what *does* he do? You come back, if you have completed Novice training, with, uh, well, he heels real good. And he comes when I call him. And he stays there when I tell him to. From there the situation degenerates rapidly.

We suspect that even if you told an uninitiated friend that your dog could beat him two sets out of three at tennis, tell his fortune, and serve him coffee without slopping it into the saucer, you would get a reply something on the order of, "Yeah, yeah, but can he maybe sit up and beg?" Whatever your reason for training your dog to do the common tricks, be it in self defense or just because you plain want to, here is the way to go about it.

SHAKE HANDS

Probably the easiest of all tricks to teach, this can be given to even a very young dog, for it involves no more than the lifting of the right forepaw on command. With your dog or puppy sitting anywhere in the house or out, reach down and take hold of his right paw with your right hand and lift it gently. Tell him "Shake!" as you do it. Lift the paw until it is on the level of his chest, and then shake it gently just as though you were shaking hands with him. Praise him highly as you are shaking his paw, and give him an extra word of commendation when it is over. Do this half a dozen times a day for a few days, then try just reaching for his paw as you give the command. If he lifts it even a little, take it and shake it, praising him effusively. With application and a little practice he will soon be lifting it quite high for you.

ROLL OVER

Next in ease of teaching, the "roll over" can also be learned quite young, for it requires little muscular learning on the dog's part. Make it as much a game as possible when teaching—whenever you normally play with him, get down on the floor with him and wait until he is lying down on his side. Then put one hand in the middle of his back and the other under his chest and shoulders. Give the command "Roll Over!" and turn him gently over as you do so. When he is over praise him highly, laugh with him at what he has done and let him know what a colossal accomplishment he has managed. Do this three or four times in an evening, and once he seems to have the idea, cut down gradually on your assistance until he is doing it by himself at your command. Praise and an air of good-fellowship will make him happy and enthusiastic about rolling over, and you can, if you time your commands right, get him to go over twice, or three times, or clear across the room. Be careful, though, about overdoing either in training or in demonstration. Even in the best of humor he may become bored with it as a repeated thing, and you will have a problem getting up his interest again.

Occasionally a dog will object quite violently to being manhandled to this extent, even in the spirit of play. If you have this problem, we can only suggest that you approach the subject more cautiously the next time you try it. Get him in a receptive mood by petting and praising him as he lies on his side (don't try to whisk him over from a Sphinx-like down position with his rear legs braced—that can turn into a match for two falls out of three), get your hands sneakily into the proper position while petting him, then ease him over as you give the command in a friendly tone. If you do it right, he'll be over before he realizes he should be making an issue of it. This may work, but if not, give it up until he's older and perhaps more amenable to foolishness at your hands. Some few dogs for their own private reasons think that rolling over is a damn fool thing to do and will have no truck with it. It is not that important an accomplishment, and the same trouble will not occur with the other tricks.

SIT UP

Because sitting up is an entirely unnatural position for a dog, he will have to be helped at first. The best way is to sit him in a corner facing out. Give the command to sit up, and lift him gently by his front legs until he is in an erect sitting position. Keep him there a few moments, then release his feet and put one hand under his chin to help him keep his balance. Keep repeating to him as he sits, "Up, Up" or whatever command you choose. Hold him there for only a few seconds, then let him down with much praise. Repeat this half a dozen times a day until he will stay without your help once you have got him up, then keep working on it until he goes up by himself. A sufficient number of repetitions, along with praise to let him know he is doing something good when he raises himself up, will give him the idea.

Because sitting up requires the development of certain back muscles ordinarily not used in that way, be sure to go cautiously with this training. If you try to keep him in the sit-up position too long too early, he will slump over simply because he physically cannot hold it any longer. Once that has happened, he will become discouraged with trying, and your training will suffer a severe setback. If on the first time you try it he simply slumps down and your hand under his chin does not help, you will know that he is too young for this training— at too early an age a puppy can no more hold himself erect than can a human child. Let the sit-up training go for a month or two until he is older and stronger.

When he will finally do the sit-up by himself, on command, try him in the center of the room. If at your command he runs over to the corner and sits up there, he is being only too logical and following out what he thinks you want, so praise him, do not reprimand him. Take hold of his legs the next time before you give the command, and assist him in sitting up where he is. A few repeats of this and he will come to understand that he is to sit up wherever he is at the time of your command.

CATCH

A great many dogs will do this quite naturally, catching any tidbit of food you throw them. To sharpen him up and make him realize that consistency and accuracy are important, give him a little practice just before his meal when he is hungry. Stand quite close in front of him and toss to him small bits of food, saying "Catch" as you throw them. What he catches he will of course eat—what he misses you must be quick to get and not allow him to touch. Before long he will have the idea that the more catches he makes, the more he gets to eat, and there you have the training. Make it as easy as possible for him. Get in a little practice in pitching before you start with him—you don't want him to have to make shoestring catches, just plain easy ones. Later you can progress to systematic catching of a small soft ball or any other soft toy, from an appreciable distance. Praise him when he makes each catch and the training incentive will be doubled.

SAY YOUR PRAYERS

This is one which is particularly appealing to children, and is quite easy to teach. Select a chair in the house for your dog to use, one heavy enough so that it will not slide when he leans against it, and just high enough for him to rest his forepaws on comfortably. Take him to it and sit him in front of the chair and give the command "Say Your Prayers!" As you do this, lift his front feet and place them on the edge of the chair, and gently lower his head until his chin is resting on his paws. Soothe him with kind words as you do this, hold him there a few moments, then release him with much praise.

Next time, give him the command wherever he is. He will not, naturally enough, understand you, but when you have given him the command lead him over to the selected chair and put him in position again. As with all the other tricks, it is simply a matter of repetition until he gets the idea and performs it himself. One of the difficulties you are likely to run into is the placement of the head. Holding the head in a certain position at command is something quite foreign to dogs, and it may take many repetitions before he understands this particular part. But keep at it with patience and praise until he catches on. Obedience training in the "stay" is helpful here.

BRING THE SLIPPERS

Here tricks veer into the area of usefulness, for it is a handy thing indeed to have your dog bring your slippers, or a pipe, or cigarettes, or whatever you happen to want and are too lazy or tired to get up and get yourself. Once your dog has learned the basics of getting and bringing to you any one thing, he can be taught to recognize the word for and bring you any number of items.

First, he must learn the simple retrieve. Without going into the regular obedience retrieve, you can get the idea across to your dog by simply playing ball with him. Throw his ball and let him bring it back to you in play, and go on from this to throwing a stick, a rolled-up newspaper, a glove and even your wallet. When you find that he will chase and bring back almost any object you throw for him, take the glove or paper or whatever and give it to him as he sits near you, and coax him to follow you with it. If done in the spirit of play, and gently, this will present no difficulties.

When he is carrying things happily for you, take him to the bedroom and give him one of your slippers to carry. Give him the command "Bring the Slippers!" or "Fetch the Slippers!" or whatever you like, and coax him to follow you into the living room, carrying the slipper in his mouth. Sit down and put it on, then give him the command again. He won't understand, of course, but after you have given him the command, go with him again to the bedroom and repeat the process with the second slipper. When you have both on, praise him and let it go for that day.

The next night when you come home, tell him again to bring the slippers, pointing to the bedroom, and going along with him to repeat the lesson of the night before. After a week or ten days you will begin to see progress. The first time he does go all by himself and bring one of your slippers, heap the praise on him, for he has managed a very considerable thing, and you should let him know it. Insist, then, that he go get the other one, and keep this up every night until it takes only one command for him to get both. Soon, in fact, you may find him going to get your slippers as soon as you get inside the house, with no command. If he does this, stop whatever you are doing and put them on so that he sees that all is as before, and praise him as always.

From the slippers you can progress to fetching almost anything that is normally kept in the same place. Work just as before with each item you want him to bring. When you first switch from the slippers to, say, a pipe or pack of cigarettes, you will probably encounter some small confusion on his part, for he will automatically react to the "Bring" part of the command by dashing for your slippers. Praise him even if he brings back the wrong thing—any reprimand on your part will make him think that it was the bringing part of the operation that you suddenly disapprove of—and repeating the command, take him to the right object. Soon he will learn to distinguish between the names of the objects, and will bring you what you want, infallibly.

WALK THROUGH

This is quite a difficult trick to teach, but it is one of the most impressive with which to show off your dog's abilities. It is, for the most part, limited to small dogs, but if you have a Great Dane or an Irish Wolfhound and feel reckless and agile, go ahead and try it, but don't say we didn't warn you.

He doesn't need to know how to heel, but it is a help. In any case, he must be able to work on the collar and leash, and know them well enough to respond to urgings of the leash without fighting it. Get him walking on your left side more or less even with you. After a few steps, stop with your left foot well out ahead. Pass the leash between your legs and as you give the command "Walk Through!" guide him through to your right side. Praise him as he comes through, but get him through by gentle tugs on the lead. Don't tug and haul him through— remember that it is a strange and curious situation to him, so introduce him gently to the idea. Then when he is on your right side move your right foot forward until it is well out in front and get him back through to your left side again. Take a few more normal steps and then slow down to try it again.

That is really all there is to it in the explanation. It is a good deal harder in practice, but with time and patience he will learn to slip through your legs like an eel and back through again. Each time he is to pass through give him the command—and always do it double, from left to right and back to left again before taking your normal walk up again. Whether or not you have any intention of teaching him heeling, you don't want him learning that it is a good thing to walk at your right side, even for a few steps in the midst of a trick. And of course don't try to do it full speed—a small miscalculation could get him hurt, and once hurt trying to go between your legs he will think twice before trying it again.

Also, make sure, quite sure, that he does this particular business only on command. You can easily see the unpleasant consequences of his performing a quick walk-through as you are walking rapidly down the street with him. The resale value of this book as kindling will come nowhere near paying the medical bills.

TRICKS FROM OBEDIENCE

For the fully trained obedience dog, and by this we mean one at the Utility level, there are many "tricks" that can be worked out—the number limited only by your ingenuity. The two we suggest here actually require no new training. What they do require is a small amount of work with the new apparatus involved, but the Utility dog will find no difficulty in this.

Find the Dollar—here you need a fairly good sized grassy field, a dog trained in either the seek-back or tracking, and a dollar bill. Get him used to the idea of carrying a crumpled dollar bill in his mouth, then practice a few seek-backs or short tracks with the dollar. With that you are ready to demonstrate to friends just how valuable your trained dog is. Leave him at the edge of the field and walk out into the middle with the crumpled bill and drop it, returning over the same path. Send your dog out to find it, and hope for the best. If he is a good worker and you feel like living dangerously, try it with a ten or a twenty. It adds a certain something to the exercise, because a crumpled bill in a large grassy field is almost invisible and unfindable by you, even if you think you know where you dropped it.

Mind Reading—this is an exceptionally effective trick, but it consists of misdirection and can only be worked on friends who are not familiar with scent discrimination. In setting up the trick, you have half a dozen children's blocks with letters of the alphabet on one side. You ask one of your spectators to place them in a line on the floor or ground, and to bring you the block he wants your dog to be mentally instructed to find. When you get the block, you hold it against your forehead and do a bit of acting along the lines of "fierce concentration," then hand the block back to be placed in line with the others while you and your dog face away. You turn and send your dog with no other word to him but "Find It" and, lo, he comes back with the proper block in his mouth!

The mechanism is simple enough—all you must do is train your dog to work scent discrimination with the blocks. In this practice, work with an assistant handling all the blocks, including the one that is handed to you and replaced in line. With a little work your dog will learn to ignore the assistant's smell on all the blocks and find the one that also has your smell on it. Your smell, of course, was well and fully given to the block while you went through the business of holding it to your forehead and "concentrating" on your mental instructions. When the blocks are put in the line, have them placed with the letter face up, and when your dog sniffs along the line it will look to the uninitiated as though he were actually peering nearsightedly at the letters to find the right one. If you do it skillfully, it will puzzle your friends for months to come.

APPENDIX

APPENDIX

AMERICAN KENNEL CLUB OBEDIENCE REGULATIONS

CHAPTER I

Special Regulations and Awards Applying to Dogs Competing in Obedience Trials

SECTION 1. If a club or association wishes to hold an Obedience Trial at which points towards a title may be awarded, it must make application to the American Kennel Club for leave to hold such trial. *Such a trial may be held either in connection with a dog show or as a separate event, (if an all breed trial is held apart from a dog show it can be given only by an obedience club) but in either case all of the rules applying to dog shows, where applicable, shall govern the conducting of obedience trials and shall apply to all persons participating in them excepting as the following Regulations and Standards for Obedience Trials may provide otherwise and excepting that castrated dogs and spayed bitches may be entered in obedience trials.* The application shall contain such information as the American Kennel Club may require, and the club or association shall make a deposit of an amount which shall be determined by the American Kennel Club. Such club will be required to make only one date deposit for the two events. If the club is not a member of the American Kennel Club, it shall also pay a license fee for the privilege of holding such trial, the amount of which shall also be determined by the American Kennel Club. The American Kennel Club will notify the club or association of its approval or disapproval of the application. If the club or association shall fail to hold its trial at the time and place which have been approved, the deposit shall become the property of the American Kennel Club,

but the amount of any license fee paid will be returned.

(At present the license fee required to be paid for holding an Obedience Trial under above Section 1, by a club that is not a member of the American Kennel Club, is $25.00. The deposit required from each club is $25.00.)

SECTION 2. *If an obedience trial is held by an obedience club, an obedience trial committee must be appointed by the club, and this committee shall exercise all the authority vested in a bench show committee. If an obedience club holds its obedience trial in conjunction with a dog show, then the obedience trial committee shall have sole jurisdiction only over those dogs entered in the obedience trial; provided, however, that if any dog is entered in both obedience and breed classes, then the obedience trial committee shall have jurisdiction over such dog, its owner, and its handler, only in matters pertaining to the Regulations and Standards for Obedience Trials, and the bench show committee shall have jurisdiction over such dog, its owner and handler, in all other matters.*

When an obedience trial is to be held in connection with a dog show by the club or association which has been granted permission to hold that dog show, the club's bench show committee shall include one person to be designated as "obedience chairman." *At this event the bench show committee of the show-giving club shall have sole jurisdiction over all matters which may properly come before it, regardless of whether the matter has to do with the dog show or with the obedience trial.*

SECTION 3. A club or association which has been granted permission to

349

hold a dog show may also be granted permission to hold in connection with the show any or all of the obedience classes defined in this chapter, except Tracking Tests, if in the opinion of the Board of Directors of the American Kennel Club such club or association is qualified to do so.

SECTION 4. *A club or association may hold an obedience match by obtaining the sanction of the American Kennel Club. Sanctioned obedience matches shall be governed by such regulations as may be determined from time to time by the Board of Directors of the American Kennel Club. No score made at a match shall be considered as "qualifying" or as a 'leg" toward a degree.*

SECTION 5A. *In the following sections 5, 6, 10, 11 and 16 (as renumbered) of Chapter I, "any breed" shall mean only those breeds eligible for registration in the American Kennel Club Stud Book or for entry in the Miscellaneous Class at American Kennel Club shows.*

SECTION 5. (Novice Class A). The Obedience Novice Class A shall be for pure-bred dogs of any breed and of either sex which have not won the title of "C.D." (Companion Dog). One dog only may be entered in this class by any one exhibitor and every dog in the class must have a separate handler. Dogs entered in this class must be exhibited by the owner or a member of his immediate family. No licensed handler, no trainer nor any kennel employee shall be allowed to compete as exhibitor or otherwise.

SECTION 6. (Novice Class B). The Obedience Novice Class B shall be for pure-bred dogs of any breed and of either sex which have not won the title of "C.D." (Companion Dog). Dogs in this class may be handled or exhibited by the owner or any other person. Exhibitors may enter more than one dog in this class, but each dog must have a separate handler for the "Sit" and "Down" exercises when judged together. No dog may be entered in both Novice Class A and Novice Class B at any one trial.

SECTION 7. The tests and scores for a perfect performance in the Novice Classes shall be:

1. Heel on Leash .... 35 points
2. Stand for Examination . 30 points
3. Heel Free .... 45 points
4. Recall .... 30 points
5. Long Sit .... 30 points
6. Long Down .... 30 points

Maximum Total Score.... 200 points
(Less Penalty for Misbehavior)

SECTION 8. The American Kennel Club will permit the use of the letters "C.D.", signifying "Companion Dog", to be used in connection with and after the name of each dog which shall be certified by Judges of Obedience Trials to have received scores of more than 50% of the available points in each of the six exercises and total scores of 170 or more points in Obedience Novice Classes.

SECTION 9. The total number of dogs required to compete in the Novice Class A and Novice Class B combined and the number of Obedience Novice Classes in which a dog must receive a score of more than 50% of the available points in each of the six exercises and a total score of 170 or more points in order to be permitted to use the letter "C.D." shall be fixed and determined by the Board of Directors of the American Kennel Club.

At present, to be permitted to use the letters "C.D.", a dog must receive a score of more than 50% of the available points in each of the six exercises and a total score of 170 or more points in Novice Classes at three Obedience Trials in which the combined number competing in Novice Class A and Novice Class B at each trial shall be six or more dogs. This applies to Division No. 1 (East and North); Division No. 2 (West and South); Division No. 3 (California); Division No. 4 (Pacific Northwest; and Division No. 5 (Hawaii).

SECTION 10. (Open Class A). The Obedience Open Class A shall be for pure-bred dogs of any breed and of either sex which shall have won the title of "C.D." (Companion Dog) in Obedience Novice Classes. One dog only may be entered in this class by any one exhibitor and every dog in the class must have a separate handler who is to handle his dog in all exercises including the "Sit" and the "Down"; dogs entered in this class must be exhibited by the owner or a member of his immediate family. No licensed handler, no trainer nor any kennel employee shall be allowed to compete as exhibitor or otherwise. No dog that has won the title of "C.D.X." shall be entered in this class.

SECTION 11. (Open Class B). The Obedience Open Class B shall be for pure-bred dogs of any breed and of either sex which shall have won the title of "C.D." (Companion Dog). Dogs in this class may be handled or exhibited by the owner or any other person. Exhibitors may enter more than one dog in this class, but the same handler who handled each dog in the first five exercises must handle each dog in the "Sit" and "Down" exercises, except that where a handler has handled more than one dog in the first five exercises, he must have an additional handler for each additional dog when judged together. No dog may be entered in both Open Class A and Open Class B at any one trial.

SECTION 12. The tests and scores for a perfect performance in the Open Classes shall be:
1. Heel Free .... 40 points
2. Drop on Recall .... 30 points
3. Retrieve on Flat ...... 25 points
4. Retrieve over High Jump 35 points
5. Broad Jump .... 20 points
6. Long Sit .... 25 points
7. Long Down .... 25 points

Maximum Total Score ..200 points
(Less Penalty for Misbehavior)

SECTION 13. The American Kennel Club will permit the use of the letters "C.D.X.", signifying "Companion Dog Excellent", to be used in connection with and after the name of each dog which shall be certified by Judges of Obedience Trials to have received scores of more than 50% of the available points in each of the seven exercises and total scores of 170 or more points in Obedience Open Classes.

SECTION 14. The total number of dogs required to compete in the Open Class A and Open Class B combined and the number of Obedience Open Classes in which a dog must receive a score of more than 50% of the available points in each of the seven exercises and a total score of 170 or more points in order to be permitted to use the letter "C.D.X." shall be fixed and determined by the Board of Directors of the American Kennel Club.

At present, to be permitted to use the letters "C.D.X.", a dog must receive a score of more than 50% of the available points in each of the seven exercises and a total score of 170 or more points in Open Classes at three Obedience Trials in which the combined number competing in Open Class A and Open Class B at each trial shall be six or more dogs in Division No. 1 (East and North) and Division No. 3 (California), four or more dogs in Division No. 2 (West and South) and Division No. 4 (Pacific Northwest) and three or more dogs in Division No. 5 (Hawaii).

SECTION 15. A dog may continue to compete in the Obedience Open Class B after having won the title of "C.D.X." and/or "U.D.", and may continue to compete in the Utility Class after having won the title of "U.D."

SECTION 16. (Utility Class). The Obedience Utility Class shall be for pure-bred dogs of any breed and of either sex which shall have won the title of "C.D.X." (Companion Dog Excellent) in Obedience Open Classes. Handlers, trainers and kennel employees may compete in this class. Exhibitors may enter more than one dog in this class, but each dog must have a separate handler for the "Group Examination" exercise when judged together.

SECTION 17. The tests and scores for a perfect performance in the Utility Classes shall be:
1. Scent Discrimination—
Article #1 .... 20 points

2. Scent Discrimination—
   Article #2 .... 20 points
3. Scent Discrimination—
   Article #3 .... 20 points
4. Seek Back .... 30 points
5. Signal Exercise .... 35 points
6. Directed Jumping ..... 40 points
7. Group Examination .... 35 points
   ———
   Maximum Total Score ..200 points
   (Less Penalty for Misbehavior)

SECTION 18. The American Kennel Club will permit the use of the letters "U.D.", signifying "Utility Dog", to be used in connection with, and after the name of each dog which shall be certified by Judges of Obedience Trials to have received scores of more than 50% of the available points in each of the seven exercises and total scores of 170 or more points in the Obedience Utility Class.

SECTION 19. (Utility Class). The total number of dogs required to compete in the Utility Class and the number of Obedience Utility Classes in which a dog must receive a score of more than 50% of the available points in each of the seven exercises and a total score of 170 or more points in order to be permitted to use the letters "U.D." shall be fixed and determined by the Board of Directors of the American Kennel Club.

At present, to be permitted to use the letters "U.D.", a dog must receive a score of more than 50% of the available points in each of the seven exercises and a total score of 170 or more points in the Utility Class at three Obedience Trials in each of which classes three or more dogs were competing. This applies to Division No. 1 (East and North), Division No. 2 (West and South), Division No. 3 (California), Division No. 4 (Pacific Northwest) and Division No. 5 (Hawaii).

SECTION 20. (Tracking Test). This test must be judged by two judges and is open only to pure-bred dogs. With each entry form of a dog which has not passed a "Tracking Test", there must be filed a written statement by a person who is accredited by the American Kennel Club to judge a "Tracking Test", that the dog is considered by him to be ready for such a test. Handlers, trainers and kennel employees may compete. An exhibitor may enter more than one dog. The holding of other titles, including "T.D.", shall not bar a dog from competition in this test.

This test cannot be given indoors nor at a dog show. The duration of this test may be one day or more, within a fifteen day period from the original date, in the event of an unusually large entry, or other unforeseen emergency, provided that the change in date is satisfactory to the exhibitors affected.

SECTION 21. The American Kennel Club will permit the use of the letters "T.D.", signifying "Tracking Dog" to be used in connection with, and after the name of each dog which shall be certified by the two Judges to have passed a Tracking Test at which at least three dogs have competed.

In case of dogs holding both the "Utility Dog" and "Tracking Dog" titles, these titles may be combined, as "U.D.T." signifying "Utility Dog Tracker".

SECTION 22. The following colors shall be used for prize ribbons in all classes except at sanctioned obedience *matches*:

First Prize .... Blue
Second Prize .... Red
Third Prize .... Yellow
Fourth Prize .... White

All prize ribbons shall have the words "Obedience Trial" printed on them.

SECTION 23. If ribbons are given at sanctioned obedience *matches,* they shall be of the following colors:

First Prize .... Rose
Second Prize .... Brown
Third Prize .... Light Green
Fourth Prize .... Gray

All prize ribbons shall have the words "Obedience Trial" printed on them.

SECTION 24. Bitches in season are not permitted to compete. The Judge of an Obedience Trial or Tracking Test must remove from competition any bitch in season, any dog which does not obey its handler, any handler who interferes wilfully with another competitor, or his dog, and may expel from competition any dog which he considers unfit to compete, or any bitch which appears so attractive to males as to be a disturbing element. In case of doubt an official veterinarian shall be called to give his opinion.

SECTION 25. The owner or agent entering a dog in an Obedience Trial does so at his own risk and agrees to abide by the rules of the American Kennel Club, and the regulations and Standards for Obedience Trials.

SECTION 26. The decisions of the Obedience Trial Committee or the Bench Show Committee, if the trial be held by a show-giving club, shall be conclusive in all matters arising at the trial and shall bind all parties, subject however, to the rules of the American Kennel Club.

SECTION 27. Any dog entered and received at an Obedience Trial must compete in all exercises of all classes in which it is entered, unless expelled by the Judge or excused by the official veterinarian. *The excuse by the official veterinarian must be in writing and attached to the show or trial report sent to the American Kennel Club by the superintendent, show secretary or trial secretary. If a dog is expelled by a judge, the reason shall be stated in the Judge's book.*

SECTION 28. No dog belonging wholly or in part to any Judge, or to any member of the immediate family or household of any Judge, shall be entered or exhibited in any dog show, Obedience Trial or Tracking Test at which such person may judge. This applies to both obedience and dog show Judges when an Obedience Trial is held in conjunction with a dog show. However, a Tracking Test held on a different day shall be considered a separate event for the purpose of this section.

SECTION 29. No entry shall be made at any Obedience Trial or Tracking Test under a Judge of any dog which the Judge, or any member of his immediate family, or household, has owned, sold, held under lease, handled in the ring, boarded, trained, or instructed regularly, within one year prior to the date of the trial. This includes Judges who train professionally, or as amateurs, and applies equally to judges who trained individual dogs, and those who train dogs in classes with or through their handlers. However, the above limitations as to trainers shall not apply at sanctioned matches.

SECTION 30. In order to win a "C.D.", "C.D.X.", or "U.D." degree, qualifying scores must be obtained under at least three different Judges.

SECTION 31. At outdoor tests held at dog shows a separate ring (rings) shall be provided for obedience classes and a sign forbidding any dog to enter such rings, except when being judged, shall be erected by the Superintendent and it shall be his duty as well as that of the Obedience Trial (or Bench Show) Committee to enforce this regulation. At indoor tests where limited space does not permit the exclusive use of rings for obedience tests, the same regulations will apply after the obedience rings have been set up.

SECTION 32. Where any of the foregoing sections of the Regulations excludes from a particular Obedience Class dogs which have won a particular Obedience title, eligibility to enter that class shall be determined as follows: A dog may continue to be exhibited in such a class after his handler has been notified by three different Judges that he has received three qualifying scores for such title, but may not be entered or exhibited in such a class in any Obedience Trial of which the closing date for entries occurs after the owner has received official notification from the American Kennel Club that the dog has won the particular Obedience title.

SECTION 33. Where any of the foregoing sections of the Regulations requires that a dog shall have won a particular Obedience title before being entered in a particular Obedience class, a dog may not be entered or exhibited in such class at any Obedience Trial for which entries have closed before the owner has received official notification from the American Kennel Club that the dog has won the required title.

SECTION 34. *Prizes and trophies at an Obedience Trial must be offered to be won outright and to be awarded automatically on the basis of scores attained by dogs competing at the Trial with the exception that a trophy or prize which requires three wins by the same exhibitor, not necessarily with the same dog, for permanent possession, may be offered for the highest scoring dog in the trial or the highest scoring dog in one of the classes.*

Class prize ribbons and trophies offered for the four official placings in a class shall be awarded on the basis of total final scores without regard to more than 50% of the points required for a qualifying score in each exercise.

Such other trophies and prizes as are offered for outright and automatic award in any class, or in any section of a split class, including prizes or trophies for the highest scoring dog in the trial or for the dog with the highest combined score in the Open "B" and Utility Classes, may stipulate a condition that the score or scores be "qualifying."

SECTION 35. A club or association holding an Obedience Trial (either a separate event or in combination with a dog show) must prepare, after the entries have closed and not before, a program showing the time scheduled for the judging of the various classes.

This program shall be based on the judging of eight Novice entries, seven Open entries or six Utility entries per hour which will be considered a reasonable average and no judge should be called upon to exceed those averages during the period of the advertised hours of a show's and/or trial's duration, less reasonable intermissions for meals. The advertised hours of a show's and/or trial's duration shall be considered the time from the start of judging to the closing of the show.

Each judge's assignment must be scheduled so as to insure the completion of the judging (based on the formula above) prior to the closing hour of the show and/or trial.

If indications point to a probable entry in any or all classes in excess of a club's facilities, it may limit entries in any or all classes by prominent announcement on the title or cover page of its premium list (or immediately under the obedience heading in the premium list of a combined dog show and Obedience Trial) that entries in such class, classes or trial, automatically will close when a certain limit, determined as above, for such class, classes or trial has been received, even if the official closing date for entries has not arrived.

If a club chooses not to so limit its entries and if, upon the closing of entries, it is determined that the entries of any Judge exceed the above hourly averages by more than 15%, then the club shall immediately obtain the approval of the American Kennel Club (a) for a reassignment of its advertised Judges so that the duties of no Judge shall exceed the above schedule by more than 15% or (b) for the appointment of an additional Judge to share the class assignment with the advertised Judge whose entries are excessive. In the latter case, immediately after obtaining approval of such additional Judge, the Obedience Trial (or bench show) committee shall, by the drawing of lots, divide the entry between the two Judges. Immediately after obtaining approval of either such change, the club shall mail to the exhibitor of each entry so affected, a notification of the change of Judge and the exhibitor shall be permitted to withdraw such entries at any time prior to the opening day of the show and the entry fees paid for entering such dogs shall be refunded. The club, in such notice to exhibitors, shall also announce which of the two Judges of a given class will judge the run-off of any tie scores which may finally develop as between the two groups of dogs. Each Judge, however, shall first conduct the run-off of any ties developing in his own group of dogs.

A club may choose to announce two Judges for a given class in its premium list. In such case the entries shall be divided by lot as above provided, but no announcement of such drawing need be made to exhibitors in advance of the trial and no exhibitor shall be entitled to a refund of entry fee.

One of the Judges so announced shall be designated in the Premium List as the Judge for the run-off of any tie scores which may finally develop as between the two groups of dogs or if the club desires, and so indicates in its Premium List, a third Judge may be announced for the run-off of such ties.

A club which gives a split class shall not award American Kennel Club official ribbons in either section, but may offer prizes and trophies on the basis of scores made within each section. The four dogs with the highest scores in the class (regardless of the section in which they were made) shall be called back into the ring and awarded the four American Kennel Club official ribbons, by at least one of the Judges of the class, who shall be responsible for recording the entry numbers of the four placed dogs in one of the Judges' Books.

CHAPTER II

Standard for Obedience Trials

SECTION 1. The purpose of Obedience Trials is to demonstrate the usefulness of the pure-bred dog as the companion and guardian of man, and not the ability of the dog to acquire facility in the performance of mere tricks. The classification which has been adopted is progressive, with the thought in mind that a dog which can be termed a utility dog has demonstrated his fitness to a place in our modern scheme of living.

SECTION 2. *If the exercises take place indoors, the ring should be at least 30' wide and 50' long and shall under no circumstances be less than 30' wide and 40' long. The ring must be thoroughly cleaned immediately before the judging starts if it has previously been used for breed judging.* The floor shall have a surface or covering adequate to provide firm footing for the largest dogs and rubber or similar non-slip material for the take-off and landing at all jumps. If the exercises take place out-of-doors the ring shall be at least 40' wide and 70' long. The ground shall be level and the grass, if any, shall be cut short.

If inclement weather at an outdoor event makes necessary the judging of Obedience Classes under shelter, all requirements as to ring size shall be waived.

SECTION 3. A word of praise is allowed between exercises and between separate parts of individual exercises after the Judge has said "Exercise finished", but no offering of any kind of food may be given in the ring. All exercises, except "Heel on Leash", "Stand for Examination" and "Tracking", shall be performed off leash.

In the Novice and Open Classes the dog may be put on leash or guided gently by the collar between exercises and to get it into proper position for the next exercise. In the Utility Class the dog shall not be put on the leash or guided or controlled by the collar at any time, and the leash shall be left on the Judge's table from the time the dog enters the ring until it leaves.

Imperfections in heeling between exercises will not be judged, but any disciplining by the handler in the ring, or any uncontrolled behavior of the dog, such as snapping, unjustified barking, or running out of the ring, even between exercises, will be severely penalized by deducting points from the total score, and the Judge may bar the dog from further competition at that trial.

SECTION 4. In all parts of all exercises performed in the ring, a single command or signal only may be given by the handler, and any extra commands or signals, or the giving of a command and a signal must be penalized; except that wherever the standard specifies "command and/or signal" the handler may give either one or the other, or both "command" and "signal" simultaneously. Where a signal is permitted and given, it must be a single gesture with *one* arm and hand only and the arm must be promptly returned to its normal position, *except that both arms may be used simultaneously to call the dog in the Recall Exercises.* Signals must be inaudible and the handler shall not touch the dog. Signaling correction to the dog from a distance is forbidden and must be penalized. Any unusual noises or motions may be considered to be signals. The dog's name may be used once immediately before any verbal command *but may not be used when a signal is employed even though the standard specifies "command and/or signal".* Whistling or the use of a whistle is prohibited.

SECTION 5. HEEL ON LEASH: In the Novice classes the handler shall enter the ring with his dog on a loose leash and shall stand still with dog sitting at heel at the handler's left side until the Judge asks if the handler is ready and then gives the order "Forward", at which order the handler may attract his dog's attention by saying his name and will give the command to Heel, and at the same time start walking briskly with the dog on loose leash. At the command or signal to Heel the dog shall walk close to the left side of the handler without crowding, permitting the handler freedom of motion at all times. At each order to "Halt", the handler will stop and his dog shall sit smartly at heel without command or signal and not move until ordered to do so. It is permissible after each halt before moving again for the handler to give the command or signal to Heel. Any tightening or jerking of the leash or any act, signal or command which in the opinion of the Judge gives the dog unnecessary or unfair assistance shall be penalized. The Judge will give the orders, "Forward", "Halt", "Right turn", "Left turn", "About turn", "Slow", "Normal" and "Fast" which last order signifies that the handler and dog must run. These orders may be given in any sequence and may be repeated if necessary. In executing the "About turn" the handler will do a "Right about turn" in all cases. The Judge will order the handler to execute the "Figure eight" which signifies that the handler shall walk around and between the two stewards who shall stand about 8 feet apart, or if there is only one steward, shall walk around and between the Judge and the steward. The "Figure eight" in the Novice Classes shall be done on leash only. The Judge will say "exercise finished" after the heeling and then, "Are you ready?" before starting the "Figure eight". There shall be no "About turn" in

the "Figure eight" but the handler and dog shall go twice completely around the "Figure eight" with at least one halt during and another halt at the end of the exercises.

SECTION 6. STAND FOR EXAMINATION: The Judge will give the order for examination and the handler will stand or pose his dog, give the command and/or signal to "Stay", walk in front of his dog, turn around, and stand facing his dog at the end of a loose leash. The Judge will touch the dog's head, body and hind quarters only and then give the order, "Back to your dog", whereupon the handler will walk around behind his dog to the heel position. The dog must remain in a standing position until the Judge says, "Exercise finished". The dog must show no shyness nor resentment.

SECTION 7. HEEL FREE: This shall be executed in the same manner as "Heel on Leash" except that the dog is off the leash. The leash shall be left on the Judge's table for all work done in the "Heel Free" exercise. Heeling in both Novice and Open Classes is done in the same manner except that in the Open Classes the dog does not heel on leash but all work is done off leash, including the "Figure eight".

SECTION 8. RECALL: To execute the "Recall" to handler, upon order or signal from the Judge, "Leave your dog", the dog is given the command and/or signal to stay in the sitting position while the handler moves *towards* the other end of the ring, the distance to be about 40 feet. Upon order or signal from the Judge, "Call your dog", the handler calls or signals the dog, which in the Novice Class must come straight in at a smart pace and sit immediately in front of the handler. Upon order or signal from the Judge to "Finish", the dog on command or signal must go smartly to heel. In the Open Class, at a point designated by the Judge, the dog must drop on command or signal from the handler, and then on order or signal from the Judge, the handler calls or signals the dog which must rise and come straight in at a smart pace and sit immediately in front of the handler. Upon order or signal from the Judge to "Finish", the dog on command or signal must go smartly to heel.

SECTION 9. LONG SIT: In the "Long Sit" in the Novice Classes all the competing dogs in a class take this exercise together, except that if there are more than fifteen dogs, they shall be split into groups of not less than six nor more than fifteen dogs. Where the same Judge does both classes the separate classes may be combined. The dogs which are in the ring shall be lined up in catalog order. Handlers' armbands, weighted with leashes, or other articles, if necessary, shall be placed behind the dogs. On order from the Judge the handlers shall sit their dogs and on further order from the Judge to "Leave your dogs" the handlers shall give the command and/or signal to stay and immediately leave their dogs, go to the opposite side of the ring, and line up in front of their respective dogs. In the Novice Classes the Judge shall take a position in the ring where he can observe both the dogs and the handlers. After one minute from the time he has ordered the handlers to leave their dogs, the Judge will order the handlers "Back to your dogs" whereupon the handlers must return promptly to their dogs each walking around and in back of his own dog to the heel position. The dogs must not move from the sitting position until permission has been given by their respective handlers after the Judge says 'Exercise finished".

SECTION 10. LONG DOWN: The "Long Down" in the Novice Classes is done in the same manner as the "Long Sit" except that instead of sitting the dogs the handlers, on orders from the Judge, will down their dogs, and except further, that the time is three minutes. The dog must stay in the down position until after the Judge says, "Exercise finished". The dogs are not required to sit.

SECTION 11. The "Long Sit" and "Long Down" exercises in the Open Classes are performed in the same manner as in the Novice Classes except that after leaving their dogs the handlers

must immediately leave the ring and go to a place designated by the Judge out of sight of their dogs, where they must remain until the time limit of three minutes in the "Long Sit" and five minutes in the "Long Down" (from the time the Judge gave the order to "Leave your dogs") has expired.

SECTION 12. RETRIEVE ON FLAT: In "retrieving the Dumbbell on the Flat", the orders given by the Judge shall be "Throw it", whereupon the handler must give the command and/or signal to stay and throws the dumbbell: "Send him", whereupon the handler gives a command or signal to his dog to retrieve; "Take it", whereupon the handler may give a command or signal and takes the dumbbell from the dog; "Finish", whereupon the handler gives the command or signal to heel. The dog shall not move forward to retrieve nor deliver to hand on return until ordered by the handler. The retrieve shall be executed at a fast trot or gallop, without unnecessary mouthing or playing with the dumbbell. After delivering the dumbbell from in front of the handler, the dog upon command or signal from the handler shall go to heel position. The size of the dumbbell may vary with the size of the dog.

SECTION 13. RETRIEVE OVER HIGH JUMP: In "Retrieving the Dumbbell over the High Jump", the exercise is executed in the same manner as the "Retrieve on the Flat", except that the dog must jump the obstacle both going and coming. The high jump shall be jumped clear and the jump shall be as nearly as possible one and one-half times the height of the dog at the withers or 3 feet, whichever is less. This applies to all breeds except those listed below for which the jump shall be once the height of the dog at the withers or 3 feet, whichever is less: Bull-Mastiffs, Great Danes, Great Pyrenees, Mastiffs, Newfoundlands and St. Bernards.

The side posts of the "High Jump" shall be 4 feet high and the jump shall be 5 feet wide and shall be so constructed as to provide adjustment for each 2 inches from 12 inches to 36 inches. It is suggested that the jump have a bottom board 8 inches wide including the space from the bottom of the board to the ground, together with three other 8 inch boards, one 6 inch board, and one 4 inch board. The jump shall be painted a flat white. The width in inches shall be painted on each side of each board in black 2 inch figures, the figure on the bottom board representing the distance from the ground to the top of the board.

SECTION 14. BROAD JUMP: In the "Broad Jump", the handler will stand with his dog at the heel position in front of and within 10 feet of the jump. On order from the Judge to "Leave your dog", the handler will give his dog the command and/or signal to stay and go to a position facing the right side of the jump, about 2 feet from the jump, and within the range of the first and last hurdles. On order from the Judge, the handler shall give the command or signal to jump and the dog shall clear the entire width of the broad jump without touching and, without further command or signal, return to a sitting position immediately in front of the handler as in the "Recall". The handler shall change his position while the dog is in midair by executing a right face. On order from the Judge, the handler will give the command or signal to heel and the dog shall finish in the prescribed manner. The Broad Jump shall consist of four separate hurdles, built to telescope for convenience, the largest measuring about 5 feet wide and 7 inches high at the highest point and painted a flat white. When set up, they shall be spaced so as to cover a distance equal to twice the height of the high jump as set for the particular dog. Hurdles shall be removed in proportion to the height of the dog and the highest hurdles shall be removed first.

SECTION 15. SCENT DISCRIMI-NATION: In each of these three exercises, the dog must select by scent alone and retrieve an article which has been handled by his handler. The articles shall be provided by the handler and these shall consist of three sets, each comprised by five identical articles, one set being wood, one metal and one leather. The articles in a set must be legibly numbered one to five. The handler shall present all the articles to the Judge and the Judge shall designate one article from each of the three sets. These handlers' articles shall be kept on the Judge's table until picked up by the handler who shall hold in his hand only one article at a time. Immediately after picking up an article, and before imparting the scent, the handler must show the number on the article to the Judge and one of the stewards. The handler's scent may be imparted to the article only from his hands which must remain in plain sight. The handler may pick up his articles in any order. At the start of the "Scent Discrimination" exercises, the remaining twelve articles will be placed at random in the ring about 6 inches apart. The handler will stand about 15 feet from the articles with the dog sitting at heel position with its back to the articles, and on order from the Judge, the handler immediately will place his article on the Judge's book and the Judge will place it among the other articles. On order from the Judge to "Send him", the handler and the dog will turn to face the articles, and the handler may place his hand gently over the dog's nose and shall give the command or signal to get it. The dog shall go at a brisk pace to the articles, but may take any reasonable time to select the right article provided he works continuously and does not pick up any article other than his handler's. After picking up the right article the dog shall bring it smartly to his handler, and the exercise is completed as in the retrieve exercises. The same procedure is followed in each of the three "Scent Discrimination" exercises. Should a dog retrieve a wrong article in any of the three exercises, it shall be placed on the Judge's table, and the handler's article must also be taken up from the remaining articles. The remaining exercises shall then be completed with fewer than twelve articles left in the ring. At the close of these exercises, the articles shall be removed from the ring.

SECTION 16. SEEK BACK: In the "Seek Back" the handler will stand with his dog in the heel position and, on order from the Judge, will signal or command his dog to walk at heel, and then on specific order or signal from the Judge will execute such portions of the "Heel Free" exercise as the Judge may order. On order from the Judge to drop it, the handler will surreptitiously drop an article as he is walking with his dog at heel. The article must be approved by the Judge and must not be a conspicuous one nor white in color. After the handler and dog have proceeded about 30 feet following the dropping of the article, on order or signal from the Judge, the handler will halt with his dog. Then on order or signal from the Judge the handler gives the command to seek back and retrieve the article. The handler should not point to the object but may point in the direction of the trail, and he is to remain in the place from which the dog is sent. The dog may retrieve either by sight or scent and is expected to find the article, pick it up, promptly return to the handler and sit in front of him, holding the article. On command or signal from the Judge, the handler takes the article and may signal or command the dog to give it up. After delivering the article from in front of the handler, the dog, upon command or signal from the handler, shall go to heel position.

SECTION 17. SIGNAL EXERCISE: In the "Signal Exercise" the heeling is done in the same manner as in the "Heel Free" exercise except that throughout the entire exercise the handler uses signals only and must not speak to his dog at any time. On order or signal from the Judge "Forward", the handler signals his dog to walk at heel and then, on specific order or signal from the Judge in each case, the handler and dog, execute a "Left turn", "Right turn", "About turn", "Halt", "Slow", "Normal", "Fast". These orders may be given in any sequence and may be repeated if necessary. Then, on order or signal from the Judge, the handler signals his dog to "stand" in the heel position near the end of the ring, and on further order or signal from the Judge "Leave your dog", the handler signals his dog to stay, goes to the far end of the ring, and turns to face his dog. Then, on separate and specific signals from the

Judge in each case, the handler will give the signals to drop, to sit, to come to a sit in front, and to finish, after which the Judge will say "Exercise finished". During the heeling part of this exercise the handler may not give any signal except where a command or signal is permitted in the Heeling Exercises.

SECTION 18. DIRECTED JUMPING: In the "Directed Jumping" exercise the jumps shall be placed midway the ring and as close to the sides *as is practicable and between 20 and 30 feet apart.* (The Bar Jump on one side, the Hurdle on the other.) The handler from a position on the center line of the ring and about 20 feet from *the line of* the jumps, stands with his dog in the heel position. On order or signal, "Send him" from the Judge, he commands and/or signals his dog to go forward at a smart pace to the other end of the ring to an equal distance beyond the jumps and in the approximate center where the handler stops his dog by command, whereupon the dog must stop and sit, with his attention on the handler (the dog need not sit squarely at this point). The Judge will then designate which jump is to be taken first by the dog, whereupon the handler commands and/or signals his dog *to return to him over the designated jump, the dog sitting in front of the handler and finishing as in the "Recall".* The handler may also give a command to jump at each jump, but the *word used must be different from the word used to call the dog.* A signal used in either case, must be a single gesture with the arm and hand only, and the arm must be promptly returned to its normal position. While the dog is in midair the handler may turn to right or left so as to be facing the dog when it lands from the jump. *The Judge will say "Exercise Finished" after the dog has returned to the heel position, at which time a word of praise is permitted. When the dog is again in heel position for the second part of the exercise, the Judge will ask "Are you ready?" before giving the order or signal "Send him" for the second jump.* The same procedure is to be followed for the dog taking the opposite jump. It is optional with the Judge which jump is taken first but both jumps must be taken to complete the exercise and the Judge must not designate the jump until the dog is at the far end of the ring. The height of the jumps shall be the same as required in the Open Classes. The high jump shall be the same as that used in the Open Classes, and the bar jump shall consist of a bar between 2 and 2½ inches in diameter, painted black and white in alternate sections of about 3 inches each. The bar shall be supported by two 4 foot upright posts at least 5 feet apart. The bar shall be adjustable for each 2 inches of height from 12 inches to 36 inches and shall be so constructed that the bar can be knocked off without disturbing the uprights. The dog shall clear the jumps without touching them.

SECTION 19. GROUP EXAMINATION: All the competing dogs take this exercise together, except that if there are more than fifteen dogs, they shall be split into groups of not less than six nor more than fifteen dogs. The handlers and dogs which are in the ring shall line up in catalog order, side by side down the center of the ring with the dogs at heel position. Each handler shall place his armband, weighted if necessary, behind his dog. On order from the Judge to "Stand your dogs", all the handlers will stand or pose their dogs, and on order from the Judge, "Leave your dogs", all the handlers will give the command and/or signal to "Stay" and walk forward to the side of the ring, then about turn and face their dogs. The Judge will approach each dog in turn from the front and examine each dog as in conformation judging. After all dogs have been examined, and after the handlers have been away from their dogs for at least three minutes, the Judge will order the handlers, "Back to your dogs", and the handlers will walk around behind their dogs to the heel position, after which the Judge will say, "Exercise finished". Each dog must remain standing at his position in the line, from the time his handler leaves him until the end of the exercise, and must show no shyness nor resentment.

SECTION 20. TRACKING: The tracking test must be performed with the dog on leash, the length of the track to be not less than 440 yards nor more than 500 yards, the scent to be not less than one half hour nor more than two hours old and that of a stranger who will leave a leather glove or wallet to be found at the end of the track. The tracklayer will follow the track (which has been staked out with flags a day or more earlier) collecting all the flags on the way with exception of one flag at the start of the track and one flag not more than 30 yards from the start of the track to indicate the direction of the track; then deposit the article at the end of the track, and leave the course, proceeding straight ahead at least 50 feet. The tracklayers must wear leather-soled shoes. The length of the leash used in tracking must be 30 to 60 feet and the dog must work at this length with no help from the handler. A dog may, at the handler's option, be given one, and only one, second chance to take the scent between the two flags at the start, provided he has not passed the second flag.

CHAPTER III

Standards for Obedience Trial Judging

Standardized judging is of paramount importance. Judges are not permitted to inject their own variations into the exercises, but must see that each handler and dog executes the various exercises exactly as described in the Standard. A handler who is familiar with the Standard should be able to enter the ring under any Judge without having to inquire as to how the particular Judge wishes to have any exercise performed. Judges must adhere to the Regulations and Standards in every respect, and must not qualify dogs that do not meet the minimum requirements as described below.

SECTION 1. The responsibility for making the tests interesting to the gallery and worth while to the exhibitor is left to the Judge, who must not permit the judging to drag so that the handlers and those watching become bored and the competing dogs tired.

SECTION 2. The Judge shall not judge any dog until he has entered in the official Judge's book the scores of all dogs judged previously and until he has sub-totaled such scores. Scores for the "Long Sit", "Long Down", and "Group Examination" exercises must be entered in the official Judge's book immediately after each group of dogs has been judged. No score may be changed except to correct an arithmetical error. All totals must be entered in the Judge's book before prizes are awarded. No person other than the Judge may make any entry in the Judge's book.

SECTION 3. The Judge must remember that he is judging the dogs ONLY on their ability to perform the tests set for them and not upon their show points or conformation.

SECTION 4. The Judge must test each contestant separately (except for the "Sit", "Down" and "Group Examination", where groups of dogs are in the ring together) and as provided in Section 8. As each handler enters the ring, the Judge shall ask if he has knowledge of the Rules and Regulations and shall see that the dog has on either a plain or chain choke collar, as no spiked collars are allowed.

SECTION 5. If a dog has failed in a particular part of an exercise, he shall not ordinarily be rejudged nor given a second chance. But, if in the Judge's opinion, the dog's performance was prejudiced by peculiar and unusual conditions, the Judge may, at his own discretion, rejudge the dog on the entire exercise. The Judge shall not permit any handler to train his dog or practice any exercise in the ring either before or after he is judged.

SECTION 6. The Judge shall carry a mental picture of the theoretically perfect performance in each exercise and shall score each dog against this visualized standard of perfection, which shall combine the utmost in willingness, enjoyment and precision. Each fault or deviation from this standard must be penalized. There shall be no penalty of less than ½ point or multiple of ½ point.

SECTION 7. When giving orders (especially for heelwork), the Judge shall not stand at one end of the ring, but shall follow the handler at a discreet distance so that he may observe any signals or undertones given by the handler to the dog.

SECTION 8. In the case of a tie, the dogs shall be tested again by having them perform at the same time one or more of the regular exercises in that class, which will prove to the Judge which dog is the most obedient. In the case of a tie in Utility, the dogs shall be tested again, by performing at the same time, all or some part of the Signal Exercise. However, the scores already awarded shall not be changed.

SECTION 9. After the scores are totaled and winners decided before awarding the prizes, the Judge shall inform the public as to the total number of points required for a perfect score. He shall then call out each winner separately and announce the scores.

SECTION 10. The Judge must look for the following in testing each dog and score accordingly:

a. Enjoyment and willingness should be taken into consideration over a better worker that shows fear and dislike of his work.

b. Talking to the dog by the handler, snapping of fingers, slapping of sides and stamping of feet are decidedly out of order.

c. Signaling correction to dog from the distance, especially during the "Sit" and the "Down", is forbidden.

d. During the dog's heel-work, the handler should always walk briskly with dog on left side and with a completely loose leash. Guiding the dog by means of leash is to be penalized.

e. Gentleness and smoothness of handling is to be greatly desired.

f. The dog should never anticipate

the handler's orders, but should wait for the commands or signals.

g. In "the finish", the method in which a dog goes to heel shall be optional with the handler provided it is done smartly.

SECTION 11. No Judge shall require any dog or handler to do anything, nor penalize a dog or handler for failing to do anything, which is not required by these Regulations and Standards, such as requiring a dog to sit at the conclusion of "Stand for Examination", "Group Examination" and "Long Down".

SECTION 12. A dog which fails to execute a principal designated feature of an exercise shall in no case be given a qualifying score for the exercise.

A dog which, in the Judge's opinion, would have failed to do a principal designated feature of an exercise had the handler not given additional commands or signals not permitted by the Standard, shall be scored as though he had failed to do that particular feature of the exercise.

SECTION 13. All orders or signals given to handlers shall be sufficiently clear and distinguishable for everyone to follow the judging and, at the end of each test, the Judge shall say, "Exercise finished".

THE ORDERS FOR THE EXERCISES AND THE STANDARDS FOR JUDGING ARE AS FOLLOWS

The orders for the exercises and the standards for judging are set forth in the following sections. The lists of faults are not intended to be complete but minimum penalites are specified for most of the more common and serious faults. A dog which makes none of the errors listed may still fail to qualify or may be scored zero for other reasons.

SECTION 14. HEEL ON LEASH: The orders for this exercise are "Forward", "Halt", "Right turn", "Left turn,", "About turn", "Slow", "Normal", "Fast", "Figure eight". These orders may be given in any order and may be repeated, if necessary, to conform to the size and shape of the ring, but the Judge shall attempt to standardize the heeling routine for all dogs in any class. The principal feature of this exercise is the ability of the dog to work with his handler as a team. A dog which is unmanageable must be scored zero. Where a handler continually tugs on the leash or adapts his pace to that of the dog, the Judge must score such a dog less than 50% of the available points. Minor deductions shall be made for such things as poor sits, occasionally guiding dog with the leash, heeling wide, and other imperfections in heeling.

SECTION 15. STAND FOR EXAMINATION: The orders for this exercise are "Stand your dog for examination", "Back to your dog", Exercise finished". The principal features of this exercise are to stand in position before and during examination and to show no shyness nor resentment. A dog that sits before or during the examination or growls or snaps must be marked zero. A dog that moves away from the position in which he was left before or during the examination, or a dog that shows shyness or resentment must receive less than 50% of the available points. Depending on the circumstances in each case, minor or substantial deductions must be made for any dog that moves his feet, or sits, or moves away at any time after the examination is completed. The examination shall consist of touching the dog's head, body and hindquarters only.

SECTION 16. HEEL FREE: The orders and scoring for this exercise shall be the same as for "Heel on Leash" except that the "Figure eight" is omitted in the "Heel Free" exercise in the Novice Classes. The leash must be placed on the Judge's table during this exercise.

SECTION 17. RECALL: The orders for this exercise are "Leave your dog", "Call your dog", "Finish". The principal features of this exercise are the prompt response to the handler's command or signal to come, and the "stay" until the handler calls the dog. A dog which does not come on the first command or signal must be scored zero. A dog which does not stay without extra command or signal, or which moves from the place where he was left, from the time the handler leaves until he is called, must receive less than 50% of the points. Substantial deductions shall be made for a slow response to the "come", depending on the specific circumstances in each case; for extra commands or signals to "stay" if given before the handler leaves the dog; for extra commands or signals to "finish", and for failure to sit or finish. Minor deductions shall be made for poor "sits" or finishes".

SECTION 18. SIT AND DOWN:

The orders for these exercises are "Sit your dogs" (or "Down your dogs"), "Leave your dogs", "Back to your dogs", "Exercise finished". The principal features of these exercises are to stay, and to remain in the sitting or down position, whichever is required by the particular exercise. A dog which, at any time during the exercise, moves a substantial distance away from the place where he was left, or goes over to any other dog, must be marked zero. A dog which fails to remain in the sitting or down position, whichever is required by the particular exercise, for at least three quarters of the specified time in the Novice Classes, or until the handler has returned to the heel position in the Open Classes, must receive less than 50% of the available points. A substantial deduction shall be made for any dog that moves even a minor distance away from the place where he was left. In the Novice classes, a substantial deduction shall be made for any dog that fails to remain in the sitting or down position, whichever is required by the particular exercise, until the handler has returned to the heel position. Depending on the circumstances in each case, minor deductions shall be made in both Novice and Open Classes, for minor movements from the position in the ring, and for sitting after the handler is in the heel position but before the Judge has said "Exercise finished" in the "down" exercises. The dogs shall not be required to sit at the end of the "down" exercises. If a dog gets up and starts to roam, the Judge shall instruct the handler or one of the stewards to take the dog out of the ring or away from the other dogs.

SECTION 19. DROP ON RECALL:

The orders for this exercise are the same as for the "Recall", except that the dog is required to drop when coming in at a point designated by the Judge, and except that an additional order or signal to "Call your dog" is given by the Judge after the "drop". The "drop" is a principal feature of this exercise, in addition to the prompt response and the "stay" as described under "Recall" above. A dog which does not stop and drop on a single command or signal must be scored zero. Minor or substantial deductions shall be made for a slow drop, depending on whether the dog is just short of perfection in this respect, or very slow in dropping, or somewhere between the two extremes. All other deductions as listed under "Recall" above, shall also apply. The Judge may designate the point at which the dog is to drop by some marker, placed in advance, which will be clear to the handler but not obvious to the dog; or he may give the handler a signal for the drop, but such signal must be given in such a way as not to attract the dog's attention.

SECTION 20. RETRIEVE ON FLAT:

The orders for this exercise are: "Throw it", "Send your dog", "Take it", "Finish". The principal feature of this exercise is to retrieve promptly. Any dog which fails to go out on the first command or a dog which fails to retrieve, shall be marked zero. A dog which goes to retrieve before given the command or signal must receive less than 50% of the points. Depending on the specific circumstances in each case, substantial deductions shall be made for a dog which is excessively slow, for excessive mouthing, dropping of dumbbell, failure to sit in front, and for extra commands or signals to "finish". Minor deductions shall be made for poor "sits" and/or "finishes".

SECTION 21. RETRIEVE OVER HIGH JUMP:

The orders for this exercise are "Throw it", "Send your dog", "Take it" and "Finish". The principal features of this exercise are that the dog must go out over the jump, pick up the dumbbell and promptly return with it over the jump. A dog which, on a single command or signal, fails to go out, or to retrieve, or which fails both going and returning to go over the high jump must be marked zero. A dog which retrieves properly but goes over the high jump in only one direction, or a dog which anticipates the handler's command or signal to retrieve, must receive less than 50% of the available points. Substantial deductions must be made for a dog which climbs the jump or uses the top of the jump for aid in going over (in contrast to a dog which merely touches the jump), or for failure to sit in front of the handler, or to finish. Depending on the specific circumstances in each case, minor or substantial deductions shall be made for slowness, mouthing or playing with the dumbbell, dropping the dumbbell, or for slowness in releasing the dumbbell to the handler. Minor deductions shall be made for touching the jump in going over, and for poor sits or finishes. The Judge must make certain in all cases that the jump is set at the proper height for each dog, and shall measure any dog if there is any question as to the proper height.

SECTION 22. BROAD JUMP: The orders for this exercise are, "Leave your dog", "Send him", and "Finish". Any dog which refuses the jump on the first command or signal or walks over any part of the jump must be marked zero. A dog which jumps at the first command but fails to clear the full distance, or a dog which fails to wait for the handler's command or signal before jumping, shall be penalized a lesser amount depending on the circumstances each case; and there shall be minor penalties for failure to return smartly to the handler and to sit straight in front of the handler or finish correctly. It is the Judge's responsibility to see that the distance jumped is that required by the Standard for the particular dog.

SECTION 23. SCENT DISCRIMINATION: The orders for each of these exercises are "Send your dog", "Take it", and "Finish". The principal features of these exercises are the selection of the handler's article from among the other articles by scent alone, and the prompt carrying of the right article to the handler after its selection. A dog which fails to go out to the group of articles, or which retrieves a wrong article, or which fails to bring the right article to the handler, must be marked zero for the particular exercise. Substantial deductions shall be made for a dog that is excessively slow going out or returning, or which picks up a wrong article, even though he puts it down again immediately. Minor or substantial deductions, depending on the circumstances in each case, shall be made for a dog that is slow or inattentive, or that does not work continuously, or that plays excessively with the article or refuses to give it up to his handler. Minor deductions shall be made for mouthing the article and for poor "sits" or "finishes". There shall be no penalty for a dog that takes a reasonably long time examining the articles, provided he is working smartly and continuously. The handler may give the Judge his articles in any order he may choose and is responsible for seeing that the Judge and a steward have noted the number on each. The handler must give up each article immediately when ordered by the Judge. The Judge must see to it that the handler imparts his scent to the article only with his hands and that, between the time the handler picks up each article and the time he gives it to the Judge, the article is held continuously in the handler's hands which must remain in plain sight. The Judge must also make sure that the articles on the floor are properly separated before sending the dog out, so that there may be no confusion of scent between articles.

SECTION 24. SEEK BACK: The orders for this exercise are: "Forward" (followed by any other orders which the Judge may give from the heel free routine), "Drop it", "Halt", "Send your dog", "Take it", and Finish. The principal features of this exercise are that the dog, on command, must seek and retrieve the article promptly. A dog which does not leave his handler promptly, which does not continue to seek while away from his handler, which does not find and pick up the article or which does not leave his handler handler with the object must be marked zero. Substantial or minor deductions according to the circumstances in each case shall be made for poor heel work, playing with the article, lack of interest or failure to surrender the article promptly.

SECTION 25. SIGNAL EXERCISE: The orders for this exercise are: "Forward", "Left turn", "Right turn", "About turn", "Halt", "Slow", "Normal", "Fast", "Stand", and "Leave your dog", and in addition the Judge must give the handler signals to signal his dog to drop, to sit, to come, to finish. The Judge may use signals instead of any of the verbal orders, but must advise the handler of his intention in advance. The orders or signals for those parts of the exercise, which are done with the dog at heel, may be given in any order and may be repeated if necessary, but the signals given the handler after he has left his dog in the "stand" position shall be given in the order specified above. The principal features of this exercise are the heeling of the dog as described for the "Heel" exercises, and the prompt response to the handler's signals given to the dog at a distance. A dog which fails, on a single signal from the handler, to stand or remain standing where left, or to drop, or to sit and stay, or to come, or which receives a command or audible signal from the handler to do any of these parts of the exercise, shall receive less than 50% of the available points All of the deductions listed under the "Heel" and "Recall" exercises above shall also apply to this exercise.

SECTION 26. DIRECTED JUMPING: The Judge's first order is "Send him", then after the dog is sitting at the far end of the ring, the Judge shall designate which jump is to be taken by the dog, whereupon the handler commands and/or signals his dog *to return to him over the designated jump, the dog sitting in front of the handler and finishing as in the "Recall"*. After the dog returns to the handler the order "Finish" is given *followed by "Exercise Finished"*. The

same sequence is then followed for the other jump. The principal features of this exercise are that the dog goes away from the handler in the direction indicated, stops when commanded and jumps as directed. A dog which does not leave his handler, does not go substantially in the right direction, does not stop on command, does not jump as directed, in the first half of this exercise must be scored zero. A dog which does not leave his handler, does not go substantially in the right direction, does not stop on command, does not jump as directed, in the second half, must receive less than 50% of the available points. Substantial or minor deductions shall be made for faults such as slowness in going out or returning, slow response to direction or poor finishes, depending on the specific circumstances in each case.

SECTION 27. GROUP EXAMINATION: The orders for this exercise are "Stand your dogs", "Leave your dogs", and "Back to your dogs". The principal features of this exercise are that the dog must stand and stay, and must show no shyness nor resentment. A dog that moves a substantial distance away from the place where it was left, or that goes over to any other dog, or that sits or lies down before the handler returns to the heel position, or that growls or snaps at any time, must be marked zero. A dog that remains standing but that moves a minor distance away from the place where it was left, or a dog that shows shyness or resentment, must receive less than 50% of the available points. Depending on the specific circumstances in each case, minor or substantial deductions must be made for any dog that moves its feet at any time during the exercise, or sits or lies down after the handler returns to the heel position. The dogs are not required to sit at the end of this exercise. The examination shall be conducted as in conformation judging. The Judge must make a written record of any deductions immediately after examining each dog, subject to further deduction of points for subsequent faults. The Judge must instruct one or more stewards to watch the other dogs while he conducts the individual examinations, and to call any faults to his attention.

SECTION 28. TRACKING TESTS: For obvious reasons these tests cannot be held at a dog show, and a Judge, though he may be qualified to judge the other Obedience Classes, is not necessarily capable of judging a Tracking Test. No Judge shall accept an appointment to judge a Tracking Test unless he is familiar with the various conditions that may exist when a dog is required to do nosework. Scent conditions, weather, lay of the land, etc., must be taken into consideration, and a thorough knowledge of this work is necessary. One or both of the Judges must personally lay out, or walk over each track after it has been laid out, a day or so before the test, so as to be completely familiar with the location of the track, landmarks and ground conditions. At least two of the major turns shall be well out in the open country where there are no fences or other boundaries to guide the dog. No major part of any track shall follow along any fence or boundary within 10 yards of such boundary. The track shall include at least two turns each approximating a right angle. No conflicting tracks shall be laid. No track shall cross any body of water. The Judges shall make sure that the track is no less than 440 yards and that the tracklayer is a stranger to the dog in each case. There is no time limit, provided the dog is working, but a dog that is off the track and is clearly not working should not be given any minimum time just on the chance that it

might pick up the track again. The handler may not be given any assistance by the Judges or anyone else. In case of unforeseen circumstances, the Judges may in rare cases, at their own discretion, give a handler and his dog a second chance on a new track. A dog that is working too fast for the conditions may be restrained gently by the handler at the end of the leash, but any leading or guiding of the dog constitutes grounds for calling the handler off and marking the dog "failed". A track for each dog entered shall be plotted on the ground not less than one day before the test, the track being marked by flags which the tracklayer can follow readily on the day of the test. A chart of each track shall be made up in duplicate, showing the approximate length in yards of each leg, major landmarks and boundaries, if any. Two of these charts shall be marked, one by each of the Judges at the time the dog is tracking, so as to show the approximate course followed by the dog. Upon completion of the meet, the Judges shall forward the marked copies of each chart to the American Kennel Club. The Judges shall sign each chart forwarded, and show on each whether the dog "passed" or "failed", the time the tracklayer started, the time the dog started and finished tracking, a brief description of ground, wind and weather conditions, the wind direction, and a note of any steep hills or valleys. If a dog is not trailing, it shall not be marked "passed" even though it may have found the article.

CONSTRUCTION OF OBEDIENCE EQUIPMENT

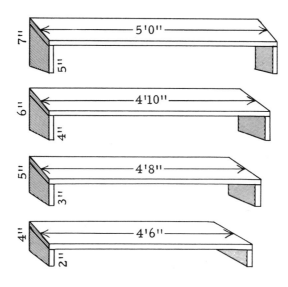

THE BROAD JUMP

THESE JUMPS ARE MADE OF 1 x 8 BOARD, ANY WOOD. THE DECREASING DIMENSIONS ENABLE YOU TO "NEST" THEM FOR STORAGE OR CARRYING. ANGLE BRACKETS UNDERNEATH ADD STRENGTH, BUT ARE NOT NECESSARY. PAINT THE JUMPS FLAT WHITE, AND IN USE ARRANGE THEM IN ORDER OF INCREASING HEIGHT, WITH THE LOWEST NEAREST TO YOUR DOG.

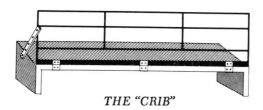

THE "CRIB"

WE RECOMMEND YOU MAKE THIS OF METAL (IRON, ALUMINUM) IN ROUGHLY THE DESIGN PICTURED HERE. IT CAN BE MADE OF DOWELS, 1 x 1 STICKS OR LATH, BUT A WOODEN VERSION WILL NOT BE TOO STRONG. DIMENSIONS ARE 8″ BY 4′8″, WITH THE HOLED BAR AT LEFT FOR CHANGING THE ANGLE OF THE CRIB. MOUNT IT AT THE FRONT OF THE SECOND JUMP, AS PICTURED HERE

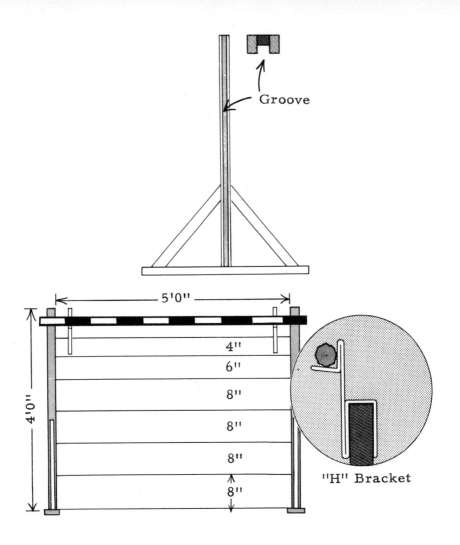

Groove

5'0"

4'0"

4"
6"
8"
8"
8"
8"

"H" Bracket

THE HIGH JUMP UPRIGHTS CONSIST OF TWO 1"x3" AND ONE 1"x2" PIECES NAILED TOGETHER, WITH THE 1"x2" FORMING THE GROOVE FOR THE JUMP BOARDS TO SLIDE INTO. THE BOARDS ARE 5' LONG, OF 1"x8" STOCK. THE BOTTOM 8" BOARD IS SLIGHTLY LESS THAN 8"—JUST WIDE ENOUGH TO MEASURE 8" FROM THE GROUND TO THE TOP OF THE BOARD. PAINT THE ENTIRE JUMP FLAT WHITE.

THE BAR JUMP STANDARDS ARE TWO 3"x3" PIECES, 4' LONG, BRACED AT THE BOTTOM AS ILLUSTRATED FOR THE HIGH JUMP STANDARDS. DRILL SLIGHTLY SLANTING HOLES AT ONE OR TWO INCH INTERVALS DOWN THE "FAR" SIDE OF EACH STANDARD, AND HAVE TWO NAILS OR PEGS TO SLIP INTO THE HOLES TO SUPPORT THE BAR AT VARYING HEIGHTS. THE BAR IS 6' LONG, 2 TO 2½ INCHES IN DIAMETER, PAINTED BLACK AND WHITE IN ALTERNATE SECTIONS OF ABOUT 3 INCHES. THE STANDARDS ARE FLAT WHITE.

THE "H" BRACKETS ARE MADE AS SHOWN IN THE INSET, OF IRON OR WOOD, TO HOLD THE BAR ON TOP OF THE HIGH JUMP BOARDS IN EARLY JUMP TRAINING (SEE ILLUSTRATION HERE, AND OPEN TEXT). YOU WILL NOT NEED THESE IF YOU DRILL THE HIGH JUMP STANDARDS TO CARRY THE BAR AS WELL AS THE BOARDS.

SCENT DISCRIMINATION ARTICLES

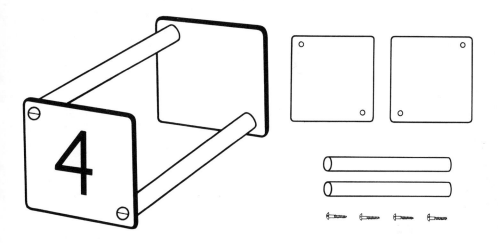

THE SIZE OF THESE DEPENDS ON YOUR DOG. MAKE THE BARS ABOUT ONE INCH LONGER THAN THE WIDTH OF YOUR DOG'S MUZZLE JUST BEHIND THE LONG CANINE TEETH, AND THE REMAINDER OF THE ARTICLE IN PROPORTION AS DRAWN HERE. MAKE SIX OF EACH KIND, AND NUMBER THEM FROM 1 TO 6 ON THE ENDS, USING #6 AS YOUR PRACTICE ARTICLE.

Wood: CUT PLYWOOD SQUARES TO SIZE, ROUND THE CORNERS SLIGHTLY, DRILL SCREW HOLES IN OPPOSITE CORNERS. SAND END-PIECES AND DOWELS WELL BEFORE ASSEMBLING, TO AVOID SPLINTERS IN YOUR HANDS WHEN SCENTING, AND IN THE DOG'S MOUTH. THEN SCREW THE END PIECES ONTO THE DOWELS TO MAKE AN ARTICLE AS PICTURED HERE. *Do not paint!*

Metal: CUT THIN ALUMINUM SHEET TO SIZE FOR ENDS, CUT PROPER SIZE OF ALUMINUM TUBING TO SIZE FOR BARS, DRILL HOLES IN OPPOSITE CORNERS OF END PIECES. THEN CUT DOWELS (SLIGHTLY SMALLER THAN INSIDE DIAMETER OF TUBING) ¼ INCH SHORTER THAN TUBING BARS. WITH THE DOWELS INSIDE THE BARS, SCREW THE END PIECES ON, WITH THE SCREW THROUGH THE END-PIECE HOLE AND INTO THE END OF THE DOWEL. YOU MAY NOT BE ABLE TO DO THE METALWORK, BUT A LOCAL SHOP WILL DO IT QUITE CHEAPLY.

Leather: GET HEAVY SOLE LEATHER FROM A SHOEMAKER AND CUT IT INTO PROPER SQUARES FOR END PIECES, WITH ROUNDED CORNERS AND SCREW-HOLES. GLUE STRIPS OF THIN LEATHER AROUND DOWELS, BUTTING THE ENDS FOR A SMOOTH SINGLE LAYER OF LEATHER. SCREW THE END-PIECES TO THE DOWELS.

INDEX

Age, for training, 60; best for buying, 12
Aggression, 33, 69
American Kennel Club (AKC), 4;
    breeder information, 14;
    "Complete Dog Book", 6;
    groups, 6;
    obedience regulations, Appendix;
    "Pure Bred Dogs" magazine, 14;
    registration, 17, 19

Bar jump, *170-171*
    construction, *see Appendix*
Bathing, 308
Benching, 192
Boarding kennels, 328
Brace, *210-214*
Broad jump, *146-151*, 202;
    construction, *see Appendix*
    problems, 281-283

Cars, 54-55; riding in, 55-57;
    travelling in, 319-323
Chewing, 42, 43
Classes, training, 114-116
Climbing jump, prevention, 144, 145
Coddling, 39-42
Collar and leash introduction, 47-49
Commands, 97, 205-206
Control, 99-101, 113
Corrections, *63-65*, 206-207
Crib, 146
    construction, *see Appendix*

Directed jumping, *169-177*, 205;
    problems, 283-287
Discipline, 39, *62*
Down, *84;* problems, 268-269
Down stay, *85-90*, 154, 200, 203
Drop on recall, *120-126*, 201;
    problems, 274-275
Dumbbell selection, 126-129

Electric wire chewing, 43, 316

Feeding, adults, 299-301

Feeding, puppies, 294-299
Feeding schedules, 298
First aid, 312-318
Food refusal, 57
Foreign travel, 327
Furniture, 39

Give, *36-38*, 58
Go to heel, *92-96*
Grooming, 309-311

Handling, 195-207
Harness, 51
Health, adults, 308-309
Health, puppies, 294-299
Hearing, 334-337
Heeling off lead, 103, 120, 197;
    problems, 264-266
Heeling on lead, *67-72*, 195
High jump, *136-142*
    construction, *see Appendix*
Housebreaking, 11, 25, *26-31*
Hurdle retrieve, *136-146*, 202-203;
    problems, 279-281
Hurdles, 137

Identification, 330-331
Insurance, 331-332
Intelligence, 5, 24

Judges, 208-209
Jumping, bar, 170-171;
    broad, 146-151;
    directed, 169-177, 205;
    high, 136-142;
    problems, 279-287
Kennels and breeders, 14-19
Kennels, boarding, 328-330

Leash selection, 52
Leash and collar introduction, 47-49

Match shows, 189, 191, 207
Medicines, administration, 313
Mongrels, 5

Obedience aptitude, 12, 13
Obedience regulations, *Appendix*

Parasites, 311-312
Pedigrees, 20, 21
Pills, administration, 313
Plane travel, 325
Play, 33, 65
Praise, 65-66, 186, 293
Preventive shots, 302-303
Protection, 44-46

Recall, *90-92*
Recall off lead, *109-113*, 197-198;
    problems, 270-274
Retrieve, *126-136*, 202;
    problems, 275-279
Running away, 104

Scent article board, 160
Scent articles, 159-160
    construction, *see Appendix*
Scent discrimination, *158-169*, 203-204;
    problems, 287-290
Scent in tracking, 227-229, 256-260
Scoring, 207-208
"Season" in females, 9, 306
Seekback, *177-179*, 204;
    problems, 290-291 ·
Sendaway, *171-173*
Shipment, 327
Senses; hearing, 334-337;
    smell, 337-338;
    vision, 333-334

Show entries, 189-191
Signals, 121, 173, *179-185*, 204;
    problems, 291-292
Sit, *72-76*; problems, 266-268
Sit stay, *83-84*, 151, 199, 203
Smell, 337-338
Spaying, 307-308
Stand, *78-83*, 185-186
Stand for examination, *106-109*,
    185-186, 197, 205;
    problems, 269-270
Stays off lead, 103, 199, 200, 203
Street and yard behavior, 32

Table manners, 57
Team, *214-223*
Teething, 35, 305
Temperament, 7, 8
Temperature, normal, 16, 304
Toys, 35
Tracking, *226-261*
Tracking equipment, 229-231
Tracking tests, 260-261
Tracking theory, 227-229, 232
Train travel, 323-325
Training classes, 114-116
Training collar, 49
Tricks, 338-346

Veterinarians, 17, 301
Vision, 333-334

Worms and worming, 303-304